Hampton-Brown

edge™

Reading, Writing & Language

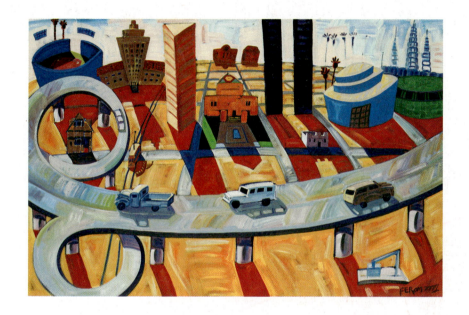

Program Authors

David W. Moore

Deborah J. Short

Michael W. Smith

Alfred W. Tatum

Hampton-Brown

NATIONAL GEOGRAPHIC

Acknowledgments

Grateful acknowledgment is given to the authors, artists, photographers, museums, publishers, and agents for permission to reprint copyrighted material. Every effort has been made to secure the appropriate permission. If any omissions have been made or if corrections are required, please contact the Publisher.

Cover Art: *Downtown*, 2001, Frank Romero, oil on canvas, 48" x 72"

Arenas Street Publishing: The photos and text from the following pages, 367-370, are excerpted from HIGH SCHOOL by Jona Frank, copyright Arenas Street Press, 2004. Published by permission.

Acknowledgments and credits continue on page 650.

Neither the Publisher nor the authors shall be liable for any damage that may be caused or sustained or result from conducting any of the activities in this publication without specifically following instructions, undertaking the activities without proper supervision, or failing to comply with the cautions contained herein.

Published by National Geographic School Publishing & Hampton-Brown
Sheron Long, Chief Executive Officer
Samuel Gesumaria, President

Editorial: Linda Alders, Amy Barbour, Lisa Berti, Chris Beem, Michael Beets, Renee Biermann, Ela Aktay Booty, Janine Boylan, Susan Buntrock, Karen Cardella, Kristin Cozort, Darin Derstine, Amanda Gebhardt, Toni Gibbs, Trudy Gibson, Greta Gilbert, Nadine Guarrera, Margot Hanis, Rachel Hansen, Fred Ignacio, Joan Johnson, Anne Kaske, Robin Kelly, Phillip Kennedy, Sarah Kincaid, Jennifer Kleiman, Jennifer Krasula, Joel Kupperstein, Phil Kurczewski, Mary Catherine Langford, Julie Larson, Kathleen Laya, Robin Longshaw, Dawn Liseth, Daphne Liu, Nancy Lockwood, Jennifer Loomis, Kathleen Maguire, Cheryl Marecki, Andrew McCarter, Joyce McGreevy, Mimi Mortezai, Kimberly Mraovich, Amy Ostenso, Barbara Paulsen, Juan Quintana, Katrina Saville, Debbie Saxton, Thomas Schiele, Elizabeth Sengel, Heather Subba, Lin Sullivan, Seija Surr, Honor Teoudoussia, Jennifer Tetzloff, Joy Triche, Marietta Urban, Sharon Ursino, Beatrice Villar, Davene Wasser, Nora Whitworth, Lori Wilkinson, Virginia Yeater, Brown Publishing Network, Mazer Creative Services

Art, Design, and Production: Marcia Bateman, Christy Caldwell, Andrea Cockrum, Kim Cockrum, Jen Coppens, Darius Detwiler, Donna Jean Elam, Michael Farmer, Chanté Fields, Kathryn Glaser, Raymond Ortiz Godfrey, Raymond Hoffmeyer, Annie Hopkins, Karen Hunting, Jeri Gibson, Rick Holcomb, Cynthia C. Lee, Ernie Lee, Douglas McLeod, Mary McMurtry, Melina Meltzer, Rick Morrison, Russ Nemec, Marian O'Neal, Andrea A. Pastrano-Tamez, Leonard Pierce, Andrea Erin Thompson, Cathy Revers, Stephanie Rice, Scott Russell, Susan Scheuer, Janet Sandbach, Jeanne Stains, Sumer Tatum-Clem, Andrea Troxel, Ana Vela, Alex von Dallwitz, Language Works, Mapping Specialists, Mazer Creative Services

The National Geographic Society
John M. Fahey, Jr., President & Chief Executive Officer
Gilbert M. Grosvenor, Chairman of the Board

Manufacturing and Quality Management, The National Geographic Society
Christopher A. Liedel, Chief Financial Officer
George Bounelis, Vice President

National Geographic School Publishing
Hampton–Brown
P.O. Box 223220
Carmel, California 93922
800-333-3510
www.NGSP.com

Printed in the United States of America

ISBN 13: 978-0-7362-6163-0
ISBN 10: 0-7362-6163-X

08 09 10 11 12 13 14 15 16 17 10 9 8 7 6 5 4 3 2

CONTENTS AT A GLANCE

REVIEWERS

We gratefully acknowledge the many contributions of the following dedicated educators in creating a program that is not only pedagogically sound, but also appealing to and motivating for high school students.

Teacher Reviewers

Felisa Araujo-Rodriguez
English Teacher
Highlands HS
San Antonio, TX

Barbara Barbin
Former HS ESL Teacher
Aldine ISD
Houston, TX

Joseph Berkowitz
ESOL Chairperson
John A. Ferguson Sr. HS
Miami, FL

Dr. LaQuanda Brown-Avery
Instructional Assistant Principal
McNair MS
Decatur, GA

Troy Campbell
Teacher
Lifelong Education Charter
Los Angeles, CA

Susan Canjura
Literacy Coach
Fairfax HS
Los Angeles, CA

John Oliver Cox
English Language
Development Teacher
Coronado USD
Coronado, CA

Clairin DeMartini
Reading Coordinator
Clark County SD
Las Vegas, NV

Lori Kite Eli
High School Reading Teacher
Pasadena HS
Pasadena, TX

Debra Elkins
ESOL Teamleader/Teacher
George Bush HS
Fort Bend, IN

Lisa Fretzin
Reading Consultant
Niles North HS
Skokie, IL

Karen H. Gouede
Asst. Principal, ESL
John Browne HS
Flushing, NY

Alison Hyde
ESOL Teacher
Morton Ranch HS
Katy, TX

Dr. Anna Leibovich
ESL Teacher
Forest Hills HS
New York, NY

Donna D. Mussulman
Teacher
Belleville West HS
Belleville, IL

Rohini A. Parikh
Educator
Seward Park School
New York, NY

Sally Nan Ruskin
English/Reading Teacher
Braddock SHS
Miami, FL

Pamela Sholly
Teacher
Oceanside USD
Oceanside, CA

Dilmit Singh
Teacher/EL Coordinator
Granada Hills Charter HS
Granada Hills, CA

Beverly Troiano
ESL Teacher
Chicago Discovery Academy
Chicago, IL

Dr. Varavarnee Vaddhanayana
ESOL Coordinator
Clarkston HS
Clarkston, GA

Bonnie Woelfel
Reading Specialist
Escondido HS
Escondido, CA

Pian Y. Wong
English Teacher
High School of American Studies
New York, NY

Izumi Yoshioka
English Teacher
Washington Irving HS
New York, NY

PROGRAM AUTHORS

David W. Moore, Ph.D.
Professor of Education
Arizona State University

Dr. David Moore taught high school social studies and reading in Arizona public schools before entering college teaching. He currently teaches secondary school teacher preparation courses in adolescent literacy. He co-chaired the International Reading Association's Commission on Adolescent Literacy and is actively involved with several professional associations. His twenty-five year publication record balances research reports, professional articles, book chapters, and books. Noteworthy publications include the International Reading Association position statement on adolescent literacy and the *Handbook of Reading Research* chapter on secondary school reading. Recent books include *Teaching Adolescents Who Struggle with Reading (2nd ed.)* and *Principled Practices for Adolescent Literacy*.

Deborah J. Short, Ph.D.
Senior Research Associate
Center for Applied Linguistics

Dr. Deborah Short is a co-developer of the research-validated SIOP Model for sheltered instruction. She has directed quasi-experimental and experimental studies on English language learners funded by the Carnegie Corporation, the Rockefeller Foundation, and the U.S. Dept. of Education. She recently chaired an expert panel on adolescent ELL literacy and prepared a policy report: *Double the Work: Challenges and Solutions to Acquiring Language and Academic Literacy for Adolescent English Language Learners*. She has also conducted extensive research on secondary level newcomer programs. Her research articles have appeared in the *TESOL Quarterly*, the *Journal of Educational Research*, *Educational Leadership*, *Education and Urban Society*, *TESOL Journal*, *Social Education*, and *Journal of Research in Education*.

Michael W. Smith, Ph.D.
Professor, College of Education
Temple University

Dr. Michael Smith joined the ranks of college teachers after eleven years of teaching high school English. He has won awards for his teaching at both the high school and college levels. His research focuses on how experienced readers read and talk about texts, as well as what motivates adolescents' reading and writing both in and out of school. He has written eight books and monographs, including *"Reading Don't Fix No Chevys": Literacy in the Lives of Young Men*, for which he and his co-author received the 2003 David H. Russell Award for Distinguished Research in the Teaching of English. His writing has appeared in such journals as *Communication Education*, *English Journal*, *Journal of Adolescent & Adult Literacy*, *Journal of Educational Research*, *Journal of Literacy Research*, and *Research in the Teaching of English*.

Alfred W. Tatum, Ph.D.
Associate Professor, Literacy Education
Northern Illinois University

Dr. Alfred Tatum began his career as an eighth-grade teacher, later becoming a reading specialist and discovering the power of texts to reshape the life outcomes of struggling readers. His current research focuses on the literacy development of African American adolescent males, and he provides teacher professional development to urban middle and high schools. He serves on the National Advisory Reading Committee of the National Assessment of Educational Progress (NAEP) and is active in a number of literacy organizations. In addition to his book *Teaching Reading to Black Adolescent Males: Closing the Achievement Gap*, he has published in journals such as *Reading Research Quarterly*, *The Reading Teacher*, *Journal of Adolescent & Adult Literacy*, *Educational Leadership*, the *Journal of College Reading and Learning*, and *Principal Leadership*.

ALL
ABOUT
ME

Language Development

Reading Strategy
Visualize

EQ **ESSENTIAL QUESTION:**
Who Am I?

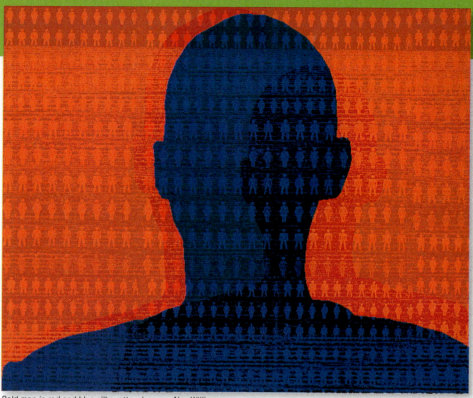

Bald man in red and blue silhouette, close up, Alex Williamson.

UNIT 2

WISDOM OF THE AGES

EQ **ESSENTIAL QUESTION:**
What Makes Us Wise?

Turkana Afternoon © 1994, Tilly Willis. Oil on canvas.

WRITING PROJECT

Expository Writing

GLOBAL VILLAGE

EQ **ESSENTIAL QUESTION:**
What Makes Us the Same? What Makes Us Different?

Ensemble © 1994, Stéphan Daigle. Acrylics on paper support.

WRITING PROJECT

Descriptive Writing

Language Development

Reading Strategy
Plan and Monitor

Survival

EQ ESSENTIAL QUESTION:
What Does It Take to Survive?

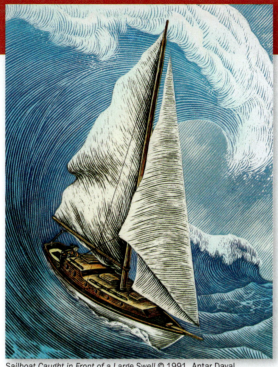

Sailboat Caught in Front of a Large Swell © 1991, Antar Dayal.
Colored scratchboard, Dayal Studio, Inc.

WRITING PROJECT

Expository Writing

UNIT 5

FITTING IN

EQ ESSENTIAL QUESTION:
How Important Is It to Fit In?

Golconde © 1953, René Magritte.

WRITING PROJECT

Expressive Writing

WHAT MATTERS MOST

EQ ESSENTIAL QUESTION:
What Is Most Important in Life?

For Dragonboat Festival © 1994, Komi Chen.

Narrative Writing

WRITING PROJECT

RESOURCES

Language and Learning Handbook
Language, Learning, Communication

Reading Handbook
Reading, Fluency, Vocabulary

Writing Handbook
Writing Process, Traits, Conventions

GENRES AT A GLANCE

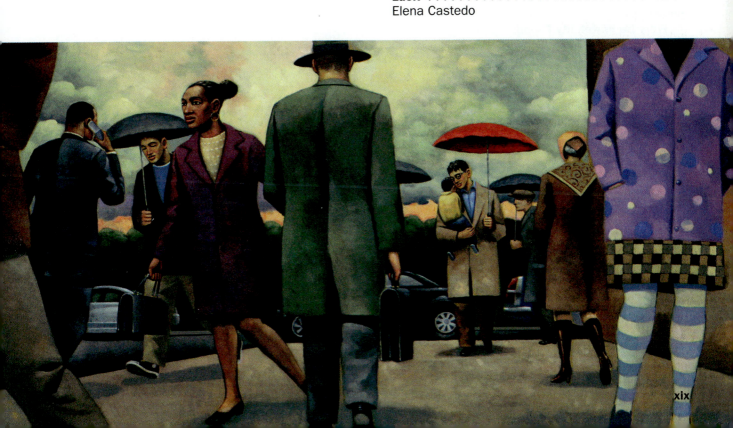

NONFICTION (continued)

ALL ABOUT ME

EQ ESSENTIAL QUESTION:

Who Am I?

The child of a snake is also a snake.

—African (Bemba) Proverb

Be friends with good people and you will become a good person.

—Mexican Proverb

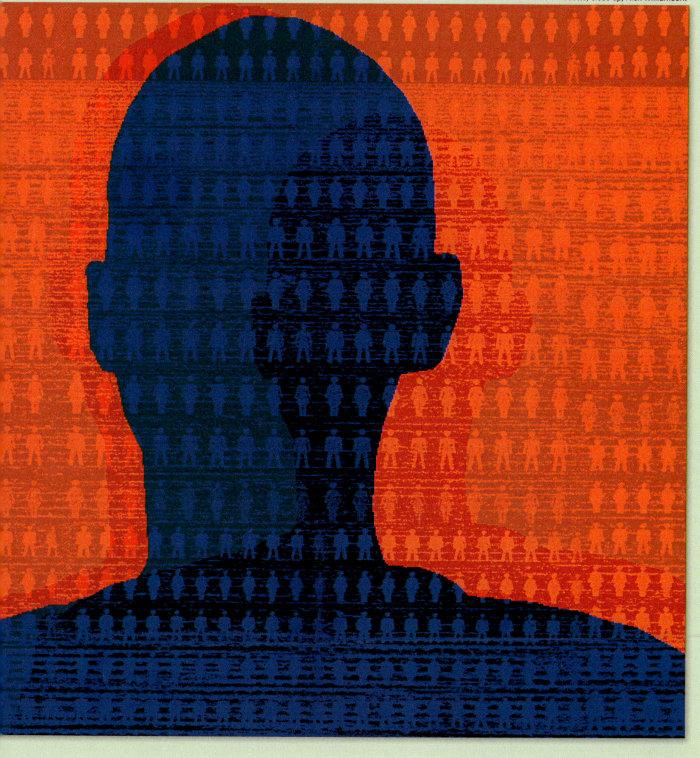

Bald man in red and blue silhouette, close-up, Alex Williamson.

EQ ESSENTIAL QUESTION:
Who Am I?

Study the Photos

Who are they?

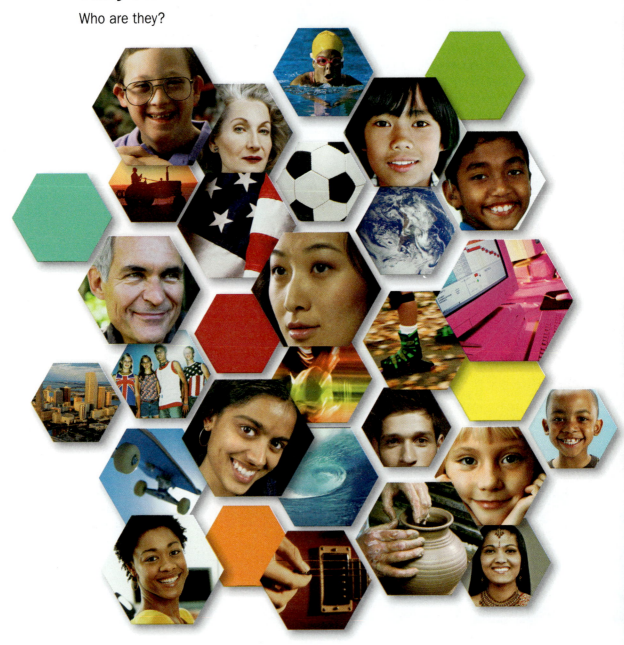

EQ **ESSENTIAL QUESTION**
In this unit, you will explore the **Essential Question** in class. Think about the question outside of school, too.

1 Study the Concept

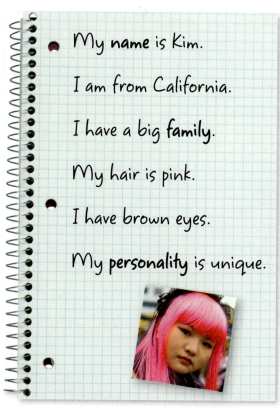

My name is Kim.

I am from California.

I have a big family.

My hair is pink.

I have brown eyes.

My personality is unique.

1. Choose a photo on page 4. Imagine who the person is. What is his or her **personality**?

2. What is the person's **name**? Where is the person from? Does the person have a big or small **family**?

3. Tell a partner about the person.

2 Choose More to Read

Choose something to read during this unit.

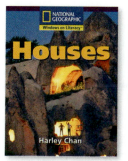

Houses
by Harley Chan

Learn about the different kinds of houses that people live in.

▶ NONFICTION

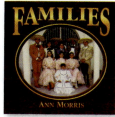

Families
by Ann Morris

Visit families around the world. Learn how they live, work, and celebrate.

▶ NONFICTION

www.hbedge.net
- Write your name in an ancient alphabet.
- Listen to music from around the world.

Relate Words

Some words connect, or relate, to each other. When you relate words, you can understand them better.

Word Web

This **category** tells how the words are related.

happy = content

These words are related. They have about the same meaning. They are **synonyms**.

happy ≠ sad

These words have opposite meanings. They are **antonyms**.

Practice Relating Words

Answer the questions based on the words above.

1. How do *happy*, *scared*, and *sorry* relate to each other?

2. Which word belongs to the feelings category: *sad* or *music*?

3. How do the words *happy* and *content* relate to each other?

4. How do the words *happy* and *sad* relate to each other?

Put the Strategy to Use

Work with a partner. Answer each question. Choose a word from the box.

5. Which word relates to clothing?

6. Which word relates to a place?

7. Which word means the opposite of *inside*?

8. Which word is a good category for the words below?

| family |
| home |
| outside |
| pants |

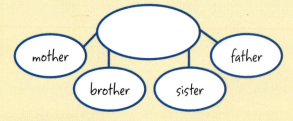

Give Information

Listen to the conversation.

1 TRY OUT LANGUAGE
2 LEARN GRAMMAR
3 APPLY ON YOUR OWN

Conversation

Nice to Meet You!

Ricardo:	Hi, I'm Ricardo.
Antonio:	Hi, Ricardo. I'm Antonio.
Ricardo:	Nice to meet you, Antonio.
Antonio:	This is my friend Mei. She is from Japan.
Ricardo:	Japan? Are you a student?
Mei:	Yes, I am here for one year. It is nice to meet you.

Use the Verb *Be*

The verb **be** has three forms: **am**, **is**, and **are**. Use these verbs to talk about yourself and others.

WHO	USE	EXAMPLE	WHO	USE	EXAMPLE
yourself	**I + am**	**I am** Ricardo.	yourself and another person	**we + are**	Antonio and I are friends. **We are** in the same class.
someone you speak to	**you + are**	**You are** my friend.	two or more people you speak to	**you + are**	**You are** my best friends.
one other person	**he + is** **she + is**	Antonio is from Cuba. **He is** a student. Mei is from Japan. **She is** a student, too.	two or more people or things	**they + are**	Antonio and Mei are new here. **They are** friendly.
one thing	**it + is**	Our classroom is an exciting place. **It is** new.			

Say It

Talk with a partner.

1–2. Tell your partner two things about yourself. Say:

   I am _____.

3–5. Tell your partner three things about your friends. Say:

   He is _____.

   She is _____.

   They are _____.

We are new students.

Write It

Choose the correct word and write each sentence.

   6. I (am/are) a new student.

   7. Like me, you (is/are) a new student, too.

   8. Lisa (is/are) also a new student.

   9. We (am/are) friends.

   10. Lisa has two brothers. They (is/are) new students, too.

Talk About a Friend

1 TRY OUT LANGUAGE
2 LEARN GRAMMAR
3 APPLY ON YOUR OWN

Talk with a group and find out about a classmate. Write down the information. Tell the class about your new friend.

Follow these steps to report the information to your class:

HOW TO GIVE INFORMATION

1. Say your classmate's name.

2. Say your classmate's age and favorite color.

3. Say more about your classmate.

My classmate's name is Mona. She is 15 years old. Her favorite color is blue. She is friendly and smart.

Use is to tell about one other person.

To gather the information, first talk with the people in your group. Find out:
- name
- age
- favorite color
- what they like to do

Then tell the rest of the class about your friend.

They are all 15 years old.

EQ ▶ **Who Am I?**
Think about your name.

Learn Key Vocabulary

Pronounce each word and learn its meaning.

Key Words

call (cawl) *verb*
▶ pages 14, 22, 24

To **call** means to use a name for someone or something. She is Rebecca. We **call** her Becky.

different (di-frunt) *adjective*
▶ pages 12, 15, 24

Different means not like someone or something else. The two shoes are **different**.

everyone (ev-rē-wun) *pronoun*
▶ page 14

Everyone means all the people in a group. **Everyone** in the picture is smiling.

everywhere (ev-rē-wair) *adverb*
▶ page 14

Everywhere means in all places. In the library, books are **everywhere**.

friend (frend) *noun*
▶ pages 12, 16, 19

A **friend** is someone you care about. The **friends** play video games.

like (līk) *verb*
▶ pages 12, 18, 25

When you **like** people or things, you feel good about them. She **likes** pizza.

other (u-thur) *adjective*
▶ pages 12, 15

Other means someone or something else. Many apples are red. The **other** apple is green.

unique (yū-nēk) *adjective*
▶ pages 18, 19, 25

Something is **unique** when it is the only one of its kind. The orange fish is **unique** in this school of blue fish.

Practice the Words Make a **Vocabulary Study Card** for each Key Vocabulary word. Then compare cards with a partner.

> different
> **What it means:** not the same
> **Example:** You and I are different.

BEFORE READING **First Names**

photo essay by Greta Gilbert

Visualize

When you read, you can use the words to see pictures in your mind. The pictures help you understand what you read.

HOW TO FORM MENTAL IMAGES

1. Turn the pages. Look at the pictures.
2. Focus on details. Think about what they make you imagine.
3. Add what you know from your life. Think about people you know.
4. To build your understanding, make a quick drawing. Show what you visualize.

Look at the text. See how one reader formed mental images.

Look Into the Text

> The girl looks like my cousin Maria. She has a smile like Maria's. I picture her at lunch with me.

Try It

Read "First Names." Visualize the people you read about.

Build Background

All people have names. Where do their names come from? Parents usually name their babies. Some parents name their baby for a **friend** or a family member. **Other** parents choose a name with a special meaning, like Joy.

Think about your name. Where does your name come from? Does it tell what you are like? Read about **different** names in "First Names." Which ones do you **like**?

www.hbedge.net
- Download and design a nametag.
- View photos of naming ceremonies from cultures around the world.

First Names

by Greta Gilbert

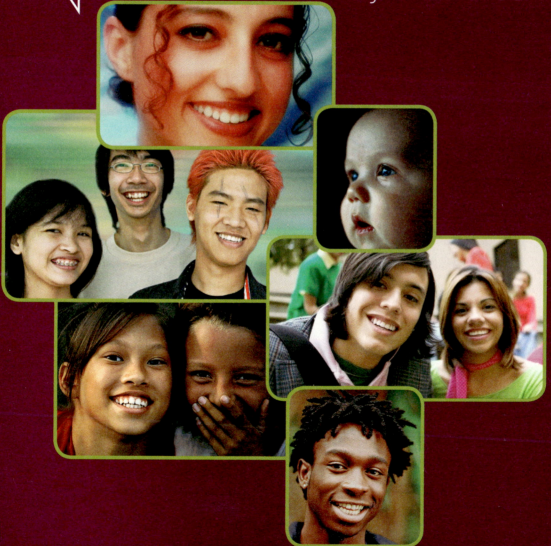

Everyone, **everywhere**, has a name.
Call our names, and we will answer.

We have the same first name—Amy. Amy means "**loved**." We are loved. There are **other** Amys. But we are all **different**.

Monitor Comprehension

Describe
How are both Amys the same? How are they different?

My name is Ernesto. My **friends** call me Ernie.

My name is also the name of a **hurricane**.

Key Vocabulary
friend *noun*, someone you care about

In Other Words
hurricane big storm

Surya is **the Hindu god of the sun**.

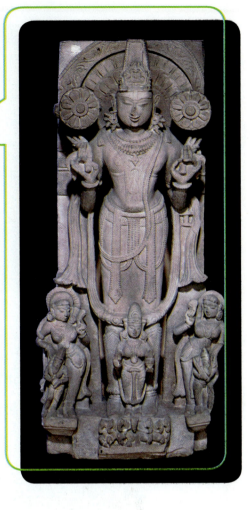

I am Surya, too.

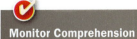

Monitor Comprehension

Explain
What is the name of
the hurricane? How do
you know?

My first name is Kofi. It means "**born** on Friday."
I was not born on Friday. But I **like** my first name.
It is **unique**. I am, too. ❖

Key Vocabulary
like *verb*, to feel good about
unique *adjective*, the only one of a kind

In Other Words
born started life

ANALYZE First Names

1. **Explain** What does Kofi's name mean?

2. **Vocabulary** What are your **friends'** names? Who has a **unique** name?

3. **Reading Strategy** **Visualize** You learned the meanings of four names. Draw a picture to show what you visualize for each name. Use your pictures to explain the meanings to a friend.

Amy	Ernesto	Surya	Kofi

Return to the Text

Reread and Retell Reread the selection. Use your own words to say what two of the names mean.

Characters in a Play

The writer of a story or a play creates **characters**. The characters are often people who seem like us. They look like real people. They have feelings like real people.

HOW TO UNDERSTAND CHARACTERS

Actors play the parts of the characters in a play. The names of the characters are in dark type. The words the characters say come after their names. These words are called dialogue.

1. To identify the characters, find the names.

2. To learn what a character is like, think about what the character says and does.

Read the text from the play. Identify the character. See how one reader learns how Juliet feels.

Look Into the Text

The **characters** are the people in a play.

Dialogue is what the characters say.

JULIET. [*looking down from above*]

Oh, Romeo, Romeo! Why is your name "Romeo Montague"?

Change your name.

Or, just say you love me.

And I will change my name. I will no longer be a Capulet.

When I read that Juliet wants to change her name, I can tell she loves Romeo.

Try It

When you read "Romeo and Juliet," look to see which character is speaking. Read the dialogue to learn about the character.

Connect Across Texts
In "First Names," people say what their names mean. Now read an excerpt from a famous play. Romeo and Juliet are in love. What do the characters think a name means?

FROM

ROMEO *and* JULIET

ACT 2, SCENE 2

by William Shakespeare

Romeo and Juliet is a very famous play. William Shakespeare wrote it more than four hundred years ago. But people still read and watch it today.

The play tells a sad story. The Capulet family and the Montague family hate each other. But Juliet Capulet and Romeo Montague fall in love. Do their names make them who they are?

JULIET. [*looking down from above*]

Oh, Romeo, Romeo! Why is your name "Romeo
Montague"?

Change your name.

Or, just say you love me.

And I will change my name. I will **no longer be**
a Capulet.

ROMEO. [*to himself*]

Should I wait to hear more or should I speak?

JULIET. [*continues*]

My family hates the name "Montague."

If you change your name, you will still be the
man I love.

What is a name? A rose is a rose

Even if it is not **called** "rose."

And Romeo is Romeo

even if he is not called "Romeo."

Romeo, give up your name.

If you do,

Then I will give you my heart.

Key Vocabulary
call *verb*, to use a name for
someone or something

In Other Words
no longer be stop being

ROMEO. [*looking up at Juliet*]

Your words of love are all I need to hear.

No longer call me "Romeo." Call me "love."

Then I will have a new name and a new life. ❖

Many actors around the world play Juliet.

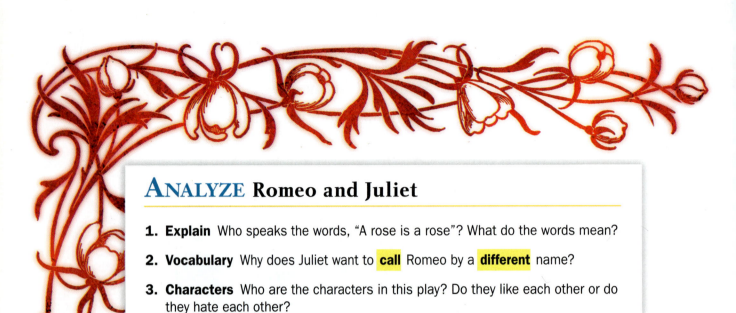

ANALYZE Romeo and Juliet

1. **Explain** Who speaks the words, "A rose is a rose"? What do the words mean?

2. **Vocabulary** Why does Juliet want to <mark>call</mark> Romeo by a <mark>different</mark> name?

3. **Characters** Who are the characters in this play? Do they like each other or do they hate each other?

Return to the Text

Reread and Retell Reread Romeo's dialogue. What does he mean when he says, "Then I will have a new name and a new life"?

About the Writer

William Shakespeare (1564–1616) is one of England's most famous writers. He wrote poems and plays. His plays are still performed around the world. Many of Shakespeare's plays are now movies, too. *West Side Story* tells a similar story. It is a musical play by a different writer.

EQ **Who Am I?**

Talk About Literature

Fluency

Listen to a reading. Practice fluency. Use the Reading Handbook, page 531.

1. **Generalize** How can you be **unique** if you have the same name as another person?

    I am unique because _____ .

2. **Explain** Why does Juliet want Romeo to give up his name?

EQ 3. **Analyze** "First Names" and "Romeo and Juliet" tell about names. Does your name make you who you are?

    Names are _____ (important/not important) because _____ .

Review Key Vocabulary

Choose the correct vocabulary word to complete each sentence.

1. My best _____ is my twin sister, Angelica. (everyone/friend)

2. Our parents _____ her Angie. (call/like)

3. Although we look the same, we are very _____. (different/other)

4. I _____ cats, but she prefers dogs. (call/like)

5. Angie swims every day. Her _____ interest is soccer. (other/different)

6. She is not like anyone else I know. She is really _____! (other/unique)

7. Angie and I go _____ together. (everyone/everywhere)

8. She is friendly to _____ she meets. (everyone/everywhere)

Vocabulary

- call
- different
- everyone
- everywhere
- friend
- like
- other
- unique

Write About Literature

EQ **Quickwrite** Every name relates to something in the world. Look at the names in "First Names." Think about what they relate to. Then explain what your own name relates to. Tell why you **like** or do not like your name.

My name is _____ . I have this name because _____ .
I like my name because _____ .

Grammar

Use Complete Sentences

A complete sentence has two parts: a **subject** and a **predicate**. The **subject** tells whom or what the sentence is about or who does the action.

> **Luisa** **is in my class**.
> **Abu and I** **are her friends**.
> **I** **am also her neighbor**.

The **predicate** tells more about the subject. A predicate always has a **verb**. The verb has to agree with the subject.

SUBJECT	VERB	EXAMPLE
I	am	**I am** 15 years old.
You	are	**You are** 15 years old, too.
He She It	is	**He is** older. **She is** in my class. **It is** a small class.
You	are	**You are** two happy students.
We	are	**We are** the same age.
They	are	**They are** younger.

Oral Practice Talk about yourself and your friends. Finish these sentences. First add a verb from the chart and then say more.

1. I _____ .
2. My best friend _____ .
3. My friend and I _____ .
4. Two of my friends _____ .
5. They _____ .

Written Practice Choose the correct word and write each sentence.

6. My family and I (is/are) from Mexico.
7. Mr. and Mrs. González (is/are) from Cuba.
8. I (am/are) from the United States.
9. Mei (is/are) from Japan.
10. Japan (is/are) far away.

Language Development

Give Information

Learn About an Actor Work with a partner. Find out about your favorite actor.

www.hbedge.net
• Read about a famous actor.
• Listen to an interview with the actor.

Collect facts about an actor you like. What is the actor's name? Where is the actor from? How old is he or she? What character does your actor play? Why are you interested in this actor?

Give information about the actor. Use sentences like these:

• The actor's name is _____ .
• (He/She) is from _____ .
• (He/She) is _____ years old.
• My actor is the character _____ in the movie, _____ .

Word Categories

Remember, a word category is a group of words that go together. They relate to each other in some way. The words in the list below belong to the category "Relatives."

Relatives
parents
children
grandparents
cousins

A category can be a word like "Relatives." It can also be a set of words like "People Related to Me."

The words in a category are often examples. A *cousin* is one kind of *relative*.

Work with a partner. Read the words in the box.

everyone	sun
moon	school
home	park
library	everything
everywhere	stars

Make a chart like this. Sort the words above into these categories.

Category Chart

Things in the Sky	Places in a Town	Words That Begin with "Every"

Expand the Story

"First Names" is about what names mean. Work with a small group. Talk about your name.

1. **Learn about it.** Where does your name come from? What does it mean?

   www.hbedge.net
   • Explore first names.
   • Find out what different names mean.

2. **Make notes.** You need to remember what you find out about your name. So write notes to yourself as you research.

3. **Present your information.** Tell the group your name. Say what you learned.

My name is Clara. In Spanish, it means "bright." It is a common name.

Writing

Write a Postcard

▶ **Prompt** Make a postcard. Write about yourself. Send the postcard to a friend or relative.

1 **Plan** Think about what you will write. Make some notes. Remember, a postcard does not have much space. Include these parts on your postcard.

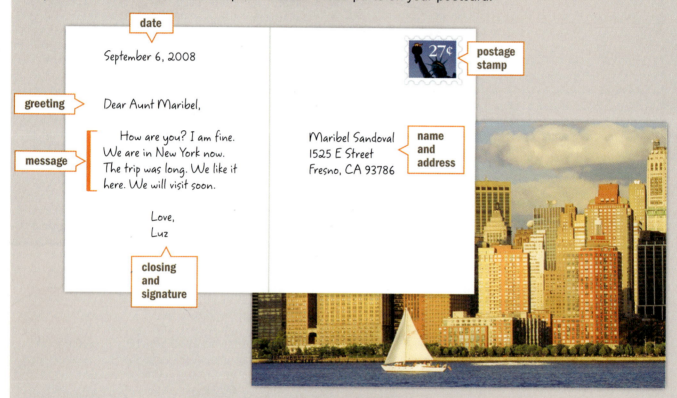

date

September 6, 2008

postage stamp 27¢

greeting Dear Aunt Maribel,

message
How are you? I am fine. We are in New York now. The trip was long. We like it here. We will visit soon.

name and address
Maribel Sandoval
1525 E Street
Fresno, CA 93786

Love,
Luz

closing and signature

2 **Write** Start with the date. Write a greeting. In the message, write sentences about yourself. When you write sentences with **am**, **is**, or **are**, use the correct form of the verb. Add your closing and signature.

3 **Share** Use a photograph or draw a picture on the other side of the postcard. Put a postage stamp in the corner. Send your postcard.

Use sentences like these:

• I went to [place] with [name].

• We had fun. We got home [when].

• How are you? I am [feeling].

• Our friends [what they are like].

Ask and Answer Questions

Listen to the conversation.

Do I Know You?

Bao: Excuse me. Do I know you?

Feng: Yes, you do! I am Feng—from China.

Bao: Wow! Do you live here in Los Angeles now?

Feng: No, I don't. I am here to visit my cousin.

Bao: Do you still live in Shanghai?

Feng: Yes, I do.

Bao: Is it still a fun city?

Feng: Yes, it is! Los Angeles is fun, too.

1 TRY OUT LANGUAGE
2 LEARN GRAMMAR
3 APPLY ON YOUR OWN

Use the Verb *Do*

The verb **do** has two forms: **do** and **does**.

• Use **do** with **I**, **you**, **we**, or **they**.

• Use **does** with **he**, **she**, or **it**.

Many questions start with **Do** or **Does**. The **subject** comes next and then another **verb**.

QUESTION	ANSWER
Do you like Los Angeles?	Yes, I **do**.
Does it feel like home?	No, it **does not**.
Do you have friends yet?	Yes, I **do**.
Do they help you?	Yes, they **do**.

When you answer, use the same verb that starts the question.
Say the **subject** first and then the verb.

Do you like Los Angeles? Yes, **I do**.

Say It

Work with a partner. Say the words in the right order to make a question.
Your partner answers the question.

1. Do you / a big city? / come from

2. in your country? / Does it / get cold

3. like / Does your family / the U.S.?

4. Do / the food here? / like / they

5. you / have / a brother or a sister? / Do

Write It

Complete each question with *Do* or *Does*. Then trade papers with a
partner and answer the questions.

6. _____ your family like the U.S.?

7. _____ you know people here from your country?

8. _____ they visit your family?

9. _____ we know them?

10. _____ it feel like home here?

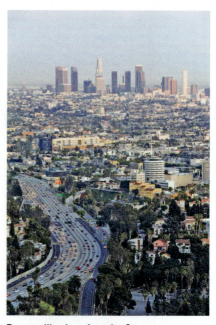

Do you like Los Angeles?

Do a Survey

Ask your family some questions and write down the answers. Then report the results to your class. Follow these tips for correct language:

HOW TO ASK AND ANSWER QUESTIONS

1. You can start a question with a verb like *Is, Are, Do,* or *Does.*

   > **Do** you like our neighborhood?

2. Name the subject next:

   I   you   he   she   it   we   they

   > Yes, I **do.**

3. When you answer, use the same verb.

The answer uses the same **verb** that starts the question.

To get ready, copy this question chart to take home.

QUESTION	YES ANSWERS	NO ANSWERS
1. Are you happy here?	1. _____	1. _____
2. Do you like our neighborhood?	2. _____	2. _____
3. Is it different from where you were born?	3. _____	3. _____
4. Does it feel the same in some ways?	4. _____	4. _____

We are happy here.

Then ask the questions and count your family's answers. Share the answers with your class.

EQ **Who Am I?**
Learn how your family and culture are part of you.

Learn Key Vocabulary

Pronounce each word and learn its meaning.

Key Words

beautiful (byū-ti-ful) *adjective*
▶ pages 43, 44

Something that is **beautiful** is pretty. The roses are **beautiful**.

grow (grō) *verb*
▶ pages 36, 45

To **grow** is to make bigger or to cultivate. A lemon tree **grows** lemons.

hard (hard) *adjective*
▶ pages 37, 41

When something is **hard**, it is not easy to do. Rock climbing is **hard**.

home (hōm) *noun*
▶ pages 34, 37, 41

A **home** is where you live. The family is happy and comfortable at **home**.

leave (lēv) *verb*
▶ pages 37, 41

To **leave** is to go away. She is happy to **leave** the group.

miss (mis) *verb*
▶ page 36

When you **miss** people or places, you are sad that you are not with them. She **misses** her little sister.

together (tu-ge-thur) *adverb*
▶ page 38

When you put things **together**, you combine them. She plants the flowers **together**.

wait (wāt) *verb*
▶ page 39

When you **wait**, you stay in one place until something happens. The people **wait** for the bus to stop.

Practice the Words Make a **Word Web** for each Key Vocabulary word. Then compare webs with a partner.

Word Web

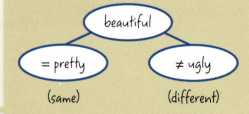

BEFORE READING Growing Together

short story by Carmen Agra Deedy

Visualize

When you read a story, try to picture what the author describes. You can visualize places in the same way that you visualize people.

Reading Strategy
Visualize

HOW TO FORM MENTAL IMAGES

1. Look for details. Find words that tell how things look, sound, smell, taste, and feel.

2. Picture the place. Ask, "What does it look like?"

3. Make a quick drawing. Show how you see the place in your mind.

Read the text. Look at the drawing.

Look Into the Text

> Some days I still miss Cuba. I miss warm breezes. I miss mango trees. I live in Georgia now. The days are cold. We only have one tree.

It is always warm in Cuba. It is not always warm in Georgia.

Try It

Visualize as you read "Growing Together." Make drawings to show the scenes you see in your mind.

Growing Together **33**

Meet Carmen Agra Deedy
(1960–   )

Carmen Agra Deedy was born in 1960 in Havana, Cuba. She came to the United States with her family in 1963. Her family moved to Georgia. Georgia is still her **home** today.

Deedy grew up in two cultures and two places. She was always trying to find her own place. Many of Deedy's stories are about people who are living in two cultures. She tells how they feel and what they experience.

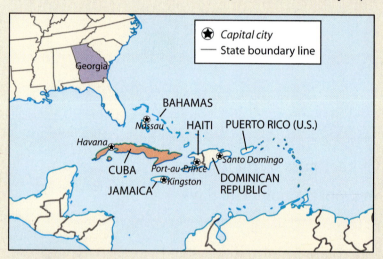

★ Capital city
— State boundary line

Georgia

BAHAMAS
Nassau   HAITI   PUERTO RICO (U.S.)
Havana
CUBA   *Port-au-Prince*   *Santo Domingo*
JAMAICA   *Kingston*   DOMINICAN REPUBLIC

Cuba is a country. It is an island in the Caribbean Sea. Georgia is a state. It is in the south part of the United States.

www.hbedge.net
- Find out more about the country called Cuba.
- Find out more about the state of Georgia.

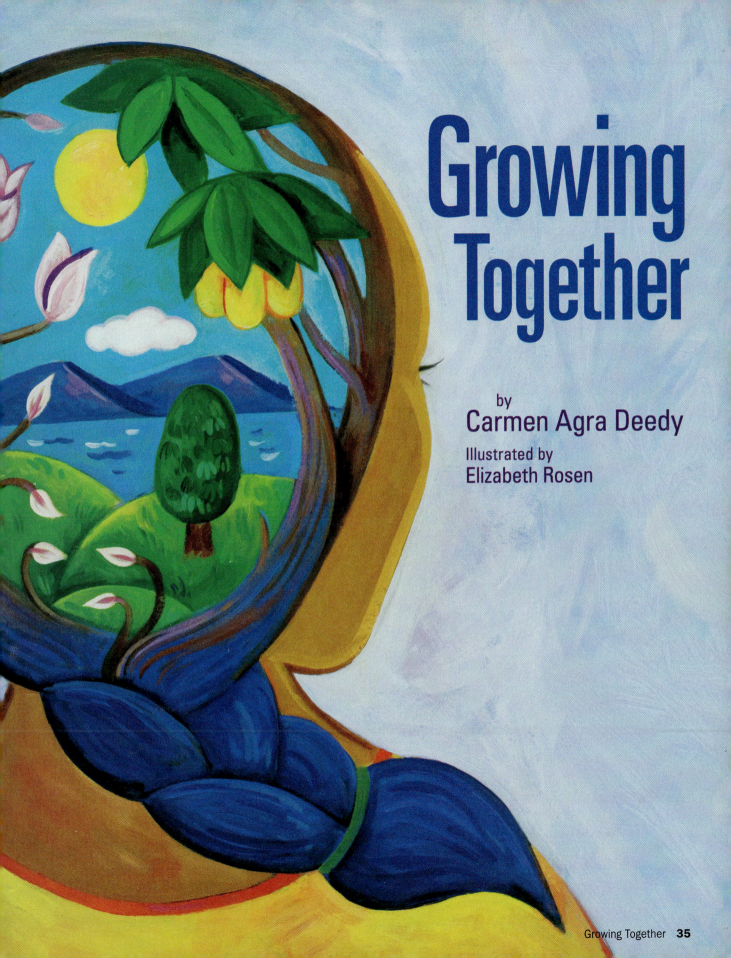

Growing Together

by
Carmen Agra Deedy

Illustrated by
Elizabeth Rosen

Some days I still **miss** Cuba. I miss warm **breezes**.
I miss **mango trees**. I live in Georgia now. The days are cold.
We only have one tree. It is a **magnolia**. It only **grows** flowers.

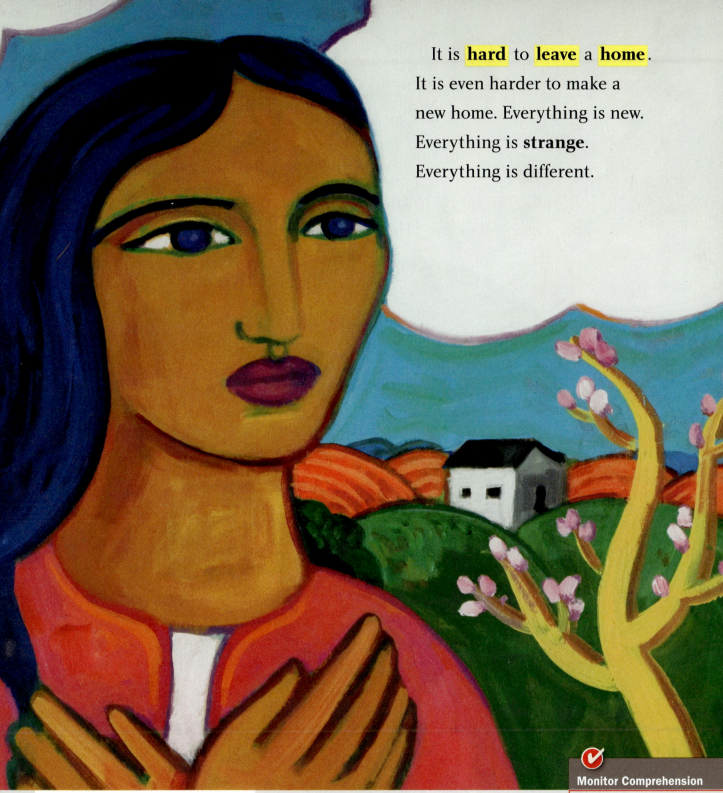

It is **hard** to **leave** a **home**.
It is even harder to make a
new home. Everything is new.
Everything is **strange**.
Everything is different.

Key Vocabulary
hard *adjective*, not easy
leave *verb*, to go away
home *noun*, place where you live

In Other Words
strange not what I know

Monitor Comprehension

Explain
Does the narrator like
her home in Georgia?
Why or why not?

I tell **Papi** how I feel.

"I **hate** it here! I am not like **them**. They are not like me!" I say.

He asks, "Carmita, do you know what it means to graft a tree?"

I **nod**. "You take a **branch** from one tree. You add it to another tree. Then they grow **together**."

Key Vocabulary
together *adverb*, with each other, combined

In Other Words
Papi Dad (in Spanish)
hate do not like
them other people in Georgia
nod move my head to say "yes"
branch part

My father says I
am the mango tree.
Georgia is the magnolia
tree. I must **wait**. The
mango and magnolia
will grow together.

Monitor Comprehension

Summarize
What does Carmita's
father tell her about
the magnolia tree and
the mango tree?

I **smile**. I will wait.
I am a tree. I grow both
mangoes and magnolias.
I am an American. ❖

In Other Words
smile show that I am happy

ANALYZE Growing Together

1. **Explain** Where does Carmita live now? Where did she live before?

2. **Vocabulary** What does Carmita mean when she says, "It is <mark>hard</mark> to <mark>leave</mark> a <mark>home</mark>"?

3. **Reading Strategy** **Visualize** Draw a picture that shows what Carmita says about the weather.

Return to the Text

Reread and Retell Why does Carmita's father talk to her about how to graft a tree? Reread the text and find details to support your answer.

poem by Langston Hughes

Elements of Poetry: Patterns

In a **poem**, the words are grouped in lines, not paragraphs. Poems are like music. In many poems, the words form patterns. A pattern can be a set of words or sounds that repeat.

HOW TO READ POETRY

1. Read the poem aloud. Ask, "How does it sound?"

2. Read the poem again slowly. Look for patterns, parts that are repeated. Listen for patterns.

3. Ask, "What do the repeated parts show is important to understand or feel?"

4. Read it again. Write your ideas on a self-stick note.

Read the lines of the poem and the self-stick note.

Look Into the Text

The night is **beautiful**.
So the faces of my people.

The stars are **beautiful**.
So the eyes of my people.

A word that repeats forms a pattern.

The poet repeats "beautiful." It shows that this is an important description of his people.

Try It

Read "My People" a few times. What do the patterns show is important? Write your ideas on self-stick notes.

Connect Across Texts

In "Growing Together," Carmita explains how she is part of two cultures. What does the speaker in this poem say about the people in his culture?

My People

by
Langston Hughes

Illustrated by
Sara Tyson

The night is beautiful,
So the faces of my people.

The stars are beautiful,
So the eyes of my people.

Beautiful, also, is the sun.
Beautiful, also, are the souls of my people.

Key Vocabulary
beautiful *adjective*, pretty, nice to look at

In Other Words
my people men, women, and children who share my background and culture
stars lights in the night sky
souls hearts and lives

ANALYZE My People

1. **Explain** What is the poem about?

2. **Vocabulary** How is the night **beautiful** ?

3. **Elements of Poetry** Find patterns in the words. How do the patterns help you understand the poem better? Explain.

🔁 **Return to the Text**

Reread and Retell Reread the poem. Name three things the poet compares to his people.

About the Poet

Langston Hughes (1902–1967) was a famous American writer. He was an important person in the Harlem Renaissance. During this time, Americans celebrated African American culture in art, writing, music, and dance.

EQ **Who Am I?**

Talk About Literature

1. **Interpret** What does Carmita mean when she says "I am a tree. I <mark>grow</mark> both mangoes and magnolias"?

2. **Compare** How are the "souls of my people" like the sun? Why?

    The souls and the sun are both _____ . This tells me that _____ .

EQ 3. **Generalize** "Growing Together" and "My People" tell about families and cultures. How do family and culture make you the person that you are?

    A person's family and culture are important because _____ .

Listen to a reading. Practice fluency. Use the Reading Handbook, page 532.

Review Key Vocabulary

Choose the correct vocabulary word to complete each sentence.

1. We lived in a _____ house in the city. (beautiful/hard)

2. At first, we did not want to _____ the city. (grow/leave)

3. It was _____ to say good-bye to our friends. (beautiful/hard)

4. Our new _____ has a big garden. (home/together)

5. We _____ flowers and vegetables. (grow/wait)

6. This year, we planted beans and corn _____ . (home/together)

7. We must _____ until they are ready for us to pick! (miss/wait)

8. We do not _____ city life any more. (wait/miss)

Vocabulary
beautiful
grow
hard
home
leave
miss
together
wait

Write About Literature

EQ **Reflection** "Growing Together" and "My People" show how places and people relate to each other. Draw a picture. Write labels and a caption to tell about your family and a place that is important to you.

This place is _____ . It is important to me because _____ . The people are _____ .

Grammar

Use Subject Pronouns

she   he   it   they

- A **pronoun** takes the place of a noun. A pronoun can be the subject of a sentence. Use the pronoun that goes with the subject.

USE	TO TELL ABOUT	EXAMPLES
she	one female	**Carmita** gardens. **She** likes to grow things.
he	one male	**Dan** watches. **He** grows things, too.
it	one thing	The **flower pot** is new. **It** is green.
they	more than one person or thing	The **friends** talk. **They** look at the garden.

- When you answer a question, use the pronoun that matches the subject.

  Does **Carmita** like the garden?   Yes, **she** does.
  Is the **garden** big?   No, **it** isn't.

Oral Practice Work with a partner. Add the correct pronoun and answer your partner's question.

1. Does Carmita like Georgia? No, _____ doesn't.
2. Does she still miss Cuba? Yes, _____ does.
3. Are the days cold in Georgia? Yes, _____ are.
4. Is it easy to leave a home? No, _____ isn't.
5. Does Papi talk to Carmita? Yes, _____ does.

Written Practice Write a short answer to each question.

6. Does Papi help Carmita understand?
7. Is Carmita the mango tree?
8. Is Carmita the magnolia tree?
9. Does Carmita wait?
10. Do the mango and magnolia trees grow together?

Language Development

Ask and Answer Questions

Play Five Questions Imagine you are from a different country. Your classmates will ask you questions that start with *Is, Are, Do,* or *Does* to guess what country you are from. Answer only with *Yes* or *No* statements. If your classmates can't guess after five questions, tell them the answer.

www.hbedge.net
- Read facts about different countries.
- View photos of different countries.

Gather information about your country. Is it big or small? Are the days cold or hot? Does it snow there? Do the people speak Spanish there? Is it in Asia?

Use these questions to help you:
1. Is your country [big/small] ?
2. Is it in [name a continent] ?
3. Does it snow there?
4. Are the days [hot/cold] ?
5. Do the people speak [name language] ?

Concept Clusters

Remember, when you relate words, you can understand them better.

A concept cluster shows information about a certain word or idea. Look at this concept cluster for *mango tree*.

Concept Cluster

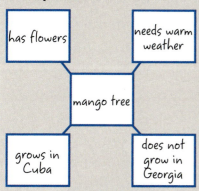

What can you add to the concept cluster?

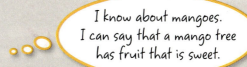

I know about mangoes. I can say that a mango tree has fruit that is sweet.

Work with a partner. Make a concept cluster for *magnolia tree*. Tell what you know about it.

- What is it?
- What does it look like?
- Where does it grow?
- What does it need?

Identify Sequence

"Growing Together" is about a girl who is learning to live in a new place. Events are the things that happen in the story. The order in which they happen is the sequence of events.

When you know the sequence of events, you can understand the story better. Copy the list to the right. Add more events to your list. Be sure to list events in order.

"Growing Together"
1. Carmita thinks about living in Cuba.
2. She tells her father how she feels.

Writing

Write an Interview

▶ **Prompt** Interview someone about a hobby. A hobby is an activity that people enjoy in their free time.

1 **Plan** Think of someone you want to interview. Call the person. Plan a time to talk with the person. Write a set of questions.

2 **Conduct the Interview** Meet with the person. Ask your questions. Write the answers. If you use **do** or **does**, be sure that the form of the verb matches the subject.

Use questions like these:
- What is your name?
- What is your hobby?
- Where do you do this hobby?
- What do you like best about it?

Interview

question → Q: What is your name?
answer → A: My name is Salvador.

Q: What do you like to do for fun?
A: I like to skateboard.

Q: How often do you skateboard?
A: My skateboarding club meets every Saturday.

Q: Where does your club go?
A: We go to the park to skate.

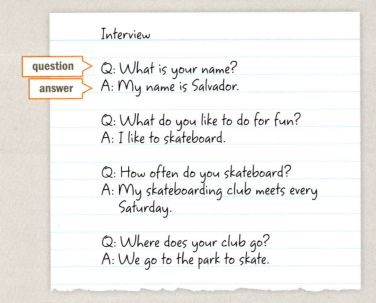

What do you like to do in your free time?

I like to collect comic books.

3 **Share** Copy the final questions and answers. Use good handwriting. Give a copy of the interview to the person you interviewed.

1 TRY OUT LANGUAGE
2 LEARN GRAMMAR
3 APPLY ON YOUR OWN

Ask for and Give Information

Listen to the rap. Where is Cynthia from?

Rap

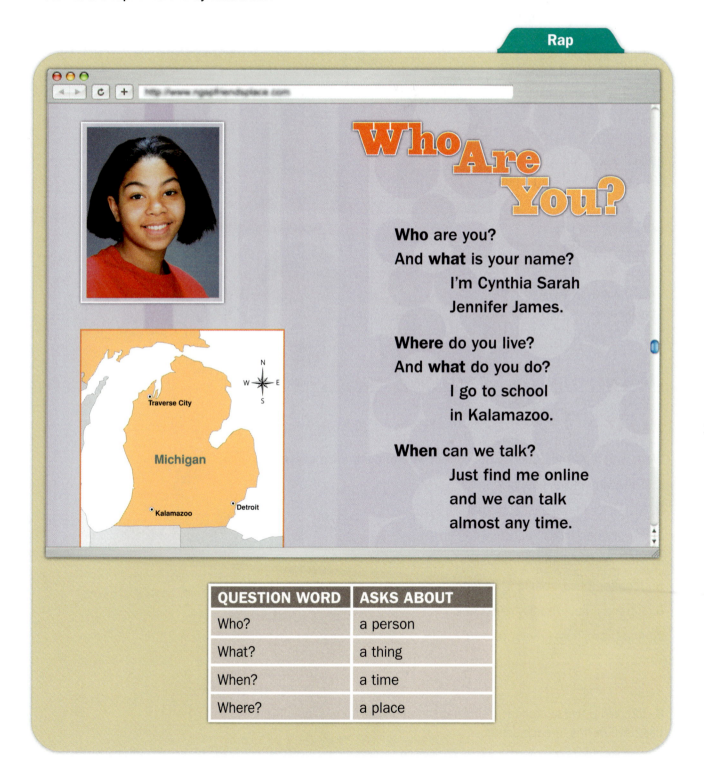

Who Are You?

Who are you?
And **what** is your name?
    I'm Cynthia Sarah
    Jennifer James.

Where do you live?
And **what** do you do?
    I go to school
    in Kalamazoo.

When can we talk?
    Just find me online
    and we can talk
    almost any time.

QUESTION WORD	ASKS ABOUT
Who?	a person
What?	a thing
When?	a time
Where?	a place

Use the Verb *Have*

The verb **have** has two forms: **have** and **has**.

• Use **have** with **I, you, we,** or **they.**

• Use **has** with **he, she,** or **it.**

See how these **verbs** agree, or go with, their **subjects** .

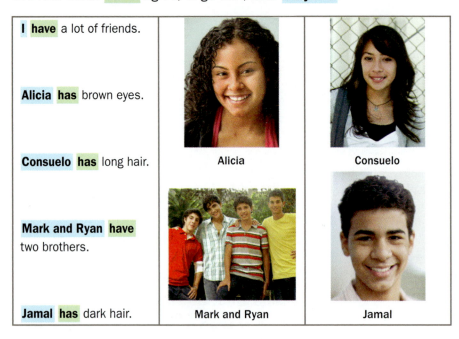

I **have** a lot of friends.

Alicia **has** brown eyes.

Consuelo **has** long hair.

Mark and Ryan **have** two brothers.

Jamal **has** dark hair.

Alicia

Consuelo

Mark and Ryan

Jamal

Say It

Work with a partner. Choose the correct verb and say each sentence.

1. The twins (have/has) blue eyes.

2. My sister (have/has) short hair.

3. My brother (have/has) curly hair.

4. We (have/has) many friends.

5. Jennifer (have/has) long fingernails.

6. Ronaldo (have/has) straight hair.

7. Ana (have/has) green eyes.

Write It

8–12. Write five sentences. Tell what you and your friends look like.
Use *have* or *has* in each sentence.

Play a Guessing Game

Work with a partner. Create "mystery cards." Then play a game to try to guess who is on the card. Ask your partner for information to find out.

Follow these tips to exchange information with your partner:

HOW TO ASK FOR AND GIVE INFORMATION

1. Decide what you want to know.

2. Form a question. Start it with the correct question word.

QUESTION WORD	ASKS ABOUT
Who?	a person
What?	a thing
When?	a time
Where?	a place

> **What** does she look like?

3. Give information in your answer.

> She **has** long hair and brown eyes.

Use **have** or **has** in some of your answers.

To make the "mystery cards," find photos of famous people. Or use photos of your classmates. Glue each photo onto an index card.

To play the game:

- Work with a partner.
- Turn the cards face down.
- Have your partner take a card.
- Ask questions to get clues about the photo. You can ask for information, but you cannot ask who the person is.
- Use clues to guess the person in the photo.

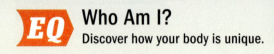

EQ ## Who Am I?
Discover how your body is unique.

Learn Key Vocabulary

Pronounce each word and learn its meaning.

Key Words

find (fīnd) *verb*
▶ pages 54, 63

When you **find** something, you learn where it is. She **finds** the book that she is looking for.

idea (ī-dē-u) *noun*
▶ pages 65, 66

When you have an **idea**, you have a thought or a plan. She has an **idea** for a paper she will write.

no one (nō-wun) *pronoun*
▶ pages 54, 57, 63

No one means no person. When you are alone, **no one** is with you.

pattern (pa-turn) *noun*
▶ pages 54, 57, 61, 65

A **pattern** is a design that repeats. There is a **pattern** on the bottom of these shoes.

scientist (sī-un-tist) *noun*
▶ pages 54, 60, 64

A **scientist** studies plants, animals, chemicals, and other things in our world.

similar (si-mu-lur) *adjective*
▶ pages 54, 56

When things are **similar**, they are almost the same. The violins are **similar**.

special (spe-shul) *adjective*
▶ pages 58, 63

If something is **special**, it is not like the others. The gold egg is **special**.

study (stu-dē) *verb*
▶ pages 54, 57, 65

When you **study** something, you look at it carefully. The boys **study** the map.

Practice the Words Work with a partner. Write a sentence for each Key Vocabulary word.

find
I <u>find</u> my pen in my bag.

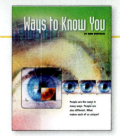

BEFORE READING **Ways to Know You**

expository nonfiction by Mimi Mortezai

Visualize

When you read about facts, you can create pictures in your mind. The pictures help you understand the ideas in the text.

Reading Strategy
Visualize

HOW TO FORM MENTAL IMAGES

1. Look first at the pictures. What pictures do you form in your own mind?

2. As you read, look for words that describe people, places, and events.
   Use those words to form more pictures in your mind.

3. Ask, "What do the pictures mean?" Use the pictures to help understand the text.

4. Write your ideas on self-stick notes.

Read the title. Look at the photos. What do they mean to you? Write the meanings on self-stick notes.

Look Into the Text

Ways to Know You
BY MIMI MORTEZAI

In my mind, I picture people's eyes. The eyes in the picture are blue, but I see eyes with different colors.

Eyes tell about us.

Try It

Visualize the text as you read "Ways to Know You." Write your ideas on self-stick notes.

Build Background

People are **similar**. We have eyes. We have hair. We have fingers. **Scientists** also **study** the details that make our bodies unique. They **find** different **patterns** in our bodies. **No one** has the same patterns as you.

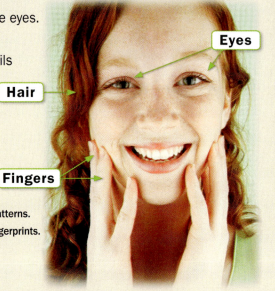

Eyes

Hair

Fingers

www.hbedge.net
- View photos of eye patterns.
- Learn more about fingerprints.

Ways to Know You

BY MIMI MORTEZAI

People are the same in many ways. People are also different. What makes each of us unique?

Fingerprints

Everyone has different fingerprints. These **triplets** look **similar**. But they have different fingerprints. Can you see the differences?

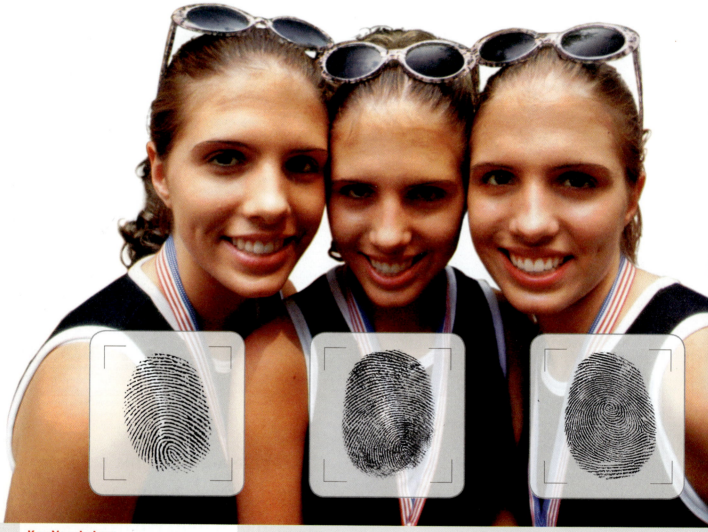

Key Vocabulary
similar *adjective*, almost the same

In Other Words
Fingerprints Lines on your fingers
triplets three brothers or sisters who were born at the same time

Fingerprints are unique in more than ten different ways. Each fingerprint has a **pattern**. **Study** your right thumb. Which patterns do you see? **No one** else has your fingerprints.

Fingerprint Patterns

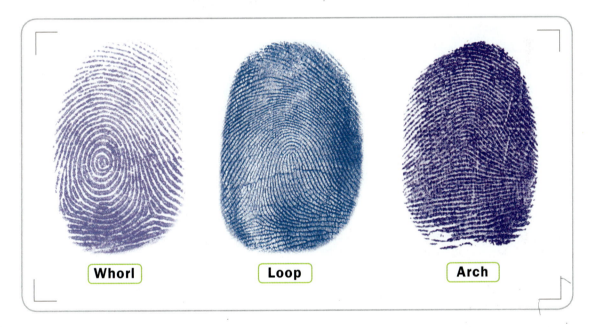

Whorl   Loop   Arch

Key Vocabulary
pattern *noun*, a design that repeats
study *verb*, to look at something carefully
no one *pronoun*, no person, nobody

In Other Words
your right thumb the short, thick finger on your right hand

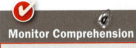
Monitor Comprehension

Explain
What is one way that people are unique?

Eyes

Everyone has different eyes. Eyes can look similar. But every eye is **special**.

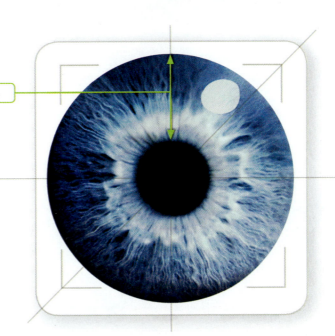

Iris

This is an iris. It has a pattern. It is unique in more than two hundred different ways.

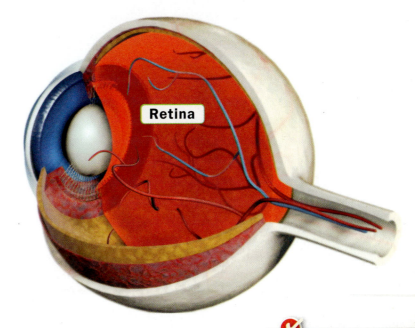

Retina

This is a retina. It has another pattern. Every eye has a different pattern.

No one else has your eyes.

Monitor Comprehension

Explain
What makes each person's eyes unique?

DNA

Everyone has DNA. **Scientists** study DNA. It is **your body's unique information**. It tells about you. It is in every part of your body. It is in your hair. It is in your fingernails. It is in your skin.

Key Vocabulary

scientist *noun*, person who studies plants, animals, chemicals, and other things in our world

In Other Words

your body's unique information information for your body only

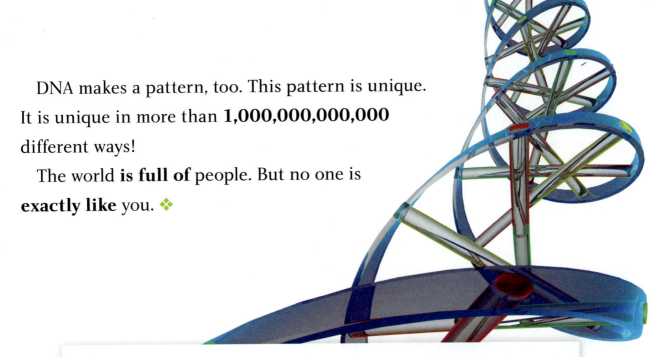

DNA makes a pattern, too. This pattern is unique. It is unique in more than **1,000,000,000,000** different ways!

The world **is full of** people. But no one is **exactly like** you. ❖

In Other Words
1,000,000,000,000 1 trillion
is full of has many
exactly like just the same as

magazine article by Joan Johnson

Text Structure: Sequence

Writers often tell about events in order. They tell what happens first, next, and last. When you follow the order of events, you will understand what you read better.

HOW TO IDENTIFY SEQUENCE

1. Read the text. Think about the **sequence**, or order, of events.

2. Write the events in a **Sequence Chart**.

3. Then use your chart to identify what happened first, next, and last.

Read the text. Look at the Sequence Chart.

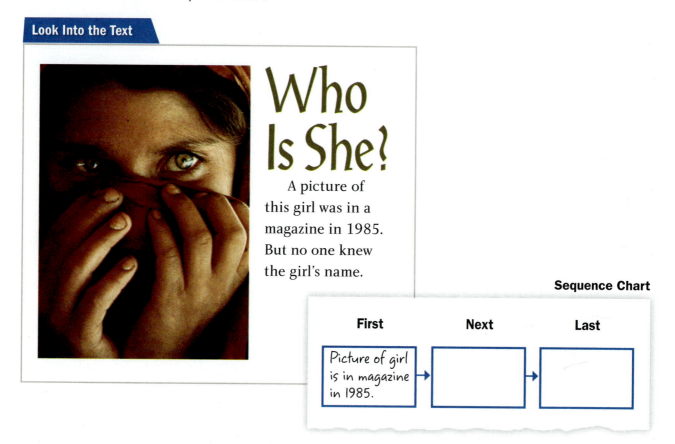

Look Into the Text

Who Is She?

A picture of this girl was in a magazine in 1985. But no one knew the girl's name.

Sequence Chart

First	Next	Last
Picture of girl is in magazine in 1985.		

Try It

Make a Sequence Chart. Add more events to your chart as you read "Who Is She?"

Connect Across Texts

"Ways to Know You" shows ways that people are **special***. In this magazine article, many people have a question. How can science help get the answer?*

Who Is She?

by Joan Johnson

A picture of this girl was in a magazine in 1985. But **no one** knew the girl's name. Years later, people wanted to **find** her. They wanted to know who she was. They looked in many places.

Key Vocabulary

special *adjective*, not like others, unique

no one *pronoun*, no person, nobody

find *verb*, to learn where a person or thing is

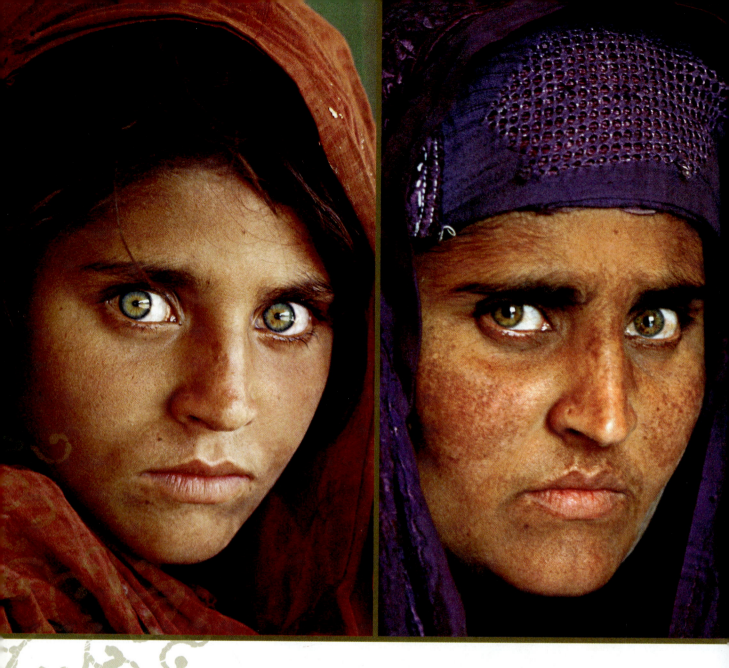

In 2002, they found her. How did
they know she was the same person?
They asked a <mark>scientist</mark>.

Key Vocabulary
<mark>scientist</mark> *noun*, person who studies
   how things work

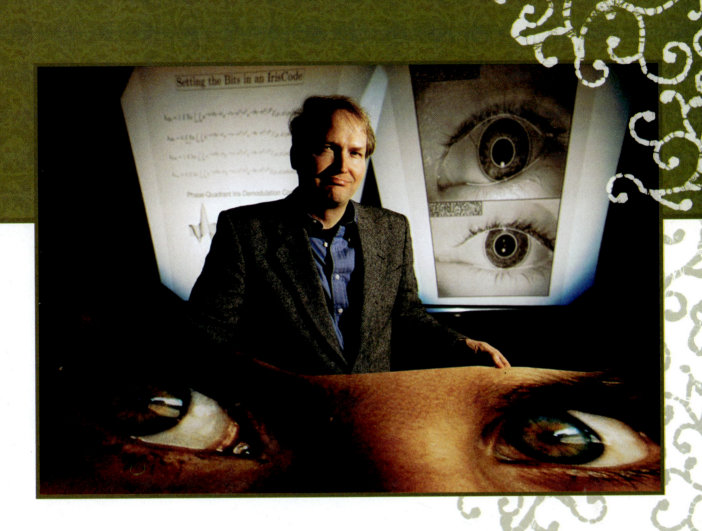

Dr. John Daugman had an **idea**. He looked at the picture of the girl. He **studied** her eyes. He found their special **pattern**. Then he studied a picture of the woman. The pattern was the same.

Monitor Comprehension

Explain
What did Dr. Daugman study? How did this help answer the question?

Key Vocabulary
idea *noun*, thought, plan
study *verb*, to look at something carefully
pattern *noun*, a design that repeats

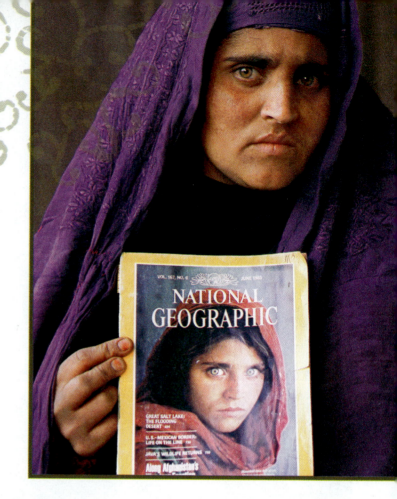

Her name is Sharbat Gula.

She is from **Afghanistan**.

She is the girl in the picture. ❖

ANALYZE Who Is She?

1. **Explain** Who is the girl in the picture?

2. **Vocabulary** What was Dr. Daugman's **idea** about the girl?

3. **Text Structure: Sequence** Look at your **Sequence Chart** with a partner. Explain how your charts help you follow the events in the selection.

↩ Return to the Text

Reread and Retell Reread the text. Name a detail that shows that the girl and the woman are the same person. Use facts from the text to support your answer.

In Other Words
Afghanistan a country in southern Asia

EQ Who am I?

Reading

Talk About Literature

1. **Summarize** What different **patterns** do fingerprints have?

   Three patterns of fingerprints are _____ .

2. **Speculate** Scientists used the pattern of Sharbat Gula's eyes to **find** her. In what other ways can eye patterns be helpful?

   Scientists can use eye patterns to _____ .

EQ 3. **Explain** How can your fingerprints, DNA, and eyes tell who you are?

Fluency

Listen to a reading. Practice fluency. Use the Reading Handbook, page 532.

Vocabulary

Review Key Vocabulary

Choose the correct vocabulary word to complete each sentence.

1. At school, I _____ math and science. (find/study)

2. I want to be a _____ someday. (idea/scientist)

3. Math is _____ to science. (similar/special)

4. Numbers have _____ , and so does DNA. (patterns/scientist)

5. Scientists use _____ tools to learn about DNA. (no one/special)

6. In my family, _____ likes science as much as I do. (no one/scientist)

7. I hope to _____ a good job. (find/study)

8. My parents like my _____ . (idea/scientist)

Vocabulary

find
idea
no one
patterns
scientist
similar
special
study

Writing

Write About Literature

EQ **Explanation** Body patterns such as fingerprints make us **special**. In what other ways are we special, or unique? Begin your answer like this:

> Our body patterns make us special. But we are special in other ways, too. For example, . . .

Grammar

Use Subject Pronouns

Use a **subject pronoun** in place of a noun.

WHO	USE	EXAMPLE	WHO	USE	EXAMPLE
Yourself	I	**I** have blue eyes.	yourself and another person	**We**	**We** have brown hair.
someone you speak to	You	**You** have brown eyes.	two or more people you speak to	**You**	**You** have different fingerprints.
one other person	He	Robert has brown eyes. **He** is tall.	two or more people or things	**They**	The friends talk. **They** laugh a lot.
	She	Lucia has long hair. **She** is smart.			
one thing	It	The DVD is new. **It** is a good movie.			

Oral Practice Work with a partner. Choose the correct subject pronoun and answer the question.

1. Do the <u>boys</u> have blond hair? No, (he/they) don't.
2. Are the <u>girls</u> tall? Yes, (she/they) are.
3. Is your <u>friend</u> short? No, (he/it) isn't.
4. Do the <u>students</u> smile? Yes, (she/they) do.
5. Does <u>Armando</u> have blue eyes? No, (he/it) doesn't.
6. Is the <u>game</u> fun? Yes, (it/they) is.

Written Practice Write about the people in the photographs on pages 56–66. Use as many different subject pronouns as possible. First, finish these sentences. Then write two more sentences.

7. Three girls are on page 56. They have _____.
8. A boy is on page 58. He has _____.

Language Development

Ask for and Give Information

Interview a Classmate Ask a partner questions to find out what makes him or her unique. Ask about home, family, and interests. Use question words.

QUESTION WORD	ASKS ABOUT
Who?	a person
What?	a thing
Where?	a place
When?	a time
Why?	reasons

www.hbedge.net
- **Learn about an activity you can do with your family.**
- **Find out about interesting hobbies.**

Ask questions like these:
- Where do you live?
- Who is in your family?
- What color is your room?

Begin questions with *Is, Are, Do,* or *Does.*

Question: Do you have brothers and sisters?
Answer: Yes, I do. I have a brother.

Synonyms and Antonyms

Remember:

- Synonyms are words with similar meanings. *Big* and *large* are synonyms.

    big = large

- Antonyms are words with opposite meanings. They are not the same. *Big* and *small* are antonyms.

    big ≠ small

Choose the synonym for each underlined word.

1. "Every eye is <u>special</u>." (unique/different)
2. "Each fingerprint has a <u>pattern</u>." (thumb/design)
3. "You are unique in many <u>big</u> and small ways." (large/special)

4. "Dr. Daugman had an <u>idea</u>." (thought/friend)

Read the word in parentheses. Find its antonym in the box. Use it to complete the sentence.

everyone	found	different	later

5. The pattern is unique in more than 200 _____ ways. (similar)
6. _____ has DNA. (no one)
7. Scientists _____ the girl in the picture. (lost)
8. Years _____, they learned the girl's name. (earlier)

Make a Time Line

Work with a partner. Make a time line to show the events in "Who Is She?"

www.hbedge.net
- See more examples of time lines.
- Learn more about Sharbat Gula.

1. Draw a dot. Write the year of the first event. Write a sentence about that event. Use words from the article.

2. Draw a line. Add another dot. Write the date of the next event. Write a sentence that tells about that event. Use words from the article.

3. Add more dots. Write about more dates and events.

Here is a sample time line. It shows part of Afghanistan's history.

Time Line

1919	1979	1989	1996	1998
Afghanistan becomes independent.	Soviet Union invades the country.	Soviet army leaves.	Taliban take over Kabul.	Earthquakes kill thousands of people.

Learn on the Job

Is a part-time job right for you? Take this career quiz to find out.

1

Career Quiz	How many times did you answer *True*?
1. I like animals and plants. ⓐ True ⓑ False **2. I am very active.** ⓐ True ⓑ False **3. I like to be outside.** ⓐ True ⓑ False	**3 times: Wow!** You are a nature lover. A part-time job outdoors is perfect for you. **1–2 times: Maybe** A part-time job outdoors may be right for you. **0 times: No thanks** A part-time job outdoors may not be right for you. Read about other part-time jobs.

2

Part-Time Jobs

Part-time jobs can help you learn about different careers. Find out which job is right for you.

3

Personality	Part-Time Jobs	Possible Careers
Nature Lover **1**	• animal shelter assistant • dog walker • park aide • garden shop sales assistant	• veterinarian • park ranger • doctor • landscape architect
Organizer **2**	• library assistant • data entry person • bookstore sales assistant • computer sales clerk	• librarian • lawyer • computer programmer
People Person **3**	• tutor • lifeguard • recreation aide • assistant coach	• community organizer • special events coordinator • teacher • psychologist

After-School Jobs

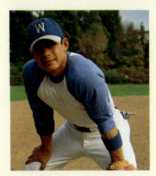

My name is Jesús. I like baseball. I work for an after-school sports program. I teach little kids. I want to be a PE teacher.

I'm Amber. Animals are great! I work at an animal shelter. I walk the dogs. I clean the cages. I want to be a veterinarian.

My name is Josh. I love to read. I work at the library. I help people use the computers. I also put books away. I want to be a computer technician.

Research Part-Time Jobs

Learn more about part-time jobs that can lead to careers.

1. Reread the list of part-time jobs in the chart on page 70.
2. Go online to **www.hbedge.net** to learn about other jobs for young people.
3. Find a job that interests you. Complete this chart.

Job	What do you like about the job?	What will you do?	What career does it lead to?

ALL
ABOUT
ME

EQ ESSENTIAL QUESTION:
Who Am I?

EDGE LIBRARY

Reflect on the Essential Question

With a group discuss the Essential Question: Who am I?

As you answer the questions, think about what you read in the selections and your choice of Edge Library books.

- What can our **names** tell others about us?
- Why are **families** important? How can they form our **personalities**?
- What can our fingerprints and retinas show others about us?

Unit Review Game

You will need:

- 2 players
- 1 **Tic-Tac-Toe** board
- question cards
- pencil, pen, or marker

Objective: Be the first player to get three Xs or Os in a row.

1. Download the **Tic-Tac-Toe** board and question cards from **www.hbedge.net**. Print out and cut apart the question cards. Mix them up.

2. **Player A** takes a card, reads the question, and answers it. If the answer is correct, player A writes **X** in a square. (If you can't agree on the answer, ask your teacher.)

4. **Player B** takes a card, reads the question, and answers it. If the answer is correct, player B writes **O** in a square.

5. Take turns to ask and answer questions.

6. The first player to have a row of **X**s or **O**s is the winner.

The way each person looks, feels, and acts is unique. For this project, you will write poetry to describe yourself and someone you know.

Write a Poem

Writers use language in special ways to express their feelings and thoughts when they write poems.

How does the writer of this poem feel about Coach Fred?

Our coach,
Coach Fred,

He's the best leader
Our team ever had.
We try to win games,
But when players fail,
He shouts, "Try again.
Don't ever give up!"

The beginning tells who the poem is about.

The next lines tell more about the topic.

Notice where the lines end.

The lines of a poem are arranged in a certain way. A line often ends, or breaks, in the middle of a sentence or a phrase.

Write Together

✓ Plan and Write

Work with a group. Write a poem together.

1 Brainstorm Ideas

Decide on a person to write about. What will you say about the person? Brainstorm ideas with your group. Jot down ideas in an **Idea Chart**.

Idea Chart

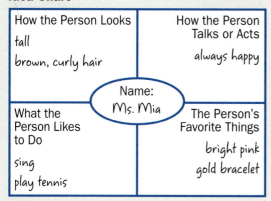

How the Person Looks	How the Person Talks or Acts
tall	always happy
brown, curly hair	

Name: Ms. Mia

What the Person Likes to Do	The Person's Favorite Things
sing	bright pink
play tennis	gold bracelet

I think I will write about . . .

2 Write the Poem

Look at your chart. Which ideas do you like best? Turn those ideas into lines for a poem. Work with your group.

> Ms. Mia, Ms. Mia, with everything pink
> What would we do without you?
> You make us smile when we feel sad.
> **Without you, what would we do?**

Use sentences like these:

- Ms. Mia loves to [verb].

- When I picture her, I think of [Make a comparison.].

- I hear her voice and imagine [noun].

- She makes us feel [descriptive word].

Write on Your Own

▶ **Prompt** Now you can write your own poem for your classmates. Tell them about you. Be sure your poem

- describes who you are, what you are like, or how you feel about a topic
- focuses on, or concentrates, one idea
- uses descriptive details.

✓ Prewrite

Make a plan for your poem. Here's how.

1 Describe Yourself

Try one of these ways to brainstorm what you will say about yourself.

- Write down everything you can think of that describes you.

- Draw and label pictures or scenes. Show yourself doing what you love best or are good at.

- Complete a chart like this one.

Idea Chart

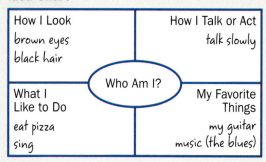

How I Look	How I Talk or Act
brown eyes	talk slowly
black hair	
What I Like to Do	**My Favorite Things**
eat pizza	my guitar
sing	music (the blues)

Who Am I?

2 Choose Your Focus

Review all of your ideas. Decide what the main focus, or point, of your poem will be. In other words, decide what it will be mainly about.

- What do you want your readers to know most about you?

- What are you most proud of?

- If you were to get an award, what would you want it to say?

✓ Draft

1 Write Your Poem

Play with words as you draft. Put words together in different ways. See how they sound. Then choose the way you like most. Try different line breaks, too.

> I'm Dan,
> the guitar man.
> My music is my soul.
> Do you want me to play for you?
> I'll play for you anywhere—yes, anytime
> the sad, sweet blues.

Here are the same words, with different line breaks.

> I'm
> Dan, the guitar man.
> My music is my soul.
> Do you want me to play
> for you?
> I'll play for you
> anywhere.
> Yes, anytime
> the sad, sweet
> blues.

2 Choose the Best Words and Details

Make your poem interesting and lively.

- Choose specific nouns to tell exactly what you mean.
- Use pronouns to communicate about people.

Which of these do you like better?

> Tommy listens to me play.
> Tommy listens every day.

> Tommy listens to me play.
> He listens every day.

**Reflect on
Your Draft**

▶ Does your poem describe something about you? Do you like the way it sounds?

✓ Make Changes

Read your poem to a partner. Fix mistakes to make your poem better.

1 Use the Correct Pronouns

Remember to use correct subject pronouns. A pronoun should match the noun it takes the place of.

> Dan loves to play guitar. ~~She~~ ^{He} practices every day.

Subject Pronouns	
Singular	**Plural**
I	we
you	you
he, she, it	they

2 Check Apostrophes in Contractions

A contraction is a short form of a word or group of words. To write a contraction, you leave out certain letters and use an apostrophe in their place.

3 Check for Sentence Punctuation

Different kinds of sentences use different end marks. Punctuation adds to the meaning of the sentence even in a poem. It tells the reader whether the sentence is a question, a statement, or an exclamation.

- Use a question mark at the end of a question.

    > What would we do without you?

- Use a period at the end of a statement or a polite command.

    > I'm Dan, the guitar man.

- Use an exclamation point to show strong feeling or surprise.

    > Don't ever give up!

What end mark did Dan change in his poem? How does it change the meaning?

Word or Group of Words	Contraction
cannot	can't
is + not	isn't
are + not	aren't
do + not	don't
does + not	doesn't
I + am	I'm
he + is	he's
she + is	she's
you + are	you're
they + are	they're

> I'm Dan,
> the guitar man.
> My music is my soul!

4 Mark Your Changes

Now edit your paper. Use these marks to show your changes.

∧	ℯ	⌐	◯	≡	╱	¶
Add.	Take out.	Replace with this.	Check spelling.	Capitalize.	Make lowercase.	Make new paragraph.

✔ Publish, Share, and Reflect

Publish and Share

Now you are ready to publish your poem. Print or write a clean copy. Then illustrate it for a Class Book of Poetry.

Read at least one poem by a classmate. What did you learn about the person that you didn't know before?

Work with your class or group to hold a poetry reading.

HOW TO HAVE A POETRY READING

1. **Practice Reading Your Poem** Try to say your poem to yourself in front of a mirror. Or read it aloud to a friend or family member.

   - Speak louder to show excitement. Speak softly to show sadness.
   - Ask your listeners how you can improve the rhythm, or beat, or the expression.

2. **Read Your Poem** Read your poem aloud for the audience. You can read it from the page or say it from memory.

Reflect on Your Work

▶ Think about your writing.

- What did you learn about writing that you didn't know before?

- What did you like best about writing a poem?

☑ Save a copy of your work in your portfolio.

WISDOM
OF THE AGES

EQ ESSENTIAL QUESTION:

What Makes Us Wise?

Our first teacher is our own heart.
—**Cheyenne Proverb**

Learning comes through work.
—**Irish Proverb**

EQ ESSENTIAL QUESTION:
What Makes Us Wise?

Study the Photos

What are these people doing?

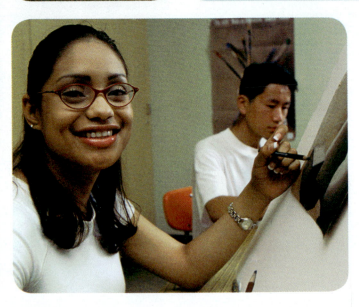

EQ **ESSENTIAL QUESTION**

In this unit, you will explore the **Essential Question** in class. Think about the question outside of school, too.

1 Study the Concept

People **learn**. They gain **wisdom**, or they become wise. Wise people give good **advice** to others.

1. Look at the photos. How do people gain **wisdom**?

2. Do you think people can **learn** to be wise?

3. Who do you learn from? Who gives you **advice**?

2 Choose More to Read

Choose something to read during this unit.

Freedom Readers
by Fran Downey

Long ago, slave owners thought a slave who could read would want freedom. They were right. Reading helped some slaves gain wisdom and freedom.
▶ **NONFICTION**

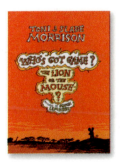

Who's Got Game?
by Toni and Slade Morrison

Lion thinks he is the "baddest in the land," until he gets a thorn in his paw. Now who is wise?
▶ **GRAPHIC NOVEL**

www.hbedge.net
• Read a cartoon about wisdom.
• Listen to a Sufi wisdom story.

Use Word Parts

Sometimes you can join two smaller words to form a **compound word**. Put the meanings of the smaller words together to understand the whole word.

compound word

birth + day = birthday

*A **birthday** is the day you were born.*

Other words are made up of a base word and a suffix. A suffix is added to the end of a word. It changes the word's meaning. The suffix **-ly** means "in that way" or "like a."

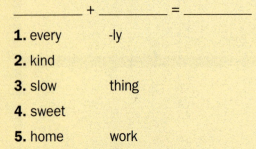

base word   suffix

friend + -ly = friendly

*The ending **-ly** means "like a." So **friendly** means "like a friend".*

Practice Using Word Parts

Put the parts together to make words. Make five different words.
Then use each word in a sentence.

_____ + _____ = _____

1. every   -ly

2. kind

3. slow   thing

4. sweet

5. home   work

Put the Strategy to Use

Work with a partner. Use what you know about word parts to figure out the meaning of each underlined word.

6. I tell my friend <u>everything</u>.

7. We talk in the <u>schoolyard</u>.

8. My friend listens to me <u>quietly</u>.

9. She <u>usually</u> gives me good advice.

Describe Actions

Listen to the interview. What does Michael's grandfather do that shows he is wise?

Interview

What Makes You Wise?

Michael: Grandpa, you seem so wise. You always know the answer. You always say the right thing at the right time. How did you get so much wisdom?

Grandpa: Well, you can't buy wisdom, that's for sure! It takes a long time to become wise. You read a lot of books. You talk to a lot of people. You ask a lot of questions.

Michael: Okay, so that's how you become wise. How do you stay wise?

Grandpa: I still read. And I still talk a lot and ask questions. I also stay healthy. I walk three miles a day. I ride my bike. You can't have a clear head if you don't have a strong body!

Use Action Verbs

1 **TRY OUT LANGUAGE**
2 **LEARN GRAMMAR**
3 **APPLY ON YOUR OWN**

- An **action verb** tells what the subject does. The tense, or time, of a verb shows when an action happens. Use the present tense to tell what the subject does now or often.

  I **read** a lot.

  I **walk** three miles every day.

  I **run** to the gym and **lift** weights.

- Add -**s** to the verb if the subject is one person or one thing (not I or You).

  My grandfather **cooks** his own meals.

  He **visits** his friends every day.

This man lifts weights to stay in shape.

Say It

1–5. Work with a partner. Match words from each column to make a sentence. Say the sentence to your partner. Make at least five sentences.

Example: I walk to Grandpa's house.

I	examines my grandfather regularly.
My grandfather	walk to Grandpa's house.
My parents	call my grandfather every day.
His friend Joe	tells him to keep exercising.
We	swims in the ocean twice a week.
Dr. Blanco	visit on Sundays.

Write It

Use a verb from the box to complete each sentence.

designs	perform	play	sings	wears

6. Grandpa also _____ with a group.

7. He _____ posters for "The Four Wise Guys."

8. I _____ the piano for the group sometimes.

9. They _____ old songs from the 1960s.

10. He _____ strange clothes.

Guess the Action

Work with a partner to act out an action. Then have a classmate guess your action. When it's your turn to guess, describe the actions you see.

Follow these steps to describe an action accurately:

HOW TO DESCRIBE ACTIONS

1. Name each person who is doing an action.
2. Use a verb to talk about the action.

Raúl and Ahmed **play** soccer.
Raúl **kicks** the ball.
Ahmed **stops** it.

Add **-s** to the **verb** when you talk about one other person, not I or you.

Here is how to play the game:

• With a partner plan an action to act out and how to act it out. You and your partner can act out different actions, or you can work together to act out one action, such as playing soccer or dancing.

• Choose one person in the class to be the "Wise One." This person has to guess what the others act out. You can take turns being the "Wise One."

• As partners act out their actions, the "Wise One" describes what action they do.

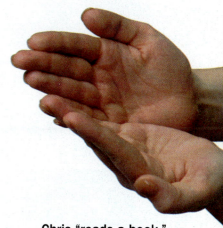

Chris "reads a book."

EQ ## What Makes Us Wise?
Find out how taking good advice makes us wise.

Learn Key Vocabulary

Pronounce each word and learn its meaning.

Key Words

angry (**ang**-grē) *adjective*
▶ page 97

If you feel **angry**, you are mad about something. The girls are **angry** with each other. *Synonym:* upset

difficult (**di**-fi-kult) *adjective*
▶ page 95

Difficult means hard or not easy to do. Chin-ups can be **difficult**.

lonely (**lōn**-lē) *adjective*
▶ page 99

If you feel **lonely**, you are not happy because you are not with other people. He is **lonely** without his friends.

problem (**prah**-blum) *noun*
▶ pages 96, 97, 100, 101

A **problem** is something that needs to be fixed. Her car has a **problem**. She needs help.

selfish (**sel**-fish) *adjective*
▶ pages 92, 97

Selfish people do not help others. The **selfish** man does not care about others around him.

share (**shair**) *verb*
▶ pages 90, 92, 99, 100

To **share** is to give part of something to others. They **share** noodles. *Synonyms:* divide, split

simple (**sim**-pul) *adjective*
▶ page 97

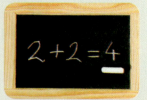

Simple means easy. Adding small numbers is **simple**. *Synonym:* clear

solution (**su**-lü-shun) *noun*
▶ pages 96, 101

A **solution** is an answer. The mechanic explains his **solution**.

Practice the Words Work with a partner. Write a question using a Key Vocabulary word. Trade papers and write an answer to your partner's question. Use a Key Vocabulary word in your answer.

Partner 1: Do you think he is angry?
Partner 2: No, I think he is lonely.

folk tale by Kofi Asare Opoku

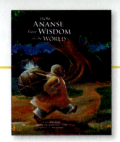

Ask Questions

Good readers do not wait for teachers to ask them questions. As you read, **ask yourself questions** about the pictures. Read the text to find the answers. This will help you understand the story better.

Reading Strategy
Ask Questions

HOW TO ASK QUESTIONS

1. Look at the pictures. Ask yourself questions about the pictures.

2. Ask questions that begin with words like *Who*? *What*? *When*? and *Where*? Write your questions on self-stick notes.

3. Read the text to find the answers.

Look at the picture and the self-stick note.

Look Into the Text

What is in the pot?

Read the text from the story. Does it answer the question?

Ananse's wife got him a large pot. Ananse put all the wisdom in the pot. He didn't tell anyone.

Try It

As you read "How Ananse Gave Wisdom to the World," write your questions about the pictures on self-stick notes. Read on to find the answers.

Genre: Folk Tales

Folk tales are stories that people tell again and again. Folk tales come from different parts of the world. The characters can be people or animals. Folk tales teach about many things. They are one way people share wisdom with each other.

www.hbedge.net

• Listen to famous folk tales.

• Find out more about "trickster" tales.

HOW ANANSE Gave WISDOM to the WORLD

BY KOFI ASARE OPOKU

COLLECTED FROM THE AKAN PEOPLE OF GHANA

ILLUSTRATED BY FRANK MORRISON

Long ago, there lived a man called Kwaku Ananse. He lived with his wife and his son. His son's name was Ntikuma.

Ananse had all the wisdom in the world. But he was **selfish**. He did not want to **share** it with anybody. He wanted to **save** the wisdom for himself.

Key Vocabulary
selfish *adjective*, not caring about others, difficult
share *verb*, to give part of something to others

In Other Words
Long ago Many years in the past
save keep

Ananse **planned to hide it** at the top of a big, tall tree. Ananse's wife got him a large **pot**. Ananse put all the wisdom in the pot. He didn't tell anyone.

Then Ananse got a rope. He tied one end around the pot and tied the other around his neck. That night, he sneaked out of the house. He walked slowly into **the forest**.

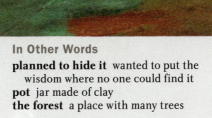

Monitor Comprehension

Explain
Why does Ananse put the wisdom in a pot?

Ananse believed **he was alone**, but he was wrong. Ntikuma saw him. He had **followed** his father into the forest. He **hid in the shadows**.

In Other Words

he was alone no one was with him
followed walked behind
hid in the shadows stayed where Ananse
   could not see him

Ananse found a tall tree. He stopped. He put the pot **on his belly**. Then he began to **climb**. The climb was very <mark>difficult</mark>. The pot was in front of him. He could not hold the **trunk**. He tried to climb the tree again and again. But he could not.

Ananse was unhappy. He stopped to think.

Monitor Comprehension

Describe
How does Ananse try to hide the pot?

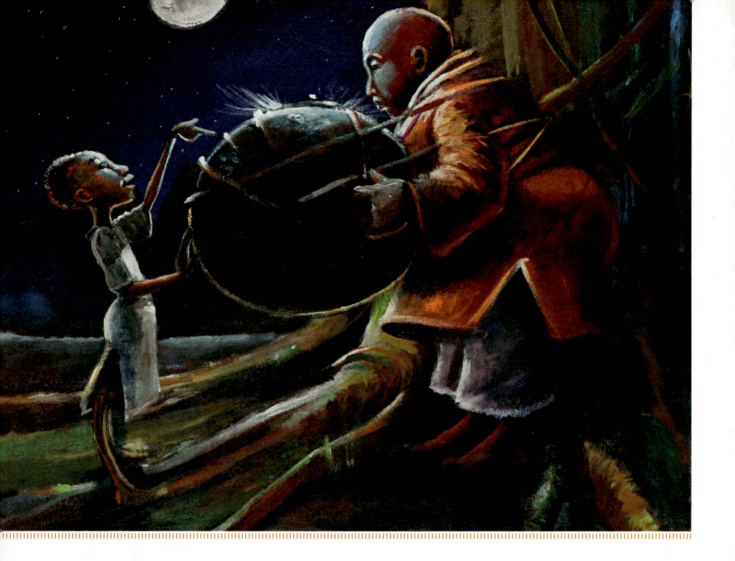

Ananse scratched his head. He **searched for** a <mark>solution</mark> to his <mark>problem</mark>.

Then he heard something. It was a loud laugh behind him. He turned around. There was his son, Ntikuma.

Ntikuma said, "Father, retie the pot. This time put it on your back. **That way**, it will be easier to climb the tree."

Key Vocabulary
<mark>solution</mark> *noun*, an answer
<mark>problem</mark> *noun*, something that needs to be fixed

In Other Words
searched for tried to think of
That way If you put the pot on your back

Ananse was **angry**. His son was right. But why didn't he think of it first? It was such a **simple** solution!

Ananse grew angrier. He threw down the pot. It **cracked**. The wisdom **spilled** from it. **It spread to all parts of the world.**

Ntikuma smiled. ❖

ANALYZE How Ananse Gave Wisdom to the World

1. **Explain** What does Ntikuma tell Ananse to do?

2. **Vocabulary** What shows that Ananse is **selfish**?

3. **Reading Strategy** **Ask Questions** Tell a partner two of the questions you asked. If you found the answers, share them, too.

⤺ Return to the Text

Reread and Retell In the story, Ananse has a plan. He finds there is a **problem** with his plan. Describe the plan. Then describe the problem.

Key Vocabulary
angry *adjective*, mad, upset
simple *adjective*, easy, clear

In Other Words
cracked broke
spilled fell
It spread to all parts of the world.
   The wisdom went everywhere.

web forum by various teens

Text Structure: Problem and Solution

Writers organize their ideas to help you understand the text. One kind of text structure, or way to organize, is a **problem and solution** pattern. Often writers describe one problem and give several solutions.

How to RECOGNIZE TEXT STRUCTURE

1. Read the title. What is the text about? How do you know? Look for a problem. Then look for text that gives ideas and solutions.

2. As you read, think about how the writer organizes the ideas. Then look for text that gives ideas about how to solve the problem.

3. Draw a chart like the one above to connect problems and solutions.

Read the title and the text. See how one reader thinks about text structure.

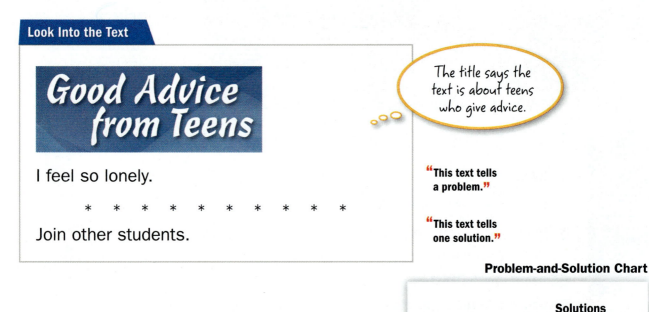

Look Into the Text

Good Advice from Teens

I feel so lonely.

* * * * * * * * * *

Join other students.

The title says the text is about teens who give advice.

"This text tells a problem."

"This text tells one solution."

Problem-and-Solution Chart

Problem — The writer feels lonely.

Solutions — Join other students

Try It

As you read "Good Advice from Teens," look for other solutions to this problem.

Good Advice from Teens

Connect Across Texts

In "How Ananse Gave Wisdom to the World," Ananse hears wisdom from his son. How is wisdom **shared** *in this web forum?*

Advice Forum

Author	Post
 **AndyBird**	**AndyBird's Question:** I just started high school. I'm in grade nine. I moved from another school. Everyone knows each other. I feel so **lonely**. No one talks to me. What can I do?
Friendly	**Friendly's Answer: Join** other students. Talk about a class you have together. Try joining **a club**. It's a good way to meet people. **Be yourself. Be confident.** I hope **all goes well**.

Key Vocabulary

share *verb*, to give part of something to others

lonely *adjective*, not happy because you are not with other people

In Other Words

Join Meet

a club a group that does things together

Be yourself. Be confident. Know that you are a good person.

all goes well you will be happy

Author	Post
 **Rosa**	**Rosa's Answer: Introduce yourself** to other students. Talk to a teacher or **counselor**. Ask them about ways to meet people. **Relax**. Go slowly. You will find some great friends.
 **Griffen**	**Griffen's Answer:** Sports! Find a sport you like to play. **It never fails**. Join a school club. Sit with a few **strangers** at lunch.

ANALYZE Good Advice from Teens

1. **Explain** What is AndyBird's <mark>problem</mark>?

2. **Vocabulary** Why does AndyBird <mark>share</mark> his problem?

3. **Text Structure: Problem and Solution** Look at your **Problem-and-Solution** Chart with a partner. How did you find the <mark>solutions</mark>?

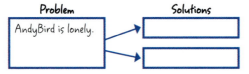

Problem

AndyBird is lonely.

Solutions

Return to the Text

Reread and Retell Who gives AndyBird the best advice? Use facts from the text to support your ideas.

In Other Words
Introduce yourself Say "hello"
counselor someone who can give you advice
Relax. Don't worry.
It never fails. Playing sports always helps.
strangers people you do not know

EQ ## What Makes Us Wise?

Talk About Literature

1. **Explain** Think about Ananse's actions. Does he really have "all the wisdom in the world"? Explain your answer.

2. **Analyze** AndyBird asks other teens for advice. Why does he do this? Why doesn't he try to solve his **problem** by himself?

   I think AndyBird asks for advice because _____.

EQ 3. **Compare** What wise advice can Ntikuma give AndyBird? What can the teens tell Ananse?

   Ntikuma can tell AndyBird _____.

   The teens can tell Ananse _____.

Listen to a reading. Practice fluency. Use the Reading Handbook, page 533.

Review Key Vocabulary

Choose the correct vocabulary word to complete each sentence.

1. The _____ was that I forgot my lunch. (problem/solution)

2. My friend would not _____ hers with me. (angry/share)

3. She was being very _____! (lonely/selfish)

4. It made me very _____. I stopped speaking to her. (angry/simple)

5. Then I felt _____ without her. (difficult/lonely)

6. My mom gave me some _____ advice. (selfish/simple)

7. "Here's one _____ to your problem," she said. (problem/solution)

8. "Don't forget your lunch." That is not so _____. (simple/difficult)

Vocabulary

- angry
- difficult
- lonely
- problem
- selfish
- share
- simple
- solution

Write About Literature

Problem-and-Solution Paragraph Reread the Web forum. Give your own **solution** to AndyBird's problem. Write a paragraph that tells the problem and the solution. Explain why your solution works. Use the chart to organize your paragraph.

1. Describe AndyBird's problem.
   AndyBird wants to make friends.

2. Write the solution.

3. Explain why your solution works.

Grammar

Use Action Verbs in the Present Tense

PAST (before now) — PRESENT (now) — FUTURE (after now)

Use the **present tense** of a verb to talk about something that happens now or often.

> I **visit** the Advice Forum site every day.
> Sometimes I **type** a question in the site.
> They never **answer** me!

Add -**s** to the verb if the subject is one person or one thing (not I or You).

> My friend Mike **writes**, and someone **answers** him right away.

To form a question, put **Do** or **Does** before the subject.

> **Do** I use the wrong words?
> **Does** Mike write interesting questions?

To form a negative statement, put **do not** (or **don't**) or **does not** (or **doesn't**) between the subject and the verb.

> Mike **doesn't** wait long for an answer.
> They just **do not** answer me!

Oral Practice Work with a partner. Use the correct verb and say each sentence.

1. AndyBird (receive/receives) a lot of good ideas on the Advice Forum.
2. Different teens (suggest/suggests) different things.
3. One teen (tell/tells) him to play sports.
4. One girl (show/shows) confidence in him.
5. All the teens (hope/hopes) good things will happen.

Written Practice Choose the correct verb and write each sentence.

6. AndyBird does not _____ all the advice. (use/uses)
7. But he _____ some of it. (follow/follows)
8. I do not _____ he can play football. (think/thinks)
9. Does he _____ soccer? (play/plays)
10. He _____ new friends all the time now. (meet/meets)

Language Development

Describe Actions

What Do You See? Work with a partner. Use the Internet, or look in newspapers or magazines, to find a picture of people who are playing sports or games.

www.hbedge.net
• View action pictures.

• Take turns. Describe what you see in the picture.
• Use as many different action verbs as you can.
• Use the correct form of the verb.

Compound Words

Remember, a compound word is made up of two smaller words.

any + body = anybody

To read a compound word:

- Break it into parts.
- Think about the meaning of each part.
- Put the meanings together to understand the whole word.

something to write with

A **chalkboard** must be a hard, flat place to write on.

chalk + board = chalkboard

a hard, flat place

Use a chart to help you figure out the meaning of each underlined word:

1. Everyone has problems.
2. I have a problem in the lunchroom.
3. I don't have anyone to sit with.
4. I feel homesick for my old school.
5. I wish someone would talk to me.

Word	Parts	Meaning
everyone	_____ + _____ =	

Describe Characters

Remember, the characters in a story are the people or animals the story is about. Look at what a character does and ask what the action shows about the character.

1. Make a **Character Chart** for the characters in "How Ananse Gave Wisdom to the World."
2. Read the story again. Think about Ananse's actions. List them in the second column. What do his actions show about his character? Write your answer in the third column.
3. Now think about Ntikuma. Complete the **Character Chart** for Ntikuma.
4. Use your chart to tell a partner about the characters in the story.

Character Chart

Character	The Character's Actions	What the Actions Show About the Character
Ananse		
Ntikuma		

Write About a Folk Tale

▶ **Prompt** When people tell folk tales, they share wisdom with each other. What folk tales do you know? Think of a folk tale that you can share. Write a short paragraph about it.

1 Plan Look through a book of folk tales. Think about your favorite folk tales. Choose one to share with your classmates. Make notes about it.

> Title: "How Ananse Gave Wisdom to the World"
> Characters: Ananse, his son Ntikuma
> What happens: Ananse puts all of the wisdom in a pot. He tries to hide the pot in a tree. Ntikuma tries to help him. Ananse gets angry and breaks the pot. All the wisdom spills out.

2 Write Use your notes to write a short paragraph about the folk tale.

- Include the title and the main characters.
- Describe what happens.
- Pay attention to the action verbs in your sentences. Be sure the verbs agree with their subjects.

Paragraph Organizer

> This folk tale is called [title] . The main characters are [names of main characters]. The first thing that happens in this story is [what happens at the beginning]. Then [what happens next]. Finally, [what happens at the end].

3 Share Copy your paragraph. Use good handwriting. Put your page in a class binder. Read the other folk tales. Discuss them with your classmates. Talk about the wisdom they share.

REMEMBER

- Add **-s** to the end of an action verb in the present tense that says what one other person or thing does.

  The student listen**s**.

- Do not add **-s** to an action verb when the subject is more than one person or thing.

  The students listen.

Express Likes and Dislikes

1 TRY OUT LANGUAGE
2 LEARN GRAMMAR
3 APPLY ON YOUR OWN

Listen to the conversation. What do you learn about Mia and David?

Conversation

Let's Talk About Sports!

Mia: Hi, David. How are you?

David: I'm fine, thanks. What are you doing this year? Are you swimming again?

Mia: No. I quit the swim team. I don't like it. It is too cold here.

David: I can't believe it! What are you doing now?

Mia: I play basketball. I really like it. All the games are indoors. I am never cold. I love it! How about you? What are you doing?

David: I am still doing martial arts. This is my fifth year!

Mia: Do you still like it?

David: It's all right. We have a new teacher. I didn't like him at first. He is very strict! But now I like him. I am learning a lot!

Language Workshop, continued

Use Present Progressive Verbs

1 TRY OUT LANGUAGE
2 LEARN GRAMMAR
3 APPLY ON YOUR OWN

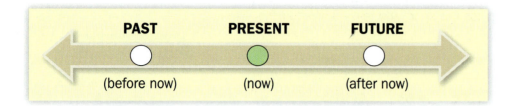

PAST	PRESENT	FUTURE
(before now)	(now)	(after now)

- Sometimes you want to talk about something that you do often. Use the **present tense**.

    I **learn** new things every day.

- At other times you want to talk about what you are doing now. Use the **present progressive** form of the verb.

    I **am trying** a new dive now.

- To form a **present progressive** verb, use **am**, **is**, or **are** plus the **-ing** form of the action verb.

    I **am practicing** the dive today.

    The coach **is helping** me.

    We **are working** together.

He is diving into the water.

Say It

1–4. Work with a partner. Look at each picture. Talk about what is happening. Use a verb in the present progressive form.

Write It

Use the present progressive form of the verb in parentheses and write the sentence.

5. I _____ to a new class this week. (go)

6. Many of my friends _____ it, too. (try)

7. Mr. Kurosawa _____ the class. (teach)

8. He _____ us some very cool moves. (show)

9. We _____ excited about it. (feel)

10. Finally, Advanced Karate _____ in our town! (happen)

Talk About a Sport

Play a game with your classmates. Perform an action that shows a sport you like. Have your classmates guess the sport and tell you whether they like it.

Follow these steps when you talk about what you like and don't like:

HOW TO EXPRESS LIKES AND DISLIKES

1. Say what you like.
2. Say why you like it.

> He **is playing** basketball. I like basketball. It is fun.

Use **is playing** to say what one person is doing now.

1. Say what you dislike.
2. Say why you dislike it.

> They **are playing** baseball. I don't like baseball. It takes too long to play.

Use **are playing** to say what more than one person is doing now.

> She **is** swinging a bat.

Her sport is baseball.

EQ ## What Makes Us Wise?
Think about the wisdom of elders and mentors.

Learn Key Vocabulary

Pronounce each word and learn its meaning.

Key Words

break (brāk) *verb*
▶ page 114

When you **break** something, you separate it into pieces or parts. He **breaks** the wood with his hand.

explain (ik-splān) *verb*
▶ pages 114, 123

To **explain** means to make something clear. The teacher is **explaining** the math problem.

fight (fīt) *verb*
▶ pages 113, 114

To **fight** is to hurt or yell at someone. The children are **fighting** in the store.

harm (harm) *verb*
▶ page 119

To **harm** means to hurt. The boys are **harming** each other.

rest (rest) *verb*
▶ pages 119, 122

When you **rest**, you do not work. She stops to **rest** during a game.

touch (tuch) *verb*
▶ page 120

When you **touch** something, you feel it. To read Braille, you must **touch** the bumps.

tough (tuf) *adjective*
▶ pages 116, 122

Tough means strong and not easily hurt. The player looks **tough**.

understand (un-dur-stand) *verb*
▶ pages 115, 117

When you **understand** something, you know how it works or what it means. The students **understand** the question.

Practice the Words Write two Key Vocabulary words in the same sentence.

> When people <u>fight</u>, they can <u>harm</u> each other.

biography by Ken Mochizuki

Ask Questions

Remember, good readers ask questions. You know how to ask questions about characters. You can ask questions about other things, too. As you read, **ask questions** about the text. Then look for the answers in the text.

HOW TO ASK QUESTIONS

1. Stop and think about the text as you read. Ask yourself questions about it.

2. Ask questions that begin with words like *Who, What, When, Where,* and *Why.* Write your questions on self-stick notes.

3. To find the answers, reread the text or read on.

Read the text and the self-stick notes. See how one reader asks questions.

Look Into the Text

Why did Bruce's family call him "never sits still"? He was always moving.

When Bruce Lee was young, he was always moving. He was always talking and running around. His family called him Mo Si Tung. It means "never sits still."

As he got older, he wanted to learn martial arts. Bruce wanted to learn from a master. The best martial arts teacher in Hong Kong was Yip Man.

I **reread** to find the answer.

Who was the best martial arts teacher in Hong Kong? Yip Man.

To find the answer, I had to **read on** in the text.

Try It

As you read "Be Water, My Friend," write your questions on self-stick notes. Reread or read on to find the answers.

Meet Bruce Lee
(1940–1973)

Bruce Lee was born in San Francisco, California, in 1940. His family returned to Hong Kong when Bruce was only a baby.

When Bruce was thirteen, he began studying kung fu. He added his own moves to the traditional kung fu moves. Later in his life, he became a teacher of his own special kind of kung fu.

His father was an opera singer and an actor, so Bruce learned to act, too. By the time he was 18 years old, he had already been in twenty movies.

Bruce was wise. He once said, "A wise man can learn more from a foolish question than a fool can learn from a wise answer."

Bruce Lee was a famous actor, dancer, and martial artist.

www.hbedge.net
• Learn about different types of martial arts.
• View a martial arts video.

from

Be Water, My Friend:
The Early Years of Bruce Lee

by Ken Mochizuki

Illustrated by
Jean-Manuel Duvivier

Many people know Bruce Lee. He studied and taught kung fu, a sport, or martial art, that uses the hands, feet, and body. Some people use martial arts to hurt others. But Bruce learned a different way.

When Bruce Lee was young, he was always moving. He was always talking and running around. His family called him Mo Si Tung. It means "never **sits still**."

As he got older, he wanted to learn martial arts. Bruce wanted to learn from a **master**. The best martial arts master in **Hong Kong** was Yip Man.

In Other Words

sits still stops moving
master very good teacher
Hong Kong an island that is part
of China

At Yip Man's school, Bruce didn't have to be still. He had to use his body. He loved it. But one day Bruce used his skills to **fight**. Yip Man was not happy.

Monitor Comprehension

Explain
Why did Bruce Lee's family call him "Mo Si Tung"?

"Then what are martial arts for?" Bruce asked.

Yip Man **explained**. "Heavy snow sometimes **breaks** big branches. But smaller plants that look weak **bend** and **survive**. Calm your mind. Do not **fight the flow of nature**. There **is gentleness** in martial arts."

"How can I be gentle while I am fighting?" Bruce asked.

Yip Man told Bruce to think about it.

Key Vocabulary
explain *verb*, to make something clear
break *verb*, to separate into pieces

In Other Words
bend let their tops move close to the ground
survive do not die
fight the flow of nature resist earth's changes
is gentleness are ways that do not harm them

Bruce went out in his boat. He started to think. Gentleness? **It didn't make sense**. He did not **understand**. He got angry. He hit the water.

Bruce hit the water again. It didn't break. It **ran through** his hands. Water was soft. But it could also break through anything in the world.

Bruce **returned** to Yip Man. "Gentleness," he said. "I think I understand."

In Other Words
It didn't make sense. It was not clear.
ran through dropped out of
returned went back

Monitor Comprehension

Summarize
What did Yip Man say to Bruce about martial arts?

It sounded easy. But it was not. One day, **Bruce's opponent** was very big. He pushed Bruce around. Bruce tried to be <mark>tough</mark>. But it didn't work. His opponent was too strong. Bruce was **losing**.

Then Bruce calmed himself. He **watched** his opponent's hands. Bruce moved his hands in a different way. He followed the flow of nature. Now his opponent had nothing to hit. Bruce won.

Key Vocabulary
<mark>tough</mark> *adjective*, strong, not easily hurt

In Other Words
Bruce's opponent the person Bruce was practicing with
losing not doing well
watched looked at

Monitor Comprehension

Explain
How did Bruce win?

Bruce knew he still had **a lot** to learn. But now he understood Yip Man. He looked down at the water. Bruce saw how water always found a way around a problem. "**Be water, my friend**," he said to himself.

ANALYZE Be Water, My Friend

1. **Explain** Why does Yip Man become angry with Bruce Lee?

2. **Vocabulary** What does Yip Man want Bruce Lee to <mark>understand</mark>?

3. **Reading Strategy** **Ask Questions** What questions did you ask? Which one was the most useful? Explain why to a partner.

Return to the Text

Reread and Retell Explain what happens in Bruce Lee's boat. Use details from the text to support your answer.

In Other Words
a lot many things
Be water, my friend I am like water

BEFORE READING Hands

short fiction by An Na

Story Elements: Character

Characters are the people in a story. Authors use description to make characters come alive. Description tells how characters look and what they do so readers can decide what they are like.

> ### HOW TO ANALYZE CHARACTERS
>
> **1.** Read the text.
>
> **2.** Write down what the character looks like. Write what the character does.
>
> **3.** Read your notes. Think about similar people. Then decide what they are like.

Read the text and study the **Character Chart**.

Look Into the Text

Uhmma's hands are as old as sand. In the mornings, they scratched across our faces. Wake up. Time for school.

At work, her hands sewed hundreds of jeans. They knew how to make a meal in ten minutes for hungry customers.

At home, they washed our dishes. They cleaned the floor. Uhmma's hands rarely rested.

Character Chart

Character	What Character Looks Like	What Character Does	What Character Is Like
Uhmma	hands as old as sand	wakes up the children works hard	

Try It

Copy the Character Chart. As you read "Hands," add more notes about Uhmma to the chart.

Connect Across Texts

In "Be Water, My Friend," Bruce Lee learns that martial arts aren't always used to **harm** others. In this short story, Young Ju learns something important from her mother.

H A N D S

by An Na

Uhmma's hands are as old as **sand**. In the mornings, they **scratched** across our faces. Wake up. Time for school.

At work, her hands **sewed** hundreds of **jeans**. They knew how to make a meal in ten minutes for hungry **customers**.

At home, they washed our dishes. They cleaned the floor. Uhmma's hands rarely **rested**.

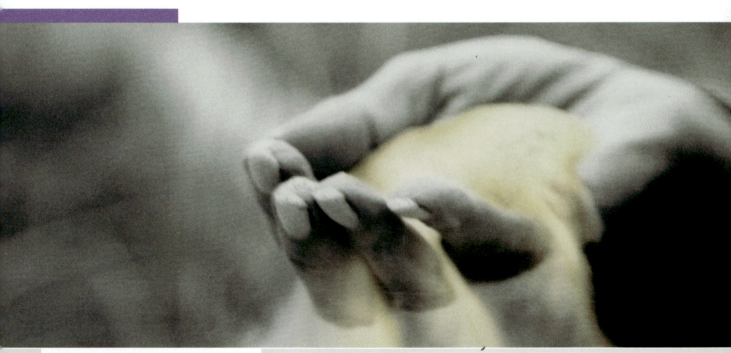

Key Vocabulary
harm *verb*, to hurt
rest *verb*, to not work

In Other Words
Uhmma's Mom's (in Korean)
sand the earth
scratched moved with a rough feeling
sewed made
jeans pants
customers people at a restaurant

But sometimes her hands opened. **Palms** up. A flower finally open to the bees.

My brother Joon and I sat on either side of her. She read stories in the lines of our palms.

Look, Young Ju, Uhmma said. Your intelligence line is strong. Maybe you will become a doctor. Uhmma **touched** the line. It **tickled**.

Joon **pushed** away my hand. Look at my intelligence line, Uhmma.

These baby hands have lines? Let me see, Uhmma said. She studied it for a moment. Then she kissed the middle. Plop. A raindrop on water. Joon **giggled**.

We were always reaching to touch Uhmma's **sandpaper** palms.

Key Vocabulary
touch *verb*, to feel

In Other Words
Palms Insides
tickled made me laugh
pushed moved
giggled laughed
sandpaper rough

Uhmma said her hands were her life. But she only wished to see our hands holding books. You must use this, she said. She pointed to her head.

I walk with Uhmma now. Her hand is held in mine.

I study these lines **of her past**. I want to remove the **scars**. I want to fill in the **cracks** in the skin. I **envelop** Uhmma's hands in my own soft palms. Close them together. Like a book. A **Siamese prayer**. I tell her, I want to **erase** these scars for you.

In Other Words
of her past that tell about her life
scars hurt places
cracks signs of hard work
envelop hold
Siamese prayer special wish
erase take away

Monitor Comprehension

Explain
Why did Uhmma look at her children's hands?

Uhmma gently **slips** her hands from mine. She **stares** for a moment at her <mark>tough</mark> skin. Then she speaks **firmly**. These are my hands, Young Ju. Uhmma puts her arm around **my waist**. We continue our walk along the beach.

ANALYZE Hands

1. **Explain** How are Uhmma's hands different from Young Ju's?

2. **Vocabulary** Why did Uhmma's hands rarely <mark>rest</mark>?

3. **Story Elements: Character** Work with a partner. Compare the notes you wrote about Uhmma on your **Character Chart**. Then compare your decisions about what Uhmma is like. How are your ideas the same or different?

🔄 Return to the Text

Reread and Retell Explain what Young Ju means when she says, ". . . she only wished to see our hands holding books." Find details in the text to support your answer.

Key Vocabulary
tough *adjective*, strong, not easily hurt

In Other Words
slips takes
stares looks hard
firmly with a strong voice
my waist the middle of my body

EQ **What Makes Us Wise?**

Fluency

Listen to a reading. Practice fluency. Use the Reading Handbook, page 534.

Reading

Talk About Literature

1. **Interpret** Bruce Lee tells himself to "be water." What does this advice mean?

   "Be water" means _____.

2. **Character** What is Uhmma's personality like? Tell how you know.

EQ 3. **Generalize** Bruce Lee and Young Ju learn important lessons from wise adults. Do you learn from wise adults? Give an example.

   One important thing I learn from a wise adult is _____. I learn it from _____.

Vocabulary

Review Key Vocabulary

Choose the correct vocabulary word to complete each sentence.

1. It is _____ to babysit my little brothers. (touch/tough)

2. They are very active. They never _____! (harm/understand)

3. Also, they do not get along. They often _____. (fight/explain)

4. I don't think they would ever _____ each other. (harm/rest)

5. But they might accidentally _____ things such as lamps. (break/explain)

6. I _____ to them that they should play outside. (explain/rest)

7. I give them wise advice, but they do not _____. (fight/understand)

8. My advice does not seem to _____ their ears. (break/touch)

Vocabulary

- break
- explain
- fight
- harm
- rest
- touch
- tough
- understand

Writing

Write About Literature

EQ **Explanation** Find these quotations in the text:

"Heavy snow sometimes breaks big branches. But smaller plants that look weak bend and survive." (page 114)

"You must use this, she said. She pointed to her head." (page 121)

Choose one quotation to **explain**. Copy the quotation. What does it mean? How can you use it in your life?

Quotations:

The quotation means . . .
In my life, I try to . . .
I also try to . . .

Use Helping Verbs

Sometimes you use two verbs that work together: a **helping verb** and a **main verb**. The **main verb** shows the action.

My grandmother **can** **speak** only Korean.

Sometimes a helping verb changes the meaning of the main verb.

- Use **can** to tell about what someone is able to do.
  I **can** **speak** two languages.
- Use **may** to tell about something that is possible. My grandmother **may** **prefer** to speak Korean.
- Use **should** to give advice or show what you believe.
  I **should** **help** her learn English.
- Use **must** to tell about something that is very important to do.
  I **must** **talk** to her right away!

Can, may, should, and **must** stay the same with all subjects. Do not add **-s**.

Grandma **can** **rest** now.
She **may** **help** me learn more Korean.

Oral Practice Work with a partner. Choose a helping verb and say each sentence. More than one answer is possible.

can	may	must	should

1. My uncle Julio _____ be more than 90 years old.
2. But he _____ lift more weight than than my dad can.
3. He _____ try to win a contest.
4. With his muscles, he _____ win any contest!
5. If I lift weights, I _____ be very careful.

Written Practice (6–10) What can you do? How may your skills help others? Write five sentences. Use **can, may, should,** and **must.**

Express Likes and Dislikes

Talk About the Selections Reread "Be Water, My Friend" and "Hands." What did you like about each selection? Why? Were there parts that you did not like? Why?

Work with a partner. Take turns. Tell your partner what you liked and what you did not like.

- Tell your partner about a part of the selection you liked.
- Give your reasons.
- Then tell your partner about a part of the selection you did not like.
- Explain why you did not like it.

Suffixes

A suffix is a word part added to the end of a word. It changes the word's meaning.

The suffix **-ly** often means "in that way" or "like a." See how it changes the meanings of these words:

WORD	MEANING
quick	fast
quickly	in a fast way
soft	gentle
softly	in a gentle way

To read a word with a suffix:

- Break the word into its parts.
- Think about the meaning of each part.
- Put the meanings together to understand the whole word.

Use a chart to help you figure out the meaning of each underlined word.

1. Our martial arts teacher speaks <u>slowly</u>.
2. I listen to his words <u>carefully</u>.
3. He explains everything <u>clearly</u>.
4. <u>Suddenly</u> it is time to practice!
5. I wait <u>nervously</u> for my turn.

Word	Parts	Meaning
slowly	_____ + _____ =	

Cause and Effect

Problem-Solution is one kind of text structure. Another kind of text structure is cause and effect. The cause is the reason something happens. The effect is what happens as a result.

Cause		Effect
Bruce wants to learn the martial arts.	→	Bruce goes to martial arts school.

Make a **Cause-and-Effect Chart** for "Be Water, My Friend." Follow these steps:

1. Copy the chart. Think about the story. Write an effect next to each cause. Add new causes and effects.
2. Use your completed chart to retell the story to a partner.

Cause-and-Effect Chart

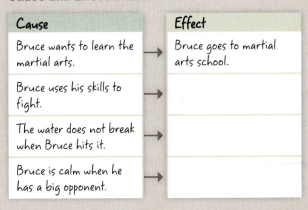

Cause		Effect
Bruce wants to learn the martial arts.	→	Bruce goes to martial arts school.
Bruce uses his skills to fight.	→	
The water does not break when Bruce hits it.	→	
Bruce is calm when he has a big opponent.	→	

Writing

Write a Comic Strip

▶ **Prompt** Make a comic strip that describes something that happened to someone. Show how someone learns a lesson.

1 **Plan** What lessons have you learned? Choose one. Draw three boxes, or panels. Decide on the characters and actions to draw. Plan your comic strip.

2 **Write** Use the panels to describe what happened in three parts.

Comic Strip

[caption]   [caption]   [caption]

- Draw a scene in each panel.

- Write what the characters say or think. Put the words inside a shape.

This shape shows what a character says.

This shape shows what a character thinks.

Use sentences like these:
- We are practicing [a sport like karate].
- Are you studying [a sport like karate]?
- I can [action word].

- Describe what is happening in each scene. Write text called a caption below the panel.

- Try to write sentences with **am, is, are, can,** and **may.** Be sure to use the verbs correctly.

3 **Share** Display your comic strip in the classroom. Read your classmates' comic strips.

> **REMEMBER**
> - Use **am, is,** or **are** + a main verb to talk about an action that is happening now. The main verb ends in **-ing.**
>
>   He **is** study**ing** karate.
>
> - Use **can** and **may** with other verbs.
>
>   You **can** kick high.

Express Needs and Wants

Listen to the poem. Pay attention to the needs and wants.

Poem

I Want to Be...

I want to be an astronaut.
> Then you need a rocket.

I want to be rich.
> Then you need a deep pocket.

I want to be an engineer.
> Then you need mathematics.

I want to be a gymnast.
> Then you need acrobatics.

I want to finish.
> Then you need to start.

I want to be loved.
> Then you need love in your heart.

Use Nouns and Verbs in Sentences

1 TRY OUT LANGUAGE
2 LEARN GRAMMAR
3 APPLY ON YOUR OWN

- A noun names a person, an animal, a place, or a thing. A noun can be the **subject** of a sentence.

  Astronauts travel into space.
  subject

- A noun can also be part of the predicate, when it relates to the verb. We call it an object.

  Astronauts ride **rockets.**
             verb   object

- Many English sentences follow the Subject-Verb-Object, or SVO, pattern.

  Astronauts take many **classes.**
  subject   verb   object

  Astronauts study **mathematics.**
  subject   verb   object

Astronauts perform dangerous missions.

Say It

Say each sentence. Talk about the underlined noun. Is it a subject or an object?

1. I am taking a new <u>class</u> this year.

2. <u>Mr. Ruiz</u> is teaching it.

3. I want an exciting <u>career</u>.

4. So I am studying <u>astronomy</u>.

5. Our <u>school</u> needs more classes like this one.

Write It

Choose a word or phrase from the box to complete each sentence.

6. I love my new _____.

7. The _____ has great pictures.

8. Mr. Ruiz _____ a lesson every night.

9. Sometimes I need a little _____.

10. My friend Eliot _____ the math homework.

Subject	Verb	Object
teacher	assigns	advice
textbook	understands	class

For That, You Need This

Work with a group. Tell your group members about something you want to have or something you want to do. Ask your classmates for ideas about what you need if you want something.

Follow these steps:

HOW TO EXPRESS NEEDS AND WANTS

1. Use **want** to talk about things you would like to have or about activities you would like to do.

> I want my own **car**.
> I want to **drive** to school every day.

When you express needs and wants, use a **noun** as the object of your sentence. Or use a **verb** with *to* before it.

2. Use **need** to talk about things or actions that are very important or necessary.

> You need a **driver's license**. You need a **job**. You need to **save** some money.

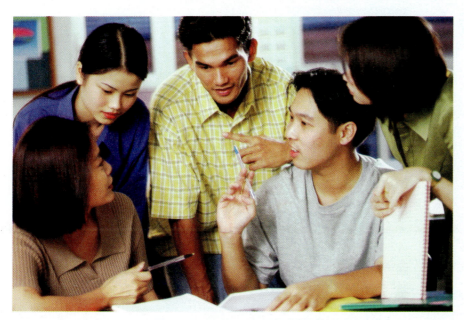

"You want to be a doctor? You need to study biology."

EQ **What Makes Us Wise?**
Think about different kinds of wisdom.

Learn Key Vocabulary

Pronounce each word and learn its meaning.

Key Words

connect (ku-**nekt**) *verb*
▶ pages 135, 144

When you **connect** people or things, you join them together. Cables **connect** the computer to the wall.

history (**his**-trē) *noun*
▶ page 143

History is what happened in the past. The grandparents share the family **history** with their granddaughter.

joy (**joi**) *noun*
▶ page 137

When you feel **joy**, you are very happy. The soccer champions smile with **joy**.

listen (**li**-sun) *verb*
▶ pages 135, 145

When you **listen** to someone, you hear what the person says. She **listens** to her friend's story.

poor (**por**) *adjective*
▶ pages 135, 139

A **poor** person has little money. The **poor** man has no money in his wallet. *Antonym: rich*

receive (ri-**sēv**) *verb*
▶ page 136

When you **receive** something, you take what someone gives you. He **receives** the gift.

remember (ri-**mem**-bur) *verb*
▶ pages 132, 138, 139, 140, 141, 142, 143, 144

When you **remember** something, you think of it again.

rich (**rich**) *adjective*
▶ pages 135, 139

A **rich** person has a lot of money. *Antonym: poor*

Practice the Words Make a drawing that shows the meaning of each Key Vocabulary word. Then compare drawings with a partner's.

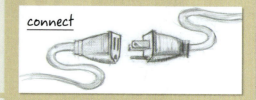

connect

memoir by Alma Flor Ada

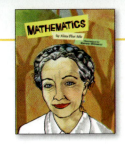

Ask Questions

As you read, you may have questions about the author's big ideas.
To understand the text better, **ask questions** about it.

Reading Strategy
Ask Questions

HOW TO ASK QUESTIONS

1. Read the text. Ask yourself questions about it.

2. Write your questions on self-stick notes about the author's big ideas.

3. Reread or read on to find the answers.

4. If an answer is not in the text, stop and think. Think about what you know from your own life to help you find the answer.

Read the text and the self-stick notes.

Look Into the Text

> Why were Mina's children's lives different? Maybe some were born when Mina was poor.

Mina had six children. Their lives were very different. Two children were rich. Two were poor. Two were comfortable. But they all had one thing in common. They loved Mina.

Mina's children visited her often. Each visitor was important to her. She shared jokes. She retold the latest news. The children drifted apart. But she connected them. Mainly, she listened.

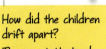

> I don't see my cousin very often.

> How did the children drift apart?
> They probably lived in different places.

Try It

As you read "Mathematics," ask questions when you don't understand the text or want to know more.

Genre: Memoir

A **memoir** describes important events in a person's life. The writer tells about events and people he or she <mark>remembers</mark>. Memoirs are based on true stories.

In "Mathematics," Alma Flor Ada shares stories about her great-grandmother. Through the memoir, we understand why the writer's great-grandmother was important to her. When you read a memoir, think about the events the writer describes.

www.hbedge.net
- Learn more about the author.
- Read an excerpt from another memoir.

MATHEMATICS

by Alma Flor Ada
Illustrated by Karen Blessen

My great-grandmother Mina never went to school. She never learned to read. She never learned to write. And she never studied **mathematics**.

One day, she heard me **recite math problems**. "Three times three is nine. Three times four is twelve."

"Child, what are you doing?" she asked. "Becoming like my Cotita?" Cotita was her **parrot**.

In Other Words
mathematics how to use numbers
recite math problems say things I had to
    learn for math class
parrot talking bird

Mina had six children. Their lives were very different. Two children were **rich**. Two were **poor**. Two were **comfortable**. But they all had one thing **in common**. They loved Mina.

Mina's children **visited** her often. Each visitor was important to her. She shared jokes. She retold the latest news. The children **drifted apart**. But she **connected** them. Mainly, she **listened**.

Monitor Comprehension

Key Vocabulary
rich *adjective*, having a lot of money
poor *adjective*, having very little money
connect *verb*, to join people or things together
listen *verb*, to pay attention to what a person says

In Other Words
comfortable not worried about money
in common that was the same
visited came to see
drifted apart did not talk to each other much

Explain
How does Mina feel about the people in her family? How do they feel about her?

Visitors never came **with empty hands**. Mina **received** their **presents** with a smile. She was **pleased by** wildflowers. She was just as pleased by a set of towels. She would then point to her closet. "On the second shelf is a can of peaches. In the drawer are new **handkerchiefs**."

Key Vocabulary
receive *verb*, to take what someone gives you

In Other Words
with empty hands without bringing something for Mina
presents gifts
pleased by happy if someone gave her
handkerchiefs cloths used for drying

One poor granddaughter gave a few oranges. She went home happily with new socks. A tired daughter brought jelly. She left excitedly with money **for rent**. The rich son received an orange. All were given with <mark>joy</mark>.

Key Vocabulary
joy *noun*, great happiness

In Other Words
for rent to pay for her house

Monitor Comprehension

Describe
What does Mina's family bring her? What does she give?

Mina never went to school. She could not read. She could not write. She never learned math. But she **remembered** the birthdays of six children. She remembered the birthdays of thirty-four grandchildren. She remembered the birthdays of seventy-five great grandchildren.

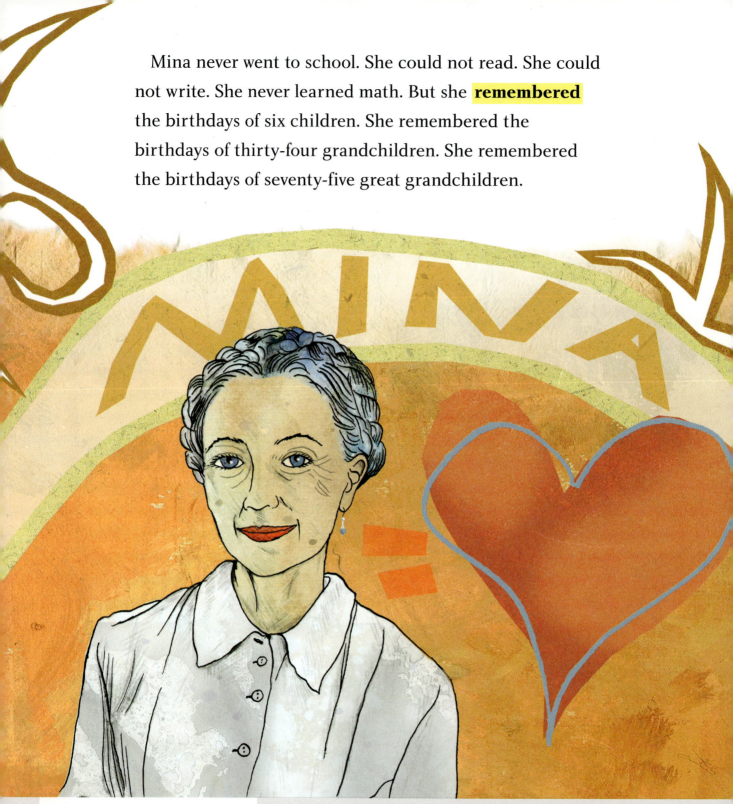

Key Vocabulary
remember *verb*, to think of something again

Mina knew a different kind of mathematics. She knew how to add and subtract. She knew how to **accept** and to give. And she knew how to share. With Mina, **the balance was always one of love**. ❖

ANALYZE Mathematics

1. **Explain** What could Mina <mark>remember</mark>? Why?

2. **Vocabulary** Was Mina <mark>rich</mark> or <mark>poor</mark>?

3. **Reading Strategy** **Ask Questions** Choose a question you asked yourself. Share it with a partner. How did it help you think about the author's big ideas?

↩ Return to the Text

Reread and Retell Explain what the author means when she says Mina knew how to add and subtract. Who does Mina add, or give, things to? Who does Mina subtract, or take, things from? Reread the text and find sentences to support your retelling.

In Other Words
accept keep something she was given
the balance was always one of love
    everyone was loved

About the Writer

Alma Flor Ada (1938–) was born in Cuba. She moved to the United States at age 17. Alma Flor Ada publishes many of her books in both Spanish and English. She says, "knowing two languages has made the world richer for me."

Elements of Poetry: Repetition

Poetry is like music. Poets often choose words because of the ways they sound. Sometimes they repeat a word or a group of words. This is called **repetition**. If a poet repeats a word or phrase, it is probably important.

> ### HOW TO APPRECIATE REPETITION IN A POEM
>
> 1. Read the poem aloud. Listen to the sounds.
>
> 2. Listen for words that the poet repeats or uses again and again.
>
> 3. Think about why the poet repeats a word or group of words. Ask, "How does the repetition show what is important to understand or feel?"

Read the lines of poetry. See how one reader learns how the poet feels about remembering.

Look Into the Text

Remember the sky you were born under,
know each of the star's stories.
Remember the moon, know who she is.

The poet repeats the word "remember." It is important to remember things.

Try It

As you read "Remember" aloud, listen for more repetition. Think about what it means.

Connect Across Texts

In "Mathematics," the author **remembers** the wisdom she learned from her grandmother. Now read this poem. What does the author want you to remember?

Remember

BY JOY HARJO

Remember the sky you were born under,
know each of the star's stories.
Remember the moon, know who she is.
Remember the sun's birth at dawn, that is the
5   strongest point of time. Remember sundown
and the giving away to night.

Key Vocabulary
remember *verb*, to think of
   something again

In Other Words
sundown the time when the sun goes down
the giving away when the sky turns dark

Remember your birth, how your mother struggled
to give you form and breath. You are evidence of
her life, and her mother's, and hers.

10   Remember your father. He is your life, also.
Remember the earth whose skin you are:
red earth, black earth, yellow earth, white earth
brown earth, we are earth.

Remember the plants, trees, animal life who all have their
15 tribes, their families, their histories, too. Talk to them,
listen to them. They are alive poems.
Remember the wind. Remember her voice.
She knows the origin of this universe.

Monitor Comprehension

Key Vocabulary
<mark>history</mark> *noun*, things that happened
  in the past

In Other Words
tribes groups
voice sounds
origin of this universe beginning of
  everything

Explain
Name some things
the poet wants you to
remember. Say why.

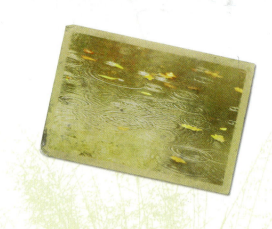

Remember you are all people and all people
20   are you.
Remember you are this universe and this
universe is you.
Remember all is in motion, is growing, is you.
Remember language comes from this.
25   Remember the dance language is, that life is.
Remember.

ANALYZE Remember

1. **Explain** Why does the poet tell us to ==remember== the plants, trees, and animal life?

2. **Vocabulary** Do you think that we should ==connect== with the Earth? Why or why not?

3. **Elements of Poetry** The poet repeats the word *remember* many times in the poem. Did the repetition get your attention? What did it make you think of? What does the poet want you to remember?

⟲ Return to the Text

Reread and Retell Look back at the poem. Tell a partner about a wise thing the poet says. How is she wise?

About the Poet

Joy Harjo (1951–) is a poet, an author, and a musician. She grew up in Oklahoma and is a member of the Muscogee Nation. She writes to bring people closer together. Harjo also writes to help people connect with nature. She says, " . . . in that way we all continue forever."

In Other Words

all is in motion everything is always changing
the dance how exciting and beautiful

EQ ## What Makes Us Wise?

Talk About Literature

1. **Explain** Author Alma Flora Ada says that "Mina knew a different kind of mathematics." Explain what she means.

    Mina knows how to _____. This is like math because _____.

2. **Visualize** Imagine the poet Joy Harjo looking at the sun as it comes up or looking hard at the night sky. What do you think she is thinking? How do you think she feels?

EQ 3. **Compare** "Mathematics" and "Remember" tell many wise lessons. Name one lesson that is similar in the two selections. Then name a lesson that is unique to each selection.

    Both selections tell the lesson _____. One lesson that "Mathematics" tells is _____. One lesson that "Remember" tells is _____.

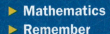

Listen to a reading. Practice fluency. Use the Reading Handbook, page 534.

Review Key Vocabulary

Choose the correct vocabulary word to complete each sentence.

1. Last year, we went to a village. There, we _____ with Dad's family after many years. (connected/received)

2. It was a great _____ to see the family! Everyone had fun. (history/joy)

3. We _____ to stories about the past. (listened/received)

4. We learned about our family's _____. (history/remember)

5. We brought gifts and we _____ presents. (connected/received)

6. Most villagers are _____, because there are not many jobs. (poor/rich)

7. The people may not have much money, but their culture is _____. (poor/rich)

8. I will always _____ the time I spent in the village. (joy/remember)

Vocabulary

- connected
- history
- joy
- listened
- poor
- received
- remember
- rich

Write About Literature

EQ **Journal Entry** In both selections, the authors describe ways of listening. To what or whom do you **listen**? How does it make you wise? Use the chart to organize your ideas.

Who or What?	Why?
I listen to . . .	It makes me wise because . . .

Use Object Pronouns

Remember that a **noun** can be the object of a verb.

I remember my **mother**. I honor my **mother**.
  verb   object   verb   object

A pronoun refers to a noun in a sentence. If the noun is the object of a verb, special forms of pronouns are used. These are called **object pronouns**.

I remember my **mother**. I honor **her**.
  verb   object   verb   object
          noun   pronoun

Study the subject and object pronouns. An object pronoun is always the object of a verb.

SUBJECT PRONOUN	I	you	he	she	it	we	they
OBJECT PRONOUN	me	you	him	her	it	us	them

Notice that the pronouns **you** and **it** are the same in both subject and object forms.

Oral Practice Work with a partner. Say each pair of sentences. Complete the second sentence with the object pronoun that refers to the underlined words.

1. Remember <u>the birds</u> of the forest. Remember _____ well.
2. Learn to love <u>the forest</u>, too. Love _____ as the home of birds.
3. Do not forget <u>your father</u>, either. Do not forget _____ ever.
4. Memorize <u>the movements</u> of the trees in the wind. Never forget _____.

Written Practice Choose the correct pronoun and write each sentence.

5. Trees always calm _____. (I/me)
6. _____ love to see them when I walk in the forest. (I/me)
7. The frogs and the snakes don't bother _____ at all. (we/us)
8. My mom says dogs like _____. (she/her)

Express Needs and Wants

Tell What They Need and Want Look in newspapers or magazines. Find pictures with people who need or want something.

- Write comments in a speech balloon. Tell what the people say.

> I want a day at the beach.
> I need to finish my report.

- Or write a caption below the picture.

This family wants some peace and quiet, but the baby needs to cry!

Suffixes

Remember, a suffix is a word part added at the end of the word. A suffix changes the meaning of the word.

See how **-ly** and **-able** change the meanings of words:

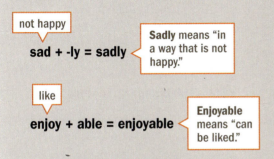

SUFFIX	MEANING
-able	can be done
-ly	in that way

Use a chart to help you figure out the meaning of each underlined word.

1. We knock <u>happily</u> on our mother's door.
2. Mother opens the door <u>quickly</u>.
3. It is so <u>enjoyable</u> to see her!
4. "Come in!" she says in a <u>kindly</u> voice.
5. "Sit down and be <u>comfortable</u>," she tells us.

Word	Parts	Meaning
happily	_____ + _____ =	

Compound Words

Remember that a compound word is made up of two smaller words.

book + bag = bookbag — A **bookbag** is a bag that you put books in.

Figure out the meaning of each underlined word.

1. I like to spend time <u>outdoors</u>.
2. I always see <u>something</u> beautiful.
3. I often see <u>sunsets</u>.
4. <u>Sometimes</u> I take a long hike.
5. I always take a <u>backpack</u>.

Kathryn likes hiking.

Education Careers

Is a job in education right for you? Take this career quiz to find out.

Career Quiz

1. I like to work with people.
- **a** True
- **b** False

2. I like to explain things.
- **a** True
- **b** False

3. I like to keep things in order.
- **a** True
- **b** False

How many times did you answer *True*?

3 times: Wow!
A job in education is perfect for you!

1–2 times: Maybe
A job in education may be right for you.

0 times: No thanks
A job in education may not be right for you. Do you know someone who would like this kind of job?

School Jobs

People who have school jobs work with students. Here are some school jobs. They have different kinds of work, or responsibilities, and need different education and training.

Job	Responsibilities	Education/Training Needed
Teacher Assistant **1**	· Helps the teacher in the classroom · Helps the students	· Associate's degree · Certificate
Teacher **2**	· Helps students learn · Records grades	· Bachelor's degree or Master's degree · Teaching credential
School Principal **3**	· Hires and supervises teachers · Helps teachers · Manages special activities	· Master's degree or doctorate

A High School Teacher

My name is Beverly Shoun. I teach English. I work at a high school.

I help my students read and understand stories, poetry, and plays.

I also give tests. My students study hard for my tests. This student is always happy to get an A.

Research School Jobs

Learn more about an education job in the United States.

1. Choose a job from the chart on page 148.
2. Go online to **www.hbedge.net**. Read about the job you chose.
3. Complete this chart.

Job	How many workers have this job?	How much money does a worker earn?	Is this a good job for the future?

WISDOM OF THE AGES

EDGE LIBRARY

Reflect on the Essential Question

With a group, discuss the Essential Question. What makes us wise?

As you answer the questions, think about what you read in the selections and your choice of Edge Library books.

- Who gives you good **advice**?
- How do people become wise? Is it something you can only **learn** as you live your life?
- Do people need to go to school to gain **wisdom**?

BINGO

B	I	N	G	O
15	18	11	21	6
24	17	3	20	10
7	13	FREE	8	16
22	5	1	9	14
12	4	2	19	23

Unit Review Game

You will need:

- 4 players
- 1 **Bingo** board for each player
- question cards
- note paper
- pencil, pen, or marker

Objective: Be the first player to mark a row of squares across or down.

1. Download **Bingo** boards and question cards from **www.hbedge.net**. Print out and cut apart the question cards. Mix them up.

2. **Player A** takes a card. He or she says the number of the card and reads the question.

3. The other players write their answers on pieces of paper. The players that get the correct answer find the number on their cards and mark it with an **X**. (If you can't agree on the answer, ask your teacher.)

4. **Player B** takes a turn. Then the other players take turns.

5. The first player to mark a row of squares says "Bingo!" This player is the winner.

When you give someone advice, you explain ways to solve problems. For this project, you will think about a problem and use your own experiences to give someone advice.

Write an Advice Column

❶ Connect Writing to Your Life

What do friends do when they have problems they cannot figure out? They ask for help.

❷ Understand the Form

Some writers help others solve problems. They answer letters in newspapers, magazines, or online. Study this example.

Dear Problem-Solver:

Every day my friend Jane sits and plays video games. How can I get her to do something else? I miss her!

—Lonely

Each letter has a greeting.

The writer states a problem.

Dear Lonely:

It is hard to compete with video games. This happened to me, too! There are things I did. Try this.

1. Tell her you miss her.

2. Ask her over to your house.

3. Suggest a new activity you can do together.

4. Keep trying.

—Problem-Solver

The person giving the advice restates the problem.

The writer suggests ways to solve the problem.

Write Together

✔ Plan and Write

Read about Couch Potato's problem. Then follow the steps.

> ### Dear Problem-Solver:
>
> I watch too much TV! I don't get enough sleep because I always stay up too late watching TV. My mom always bugs me about it. What should I do?
>
> —Couch Potato

1 Talk About the Problem

Who is asking for advice? What does the person need to know? Discuss the problem with a small group.

2 Brainstorm Solutions

Think about your experience with the problem or a similar one. Brainstorm solutions with your group. Use a **Problem-and-Solution Chart** to record ideas to solve the problem.

Problem-and-Solution Chart

"He can make a sign."

"Yes! Or he can go . . ."

Problem: watching too much TV

Solution: use "Stop—Do Not Watch" sign

Solution:

3 Write the Advice

Write a greeting. Use the notes in your **Problem-and-Solution** Chart to suggest ways the person can solve the problem. Work with your group. Sign the response with your name or a made-up one.

greeting → Dear Couch Potato:
I know it is hard to turn off that TV. Here are some things that might help.
1. Put a sign on the TV that says STOP—DO NOT WATCH.

Reflect on Your Draft

Talk with your group. What helped you write your advice column?

Write on Your Own

Your Job as a Writer

▶ **Prompt** Read the letter to Problem-Solver or go to **www.hbedge.net** and pick another letter.

Write an advice column to share with your group. Be sure to

- restate the problem
- offer solutions to the problem.

Dear Problem-Solver:

I have to pass an important test next week. But I have not been paying attention in class. Help! What can I do?

—Worried

 **Prewrite**

Get ready to give your advice.

1 Think About the Problem

Think about your experience with the problem or a similar one. What wisdom can you share with the writer?

This happened to me, too . . .

2 Brainstorm Solutions

Use a **Problem-and-Solution Chart** to record ideas to solve the problem. Add as many solutions as you can think of.

Problem-and-Solution Chart

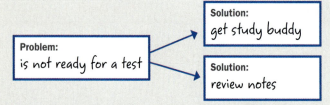

Problem:
is not ready for a test

Solution:
get study buddy

Solution:
review notes

Write

Write your response.

1 Write the Greeting

Use the made-up name of the person asking for advice in the greeting.

> Dear Worried:

2 Restate the Problem

Use the notes in your **Problem-and-Solution** Chart to start your letter. In the first sentence, restate the problem.

> Dear Worried:
>
> I totally understand what it is like not to be ready for a test.

Use sentences like these:

- I understand what it is like to [Restate the problem].

- I know what you are going through.

- I know it is hard when [Describe the problem].

3 Present the Solutions

Turn the notes in your **Problem-and-Solution Chart** into sentences. Present your advice.

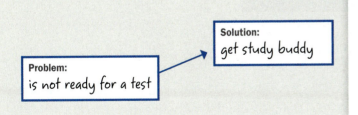

> Dear Worried:
>
> I totally understand what it is like not to be ready for a test. Here are some things you must try:
>
> 1. Get a study buddy in your class. Ask him or her to help you study.

4 Sign Your Name

End by signing your name. You can use your real name or a made-up one.

✔ Check Your Work

After you have finished your draft, make it better and check it for mistakes.

🔲 Check for Subject-Verb Agreement

Remember that the subject and verb in a sentence must agree in number. Use a plural verb with a plural noun.

> The students ~~is~~ *are* giving advice.
>
> They make*s* suggestions for how to solve problems.

🔲 Check Spelling of Plurals

Circle each word that may not be spelled right. Look it up in the dictionary or ask for help. Fix the spelling if you need to.

Rules	Examples
Make most nouns plural by adding -s to the end.	author ➔ authors crowd ➔ crowds
If the word ends in s, sh, ch, x, or z, add -es.	beach ➔ beaches bus ➔ buses
If the word ends in a y, change the y to an i and add -es.	baby ➔ babies city ➔ cities

🔲 Check for Capital Letters

The names of people, their titles, and names of places are called proper nouns.

Rules	Examples
Capitalize proper nouns.	Steve Eddins Dr. Grover
Capitalize the pronoun *I*, every time it appears in a sentence.	I was shocked when I heard about the test.

> *I*
> ~~i~~ met three friend*s* at one of our favorite beach*es*.

🔲 Mark Your Changes

∧	✗	⌐	◯	≡	╱	¶
Add.	Take out.	Replace with this.	Check spelling.	Capitalize.	Make lowercase.	Make new paragraph.

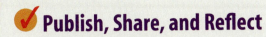

✔ Publish, Share, and Reflect

Publish and Share

Now you are ready to publish your advice column. Print or write a clean copy on a large sheet of paper. Then post it in your classroom.

Read at least one advice column by a classmate. Was that person's advice different or the same as yours? How?

Which advice for the problem do you think is the best? Discuss the advice with your classmates.

HOW TO HAVE A DISCUSSION

1. **Read Each Advice Column** Read each advice column to see if it restates the problem and presents a solution.

2. **Discuss the Advice in Your Group** Give your opinion. Listen to other opinions. Try to finish these sentences:

   I think the best advice is _____.

   I think this because _____.

3. **Don't Interrupt** Wait until another person has shared ideas before you speak.

4. **Vote on the Best Advice** Give everyone a chance to speak. Then decide which advice you all agree with. There is no single correct answer. Different advice may be better for different people. Share your group's decisions with the class.

Reflect on Your Work

▶ Think about your writing.

- What did you learn about writing that you didn't know before?

- What did you like best about writing an advice column?

☑ **Save a copy of your work in your portfolio.**

UNIT 3

GLOBAL VILLAGE

EQ ESSENTIAL QUESTION:

What Makes Us the Same? What Makes Us Different?

We are all made of the same clay.

—English Proverb

Five fingers are brothers, but all are not equals.

—Afghan Proverb

Ensemble © 1994, Stéphan Daigle. Acrylics on paper support.

EQ ESSENTIAL QUESTION:
What Makes Us the Same?
What Makes Us Different?

Study the Photos

What images can you see?

EQ **ESSENTIAL QUESTION**

In this unit, you will explore the **Essential Question** in class. Think about the
question outside of school, too.

1 Study the Concept

You are in a classroom.
Your classroom is in a school.
Your school is on a street.
The street is in a town.
The town is in a state.
The state is in a **country**.
The country is in the **world**.
The world has many **cultures**.

1. The United States is a **country** in the **world**. How many countries can you name?

2. A country's **culture** includes its art, music, and food. What are some parts of your culture? How is your culture different from other cultures?

3. People in the world need the same things to live. Name some of the things that we all need.

2 Choose More to Read

Choose something to read during this unit.

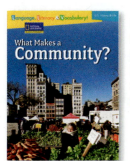

What Makes a Community?
by Janet Helenthal
Study a small community in New York City to learn what makes a community.
▶NONFICTION

Rice
by Marianne Morrison
People in many countries eat rice. Learn where it grows and how people eat it.
▶NONFICTION

www.hbedge.net
- Learn how to greet people in different countries.
- Learn about food from around the world.

Use Word Parts

Remember, some English words are made up of different parts. These parts include **base words**, **prefixes**, and **suffixes**.

You can use word parts as clues to a word's meaning. Follow these steps.

- Look for a prefix or suffix. Cover it.   Example: **hope** ful
- Read the base word or words, and think about their meaning.
- Uncover the prefix or suffix and think of its meaning.
- Put the meanings of the word parts together.

respect + -ful = respectful

| honor | full of | full of honor |

Sometimes you can combine two smaller words to form a **compound word**.

class + room = classroom

Practice Using Word Parts

Use the word parts to figure out the meaning of each word.

1. unlike
2. replay
3. readable
4. suitcase
5. backpack
6. careful

SUFFIX	MEANING	EXAMPLE
-ful	full of	hope**ful**
-able	can be done	change**able**

PREFIX	MEANING	EXAMPLE
un-	not	**un**happy
re-	again	**re**write

Put the Strategy to Use

Work with a partner. Figure out the meaning of each underlined word.

7. I reread my friend's e-mail.
8. My name is unusual.
9. He dropped a big, colorful plate.
10. The plate was breakable!

Describe People and Places

Listen to the chant.

Chant

AT THE AIRPORT

Many different people wait
At the crowded airport gate.

A young woman reads the news.
A little boy ties his shoes.

One man just stands and stares
While people sit on shiny, black chairs.

Another man with a serious face
Pulls along a blue suitcase.

Different people, yet still the same—
They all wish they were on the plane!

Use Adjectives Before Nouns

1 TRY OUT LANGUAGE
2 LEARN GRAMMAR
3 APPLY ON YOUR OWN

Adjectives are words that describe people, places, or things. You can use adjectives to describe how something looks.

> A **long line** waits at the check-in counter.

An adjective often comes before the **noun** it describes.

> Passengers cannot carry **large suitcases** on the **small plane**.

Adjectives help the reader imagine what you are writing about.

> The **large bags** must go in a special place.

Say It

Work with a partner. Look at the photo. Then say each sentence with an adjective from the box.

blue	large	small	tall	yellow

1. The first woman wears a _____ shirt.

2. The second woman wears a _____ jacket.

3. The _____ man behind her wears a hat.

4. He has a _____ suitcase.

5. It cannot fit on the _____ plane.

Passengers wait in a long line.

Write It

Write each sentence with an adjective and a noun from the box.

6. A _____ _____ carries a big bag on his back.

7. It is a _____ _____!

8. He wears shorts and _____ _____.

9. A man in a _____ _____ is at the end of the line.

10. He is next to a woman with _____ _____.

Adjectives	Nouns
black	backpack
blue	boy
huge	hair
little	shirt
long	sneakers

Describe a Picture

Where do you want to go? Work with a partner to find a picture of an interesting place. Look on the Internet or in magazines. Then write four sentences to describe the people and the things in the picture.

Follow these steps to create a good description:

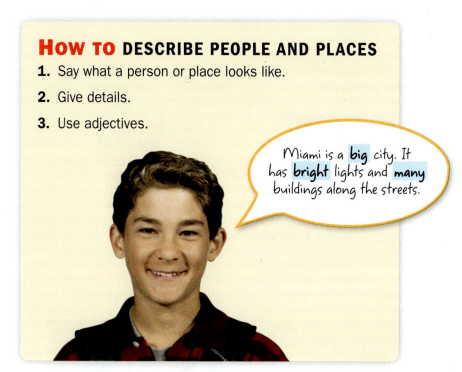

HOW TO DESCRIBE PEOPLE AND PLACES

1. Say what a person or place looks like.

2. Give details.

3. Use adjectives.

Miami is a **big** city. It has **bright** lights and **many** buildings along the streets.

Use **adjectives** when you describe people and places.

After you finish your description:

• Write your name on the back of your picture.

• Give your picture to the teacher. The teacher will show all the pictures to the class.

• Take turns with your partner. Read your sentences to the class. Can the class guess which picture is yours?

Miami is a fun city.

EQ **What Makes Us the Same? What Makes Us Different?**
Talk about how our environments make us different.

Learn Key Vocabulary

Pronounce each word and learn its meaning.

Key Words

crowded (**krow**-dud) *adjective*
▶ page 170

A **crowded** place is full of people or things. The bus is **crowded**.

decide (di-**sīd**) *verb*
▶ page 181

When you **decide** to do something, you make a choice to do it. The signs help you **decide** where to go.

enough (i-**nuf**) *adjective*
▶ pages 168, 172, 174

When you have **enough** of something, you have as much as you need. There is **enough** food in the cart for everyone.

hungry (**hung**-grē) *adjective*
▶ pages 168, 172

When you are **hungry**, you need or want something to eat. The baby birds are **hungry**.

instead (in-**sted**) *adverb*
▶ pages 168, 170

Instead means in place of something else. She is buying carrots **instead** of broccoli.

meal (mēl) *noun*
▶ page 182

A **meal** is all the food you eat at one time. Breakfast, lunch, and dinner are **meals**.

safe (sāf) *adjective*
▶ pages 174, 176

If something is **safe**, it doesn't hurt you. It is important to have **safe** water to drink. *Antonym:* dangerous

village (**vi**-lij) *noun*
▶ pages 170, 171, 172, 174, 175, 176

A **village** is a very small town. This **village** is by the ocean.

Practice the Words Make a **Study Card** for each Key Vocabulary word. Then compare cards with a partner.

> crowded
> What it means: very full
> Example: The cafeteria is crowded at lunch time.

expository nonfiction by David J. Smith

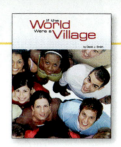

Determine Importance

A **main idea** is what the writer thinks is most important about a topic. Sometimes you can find the main idea when you look at the title, headings, pictures, and other parts of the text. When you find the author's main idea, you can figure out what is most important in the text.

Reading Strategy
Determine Importance

HOW TO DETERMINE IMPORTANCE

1. Look at the headings, pictures, and boldfaced words. Identify the topic, what the selection mostly is about. Write it in a **Main Idea Chart**.

2. Decide what the author mostly is writing about the topic. Ask, what is most important for me to know about the topic?

3. Write the most important idea.

Look at the picture and read the text. Use the **Main Idea Chart** to tell what's most important.

Look Into the Text

Food

There is a lot of food in the global village. There is enough food for everyone. But the food is not divided equally. Many people are hungry.

Main Idea Chart

Topic	The Most Important Idea about the Topic
food	There is food, but not everyone gets it

Try It

Copy the Main Idea Chart. Complete your chart as you read "If the World Were a Village."

Build Background

Did you know that many people in the world are **hungry** almost every day? Did you know that some children do not go to school because they have to work **instead**? "If the World Were a Village" is an essay about how people live around the world. Life for many people is unfair. Some people have what they need. Other people don't have **enough** food or water.

www.hbedge.net
- View photos of houses from around the world.
- Learn about projects that help people in need.

If the
World
Were a Village

by David J. Smith

Welcome to the Global Village

Earth is **crowded**. It gets more crowded every year. In 2008, the world's population was **6.7 billion**. Eleven countries each had more than **100 million** people. China had more than **1.3 billion**.

These numbers are big. They can be hard to understand. **Instead**, think of them differently. Imagine the world as a **village** of 100 people. Each person in this village **stands for** 67 million people from the real world. We can learn about these villagers. They can teach us about people in the real world. They also teach us about world problems.

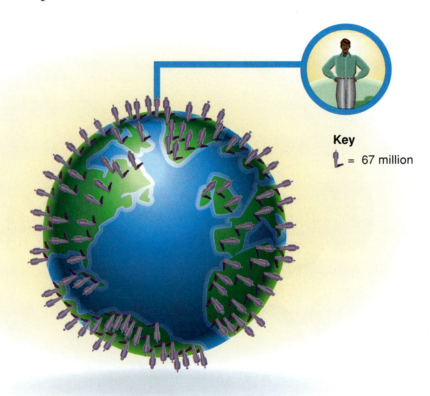

Key

🚶 = 67 million

Key Vocabulary

crowded *adjective*, full of people or things

instead *adverb*, in place of something else

village *noun*, a very small town

In Other Words

Global World
6.7 billion 6,700,000,000
100 million 100,000,000
1.3 billion 1,300,000,000
stands for equals

Languages

"Ni hao ma?" "Hello!" "Namaste!" "Zdraz-vooy-teh." "¡Hola!"
"Ahlan." "Selamat pagi." The villagers use many languages. What
languages do they speak? There are almost six thousand languages
in the global village. More than half of the people speak eight
languages.

21 speak a **Chinese dialect** (of these people,
16 speak the Mandarin dialect)

9 speak English
9 speak Hindi
7 speak Spanish

4 speak Arabic
4 speak Bengali
3 speak Portuguese
3 speak Russian

Learn to say hello in these languages. Then you can **greet** many
people in the world.

In Other Words
Chinese dialect form of Chinese from one
  of China's regions
greet say hello to

Cultural Background
"Ni hao ma?" "Namaste!" "Zdraz-vooy-teh."
"¡Hola!" "Ahlan." "Selamat pagi." These are
ways to say "hello" in Chinese, Hindi, Russian,
Spanish, Arabic, and Malay.

Monitor Comprehension

Explain
Why does the author
say it is helpful to
think of the world as
a village?

Food

There is a lot of food in the global village. There is **enough** food for everyone. But the food is not **divided** equally. Many people are **hungry**.

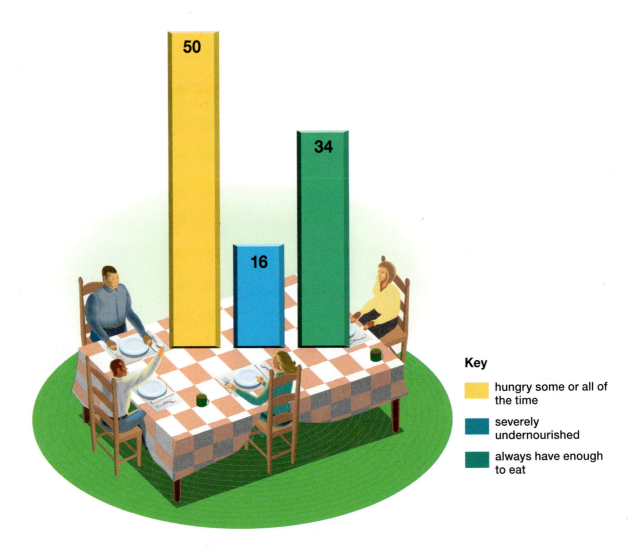

Key

■ hungry some or all of the time

■ severely undernourished

■ always have enough to eat

Enough

Women sell many kinds of vegetables in this busy market. Some people buy food here and then resell it to neighbors.

This family has a lot of food to share.

Not Enough

The men at this market sell only a few kinds of vegetables.

This family has just a little food to eat.

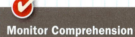

Monitor Comprehension

Explain
What does the author say about how food is divided in the village?

Air and Water

The air and water are <mark>safe</mark> in most of the village. But some air and water are **polluted**. Pollution can make people sick. Sometimes there is not enough clean water. The villagers must walk a long way to find more. How many people have safe water? How many people breathe clean air?

17 people do not have safe water in or near their homes

83 people have safe water in or near their homes

32 people breathe polluted air

68 people breathe clean air

Key Vocabulary
<mark>safe</mark> *adjective*, not dangerous

In Other Words
polluted dirty

Schooling and Literacy

A bell begins the school day. Some children in the village have no school near them. Others do. But they don't go to school. They must work instead. They help feed their families. How many people **attend** school?

36 villagers are ages 5 to 24

30 of them attend school

There is **1** teacher

Not everybody in the global village can read and write. Fifty-nine people over age 15 can read at least a little. Thirteen cannot read at all. More males than females learn how to read.

Monitor Comprehension

Explain
What are two reasons some children in the village do not go to school?

Think about **your place in the global village**. What is your life like? **How does it compare to** the lives of people around you? Get to know the world you live in. It's a small, but **precious** place that we all share. ❖

ANALYZE If the World Were a Village

1. **Explain** What things does every person in the global ==village== need?

2. **Vocabulary** Why are the air and water not ==safe== in some places in the village?

3. **Reading Strategy** **Determine Importance** What topics and important ideas did you write in your **Main Idea Chart** for each section? Share your ideas with a partner.

↪ Return to the Text

Reread and Retell Imagine you go to school in the global village. Talk about it. Include information about the students and teachers. Reread the text to find facts to support your retelling.

In Other Words
your place in the global village where you live
How does it compare to How it is like
precious very special

The Same

by Francisco X. Alarcón

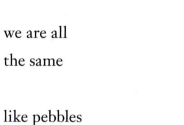

we are all
the same

like pebbles
in a riverbed

5   each of us
so different

In Other Words
pebbles little stones
a riverbed the bottom of a river

About the Poet

Francisco X. Alarcón (1954–) is a poet and a teacher. He says, "When you read poetry, you have to find new ways of looking at yourself." He writes in both English and Spanish.

magazine article by Nancy Shepherdson

Text Feature: Headings

Some text gives information about real events, people, and ideas. These texts are called nonfiction. Some nonfiction texts have sections, or parts. The **heading**, or title, for a section tells what the section is about.

> ### HOW TO USE HEADINGS
>
> 1. Read the heading to find out the topic of the section.
>
> 2. Think about what you already know about the topic. Then predict what the section is about.
>
> 3. Read the section. Check your prediction.

Read this section. See how one reader uses the heading to tell what the section is about.

Look Into the Text

heading ▷ **CHICKEN FEET**

Our grocery stores have a lot of food. There are still a lot of things that are hard to find there. Do you know what happens to chicken feet? Every week, the United States sends 30 million pounds of them to Asia. They are popular there.

> The heading tells me that this section is about chicken feet.

> And the section is about what happens to chicken feet.

Try It

As you read "Freaky Food," use the headings to decide what each section will be about.

Freaky Food

BY NANCY SHEPHERDSON

Connect Across Texts

In "If the World Were a Village," David Smith uses numbers to show how people are different. How does the author of this magazine article show differences around the world?

Have you ever eaten ants? Kids in many countries munch on fried ants. You may say "Ewww," but it's normal for them. People eat the foods of their country. They like those foods.

In Other Words
Freaky Strange
munch on eat

YOU'RE BUGGING ME!

Insects give a lot of **energy**. **Early American pioneers** ate bugs when they didn't have other food. Ask people in Africa, Australia, Europe, Asia, and America. Many people eat insects in over half the world. They say that ants taste good.

CHICKEN FEET

Our grocery stores have a lot of food. There are still a lot of things that are hard to find there. Do you know what happens to chicken feet? Every week, the United States sends 30 million pounds of them to Asia. They are popular there.

For many people, chicken feet are a delicious treat.

In Other Words

energy power to keep your brain and body active

Early American pioneers People who traveled across the United States in the late 1700s and throughout the 1800s

EAT A WEED

Did you know you can eat some kinds of dandelions? Europeans and Americans have eaten them for **centuries**. The leaves make a salad. The yellow flowers can be fried. They are eaten like French fries. Make sure to wash the flowers well before you cook them. **Seaweed is** also very popular. It is in many of the foods we eat every day. Your hamburger might have some seaweed. Your ice cream might, too. Bet you can't taste it.

WHAT'S ON THE MENU?

Different foods are eaten around the world. That is no surprise. The people of the world are very different, too. We have different cultures. We may believe different things. Our countries grow different foods. Some people are lucky. They have a lot of food. Others are not as lucky. They eat what they can find.

All of these things are important. They help us **decide** which foods to eat. They give us different **tastes**.

You can cook dandelion weeds or eat them raw.

Key Vocabulary
decide *verb*, to make a choice

In Other Words
Weed Wild plant
centuries hundreds of years
Seaweed is Plants that grow in the sea are
tastes ideas about what we like

Monitor Comprehension

Describe
Tell what some foods around the world are like.

Try a little test. At lunch today, look around. What "freaky foods" do you see? Before you say "Ewww," look at your own lunch. What would other people say? Your favorite **meal** may be a "freaky food" to **your neighbor**. That's OK. Our foods can be different and special—just like all the people in the world. ❖

ANALYZE Freaky Food

1. **Describe** What "test" does the author want you to try?

2. **Vocabulary** What are some of your favorite **meals**? Do you think some people might find them freaky?

3. **Text Feature: Headings** Explain to a partner how the headings helped you predict what the sections were about.

Return to the Text

Reread and Retell Tell about one freaky food from the text. Explain why some people eat it and what makes it strange to others. Use facts from the text to support your ideas.

Key Vocabulary
meal *noun*, all the food you eat at one time

In Other Words
Try a little test. Do something new.
your neighbor the person next to you

EQ ## What Makes Us the Same? What Makes Us Different?

Talk About Literature

1. **Make Judgments** "If the World Were a Village" tells about world problems. Explain which world problem is the worst.

   The worst world problem is _____ because _____ .

2. **Interpret** The author of "Freaky Food" says, "Our foods can be different and special—just like all the people in the world." Restate this idea in your own words.

EQ 3. **Draw Conclusions** "If the World Were a Village" and "Freaky Food" describe people around the world. Do the selections say that we are the same or different? Support your opinion with an example.

   The selections say that we are _____ . The text/image that shows this is _____ .

 Listen to a reading. Practice fluency. Use the Reading Handbook, page 535.

Review Key Vocabulary

Choose the correct vocabulary word to complete each sentence.

1. Ernesto and his family live in a small _____. (meal/village)

2. The water in Ernesto's village is _____. (safe/crowded)

3. His family has _____ food to eat. (enough/hungry)

4. They are not _____. (hungry/instead)

5. Ernesto's family _____ to share their food. (crowded/decides)

6. They make a _____ for the villagers. (village/meal)

7. The villagers go to Ernesto's house. The house is _____ because it is too small for everyone. (safe/crowded)

8. The villagers choose to eat outside _____. (instead/enough)

Vocabulary

- crowded
- decides
- enough
- hungry
- instead
- meal
- safe
- village

Write About Literature

EQ **Opinion Statement** Are people the same or different? Use the chart to organize your thoughts. Then write your opinion.

1. State Your Opinion	2. Support Your Opinion
I think people are . . .	I think this because I read . . .

Use Adjectives

Adjectives describe people, places, or things. Use adjectives to describe how something looks, sounds, feels, tastes, or smells.

> Earth is a **crowded** planet.
> **Many** people live here.

Most of the time, an adjective comes before the **noun**.

> The **hungry people** need food.

> We breathe **safe** air.

Sometimes an adjective comes after the verbs **am**, **is**, or **are**. These adjectives describe the noun in the subject.

> The rivers are **dirty**.

> The food is **freaky**.

Oral Practice Work with a partner. Add an adjective to each sentence. Say the noun that each adjective describes.

clean	difficult	dirty	hungry	poor

1. Many people in the world do not drink ____ water.
2. They breathe _____ air.
3. Their lives are _____ .
4. Some _____ children do not go to school.
5. They work to feed their _____ families.

Written Practice Rewrite these sentences. Add adjectives to describe the nouns.

delicious	different	fried	popular	salty

6. Chicken feet are a food in Asia.
7. Some people eat ants.
8. Other people like popcorn.
9. Dandelion leaves can make a salad.
10. Everyone eats food.

Describe People and Places

Describe a Person in Your Neighborhood Think of an interesting person who lives near you. It could be someone with an interesting job. Or it could be someone with a fun hobby, or special interest.

Make a list of words that describe the person and the neighborhood. These words should describe how things look, feel, or sound.

Write your words in a chart like this:

Person	Neighborhood

Use your chart to plan a description. Share the description with a partner.

Review Suffixes

Remember, a suffix is a word part added to the end of a base word. It changes the word's meaning.

SUFFIX	MEANING	EXAMPLE
-er	person who does this action	teacher
-y	having the quality of; like	snowy

To read a word with a suffix:

- Break the word into its parts.
- Think about the meaning of each part.
- Put the meanings together to understand the whole word.

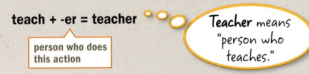

teach + -er = teacher

person who does this action

Teacher means "person who teaches."

Use a chart to help you figure out the meaning of each <u>underlined</u> word.

1. It is a <u>cloudy</u> day.
2. We walk along a <u>dusty</u> road to a village.
3. We see a <u>farmer</u> by the road.
4. We buy some <u>dirty</u> carrots from him.
5. He is a hard <u>worker</u>.

Word	Parts	Meaning
cloudy	_____ + _____ =	

Use a Bar Graph

Bar graphs give information without many ideas.

1. Find the title. It tells what the graph is about.
2. Read the labels. They tell about each bar.
3. Move your fingers up a bar. Then read across to find the number. For example, in Norway there are 313 doctors for every 100,000 people.

Answer this question about the graph at right:

How many doctors does Mexico have for every 100,000 people?

Work with a partner. Get information from other bar graphs. Ask each other questions about them.

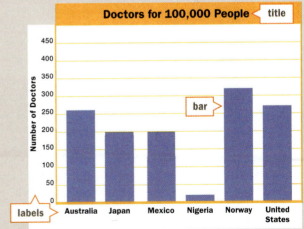

Source: United Nations Development Programme, 2007/2008 Report (Data from 2000–2004)

www.hbedge.net
- View more bar graphs.

Writing

Write a Photo Essay

▶ **Prompt** Create a photo essay about some foods in your culture. A photo essay uses photos with short descriptions, or captions, to tell a story.

1 **Plan** Use a chart to help you plan your photo essay. Find two or three photos of foods from your culture.

- Take notes about each photo. Write the name of the food. Say what it is.
- Write interesting details about the food. Or say what you think about it.
- Think of adjectives that describe how the food tastes, smells, looks, and feels.

Description Chart

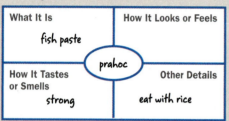

What It Is	How It Looks or Feels
fish paste	
prahoc	
How It Tastes or Smells	Other Details
strong	eat with rice

▼ **Writing Handbook**, page 599

REMEMBER
• Adjectives are words that describe.
• Adjectives usually come before nouns. We make **round** shapes.
• An adjective may come after the noun when the sentence uses *am*, *is*, or *are*. The food is **tasty**.

2 **Write** Use your notes to write captions for the photos. Include words that describe. Be sure to use adjectives correctly.

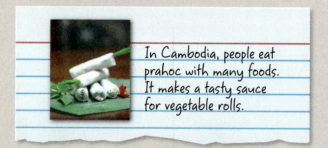

In Cambodia, people eat prahoc with many foods. It makes a tasty sauce for vegetable rolls.

Use captions like these:

- In [place] , people eat [food] .
- This is [name of food] .
- It tastes [adjective] .
- It smells [adjective] .

3 **Share** Put your photos and captions on a large sheet of paper. Post your photo essay in the classroom. Read two other photo essays. Compare them. Discuss them with the writers.

Make Comparisons

1 TRY OUT LANGUAGE
2 LEARN GRAMMAR
3 APPLY ON YOUR OWN

Look at the picture and listen to the description.

Description

Different, But Still Friends

My name is Farah. I go to high school in Florida. My friend Anna wears jeans and T-shirts at school. I do not wear jeans or T-shirts. I wear different clothes to follow my beliefs. We are different, but we are still friends.

All the girls at school wear watches and rings. So do I. We all go to the same classes and study the same subjects. Both Anna and I like American history. We both sing in the choir.

We are the same height, but I am older than Anna. We both have dark brown hair. The only difference is that I cover mine. Yes, we are a little different, but she is still my best friend.

Language Workshop, continued

1 TRY OUT LANGUAGE
2 LEARN GRAMMAR
3 APPLY ON YOUR OWN

Use Adjectives That Compare

You can use an **adjective** to make a comparison.

Juan is not as **tall** as Kate.

You can also change the form of the adjective to make the comparison. Add **-er** to short adjectives to compare two people, places, or things.

tall + -er = taller	Kate is **taller**.
short + -er = shorter	Juan is **shorter**.

Often, you will use the word **than** after the adjective.

Kate is taller **than** Juan.
Juan is shorter **than** Kate.

Kate and Juan stand next to each other.

Say It

1–5. Compare people and things in your classroom. Use the sentence builder to create at least five sentences. Say the sentences to a partner.

_____	is are	bigger longer shorter smaller taller	than	_____.

Write It

Write each sentence with the correct adjective.

6. Alberto is (tall/taller).

7. My friend Kim is even (tall/taller) than Alberto.

8. Rachel is (short/shorter) than Alberto.

9. She is very (short/shorter).

10. But her feet are (big/bigger) than Kim's!

Play a Comparison Game

Make adjective cards. Then play a game in which you compare things in the classroom. Follow these steps to make clear comparisons:

HOW TO MAKE COMPARISONS

1. Say how things are alike.

2. Say how things are different.

3. Use adjectives that compare.

> My desk is clean, and your desk is clean.

> Your desk is **cleaner** than my desk.

You can add -er to many adjectives to compare two things.

To make the adjective cards:

- Think of adjectives that describe objects in your classroom.

- Write each adjective on a card.

To play the game:

- Mix together the cards for the whole class.

- Take turns. Choose a card and use the adjective to describe something in the classroom.

- Challenge a classmate to make a comparison with the same adjective.

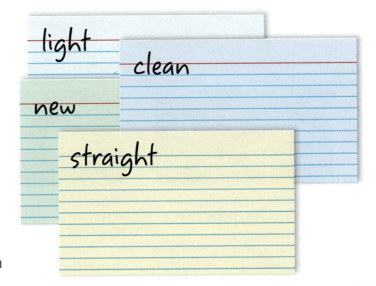

EQ What Makes Us the Same? What Makes Us Different?

Think about how the experiences we share make us the same.

Learn Key Vocabulary

Pronounce each word and learn its meaning.

Key Words

belief (bu-**lēf**) *noun*
▶ pages 192, 195

A **belief** is an idea that you think is true. People sometimes fight for their **beliefs**.

experience (ik-**spear**-ē-uns) *noun*
▶ page 194

An **experience** is something that you did or saw. The young women enjoy their **experiences** as volunteers.

forget (fur-**get**) *verb*
▶ page 194

When you **forget** something, you cannot think of it. He **forgets** how to solve the math problem.

popular (**pah**-pyu-lur) *adjective*
▶ pages 199, 202

When something is **popular**, many people like it. Soccer is **popular**.

religion (ri-li-jun) *noun*
▶ pages 192, 195

Religion is a set of strong ideas about god or gods. Christianity, Judaism, and Islam are **religions**.

sport (**sport**) *noun*
▶ pages 199, 202, 203

A **sport** is a game, such as baseball or basketball.

truth (**trüth**) *noun*
▶ pages 195, 197

Something that is a fact is the **truth**. People must tell the **truth** in court.

uncomfortable (un-**kumf**-tur-bul) *adjective*
▶ pages 192, 195

Uncomfortable means not feeling easy. This new driver is **uncomfortable**.

Practice the Words Make an **Idea Web** for three Key Vocabulary words. Write words that are related to each word you choose.

Idea Web

fun   play
sport
practice   basketball

narrative nonfiction by Philip Devitt

Determine Importance

As you read, **determine what is important** so that you can remember it. One way to do this is to summarize the paragraphs in a selection.

Reading Strategy
Determine Importance

HOW TO SUMMARIZE A PARAGRAPH

1. Identify the topic. Ask, "What is the paragraph mostly about?"

2. As you read, take notes about the important details and ideas. Use a **Summary Planner**.

3. Stop and ask, "What does the author want me to know in this part of the selection?" Write a sentence or two to retell the ideas.

Read the text and the Summary Planner.

Look Into the Text

I will never forget the week I spent in Washington, D.C. I was part of the Presidential Classroom. It's a program for high school students. It teaches about the government. The experience changed how I see the world. But what I remember most was not about government. It was the night I saw myself through the eyes of a quiet Muslim girl.

Summary Planner

Title: Behind the Veil

Topic: An unforgettable week in Washington, D.C.

Important Details and Ideas:
- author is at a program for high school students
- he remembers a certain girl more than anything
- girl is Muslim

Sum Up the Ideas: The author meets a Muslim girl in Washington, D.C., who changes his view of the world.

A summary is short—just a sentence or two.

Try It

Make a Summary Planner. As you read "Behind the Veil," use the planner to sum up the important ideas.

Build Background

People around the world wear different clothes. In many parts of the world, people wear clothes that are not common in the United States.

In some Muslim countries, people wear clothes that cover the whole body. Some Sikh men and some Jews wear head coverings. They do this because of their **religion** or their **beliefs**.

"Behind the Veil" is an essay about what the author learned from Nadia, a Muslim girl. Nadia wants to follow her beliefs, even if looking different can be **uncomfortable**.

www.hbedge.net
- Read another essay about a lesson a teen learned.
- View clothing from around the world.

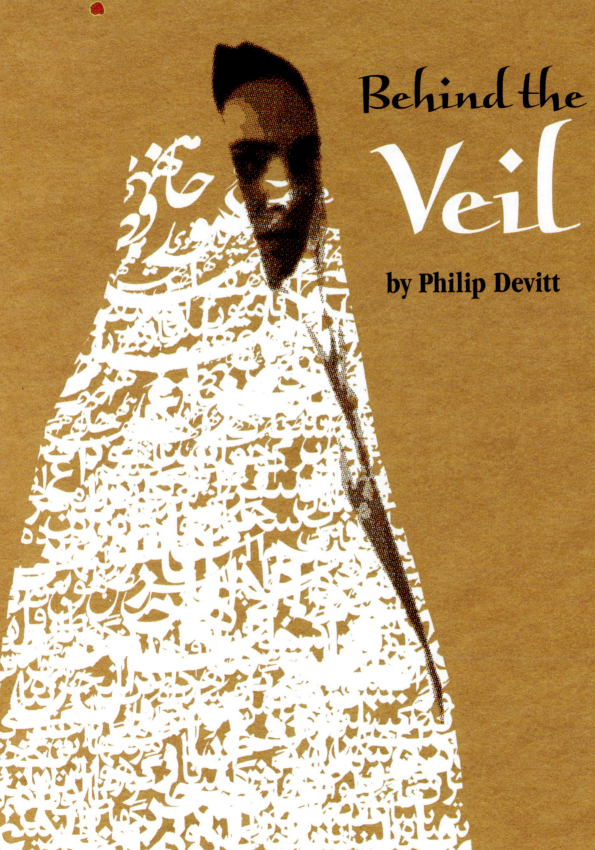

Behind the Veil

by Philip Devitt

I will never **forget** the week I spent in Washington, D.C. I was part of the Presidential Classroom. It's a **program** for high school students. It teaches about **the government**. The **experience** changed how I **see** the world. But what I remember most was not about government. It was the night I saw myself through the eyes of a quiet Muslim girl.

It was our last night. We sat in a small room. We had been there many times. But this time was different. We were there to say goodbye.

Nadia wore black clothes. Her face, arms, and legs were covered. She seemed afraid to join the group. I could not understand why.

We had all tried to make her feel welcome many times throughout the week. Sometimes she seemed **depressed**. We tried to make her laugh. Other times she seemed lonely. We tried to start conversations with her. She rarely lifted her head to look at us. When she did, we saw her sad eyes. They seemed full of **emotion**. It was waiting to **pour out**.

Key Vocabulary
forget *verb*, to not be able to think of something
experience *noun*, something that you did or saw

In Other Words
program group of special classes and meetings
the government how the country is run
see understand
depressed sad
emotion a lot of feeling
pour out come out quickly

When everyone finished speaking, Nadia slowly **rose** from the corner. She walked to the middle of the room. "This has been a **memorable week**," she said. "But it has also been one of my most **uncomfortable**."

"All of you have been wonderful to me," she said. "But I **realize** that some of you are afraid of me and my **beliefs**. I understand. You only know the Islam that you hear about **in the media**. You don't know the **truth** of our **religion**."

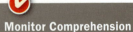

Monitor Comprehension

Explain
Why has this been a difficult week for Nadia?

Key Vocabulary
uncomfortable *adjective*, not easy
belief *noun*, an idea you think is true
truth *noun*, something that is a fact
religion *noun*, a set of strong ideas about god or gods

In Other Words
rose got up
memorable week week that I will always remember
realize understand
in the media in newspapers and on television

What she said was true. We knew about the beliefs of Islamic terrorists. But we knew nothing about the beliefs of **nonviolent Muslims**. I didn't know anything about her religion.

"The truth is that I am just like all of you. I like the same music. I like the same television shows." **A single** tear slid down her cheek. "When you laugh at something, so do I. And when you cry, I do, too."

In Other Words
nonviolent Muslims Muslim people who do not want to hurt others
A single One

Nadia's words were simple. They **meant so much** to me. Her clothing and religion did not **define her**. She was a teenager growing up in America—just like me. ❖

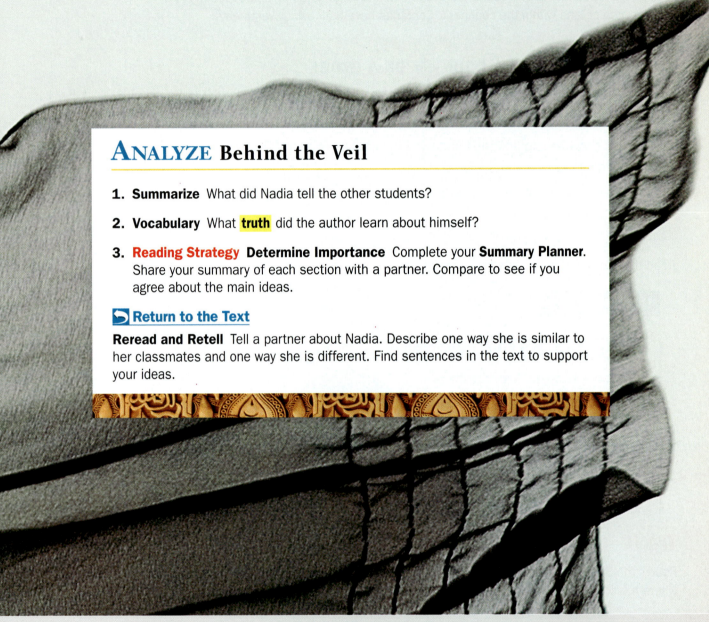

ANALYZE Behind the Veil

1. **Summarize** What did Nadia tell the other students?

2. **Vocabulary** What truth did the author learn about himself?

3. **Reading Strategy** **Determine Importance** Complete your **Summary Planner**. Share your summary of each section with a partner. Compare to see if you agree about the main ideas.

⟩ Return to the Text

Reread and Retell Tell a partner about Nadia. Describe one way she is similar to her classmates and one way she is different. Find sentences in the text to support your ideas.

In Other Words
meant so much were very important
define her tell us everything about who
she was

photo essay by Sara Chiu

Text Feature: Globes

Writers often include maps to show the location of a certain place. The maps in "The Simple Sport" look like globes. A **globe** is a model of the earth. It is shaped like a ball.

Globes show continents and countries. Continents are large areas of land. A country is a smaller area of land within the continent. Countries have their own governments.

HOW TO LOCATE A COUNTRY ON A GLOBE

1. Read the name of the country in the text.

2. Look for the country on the globe.

3. Read the labels to see what continent the country is part of. The names of continents are in capital letters.

4. Think about where the country is located. Use this information to help you understand the text.

Read the text and find the country on the globe.

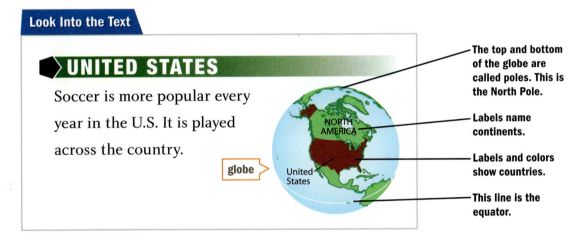

Look Into the Text

UNITED STATES

Soccer is more popular every year in the U.S. It is played across the country.

globe

United States

NORTH AMERICA

The top and bottom of the globe are called poles. This is the North Pole.

Labels name continents.

Labels and colors show countries.

This line is the equator.

Try It

Read "The Simple Sport." Find the country on each globe shown near the text. Think about where the country is located.

The Simple Sport

by Sara Chiu

Connect Across Texts

In "Behind the Veil," the author learns he has many things in common with someone from another culture. In this photo essay, learn how many countries share a love of soccer.

Call it soccer, football, or *fútbol*. It is one **sport** with many names. In the United States, we call it soccer. It's the most **popular** sport in the world.

Soccer is called "the simple sport." You can see why. It's a game anyone can play. Players are young and old. They are male and female. They are rich and poor. Soccer is a sport everyone can enjoy.

Soccer is a very old sport. The Chinese played games like soccer thousands of years ago. It was also played in Rome, Egypt, Europe, and Central America. These games changed over time. One thing has never changed. Soccer is still **exciting**.

Is soccer still popular today? Ask billions of soccer fans. They sit in crowded **stadiums**. They watch from their TVs. They **cheer** for their favorite **teams**. Ask millions of soccer players. They play in schoolyards. They play on fields. They play in stadiums. Soccer is the sport they love.

Let's see how soccer is played around the world.

Key Vocabulary
sport *noun*, game
popular *adjective*, liked by many people

In Other Words
fútbol soccer (in Spanish)
exciting a lot of fun
stadiums large, open places for playing and watching sports
cheer shout with happiness
teams groups of players

ENGLAND

England has one of the oldest national soccer teams. It started in 1872. Soccer is England's most popular sport. It's also **a big business**. England's soccer team uses this flag.

SOUTH KOREA

Many people play soccer in South Korea. It had one of the first **professional teams** in East Asia. South Korea and Japan **hosted** the World Cup in 2002.

In Other Words

a big business an activity that makes money
professional teams groups of people who were paid to play
hosted organized

Cultural Background

The World Cup is a tournament of soccer games to decide the best soccer team in the world. The World Cup takes place every four years, and a different country hosts the games each time.

ZAMBIA

Zambia's national soccer team **formed** in 1929. The team is practicing for the 2010 World Cup in South Africa.

BRAZIL

Soccer is important in the culture of Brazil. Its team has been in every World Cup final. Brazil won the World Cup for the first time in 1958. Brazil has won four more times since then.

In Other Words
formed started

Monitor Comprehension

Explain
How important is soccer in Brazil? How do you know?

▶ UNITED STATES

Soccer is more popular every year in the U.S. It is played across the country. You just need a ball and some friends. Come play "the simple sport." ❖

ANALYZE The Simple Sport

1. **Explain** Why is soccer called "the simple sport"?

2. **Vocabulary** How do you know that soccer is a **popular** **sport**?

3. **Text Feature: Globes** Look at the globes in the essay. Work with a partner. Name a country. Have your partner name the continent where the country is located. Take turns naming countries and continents.

◗ Return to the Text

Reread and Retell Tell about one country where soccer is popular. Share at least one important fact about soccer in that country.

What Makes Us the Same? What Makes Us Different?

Fluency

Listen to a reading. Practice fluency. Use the Reading Handbook, page 536.

Reading

Talk About Literature

EQ 1. Compare How are Nadia and the author of "Behind the Veil" different? How are they similar?

> One way they are different is _____. One way they are similar is _____.

2. Generalize You read about soccer in "A Simple Sport." Think about other **sports**. Describe two things that are true for most sports. Give examples from two sports.

> Many sports _____. For example, in _____, _____. And in _____, _____.

EQ 3. Analyze "Behind the Veil" and "The Simple Sport" show how people are both similar and different. Do your clothes or favorite sport make you similar to or different from other people?

Vocabulary

Review Key Vocabulary

Choose the correct vocabulary word to complete each sentence.

1. My cousin Faisal is Muslim. He says he'll never _____ the time he spent at school in New York. (truth/forget)

2. The students there understood his _____ . (religion/sport)

3. They knew a lot about Muslims. They respected his _____ . (truth/beliefs)

4. Everyone was friendly. Faisal did not feel _____ . (popular/uncomfortable)

5. His time in New York was a pleasant _____ . (experience/religion)

6. Faisal made many friends. He was very _____ . (popular/uncomfortable)

7. He went to baseball games with his friends. Baseball is Faisal's favorite _____ . (experience/sport)

8. The _____ is that Faisal wants to be a baseball player. (experience/truth)

Vocabulary

- beliefs
- experience
- forget
- popular
- religion
- sport
- truth
- uncomfortable

Writing

Write About Literature

EQ Invitation Sports teams and groups like Presidential Classroom bring different people together to reach the same goal. Reread the selections. Write an invitation to join the Presidential Classroom or a sports team.

> Join the _____ .
> Everyone in this group likes _____ .
> You can be _____ or _____ .
> Join now!

Integrate the Language Arts

Use Adjectives That Compare

To compare two things:

- Add **-er** to many **adjectives**.
  England's team is **older** than Zambia's team.

- Use **more** before long adjectives.
  Soccer is **more popular** in Europe than in the United States.

- The word **than** usually comes after the adjective.

To compare three or more things:

- Add **-est** to many adjectives.
  England has one of the **oldest** teams in the world.

- Use **the most** before long adjectives.
  Soccer is **the most popular** sport in the world.

Oral Practice Work with a partner. Say each sentence with the correct choice.

1. Ali is (strong/stronger) than Cara.
2. But Cara is (more athletic/most athletic).
3. Ali is the (taller/tallest) on her team.
4. She is also the (more powerful/most powerful) kicker on the team.
5. But she is the (slower/slowest) runner.

Written Practice Rewrite each sentence to make a comparison. Use the correct form of the adjective, and add other words as needed.

6. Soccer is _____ baseball. (interesting)
7. Soccer players are _____ baseball players. (fast)
8. They also are _____ baseball players. (skillful)
9. The goalie is usually _____ of all. (talented)
10. I think soccer players are _____ athletes in the world. (amazing)

Make Comparisons

Talk About Sports What is your favorite sport? What sport do you not like? Compare the two sports.

- Say how the two sports are alike and different.
- Use adjectives to make comparisons between the two sports.

Both basketball and baseball are great sports. But I think baseball is more relaxing.

Basketball is more exciting than baseball.

Vocabulary Study

Review Prefixes

A prefix is a word part added to the beginning of a base word. It changes the word's meaning.

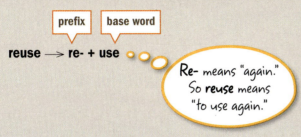

prefix   base word

reuse → re- + use

Re- means "again." So **reuse** means "to use again."

Study the meanings of the prefixes. Read the examples.

PREFIX	MEANING	EXAMPLE
un-	not	uncertain
re-	again	retell

When you come to a word you don't know, look for a prefix. Put the meaning of the prefix together with the meaning of the base word to figure out the meaning of the word.

Use a chart to find the meaning of each underlined word.

1. Nadia seemed so <u>unhappy</u>.
2. She was <u>unable</u> to speak.
3. Would she leave and not <u>return</u>?
4. It was <u>unclear</u> why she was so quiet.
5. She will tell us when she <u>regains</u> her happy mood.

Word	Parts	Meaning
unhappy	_____ + _____ =	

Comprehension

Classify and Compare

To classify means to put things that are alike into groups, or categories.

"The Simple Sport" gives facts about soccer in different countries. The **Category Diagram** shows one way to classify those facts.

Review "The Simple Sport." Look for ways to classify the facts. Then make your own Category Diagram. Write a comparison statement about two or more facts.

Category Diagram

Soccer — topic

categories ▷ Year National Team Began   World Cup Host

England: 1872   Zambia: 1929 — facts

Use your diagram. Compare facts within one category. Then write a comparison statement.

[country] started a soccer team in [date].
But [country] formed a team later, in [date].

Write a Comparison-Contrast Paragraph

▶ **Prompt** Write a paragraph that compares and contrasts two of your friends. When you **compare**, you say how people or things are alike. When you **contrast**, you say how people or things are different.

1 Plan Read the topic sentence. Write a list of words to describe two friends. Use a **Venn Diagram** to note how they are alike and different.

Topic Sentence: *My friends Ben and Juan are similar and different in many ways.*

Venn Diagram

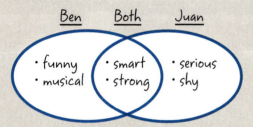

Ben   Both   Juan

- funny
- musical
- smart
- strong
- serious
- shy

Signal Words

COMPARE	CONTRAST
both	but
also	however
alike	although
too	in contrast
in the same way	on the other hand

2 Write Use your notes to write a paragraph. Include signal words to show when two things are alike and when they are different. Be sure to use adjectives correctly when you compare and contrast.

    My friends [name] and [name] are similar and different in many ways. They are both [descriptive word] and [descriptive word] . However, [name of one friend] is [adjective that compares] than [name of other friend] . On the other hand, [name of second friend] is [adjective that compares] than [name of first friend] . My friends are also different because they [tell about another difference] . These things remind me that people are alike and different in many ways.

REMEMBER

- Add **-er** to many adjectives to compare two things.
- Add **-est** to compare three or more things.
- Use **more** or **the most** before long adjectives.
- Use special forms for **good**, **bad**, and **many**.

3 Share Ask your friends to read your paragraph. Talk about your ideas.

1 TRY OUT LANGUAGE
2 LEARN GRAMMAR
3 APPLY ON YOUR OWN

Make Comparisons

Look at the pictures and listen to the description.

Description

TWO MUSICIANS

Dante and Joon both play instruments. Dante plays the guitar. Joon plays the violin. Dante plays in a rock band called "Brink Avenue." Joon plays in the Plainfield High School Orchestra.

Dante and Joon play different styles of music, but they both practice hard. They both practice their instruments for at least two hours a day.

Dante's band practices on Tuesdays and Thursdays. Joon's orchestra also practices on Tuesdays and Thursdays.

Both boys have big performances next week. Dante and his band are playing at the homecoming dance. Joon and the orchestra are performing their fall concert. They are both excited about playing for an audience.

Use Possessive Nouns

Use a **possessive noun** to show that someone owns, or possesses, something. To form a possessive with singular nouns, add **'s** to the end of the noun.

Each **person's** dream is different.

Kendall's dream is to be a famous ballet dancer.

Charles's goal is to be a great trumpet player.

Will Kendall's dream come true?

Say It

1–5. Work with a partner. Choose a word from each row. Use the words in a sentence to show possession.

Example: **Anthony's song** is beautiful.

| Anthony | audience | Christine | orchestra | man |
| cheers | hand | guitar | performance | song |

Write It

Write each sentence with the correct possessive noun.

6. Myra has beautiful ballet shoes.

_____Myra's_____ ballet shoes are beautiful.

7. Those tap shoes belong to Sam.

Those are _____ tap shoes.

8. The boy has a unique goal.

The _____ goal is unique.

9. Do not drink that water. It is for the singer.

Do not drink the _____ water.

10. Dania is having a recital. I am invited.

I am invited to _____ recital.

You Be the Judge

Find two different video performances. You might watch a TV reality show or look on a video-sharing Web site. Compare the two performances. How are they alike? How are they different?

Follow these steps to make clear comparisons:

> ## HOW TO MAKE COMPARISONS
>
> 1. Say how two people or things are different. Use words such as *but* or *different*. Use comparison words such as *louder* or *more musical*.
>
> 2. Say how two people or things are alike. Use words such as *both*, *and*, and *too*.

Dante's performance was louder than Joon's performance. Both performances were enjoyable.

Use **possessive nouns** when you make comparisons.

To get ready, fill out a chart like this.

Comparison Chart

Dante's Performance	Both Performances	Joon's Performance
loud	very good	soft
lots of kids in the audience	enjoyable	lots of grownups in the audience

Then take turns with your partner. Tell each other about your comparisons. Do you agree with each other?

Sarah's performance was the most beautiful of all.

EQ ## What Makes Us the Same? What Makes Us Different?
Find out how our hopes and dreams make us different.

Learn Key Vocabulary

Pronounce each word and learn its meaning.

Key Words

become (bi-**kum**) *verb*
▶ pages 217, 227

To **become** means to begin to be something. She is studying to **become** a doctor.

dream (drēm) *noun*
▶ pages 212, 216, 217, 221, 223, 227

A **dream** is something you hope for. Her **dream** is to be an engineer.

easy (**ē**-zē) *adjective*
▶ pages 211, 218

When something is **easy**, it is not difficult. It is **easy** for some children to ride a tricycle. *Synonym:* simple

practice (**prak**-tus) *verb*
▶ page 220

When you **practice** an activity, you do it regularly so you can improve. She **practices** tennis twice a week.

respect (ri-**spekt**) *noun*
▶ pages 220, 221

When you show **respect**, you show that you value someone or something. A bow is a sign of **respect**.

succeed (suk-**sēd**) *verb*
▶ pages 212, 223, 224, 225, 226

To **succeed** is to reach a goal. When you **succeed** at college, you graduate.

try (trī) *verb*
▶ pages 218, 223, 224, 225

To **try** means to work hard. The runners all **try** to finish the race.

victory (**vik**-tu-rē) *noun*
▶ pages 224, 226

When you have a **victory**, you win. The young man enjoys his **victory**.

Practice the Words Work with a partner. Write two sentences. Use at least two Key Vocabulary words in each sentence.

> It was not easy, but
> I finally reached my dream.

short fiction by Erika Tamar

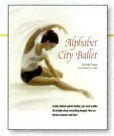

Determine Importance

Writers give you clues about which details they think are important. But only you can decide which details are important to you personally.

HOW TO DETERMINE WHAT'S IMPORTANT TO YOU

1. Look for details. Think about what the characters say. Pay attention to details that remind you of your own life. Ask, Is my life similar to this? Is it different?

2. Note these details. Make a **T Chart**. In the first column, write important words and phrases from the text.

3. In the second column, write about why the text is meaningful to you.

4. Reread your chart. Which details are the most important to you?

In this story, a brother and sister compare soccer and ballet. Read the text and the **T Chart** to see how one reader determines what is personally important.

Look Into the Text

> "Dancers have to make it *look* easy. They're tougher athletes than anybody."
>
> Luis raised his eyebrows.
>
> "Okay," Marisol said, "see if you can do this."

T Chart

What I Read	Why It Is Important To Me
"Dancers have to make it look easy."	My friends say I make playing guitar look easy, but I have to practice every day! I am glad to know dancers have this same problem.

Try It

Make a T Chart to note details. As you read "Alphabet City Ballet," decide which details are important to you.

Build Background

Ballet is a type of dance. People who **dream** of a career in ballet must work hard to **succeed** . Most professional ballet dancers start studying ballet when they are young children. Ballet is tougher than it looks! A good ballet dancer has to know about music, and be strong, healthy, and flexible. "Alphabet City Ballet" is the story of Marisol, a young woman who takes ballet very seriously.

These dancers practice for a ballet performance.

www.hbedge.net
- Learn about a performing arts school.
- View a ballet performance.

Alphabet City Ballet

by Erika Tamar
Illustrated by Chris Vallo

As kids, Marisol and her brother, Luis, were so alike.
But in high school, everything changed. How can
Marisol reconnect with him?

The **barrettes** didn't work. For the next three **ballet practices**, Marisol used a ribbon instead. The ribbon held her hair back. But it slipped during class. **It bothered her**.

One evening, she thought of the perfect thing: a **sweatband**! Her brother Luis had a blue one. He wore it for soccer. It would hold everything back, and look **professional**, too.

In Other Words
barrettes hair clips
ballet practices dance lessons
It bothered her. She did not like it.
sweatband piece of clothing for your head
professional neat

Geography Background
Alphabet City is a part of Manhattan, New York. It is called "Alphabet City" because some of the streets are named Avenues A, B, C, and D.

She heard a key in the lock. Then Luis was in the kitchen in front of her.

She bit her lip. "I want to wear your sweatband Wednesday. I wanted to try it on. For ballet."

"You don't **raise no sweat** in 'ballet.'" He said "ballet" so that it sounded like "sweat."

In Other Words
raise no sweat work that hard (slang)

Monitor Comprehension

Explain
What happens when Marisol asks for the sweatband?

Set a Purpose
**Find out why ballet
is so important to Marisol.**

Marisol was suddenly angry. "You don't know anything about it! It's *all* sweat!"

"**Whoa**. What're you mad for?" Luis asked.

"You think you're so smart! It's tougher than soccer!" she yelled.

"Okay. All right."

"I'm doing something good." Her voice **broke**. She was **on the edge of tears**.

"I didn't know **you took it that seriously**," he said.

"I do." She turned from him. "It's my  dream."

"Okay," he said.

Key Vocabulary
dream *noun*, something you hope for

In Other Words
Whoa Wait (slang)
broke stopped suddenly
on the edge of tears going to cry
you took it that seriously it was so important
   to you

"You need to have one too, Luis."

"I **got a million** of them," he said.

"What?"

"The bike, new shoes, a **dynamite** car, a big apartment with my own room, airplane tickets to go anyplace I—"

"A dream isn't about things," Marisol said. "A dream is who you want to be. Who you want to **become**."

Key Vocabulary
become *verb*, to begin to be something

In Other Words
got a million have many (slang)
dynamite really fancy (slang)

Explain
How does Marisol feel about ballet?

Set a Purpose
**Find out what happens
when Luis tries to do ballet.**

Luis looked at Marisol. The room was quiet.

"It's not tougher than soccer, though," he finally said.

"Dancers have to make it *look* **easy**. They're **tougher athletes** than anybody."

Luis **raised his eyebrows**.

"Okay," Marisol said, "see if you can do this."

She lay flat on her stomach. Then she raised one leg as high as she could behind her. And it *was* high. She was getting a lot better.

Luis lay down next to her.

"Try not to move your body," she told him. She watched as he got his leg up pretty well. "See if you can get it as high as *this*," Marisol said, "and *hold* it."

He tried **for height**. "**Jeez**," he **breathed**. "That **kills** my back."

"Now try doing that ten times."

"No, thanks." He laughed and sat up. Marisol sat up, too. They were on the floor together. Just like when they were kids, she thought.

Key Vocabulary
easy *adjective*, not hard, not difficult

In Other Words
tougher athletes better and stronger
raised his eyebrows did not believe her
for height to make his leg go higher
Jeez Wow (slang)
breathed said quietly
kills hurts

Monitor Comprehension

Describe
What happens when
Luis tries to do ballet?

"You're good," he said.

"Because I **practice** it every day," she said. "That's **preparation for the arabesque**."

He **studied** her face and smiled. "You're **gonna be terrific**, Marisol."

Finally, *finally*, he was showing **respect**. It was good to feel **tight** with him again. She wished it didn't have to make her feel so sad. ❖

Key Vocabulary
practice *verb*, to do regularly
respect *noun*, showing that you value someone or something

In Other Words
preparation for the arabesque the first part of a ballet position
studied looked closely at
gonna be terrific going to do a great job
tight connected (slang)

ANALYZE Alphabet City Ballet

1. **Describe** What does Marisol do to earn Luis's <mark>respect</mark>?

2. **Vocabulary** What is Marisol's <mark>dream</mark>?

3. **Reading Strategy** **Determine Importance** Share your **T Chart** with a partner. Talk about what is important to you.

➥ Return to the Text

Reread and Retell Does Luis have a dream? What does Marisol say about his dreams? Use details from the text to support your answer.

About the Writer

Erika Tamar (1934–) has always loved reading, so it seemed natural for her to become a writer. "My greatest interest, still and always, is writing," she said. Tamar is the author of twenty-two books for children and teenagers. She lives in New York City and has three grown children.

song lyrics by Jimmy Cliff

Elements of Poetry: Rhythm, Rhyme, and Repetition

Song lyrics, or the words of the song, are like poetry. Poets and song writers use words in different ways to make the language musical. **Rhythm**, **rhyme**, and **repetition** are three ways to make language musical.

- Rhythm is a pattern of beats.

- Rhyme is the repetition of sounds at the ends of words. For example, the words *fly* and *high* rhyme with *try*. Some poets and most song writers use rhyme to connect words or ideas.

- Poets and song writers often repeat important words, phrases, or sentences. Repetition creates patterns. The patterns of a poem or song often help us understand what the writer thinks is important.

HOW TO READ SONG LYRICS

1. Read the text aloud.

2. Notice patterns. Look for words that rhyme. Look for lines that repeat.

3. Listen for a beat, or rhythm.

4. Ask, "How does the rhythm, rhyme, or repetition add to the song? How do the lyrics make me feel?" Write your ideas on self-stick notes.

Read the text and the self-stick notes.

Look Into the Text

You can get it if you really want
You can get it if you really want
You can get it if you really want
But you must try, try and try, try and try
You'll succeed at last

The first line repeats. "Try and try" repeats. These words make me feel good.

Persecution you must bear
Win or lose you got to get your share
Got your mind set on a dream
You can get it though hard it may seem now

"Bear" rhymes with "share." "Dream" rhymes with "seem."

Try It

Look for rhythm, rhyme, and repetition in "You Can Get It If You Really Want." Write your ideas on self-stick notes as you read.

Connect Across Texts

In "Alphabet City Ballet," Marisol works hard to make her <mark>dream</mark> *come true. What do these song lyrics say about dreams?*

YOU CAN GET IT IF YOU REALLY WANT

by Jimmy Cliff

Illustrations by CJ Zea

You can get it if you really want

You can get it if you really want

You can get it if you really want

But you must try, try and try, try and try

5   *You'll succeed at last*

Persecution you must bear

Win or lose you got to get your share

Got your mind set on a dream

You can get it though hard it may seem now

Key Vocabulary
<mark>try</mark> *verb*, to work hard
<mark>dream</mark> *noun*, something you hope for
<mark>succeed</mark> *verb*, to reach a goal

In Other Words
Persecution you must bear You must deal with people who treat you badly
your share the part that you should have
set on always thinking about

10 *You can get it if you really want*

You can get it if you really want

You can get it if you really want

But you must try, try and try, try and try

You'll succeed at last

15 Rome was not built in a day

Opposition will come your way

But the harder the battle you see

It's the sweeter the victory

Key Vocabulary

<mark>**victory**</mark> *noun*, a win

In Other Words

Rome was not built in a day It may not
    happen quickly
Opposition Problems
battle work
sweeter better

You can get it if you really want

20   *You can get it if you really want*

You can get it if you really want

But you must try, try and try, try and try

You'll succeed at last

You can get it if you really want

25   *You can get it if you really want*

You can get it if you really want

But you must try, try and try, try and try

You'll succeed at last ❖

Monitor Comprehension

Explain
What does the songwriter say about Rome? Why?

ANALYZE You Can Get It If You Really Want

1. **Summarize** What is this song about? How do you know?

2. **Vocabulary** What does the songwriter think you need to do to <mark>succeed</mark>?

3. **Elements of Poetry** Describe some patterns and rhymes in the song.

Return to the Text

Reread and Retell Reread the song lyrics. What does the songwriter say about <mark>victories</mark>?

EQ What Makes Us the Same? What Makes Us Different?

Talk About Literature

EQ 1. Compare How are Marisol and her brother similar? How are they different?

One way that Marisol and Luis are similar is _____. One way they are different is _____.

2. Make Judgments Jimmy Cliff's song says that you can get what you want, if you really want it. Do you think this is always true? Give an example.

I (agree/disagree) with the song lyrics because _____. One example of this is _____.

3. Interpret Do you think Marisol would agree or disagree with the song lyrics? Why?

Marisol would _____ with the song lyrics because she _____.

Listen to a reading. Practice fluency. Use the Reading Handbook, page 536.

Review Key Vocabulary

Choose the correct vocabulary word to complete each sentence.

1. Marisol wants to be a ballet dancer. It is her _____. (victory/dream)
2. Luis thinks that ballet positions are _____ because they look simple. (easy/tough)
3. Marisol asks Luis to _____ one of the ballet positions. (become/try)
4. Marisol _____ ballet every day. (become/practices)
5. She tells her teacher that she wants to _____ a ballet dancer. (become/try)
6. Her teacher thinks that Marisol will _____. (practices/succeed)
7. Marisol also wants her brother to show her _____. (respect/succeed)
8. That will be a sweet _____, she says. (victory/respect)

Vocabulary

- become
- dream
- easy
- practices
- respect
- succeed
- try
- victory

Write About Literature

EQ Journal Entry Some people want to **become** famous. Others want to become rich. What is your **dream**? How will you get it? Use both texts to support your answer.

My dream is _____. The text tells me to _____ to reach my dreams. To reach my dream, I will _____.

INTEGRATE THE LANGUAGE ARTS

Use Possessive Adjectives

A **possessive adjective** tells who someone or something belongs to.

I → **my**	I love ballet. Ballet is **my** favorite activity.
you → **your**	What do **you** like? Is ballet **your** favorite activity, too?
he → **his**	He loves soccer. **His** soccer shoes are new.
she → **her**	**Mari** loves to play tennis. **She** just won **her** first tournament.
it → **its**	My ballet slipper is broken. **Its** strap fell off.
we → **our**	We can get it fixed. **Our** uncle repairs shoes.
you → **your**	You girls have brown eyes. **Your** eyes are all brown.
they → **their**	They can't go. They have to go to **their** piano lessons.

Match the possessive adjective to the noun or pronoun it goes with.

Janie got **her** slipper fixed.

We can go to **our** class now.

Oral Practice Work with a partner. Say each sentence with the correct possessive adjective.

1. Marisol waits for (her/his) brother Luis.
2. She asks Luis if she can use (your/his) sweatband.
3. She wants the sweatband because she likes (her/its) professional appearance.
4. Marisol and Luis talk about (their/our) dreams.
5. What about you? What's (my/ your) dream?

Written Practice (6–10) Read the story starter. Tell what happens next to Marisol and Luis. Use five possessive adjectives in your story.

Marisol stood backstage. It was her first ballet performance, and she was nervous. She peeked out into the audience to look for her brother.

Make Comparisons

Compare Characters Think about the characters in "Alphabet City Ballet." How are Marisol and Luis alike? How are they different? Talk with a partner.

- Use words such as *both*, *and*, and *too* to say how Marisol and Luis are alike.
- Use words such as *but* and *different* and comparative adjectives that compare to say how they are different.

> Both Marisol and Luis have dreams.

> Marisol's dream is more serious than Luis's dreams.

Review Prefixes, Suffixes, and Compound Words

When you read a long word, see if you can break it into parts.

> **untrue** ⟶ **un-** + **true**
>
> **predictable** ⟶ **predict** + **-able**
>
> **sweatshirt** ⟶ **sweat** + **shirt**

Study these prefixes and suffixes:

PREFIX	MEANING	EXAMPLE
un-	not	unhappy
re-	again	review

SUFFIX	MEANING	EXAMPLE
-able	can be done	breakable
-er	one who	farmer
-ly	in that way	seriously

Use what you know about word parts to figure out the meaning of each underlined word. Make a chart.

1. "One evening, she thought of the perfect thing: a <u>sweatband</u>."
2. "Marisol was <u>suddenly</u> angry."
3. "You don't know <u>anything</u> about it."
4. "<u>Dancers</u> have to make it look easy."
5. "Luis raised his <u>eyebrows</u>."
6. Marisol wants to <u>reconnect</u> with Luis.

Word	Parts	Meaning
sweatband	_____ + _____ =	

Setting

The setting of a story is when and where it takes place. Every story has a setting. You can use clues in the story to figure out the setting.

Setting Chart

Clue	Time	Place
page 214: "One evening, she thought . . ."	after school	
page 215: "Luis was in the kitchen in front of her."		at home

The setting for "Alphabet City Ballet" is after school at the home of Marisol and Luis.

Look back at some stories you have read, such as "Growing Together" or "How Ananse Gave Wisdom to the World." Find clues to help you identify the setting. Make a **Setting Chart** for one of those stories.

Look for clues that show a year, a season, or a time of day. Look for clues that show a location. Record information in your chart.

"Green" Careers

Is an environmental job right for you? Take this career quiz to find out.

1

2

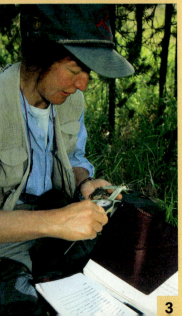

3

Career Quiz

1. Math and science classes interest me.
  ⓐ True
  ⓑ False

2. I want to make the land, water, and air safe.
  ⓐ True
  ⓑ False

3. It is important to make the world a healthy place. Environmental workers reduce pollution. That kind of work is interesting.
  ⓐ True
  ⓑ False

How many times did you answer *True*?

3 times: Wow!
An environmental job seems perfect for you!

1–2 times: Maybe
An environmental job may be right for you.

0 times: No thanks
An environmental job may not be right for you. Do you know someone who would like this kind of work?

Environmental Jobs

Here are some environmental jobs. People do different things in these jobs and need different levels of education and training.

Job	Responsibilities	Education/Training Needed
Environmental Technician **1**	• Checks and fixes the machines that environmental engineers and scientists use	• High school diploma, with a lot of math and science classes • Associate's degree
Environmental Engineer **2**	• Finds ways to make the air, water, and land safe	• Bachelor's degree
Environmental Scientist **3**	• Does research to learn about the air, water, and land	• Bachelor's degree • Master's degree (preferred) • Doctorate, if you want to do research

An Environmental Engineer

Susan Murcott shows a biosand filter.

My name is Susan Murcott. I am an environmental engineer. I teach at a university. My students and I help people get clean water to drink.

The water is dirty in some parts of Nepal and Ghana. It makes people sick. My students and I found a way to make the water clean. We made a special water filter. It does not cost a lot to make. It is easy to use. It works for a long time.

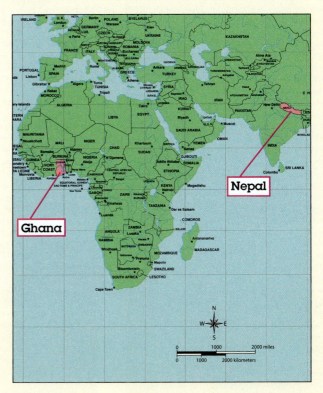

The water filter looks like a plastic box. You pour the dirty water in one end. Clean water comes out the other end. It is called a biosand filter.

We gave away hundreds of water filters. We also teach villagers how to make the water filters. I hope that everyone will have clean water one day.

Research Environmental Jobs

Learn more about an environmental job in the United States.

1. Choose a job from the chart on page 230.
2. Go online to **www.hbedge.net**. Read about the job you chose.
3. Complete the chart.

Job	How many workers have this job?	How much money does a worker earn?	Is this a good job for the future?
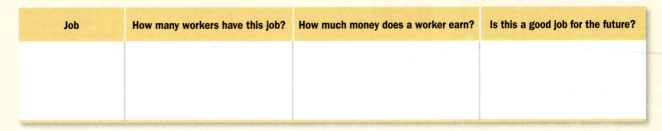			

GLOBAL VILLAGE

EQ **ESSENTIAL QUESTION:**
What Makes Us the Same? What Makes Us Different?

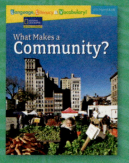

Reflect on the Essential Question

With a group, discuss the Essential Question: What makes us the same? What makes us different?

Think about what you read in the selections and your choice of Edge Library books.

- How are people in <mark>countries</mark> around the world the same?
  Do people share the same experiences? Which experiences are the same? Which experiences are different?

- How are the people of the <mark>world</mark> different?
  Does everyone live in the same environment?

- What can you learn about people from their <mark>cultures</mark>?
  Do people have the same hopes and dreams?

30 QUESTIONS

START

You worked hard, and you finished your test on time.
Go forward 1 space.

You talked to a friend when you were supposed to be listening.
Go back 1 space.

GRAMMAR MASTER ZONE

You and your friend are alike. You both use great grammar.
Go forward 1 space.

You know grammar as well as some of the adults you know.
Go forward 2 spaces.

You were late for class, but you did your homework.
Stay where you are.

While you were studying for the test, you got food on your textbook.
Miss 1 turn.

You forgot which verbs you need to know for the test.
Go back 1 space.

You looked up a new word in the dictionary.
Take an extra turn.

You love learning new vocabulary!
Take an extra turn.

Your teacher says that your grammar is better today than it was yesterday.
Take an extra turn.

Unit Review Game

You will need:

- 2, 3, or 4 players
- 1 **30 Questions** board
- question cards
- 1 coin
- a marker for each player

Objective: Be the first player to get to the Grammar Master Zone.

1. Download a **30 Questions** board and question cards from **www.hbedge.net**. Print out and cut apart the cards. Mix them up.

2. **Player A** flips the coin.

   - For "heads" , go forward 2 spaces.

   - For "tails" , go forward 1 space.

3. If player A lands on a *lucky* or *unlucky* space, he or she follows the directions. If player A lands on an empty space, he or she chooses a card and answers it.

   - If the answer is correct, player A flips again.

   - If the answer is incorrect, player B takes a turn.

4. The other players take turns.

5. The first player to get to the **Grammar Master Zone** is the winner.

People in every part of the world play sports and games. Sometimes these activities make us the same. At other times they show how we are different. In this project, you will describe a sport or game.

Write a Description

1 Connect Writing to Your Life

Think of a sport or game that you like. What do you know about it? How can you describe it to a friend?

2 Understand the Form

When you write a description, you write about something you know. You give information to help others understand what it is like.

Cricket
by Anau Palu

Cricket is one of the most popular sports in India, England, and some countries in the Caribbean Sea. It is also one of Pakistan's most popular sports. People play on a large, green field. A bowler pitches a small, hard ball. A cricket ball is a little heavier than a baseball. A batsman hits the ball with a wooden bat. Cricket matches can last for many days. Many people love to watch and play cricket. Like many popular sports, cricket connects teams, fans, and countries.

The title names what is being described.

Descriptive words help paint a picture in the reader's mind.

Comparisons help readers connect ideas and details to what they know.

Write Together

✔ Plan and Write

Work with a group. Think about a sport or game you know. Then follow the steps to write a description.

1 Collect Ideas

Decide which sport to write about. Brainstorm things you know about the sport. Make a list. As a group, decide on the most important ideas to include in your description. Make a checkmark next to each important idea.

"Baseball is popular in many countries."

"Yes, it is. Another name for baseball is 'America's pastime.'"

Baseball
- ✔ popular in many countries
- ✔ uses a bat and a hard ball
- players wear uniforms
- ✔ two teams play
- ✔ called "America's pastime"
- field is called a "diamond"
- ✔ games can be long (but shorter than cricket)
- started in the U.S. in 1845

2 Write the Description

Describe the sport. Use descriptive adjectives and action verbs to say more about it. Use comparisons to help readers connect your sport to one they know. Work with your group.

Baseball

Baseball is sometimes called "America's pastime." But it is popular in many countries. The game is played by two teams. One team bats first. The players take turns to hit a small, hard ball. The other team stands in the grassy field. They try to stop the other team. Then the teams switch places. Most baseball games are long. But they are usually shorter than cricket games. Baseball has something for everyone. That is why people around the world love the game.

Write on Your Own

▶ **Prompt** Now you can write your own description. Choose a sport you like. Describe it. Be sure to write

- the most important information about the sport
- details that help your reader understand what the sport is like.

✔ Prewrite

Plan the description you will write. Follow these steps.

1 Brainstorm Ideas

List what you know about the sport.

> **Soccer**
> players kick the ball
> some people call it "football"
> countries have national teams
> some balls are red and white
> players are great athletes
> the goalie tries to stop the ball

2 Choose the Most Important Details

Review your ideas. Decide which ideas are most important.

> **Soccer**
> ✔ players kick the ball
> ✔ some people call it "football"
>   countries have national teams
>   some balls are red and white
> ✔ players are great athletes
>   the goalie tries to stop the ball

Write

Use your ideas to write a description of the sport.

1 Write the Description

> ### Soccer
> Soccer is a sport. It is the most popular sport in the world. In some countries, it is called "football." But American fans call it "soccer." Soccer is a fun, simple game to play. You just need a team, a field, and a ball. To play soccer, you kick a ball. You try to kick it into the other team's goal. If you do, you score a point. It sounds easy. But soccer players must be strong, powerful athletes. They are stronger than baseball players. They are more powerful than football players. Soccer is simple and challenging, too. That is why it is played in so many different countries.

2 Choose Adjectives to Add

Use descriptive adjectives to say more. They can help your reader picture what you want to say.

> challenging, exciting
> Soccer is a sport.
>
> colorful
> Soccer players wear uniforms.

Adjectives
challenging
colorful
difficult
exciting
fast

Reflect on Your Draft

▶ Does your description include all the most important ideas about it? Does it use comparisons to help readers connect your sport to one they know?

✔ Check Your Work

Read your description to a partner. Fix mistakes and look for ways to make your writing better.

1 Check Apostrophes in Possessive Nouns

You can use a possessive noun to tell who or what owns something. Include an apostrophe when you write a possessive noun.

> Emre's favorite sport is football.
> Sean's soccer team is the best.

2 Check for Commas

A good description includes describing words. Add a comma between two **adjectives** that come before a noun.

> The **fast**, **talented** player scores a goal.

Do not add a comma if one of the **adjectives** is a number.

> The **two** **talented** teams play on Saturday.

3 Mark Your Changes

Now edit your own paper. Use these marks to show your changes.

∧	✗	⌐	◯	≡	╱	¶
Add.	Take out.	Replace with this.	Check spelling.	Capitalize.	Make lowercase.	Make new paragraph.

Publish, Share, and Reflect

Publish and Share

Now you are ready to share your description with the class. Use it in a presentation about your sport.

HOW TO GIVE A PRESENTATION

1. **Plan Your Presentation** Think of ways to help your class understand the sport. You can
   - find photos or videos of the sport
   - bring examples of sports equipment
   - make a poster to show the rules of the game
   - show how parts of the game are played.

2. **Present Your Sport** Read your description slowly and clearly. Point out the things you brought. Use them to explain your ideas.

3. **Discuss Sports** Ask your listeners if they have questions about the sport. Give answers that show what you know.

Listen to your classmates. Then talk together about the sports.

- Which sports are similar? How are they similar?
- How are some sports different?
- What do the sports show you about people in different cultures?

Reflect on Your Work

▶ Think about your writing.

- What did you learn about writing that you didn't know before?

- What did you like best about writing a description?

☑ **Save a copy of your work in your portfolio.**

SURVIVAL

EQ **ESSENTIAL QUESTION:**

What Does It Take to Survive?

A good friend protects you from
the storm.

—Chinese Proverb

Don't depend on other people;
do it yourself.

—Yiddish Proverb

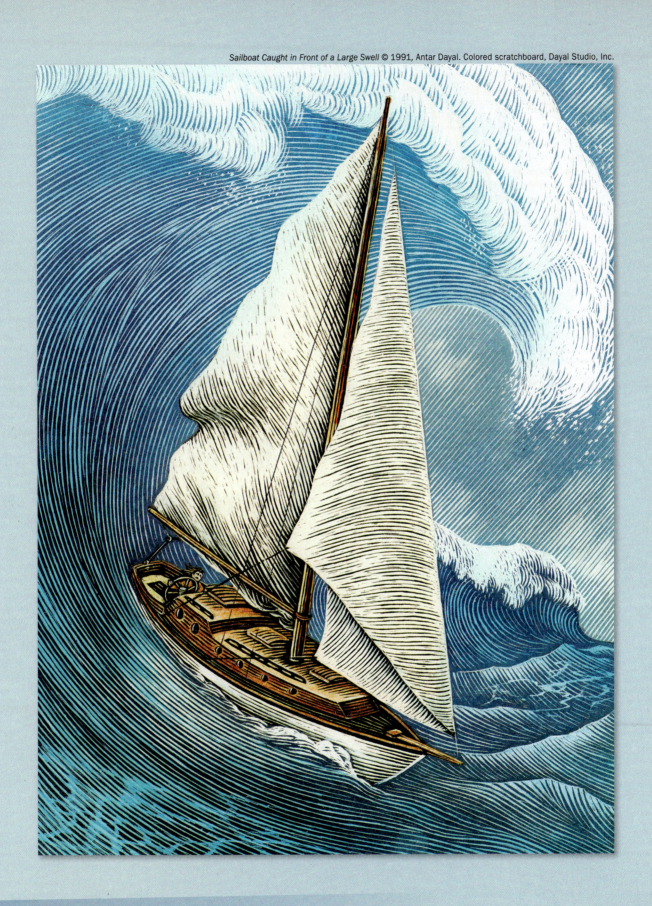

Sailboat Caught in Front of a Large Swell © 1991, Antar Dayal. Colored scratchboard, Dayal Studio, Inc.

EQ **ESSENTIAL QUESTION:**
What Does It Take to Survive?

Study the Poster

Think about what it takes to survive, or live through hard times.

Survival Facts
A PERSON CAN LIVE FOR

- **THREE MINUTES WITHOUT AIR**

- **THREE DAYS WITHOUT WATER**

- **THREE WEEKS WITHOUT FOOD**

EQ **ESSENTIAL QUESTION**

In this unit, you will explore the **Essential Question** in class. Think about the question outside of school, too.

1 Study the Concept

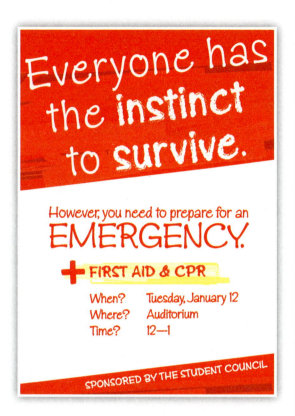

Everyone has the instinct to survive.

However, you need to prepare for an **EMERGENCY.**

+ FIRST AID & CPR

When?   Tuesday, January 12
Where?   Auditorium
Time?   12—1

SPONSORED BY THE STUDENT COUNCIL

1. What do people need to **survive**? List things you need to live. Then list things you need to be happy. Talk about how your lists are different.

2. People do many things to help others in an **emergency**. What are some ways you help others?

3. Imagine you are in an emergency. What does your survival **instinct** tell you to do?

2 Choose More to Read

Choose something to read during this unit.

Hercules
by Paul Storrie

Hercules is known for his strength. But he has a powerful enemy—the goddess Hera. She will do anything to defeat him. Hercules must perform twelve tasks to prove his strength. What helps Hercules survive?

▶ GRAPHIC NOVEL

Wicked Weather
by Beth Geiger

The winds of some tornadoes are strong enough to move houses! Learn about these dangerous storms, and how to survive them.

▶ NONFICTION

www.hbedge.net
• Read an emergency checklist.
• Learn how you can help people in need.

Use a Dictionary

When you read, you may see a word that you do not know. Use the dictionary to learn more about the word. Look at these parts of a dictionary page.

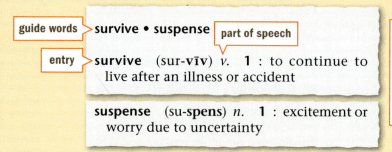

Dictionary

guide words ➤ **survive • suspense** | part of speech

entry ➤ **survive** (sur-vīv) *v.* **1** : to continue to live after an illness or accident

suspense (su-spens) *n.* **1** : excitement or worry due to uncertainty

The part of speech is usually shortened.
v. = verb
n. = noun
adj. = adjective
adv. = adverb

Follow these steps:

- Use alphabetical order to find the right page in the dictionary.
- Look at the **guide words**. They show the first and last entries on a page.
- Find the **entry** for the word on the page. Look at the spelling of the word.
- Read the **pronunciation.** It shows how to say the word.
- Read the **definition.** It tells what the word means.
- Look at the **part of speech.** It tells you how to use a word.

Practice Using a Dictionary

Read the text at right. Answer the questions for the word *survive*. Use the dictionary page above.

1. Is *survive* the first or the last entry on the page?

2. Touch the pronunciation for the word. Say it aloud.

3. What is the definition of the word?

4. What is the part of speech of the word?

5. Now say the meaning of the sentence in the text.

Police found Sam Malden last Friday. He was lost in the wilderness for three days. Police were not sure he would survive. "I'm happy to say that the suspense is finally over," the police chief said.

Put the Strategy to Use

6–10. Work with a partner. Answer the questions for the word *suspense*. Use the dictionary page above.

1 TRY OUT LANGUAGE
2 LEARN GRAMMAR
3 APPLY ON YOUR OWN

Describe an Experience

Look at the storyboard. Read the captions. What happened?

Storyboard

Run for Your Life!

A girl was on her way home from school.

She walked past a house with a large dog in the front yard.

The girl was scared of the dog. She started to run for her life. The dog started to run, too.

Suddenly, she jumped to the side, into a neighbor's yard. The dog continued to run—after a cat!

1 **TRY OUT LANGUAGE**
2 **LEARN GRAMMAR**
3 **APPLY ON YOUR OWN**

Use Past Tense Verbs

The tense, or time, of a **verb** shows when an action happens.

PAST	PRESENT	FUTURE
●	●	○
(before now)	(now)	(after now)

- A verb in the **present tense** says what happens now or often.
  The girl **walks** home from school every day.

- A verb in the **past tense** says what happened before now.
  Yesterday, she **walked** home from school.

Add **-ed** to most verbs when say what happened in the past.

walk + **-ed** = walk**ed**   jump + **-ed** = jump**ed**

She **jumped** to the side. A dog **started** to chase her.

Say It

Work with a partner. Say the sentence. Then your partner says the sentence in the past tense.

1. My sister walks home from school.
2. One day, a strange event happens to her.
3. Suddenly, the wind starts to blow hard.
4. A big gust of wind picks her up.
5. She travels more than 100 feet in the air!

Write It

Choose the correct verb and write the sentence.

6. Every day, my sister (walks/walked) home from school.
7. Yesterday, she (walks/walked) home, too.
8. On her way home, the wind (pushes/pushed) her down.
9. She (works/worked) hard to get up again.
10. Then the wind (slows/slowed) down.

The tornado passed over the house.

Tell Your Story

Have you had an unusual experience? Think about a time when you were in danger. Maybe you had to decide quickly how to survive. Describe the experience for your class.

Follow these steps to create a good description:

How to DESCRIBE AN EXPERIENCE

1. Say what happened. Use the past tense.

2. Give details.

3. Use descriptive adjectives.

It **rained** for three days and nights. The water **reached** the tops of the riverbanks. Then the river **flooded**. Our home **flooded**, too. We **climbed** to the roof for safety.

Use the **past tense** to tell about events that happened before now.

To prepare to tell your story, make a storyboard about your experience. Use photos like these to add details about the event.

Then use your storyboard to share your experience with the group.

EQ ## What Does It Take to Survive?
Think about how luck helps survivors.

Learn Key Vocabulary

Pronounce each word and learn its meaning.

Key Words

damage (**da**-mij) *noun*
▶ page 264

Damage is harm or hurt. The storm did a lot of **damage** to the chair. *Synonym:* destruction

defenseless (di-**fens**-lus) *adjective*
▶ pages 257, 259

You are **defenseless** when you cannot protect yourself from something that can hurt you.

die (dī) *verb*
▶ pages 250, 263

When a person, plant, or animal **dies**, it stops living. One of the flowers **died**.

fear (fear) *noun*
▶ pages 250, 255, 267

Fear is the feeling you get when you are afraid. The man felt **fear** when he jumped from the plane.

injured (**in**-jurd) *adjective*
▶ pages 263, 266

When your body is **injured**, it is hurt. He felt a lot of pain from his **injured** leg.

powerful (**pow**-ur-ful) *adjective*
▶ page 254

Something that is **powerful** is very strong. A lion is a **powerful** animal. *Antonym:* weak

recover (ri-**ku**-vur) *verb*
▶ pages 265, 266

To **recover** means to get better after being hurt or sick. His mom helps him **recover**. *Synonym:* improve

weak (wēk) *adjective*
▶ page 257

Weak means not strong. Baby animals are often too **weak** to stand. *Antonym:* strong, powerful

Practice the Words Make a **Vocabulary Example Chart** for each Key Vocabulary word. Then compare charts with a partner.

Vocabulary Example Chart

Word	Definition	Example from My Life
injured	hurt	falling off my bike

Plan Your Reading

Before you read a text, look it over, or **preview** it. Then **make predictions**. Try to decide what it is about and what might happen. This makes reading the text more meaningful.

Reading Strategy
Plan and Monitor

HOW TO PREVIEW AND PREDICT

1. Read the title. Look at the pictures.

2. Begin to read. Stop after every few paragraphs to make a prediction, or decide what will happen next. Record your idea in a **Prediction Chart**.

3. Read on to find out what happens. Make a note in your chart. Decide if your prediction was confirmed, or came true.

4. Keep reading. Follow these steps to make and confirm more predictions.

Look at the picture. Then read the text and the chart.

Look Into the Text

And he knew that Nimuk was hungry, too. "One of us will soon be eating the other," Noni thought. "So . . ."

Prediction Chart

What the Images and Text Tell Me	My Prediction	What Happens
The dog looks hungry. Noni thinks one of them will eat the other.	Noni will kill Nimuk.	

Try It

Make a Prediction Chart. As you read "Two Were Left," make and confirm your predictions. In your chart, write your predictions and what happens.

Into the Literature

Build Background

The story "Two Were Left" takes place in the Arctic Ocean. The Arctic is the area of land and ocean around the North Pole. It is frozen most of the year. In the spring, the Arctic sea ice breaks up. This creates large icebergs and small ice islands. People can get stranded on ice islands. Full of **fear**, they may float in the sea. If no one finds them, they will **die**.

iceberg

ice island

www.hbedge.net
- View more photos of the Arctic.
- Learn about life in the Arctic.

TWO WERE LEFT

WRITTEN BY
Hugh B. Cave

Adapted with approval from the
Hugh B. Cave Irrevocable Trust

◉

ILLUSTRATED BY
S.D. Nelson

Noni and his dog Nimuk are alone. They have not eaten in three days. What will they do?

On the third night of hunger, Noni thought of the dog. Nothing else lived on the ice island.

In the breakup of the iceberg, Noni lost everything. He had only Nimuk, his devoted, loyal husky. And now the two were alone. They were **stranded** on the ice. They **eyed each other**.

In Other Words

In the breakup of the iceberg When the ocean ice broke into small pieces
stranded left alone
eyed each other looked at each other carefully

Noni's love for Nimuk was very real. But Noni knew that the men of his village killed their dogs. They did it when there was no food. They did not think twice about it.

And he knew that Nimuk was hungry, too. "One of us will soon be eating the other," Noni thought. "So . . ."

He could not kill the dog with his bare hands. Nimuk was **powerful**. A weapon, like a knife, was needed.

Removing his mittens, he unstrapped the brace from his leg. He had hurt his leg a few weeks ago. He had made the brace from pieces of leather and iron.

He put one of the pieces into a **crack in the ice**. Then he began to **rub** the other against it. Nimuk watched him.

He worked all night. **At dawn**, his task was complete.

Monitor Comprehension

Confirm Prediction
What did Noni decide to do?

Noni loves his dog. Will he complete his plan?

Noni pulled the finished knife from the ice. He touched its edge. The sun reflected from it.

"Here, Nimuk," he called softly. The dog watched him **suspiciously**. "Come here," Noni called.

Nimuk came closer. Noni saw <mark>fear</mark> in the animal's eyes. Weakened by hunger, the dog **dragged** his body forward. Noni's heart **wept**.

Key Vocabulary
<mark>fear</mark> *noun*, the feeling you get when you are afraid

In Other Words
suspiciously like he did not trust Noni
dragged pulled
wept cried

Now! Now was the time to **strike**!

A terrible feeling came over Noni, and he started to cry. He could not hurt Nimuk. He **cursed** the knife and threw it far from him. He fell.

In Other Words
strike kill the dog
cursed said angry words about

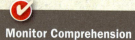
Monitor Comprehension

Confirm Prediction
Did Noni do what he planned to do? Was your prediction correct?

Predict
Noni's plan failed. How will he survive?

Now the dog **growled**. He circled the boy's body. Noni was sick with fear. Without the knife, he was <mark>**defenseless**</mark>. He was too <mark>**weak**</mark> to go get it now. And Nimuk was hungry.

The dog circled him. Noni heard his breathing from behind and knew Nimuk was getting close. He prayed for the **attack** to be fast. He felt the dog's breath against his neck. He knew this was the end.

Then he felt the dog's hot tongue. Nimuk was licking his face.

Noni's eyes opened. He did not believe it. He pulled the dog into his arms. Then he began to cry.

Key Vocabulary
defenseless *adjective*, unable to protect yourself from something that can hurt you
weak *adjective*, not strong

In Other Words
growled made an angry noise
attack fight

The plane came out of the south. The **pilot** looked down. He saw something flashing. He turned his plane. He saw a shape. It looked human. Or were there two shapes?

He set his plane down and went to them. They were a boy and a dog. The boy was **unconscious**. But he was alive. The dog **whined**. He was too weak to move.

In Other Words
pilot person in control of the plane
unconscious not awake
whined made sad sounds

A short distance away there was a shiny object. It was what caught the pilot's attention. It was a knife stuck in the ice. It moved gently in the wind. ❖

ANALYZE Two Were Left

1. **Confirm Prediction** What happened to Noni and Nimuk? Did the ending surprise you?

2. **Vocabulary** When does Noni feel **defenseless**?

3. **Reading Strategy** **Plan and Monitor** Look at the **Prediction Chart** you started on page 249. How many of your predictions did you confirm? How did you make them?

▶ Return to the Text

Reread and Retell In your own words, tell how Nimuk surprises Noni. Use facts from the text to support your ideas.

Tornado Survivor Called "the Luckiest Man on Earth"

newspaper article by Wes Johnson

Text Feature: Photos and Captions

Many texts include **photos** and **captions**. A photo shows how something looks. A caption gives more information about a photo or an illustration. Photos and captions give important information to help you understand people and events that you read about.

HOW TO USE PHOTOS AND CAPTIONS

1. Look at the photo.

2. Read the caption. Use the caption to understand what the photo shows.

3. Read the text. Connect the information from the photo and caption to the text.

4. Use all of the information to improve your understanding of the text.

Look at the photo. Then read the caption and the text. See how one reader used them to improve his understanding.

Look Into the Text

> The photo shows where Matt lived. The caption and text tell me more about the damage. That tornado was powerful!

caption > Tornado survivor Matt Suter stands in front of the remains of his home.

"The only thing left is the deck I'd been building for my grandma," Suter said. "Everything else is in the field or in the trees."

Try It

As you read "Tornado Survivor," use the photos and captions to help you understand the text.

Connect Across Texts

In "Two Were Left," Noni fights to survive. This newspaper article is about another young man who survives. Compare their stories. What did it take for them to survive?

Tornado Survivor

Called "the luckiest man on earth"

Adaptation of an article by **Wes Johnson**
News-Leader

AMAZING JOURNEY

FORDLAND, MISSOURI,   March 19, 2006—Matt Suter couldn't believe how loud the sound was. It came from outside the trailer home's walls.

The Fordland High School senior stood on a sofa. He struggled to close a window. Outside, rain and wind hit the **trailer**.

"It got louder and louder. It sounded like ten military jets were coming at us," Suter said.

"Suddenly there was lots of **pressure**. The doors blew out. I looked at my grandma. The walls were moving. The roof was moving. The floor was moving just like Jell-O. I could feel the whole trailer **tipping over**."

In Other Words
trailer small building
pressure pushing
tipping over falling on its side

A heavy lamp hit Suter in the head. He **lost consciousness**. In an instant, the tornado sucked Suter through the **collapsing** trailer walls.

Blown by **150-mile-per-hour** winds, the unconscious teen was then pulled up into the **raging blackness**.

Suter eventually landed in a field. He was **dazed** and his head was <mark>injured</mark>. But otherwise, he was not hurt.

A NEW RECORD

Suter may hold the record for the longest distance traveled by anyone picked up by a tornado who lived to tell about it: 1,307 feet (398 meters).

"I've never heard of anyone going that far in a tornado and surviving," tornado researcher Tom Grazulis said. "In more than forty thousand reports about tornadoes, I've only found one person who was carried more than a mile. But he <mark>died</mark>."

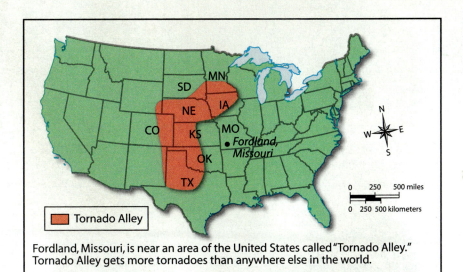

Fordland, Missouri, is near an area of the United States called "Tornado Alley." Tornado Alley gets more tornadoes than anywhere else in the world.

Monitor Comprehension

Explain
What happened to Matt Suter when the tornado hit?

Key Vocabulary
<mark>injured</mark> *adjective*, hurt
die *verb*, to stop living

In Other Words
lost consciousness fell into a deep sleep
collapsing falling
150-mile-per-hour 241-kilometer-per-hour
raging blackness dark, wild wind
dazed not sure what had happened

When Suter woke up, he **was confused**. There was blood pouring down his face from the cut in his head. "Everything was gone. I could see **debris** everywhere," he said.

Suter was **barefoot** and soaking wet from rain. He started looking for help. A neighbor found Suter at his door. He wrapped Suter in a blanket. Then the neighbor called his brother, who drove Suter back to see the **damage**.

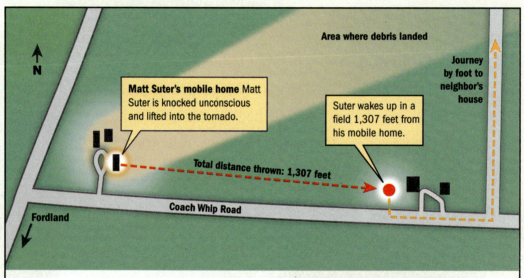

Area where debris landed

Journey by foot to neighbor's house

Matt Suter's mobile home Matt Suter is knocked unconscious and lifted into the tornado.

Suter wakes up in a field 1,307 feet from his mobile home.

Total distance thrown: 1,307 feet

Coach Whip Road

Fordland

N

Matt Suter survived being sucked up by a tornado and thrown 1,307 feet (almost five soccer fields) away. He may have set a new record for distance traveled by a tornado survivor.

Key Vocabulary
damage *noun*, harm or hurt

In Other Words
was confused did not know what had happened
debris pieces of my house
barefoot not wearing shoes

Tornado survivor Matt Suter stands in front of what remains of his home.

"The only thing left is the deck I'd been building for my grandma," Suter said. "Everything else is in the field or in the trees."

Suter's physician, Dr. Ron Buening, said that Suter will **recover** from his injuries. "He was the luckiest man on earth," Buening said.

Monitor Comprehension

Describe
What happened to Suter's home?

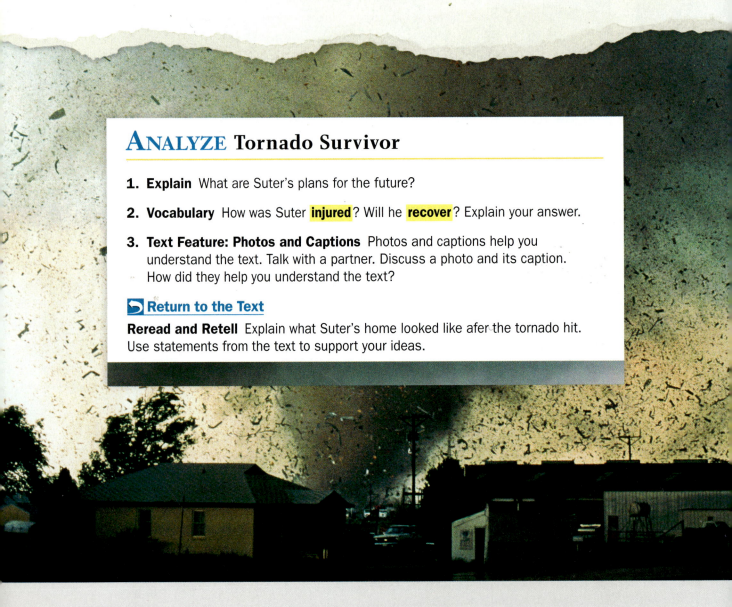

AFTER THE STORM

Suter plans to help his grandmother rebuild her home. After he graduates, he wants to join the Marines.

As for being a tornado survivor? "I've always wanted to see a tornado," he said. "But I sure didn't want to be in one." ❖

ANALYZE Tornado Survivor

1. **Explain** What are Suter's plans for the future?

2. **Vocabulary** How was Suter **injured**? Will he **recover**? Explain your answer.

3. **Text Feature: Photos and Captions** Photos and captions help you understand the text. Talk with a partner. Discuss a photo and its caption. How did they help you understand the text?

Return to the Text

Reread and Retell Explain what Suter's home looked like afer the tornado hit. Use statements from the text to support your ideas.

REFLECT AND ASSESS

► Two Were Left
► Tornado Survivor Called "the Luckiest Man on Earth"

EQ What Does It Take to Survive?

Talk About Literature

1. Explain In "Two Were Left," what caught the pilot's attention? Then what happened?

> The pilot saw _____. When he turned the plane, he saw _____.

2. Summarize How is Matt Suter's experience unique? Why do people call him the luckiest man on earth?

> Suter's experience is unique because _____. People call him the luckiest man because _____.

EQ 3. Compare Noni and Matt Suter each survived terrible events. What helped them both survive?

Listen to a reading. Practice fluency. Use the Reading Handbook, page 537.

Vocabulary
Review Key Vocabulary

Choose the correct vocabulary word to complete each sentence.

1. We felt great _damage_ when we heard that a tornado was coming.
2. When the tornado hit, it did a lot of _damage_ to our town.
3. Some people may be lost. Some of them may be _died_.
4. During the storm, the _powerful_ winds broke huge branches off the trees.
5. We were _defenseless_ and could not protect ourselves from the winds.
6. The people in our town are strong, not _powerful_.
7. We will _____ quickly from this storm.
8. No one _injured_ or was seriously hurt.

Vocabulary
- damage
- defenseless
- died
- fear
- injured
- powerful
- recover
- weak

Writing
Write About Literature

EQ Survival Guide What helps people survive when they are in danger? What personal traits help them? Look back at the texts to see how Noni and Matt Suter survived. Explain how people can face **fear** and survive danger.

> To survive danger, you need _____. If you remember _____, you will be more likely to survive. That is the most important thing.

Reflect and Assess **267**

Use Past Tense Verbs: *Was, Were*

When you talk about the past, you usually use past tense verbs.

The verb **be** has two special forms for the past: **was** and **were**.

- Use **was** with **I**, **he**, **she**, and **it**.
- Use **were** with **we**, **you**, and **they**.

The verbs agree, or go with, their subjects.

> I **was** scared.
> My sister **was** scared, too.
> She **was** afraid of the water.
> But we **were** both strong.

Oral Practice Work with a partner. Choose the correct verb and say the sentence.

1. My brother helped us. He (was/were) very strong.
2. My mother helped. She (was/were) strong, too.
3. The river flowed fast. It (was/were) 10 feet above flood level.
4. Many people needed help. They (was/were) in danger.
5. I (was/were) worried about them.

Written Practice (6–10) Write five sentences about a survivor. You can write about an imaginary survivor or one from a story. Start with this sentence and choose the correct verb. Then write more sentences.

> The experience (was/were) scary.

Describe an Experience

Learn About a Survivor Work with a partner. Find out about a survivor. What did this person do to survive?

www.hbedge.net
- View a picture of a survivor.
- Read an interview with a survivor.

Collect details about the survivor's experience. What happened? When did it happen? Where did it happen? What did the person do to survive?

> Describe the survivor's experience.
> Use sentences like these:
>
> - The survivor's name is [person's name].
> - He/she was in a/an [type of disaster].
> - It happened in [where] in [when].
> - He/she [Say what the person did to survive.]

Use a Dictionary

When you come to a word you do not know, use a dictionary to learn more about the word.

> Hurricane Katrina was a terrible <u>disaster</u>.

- Use guide words to find the right page. Then find the word.
- Read the pronunciation. Say the word.
- Learn the part of speech.
- Read the definition.
- Reread the word in the text. Use the meaning of the word to unlock the meaning of the text.

Dictionary

> **disabled • discard**

> **disaster**   (di-zas-tur) *n.*   **1** : a sudden event that causes damage, loss, or destruction

Use the dictionary page to answer the questions.

1. What is the meaning of *disaster*?
2. How do you pronounce *disaster*?
3. What part of speech is *disaster*?
4. What is the first entry on the dictionary page where *disaster* appears?

Literary Element: Plot

The plot is the order of action in a story. It is all the things that happen from the beginning to the end. The action is always related to the main problem.

1. **Beginning** Every plot begins with a **problem**.
2. **Middle**
   - **Events** make the problem worse.
   - When the problem is at its worst, something changes. This is called the **turning point**. After the turning point, the problem stops getting worse.
3. **End** The end of the story describes the **solution**.

Create a **Plot Diagram** to show what happens in "Two Were Left."

Plot Diagram

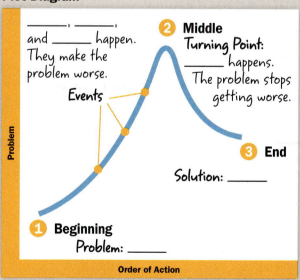

Continue the Story

▶ **Prompt** Think about what happens to Noni and Nimuk in "Two Were Left."
How might the story continue? Write a paragraph to add your own ending.

1 **Plan** Look back at the selection. Think about the predictions you made. Use
them to continue the story. Make a **Story Chart**. Say what happens at the
beginning. Say what happens next. Predict what happens after the pilot finds
Noni and Nimuk.

Story Chart

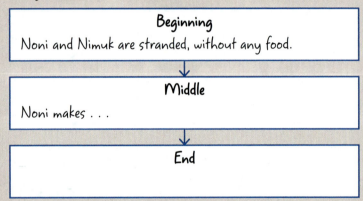

2 **Write** Write a paragraph that explains how the story might end. Begin your
paragraph like this:

> After the pilot picked up Noni and Nimuk . . .

Use past tense verbs correctly.

- Many past tense verbs end in **-ed**.

  return + **-ed** = return**ed**

- If a verb ends in silent **e**, drop the **e** before you add **-ed**.

  mov~~e~~ + **-ed** = mov**ed**

- If a verb ends in one vowel and one consonant, you usually double the consonant.

  stop + **p** + **-ed** = stop**ped**

3 **Share** Ask a partner to read your paragraph. Compare your story endings.

1 TRY OUT LANGUAGE
2 LEARN GRAMMAR
3 APPLY ON YOUR OWN

Describe a Past Event

Look at the photo and listen to the news report. What does the news report describe?

News Report

SURVIVING KATRINA

This is Amy Chen in New Orleans after Hurricane Katrina hit the city. I'm reporting at the scene of another rescue earlier today.

Ordinary citizens used their boat to help three women and a young child. First, they rescued the women and the child from the rooftop of their home. Then they took them by boat to safety. The women were able to walk to a shelter. At the shelter, they received food and a dry place to stay.

This is Amy Chen—reporting for the News Channel.

Use Past Tense Verbs: *Had*

1 **TRY OUT LANGUAGE**
2 **LEARN GRAMMAR**
3 **APPLY ON YOUR OWN**

The verb **have** has a special form to tell about the past.

PAST   PRESENT   FUTURE

(before now)   (now)   (after now)

PAST	PRESENT
Yesterday, people **had** a lot to carry.	They usually **have** things to carry.
We **had** many things to carry, too.	We **have** a lot to carry every day.
I **had** family photos.	I usually **have** a raincoat.
The woman **had** a child.	My sister **has** a backpack.
My brother **had** the dog.	My brother **has** a backpack, too.
The dog **had** a toy.	It **has** a water bottle in it.

- In the **past tense**, use **had** with all subjects.
- In the **present tense**, use **has** with **he**, **she**, and **it** and **have** with **you**, **we**, or **they**.

Say It

Work with a partner. Choose the correct word and say the sentence.

1. I usually (have/had) a lot to carry to school.

2. My friends carry a lot, too. They (have/has) backpacks and jackets.

3. Yesterday, they even (have/had) cans of food to donate.

4. My sister also carried a lot. She (have/had) bottles of water to give.

5. I imagine you (have/had) a lot to carry yesterday, too!

Write It

Choose *have*, *has*, or *had* and write the sentence.

6. Every day, TV _____ a lot of reports about rescues.

7. News shows often _____ reports about tornadoes and other storms.

8. Yesterday, they _____ a report about a winter storm.

9. I _____ other things to do, but I watched it anyway.

10. My dad _____ a lot to do, but he watched it with me, too.

Talk About a Weather Event...

1 TRY OUT LANGUAGE
2 LEARN GRAMMAR
3 APPLY ON YOUR OWN

Watch the news and listen for a story about a severe, or dangerous, weather event. It could be a hurricane, a cyclone, a tornado, a flood, or a winter storm. Take notes about what happened. Then use the notes to report on the event to the class.

Follow these steps to describe the event accurately:

HOW TO DESCRIBE A PAST EVENT

1. Say what happened.

2. Say when and where it happened.

3. Give details.

> Yesterday, there **was** a severe winter storm in the mountains west of Denver, Colorado. The snow **forced** the cars and trucks to stop on I-70. The police **closed** the roads and **helped** people find shelter in schools. They **had** food and water for them, too.

Use past tense verbs when you describe an event that happened in the past.

Police closed many roads because of the storm.

EQ **What Does It Take to Survive?**
Find out how creative thinking can help people survive.

Learn Key Vocabulary

Pronounce each word and learn its meaning.

Key Words

choice (chois) *noun*
▷ page 281

You make a **choice** when you pick between two or more things. His **choice** is between the two sandwiches.

disaster (di-**zas**-tur) *noun*
▷ pages 276, 279, 281, 285, 289

A **disaster** is an event that harms a lot of people, animals, or things. A flood is a **disaster**.

neighbor (nā-bur) *noun*
▷ page 278

Your **neighbor** is someone who lives near you. These friends are also **neighbors**.

obstacle (**ob**-sti-kul) *noun*
▷ pages 278, 286, 288, 289

An **obstacle** is something that stops you from doing what you want to do. Lava is an **obstacle** on this road.

safety (**sāf**-tē) *noun*
▷ pages 279, 280, 282

Safety is when you cannot be hurt. She wears a helmet and pads for **safety**.

save (sāv) *verb*
▷ page 281

To **save** is to stop someone or something from being hurt or destroyed.

stranger (**strān**-jur) *noun*
▷ pages 280, 289

A **stranger** is someone you do not know. **Strangers** often sit next to each other on the bus.

victim (**vik**-tum) *noun*
▷ pages 276, 280, 282

A person who has been hurt by someone or something is a **victim**. The flood **victim's** home is ruined.

Practice the Words Make an **Example Web** for each Key Vocabulary word. Write words or phrases to connect with the word.

Example Web

selection — choice — decision

BEFORE READING Surviving Katrina

news feature by Daphne Liu

Plan Your Reading

When you read, you always read for a reason. For example, you read to check information or to learn something.

Reading Strategy
Plan and Monitor

HOW TO PREVIEW AND SET A PURPOSE

1. Look quickly at the text. Notice headings, pictures, and other visuals.

2. Look at the title and cover. Ask, "What is the text about?"

3. Read the first few sentences. Think some more on what the text is about.

4. Ask, "What do I want to find out?" Your answer is your purpose for reading.

Look at the cover. Then read the title and the text. See how one reader previewed and set a purpose before reading.

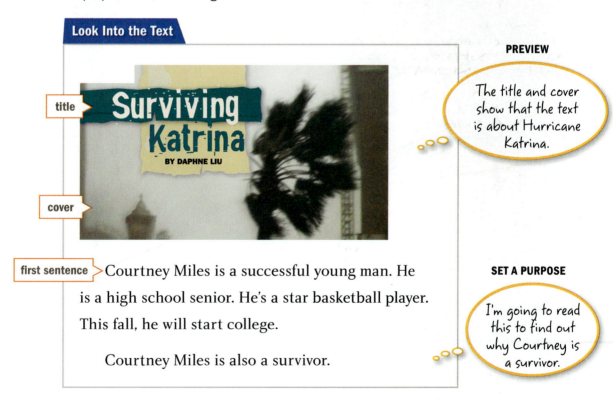

Look Into the Text

title

cover

PREVIEW

The title and cover show that the text is about Hurricane Katrina.

first sentence > Courtney Miles is a successful young man. He is a high school senior. He's a star basketball player. This fall, he will start college.

Courtney Miles is also a survivor.

SET A PURPOSE

I'm going to read this to find out why Courtney is a survivor.

Try It

Now it's your turn. Preview the text and set a purpose for reading "Surviving Katrina." Discuss your purpose with a partner.

Build Background

Hurricane Katrina hit the city of New Orleans, Louisiana, in August 2005. It caused one of the worst **disasters** in United States history. Floods destroyed homes, and people died.

What caused the disaster? New Orleans is bordered by Lake Pontchartrain and the Mississippi River. The city uses levees, or seawalls, to keep the lake and the river out. Hurricane Katrina brought a lot of rain. The levees broke.

levee

Water flooded New Orleans. It damaged much of the city. But many people survived. People all over the country helped the **victims** of Katrina. Some traveled to the disaster areas to help. Others donated clothes, food, water, and medical equipment. These volunteers helped the victims rebuild their lives.

www.hbedge.net
- Read about organizations that help in disasters.
- Learn about hurricane safety.

Surviving Katrina

BY DAPHNE LIU

Courtney Miles is a successful young man. He is a high school senior. He's a star basketball player. This fall, he will start college.

Courtney Miles is also a survivor.

A Troubled Past

In 2005, Courtney was living in New Orleans. His father had moved across the country. His mother was in jail. Courtney stayed with his grandmother, but she moved away, too. The teenager was on his own, with no food or money. Life was hard.

"I was trying to **go down a straight street**, but I had all these **obstacles**," Courtney says. **Neighbors** offered to help, but he usually **refused**. He wanted to take care of himself.

Key Vocabulary
obstacle *noun*, something that stops you from doing what you want to do
neighbor *noun*, someone who lives near you

In Other Words
go down a straight street be good
refused said no

A Disaster

Then Hurricane Katrina **struck**. Courtney's neighborhood was **flooded**. There was no electricity. People had no food or clean water. The flood waters were knee high. "**Man**, we have to do something to get out of here," Courtney told his friends.

What Courtney did next makes some people call him a **hero**. Others call him a **criminal**. But Courtney and his friends knew what they had to do. One night, they **broke into** a bus station. Courtney didn't have a driver's license, but he took a bus anyway. He drove back to his neighborhood and picked up his neighbors. Then he brought them to <mark>safety</mark>.

Key Vocabulary
<mark>disaster</mark> *noun*, an event that harms a lot of people, animals, or things
<mark>safety</mark> *noun*, a place where you cannot be hurt

In Other Words
struck happened
flooded covered with water
Man Hey, everyone (slang)
hero brave person
criminal person who breaks the law
broke into illegally entered

Monitor Comprehension

Explain
What did Courtney decide to do? Why did he do it?

The Road to Safety

Along the way, <mark>strangers</mark> begged for a ride. Courtney could not leave them behind, so he let them get in, too.

Courtney and his friends drove to the Cajun Dome in Lafayette. It was a **shelter** for thousands of hurricane <mark>victims</mark>. But Courtney's work was not done. Soon he was back on the bus. "The only thing I kept thinking about was the people I had left behind," he explains.

In the end, Courtney brought nearly four hundred people to safety.

Eventually, the storm waters went down. But Courtney's life had changed forever. He had no home. All his **belongings** were gone. He couldn't even go to school.

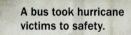

A bus took hurricane victims to safety.

Floods destroyed many neighborhoods.

Key Vocabulary

stranger *noun*, someone you do not know

victim *noun*, a person who has been hurt by someone or something

In Other Words

shelter safe place
Eventually In the end
belongings possessions

Courtney Miles started a new life in Oakland.

A New Life

Courtney moved to Oakland, California, to live with a grandfather he had never met. When Courtney arrived, he had little more than the clothes **on his back**. "I was upset," he explains. "But there's no way I can go back to that. I just have to move on and accept it."

At his new school, Courtney **got to work**. He spent every day in study hall. He joined the basketball team and led them to victory. Now he looks forward to college.

When Courtney looks back at Hurricane Katrina, his feelings are mixed. "In a way [Katrina] was bad. But in a way it **saved** me."

It takes more than a disaster to stop this young man. When trouble comes, he makes hard **choices**. Then he does what he has to do.

That makes Courtney Miles a survivor. ❖

Key Vocabulary
save *verb*, to stop someone or something from being hurt or destroyed
choice *noun*, the decision you make when you pick between two or more things

In Other Words
on his back he was wearing
got to work worked hard

Monitor Comprehension

Explain
How many people did Courtney help? How did he do it?

ANALYZE Surviving Katrina

1. **Explain** What did Courtney do when he moved to Oakland, California?

2. **Vocabulary** Where did Courtney find <mark>safety</mark> for himself and other <mark>victims</mark> of Katrina?

3. **Reading Strategy Plan and Monitor** Work with a partner. Review your purpose for reading. Did you have the same purpose? How did setting a purpose affect your understanding?

Return to the Text

Reread and Retell Retell Courtney's story in your own words. Use facts from the text to support your ideas.

Maps

Maps give information about places. Different maps
are made for different reasons, or purposes.

How to Read a Map

1. Look for its title. It tells what the map is about.
2. Study all the parts: the scale, compass rose, and legend.
3. Look at the colors and labels. They will help you understand the map.

Different Kinds of Maps

Political Map

A **political map** shows **boundaries** between
states and countries. It also shows other
major cities. The **legend** shows what pictures
stand for.

Physical Map

A **physical map** shows natural features such
as lakes, rivers, and mountains. The **compass
rose** shows the directions north, south, east,
and west. The **scale** shows how the distance
on the map compares to the real distance.

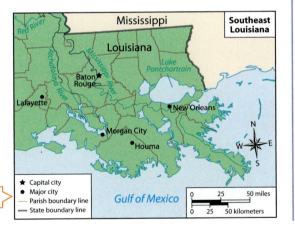

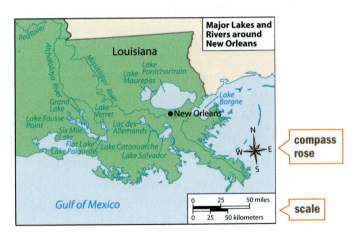

magazine article by Nick D'Alto

Monitor Your Reading

When you read, make sure you understand the text. If you don't understand it, reread or read on to make it clear, or **clarify ideas**.

Reading Strategy
Plan and Monitor

HOW TO CLARIFY IDEAS

1. Stop reading after difficult sentences or paragraphs. Ask yourself, "What is the writer saying?" Explain the text to yourself in your own words. If you still do not understand, reread those sections.

2. If rereading doesn't help you, read on. You might find information later in the text that will help you understand.

3. Read at the right speed. You might need to read some texts more slowly.

Read the text and the self-stick notes to see how one reader clarified ideas.

Look Into the Text

CHALLENGE 1

A boat sank. Three friends were stuck on an island. Their radio was gone. Their cell phone wouldn't work. Yet they rescued themselves by using a credit card. How was it possible?

That credit card was valuable—but only if you think laterally. Credit cards are made from plastic. They're usually shiny on one side. One friend used the credit card to reflect sunlight.

* * * * * * * * *

At first, the card didn't reflect strongly enough. So the friends dunked the card in sea water. This made it shinier. Then they used their fingers to help aim the signal as a plane flew overhead.

They used the card like a mirror. They reflected the sun with it.

They had to get the card wet. Then they pointed it at an airplane.

Try It

Clarify ideas as you read "Test Your Survival Skills." Use self-stick notes to ask questions, explain to yourself, or draw pictures.

Connect Across Texts

In "Surviving Katrina," you learn how Courtney Miles survived a **disaster**. Read this magazine article to see how you could survive a disaster.

TEST YOUR SURVIVAL SKILLS

BY NICK D'ALTO
Odyssey, December 1, 2005
ILLUSTRATIONS BY CHRIS VALLO

Survival experts often say that the way you think might be your most important survival tool. In an emergency, you need to be able to see ordinary things in extraordinary ways. Experts call this "**lateral thinking**."

Here are two true survival stories. Read about each situation. Then brainstorm. How did each survivor "think" his or her way out of **danger**?

CHALLENGE 1

CREDIT THESE GUYS WITH GENIUS

A boat sank. Three friends were stuck on an island. Their radio was gone. Their cell phone wouldn't work. Yet they rescued themselves by using a credit card. How was it possible?

Key Vocabulary
disaster *noun*, an event that harms a lot of people, animals, or things

In Other Words
lateral thinking thinking in new and different ways
danger the situation that could harm the survivor

ANSWER

That credit card was valuable—but only if you think laterally. Credit cards are made from plastic. They're usually shiny on one side. One friend used the credit card to reflect sunlight. The flashes were noticed by a passing plane. (Sometimes, reflected sunlight can be spotted 100 miles, or 160 kilometers, away.)

At first, the card didn't reflect strongly enough. So the friends **dunked** the card in sea water. This made it shinier. Then they used their fingers to help aim the signal as a plane flew overhead.

The lesson? When they looked at the credit card, the friends saw more than just a useless piece of plastic. And then they turned their worst <mark>obstacles</mark>—water and the blazing sun—into a way to improve their plan for survival.

Key Vocabulary
obstacle *noun*, something that stops you from doing what you want to do

In Other Words
dunked put

CHALLENGE 2

WISDOM TEETH

A plane crashed into a mountain. The pilot and **his elderly passenger** were badly hurt. They had no food or water. The pilot finally found a **stream**. But his hands were very burned. He could not **scoop up** the water. The passenger was too weak to reach the stream. Yet the passenger's age helped them get water. Can you guess how?

ANSWER

It's **gross**. The passenger wore dentures, or false teeth. The pilot removed the dentures and turned them upside down. He used them as a cup to lift water from the stream. Now he and the passenger could drink. **Disgusting**? You do what you have to do to survive.

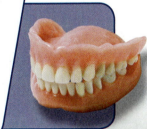

In Other Words
his elderly passenger the old person on the plane
stream small river
scoop up use his hands to pick up
gross awful
Disgusting Awful

Monitor Comprehension

Explain
Why were the pilot and passenger hurt? How did they survive?

Your only tool is a garbage bag. How many survival uses for it can you think of? Could you make a **poncho** to keep dry? A **kite** to call **rescuers**? **A stretcher to move** the injured? Use lateral thinking. How many possible uses can you think of? ❖

ANALYZE Test Your Survival Skills

1. **Explain** What does it mean to use "lateral thinking"?

2. **Vocabulary** What obstacles did the friends on the island face?

3. **Reading Strategy** **Plan and Monitor** Work with a partner. Which ideas did you explain in your own words? How did it help you understand the text?

🔊 Return to the Text

Reread and Retell Reread the whole text. Choose the survival story you like best. Explain how thinking creatively helped people survive.

In Other Words
poncho rain coat
kite flying object
rescuers people who can help you
A stretcher to move An object to carry

EQ **What Does It Take to Survive?**

Reading

Talk About Literature

1. **Describe** What **obstacles** did Courtney Miles face before the hurricane? Tell what was hard about his life.

   Courtney's life was hard because _____ .

EQ 2. **Infer** How does lateral thinking help people survive?

   Lateral thinking helps people survive because _____ .

3. **Analyze** How did Courtney Miles use lateral thinking?

   Courtney Miles used lateral thinking by _____ .

Fluency

Listen to a reading. Practice fluency. Use the Reading Handbook, page 538.

Vocabulary

Review Key Vocabulary

Choose the correct vocabulary word to complete each sentence.

1. As a firefighter, Oscar knew about fires, floods, and other _____ .

2. He had rescued many _____ from burning buildings.

3. But those people were _____ to him. He did not know them.

4. One day, Oscar saw smoke next door. His _____ was at home.

5. The house was on fire. Oscar had to _____ the family inside.

6. Metal bars on the windows were an _____ , though.

7. Oscar made a difficult _____ . He broke down the door.

8. Then he pulled the family to _____ .

Vocabulary
- choice
- disasters
- neighbor
- obstacle
- safety
- save
- strangers
- victims

Writing

Write About Literature

Opinion Statement Why do **strangers** help each other during a **disaster**? Support your opinion with examples from both selections. Use a chart to organize your thoughts.

1. State Opinion	2. Support Opinion
I think strangers help each other because . . .	I think this because I read . . .

Grammar

Use Irregular Past Tense Verbs

We add **-ed** to most verbs to show that an action happened before now.

Hurricane Katrina flood**ed** the city fast.

But, some verbs have a special form for the past tense. These verbs are irregular.

PRESENT	PAST	EXAMPLE
come, comes	came	The water **came** toward us fast.
do, does	did	We **did** what we had to do.
go, goes	went	My brother **went** for help.
have, has	had	He **had** no time to waste.
run, runs	ran	We **ran** as fast as we could.

Oral Practice Work with a partner. Say each sentence. Then have your partner say the sentence in the past tense.

1. We run fast to higher ground.
2. My family has some blankets.
3. My dad goes for help.
4. My little sister does her best to help.
5. Help comes quickly.

Written Practice Change the verb in parentheses to the past tense and write the sentence.

6. People _____ to help us. (run)
7. They _____ from all over the city. (come)
8. My brother _____ to find food and water. (go)
9. We _____ the desire to live. (have)
10. We _____ our best to survive. (do)

Language Development

Describe a Past Event

Find Out More About Katrina Work with a partner. Use "Surviving Katrina" and the Internet to find out more about this disaster. Then describe the event to your partner.

www.hbedge.net
• Find out more about Hurricane Katrina.
• Research the number of people who returned to New Orleans after the storm.

First, decide who will gather which information: What else happened? When did it happen? Where did it happen? How did people survive? Did they return to the city later? Then research the information about the hurricane.

Describe the events in the order in which they happened. Use sentences like these:

First, Hurricane Katrina hit land in _____. This happened on _____. People _____ to survive. _____ percent of the people of New Orleans returned later.

Multiple-Meaning Words

Many English words have more than one meaning. The meanings are numbered in the dictionary. They often show different parts of speech.

> **flood** (flud) *n.* **1** : a great flow of water *v.* **2** : to cover or fill with water

The word *flood* has more than one meaning. Read the dictionary entry above. Think about what *flood* means in this sentence:

"Floods destroyed many neighborhoods."

In this sentence, **flood** is a noun. It means "a great flow of water."

Tell which dictionary meaning fits each sentence.

1. "Hurricane Katrina hit the Gulf Coast states."

> **state** (stāt) *n.* **1** : one of the units of a nation *v.* **2** : to express in words

2. "His father had moved across the country."

> **country** (kun-trē) *n.* **1** : a nation **2** : an open area of land outside of cities and towns

3. "Neighbors offered to help, but he usually refused."

> **offer** (ah-fur) *n.* **1** : an act of giving *v.* **2** : to give

Compare Fiction and Nonfiction

Stories about imaginary people, places, things, and events are called fiction. "Two Were Left" is an example of fiction.

Texts that give information about real people, places, things, and events are called nonfiction. "Surviving Katrina" is an example of nonfiction.

Work with a partner. Copy the **Venn Diagram** and then add more ideas that compare fiction and nonfiction.

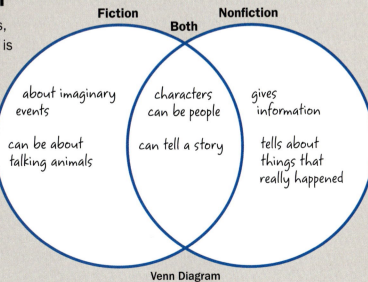

Fiction — about imaginary events; can be about talking animals

Both — characters can be people; can tell a story

Nonfiction — gives information; tells about things that really happened

Venn Diagram

Write About a Challenge

▶ **Prompt** Hurricanes, floods, and tornadoes are major challenges. Most people do not have to face disasters like those. But people face smaller challenges every day. What challenges have you faced? Choose one. Write a paragraph about a challenge that you faced.

1 **Plan** Think of a challenge or a difficult situation in your life. Make a **Problem-and-Solution Chart**. Use it to plan your paragraph.

Problem-and-Solution Chart

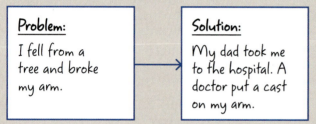

2 **Write** Tell about the challenge you faced. Use the Paragraph Organizer to help you. Be sure to use the correct verb tenses in your paragraph.

REMEMBER
• Use the past tense to tell about something that happened before now.
• Many past tense verbs end in **-ed**.
• The verbs **do** and **have** use special forms to tell about the past.

Paragraph Organizer

    Everyone faces challenges sometimes. One challenge I faced was [what] . It happened [when] , in [where] . The situation was difficult because [reason] . I overcame this challenge when [Describe the solution.] . Many people grow stronger when they overcome a challenge. This [did or did not] happen for me.

3 **Share** Ask a partner to read your paragraph. Discuss the challenge that each of you faced. Compare how you overcame your challenges.

Give and Carry Out Commands

1 TRY OUT LANGUAGE
2 LEARN GRAMMAR
3 APPLY ON YOUR OWN

Look at the photo and listen to the rap. What can this person do?

Rap

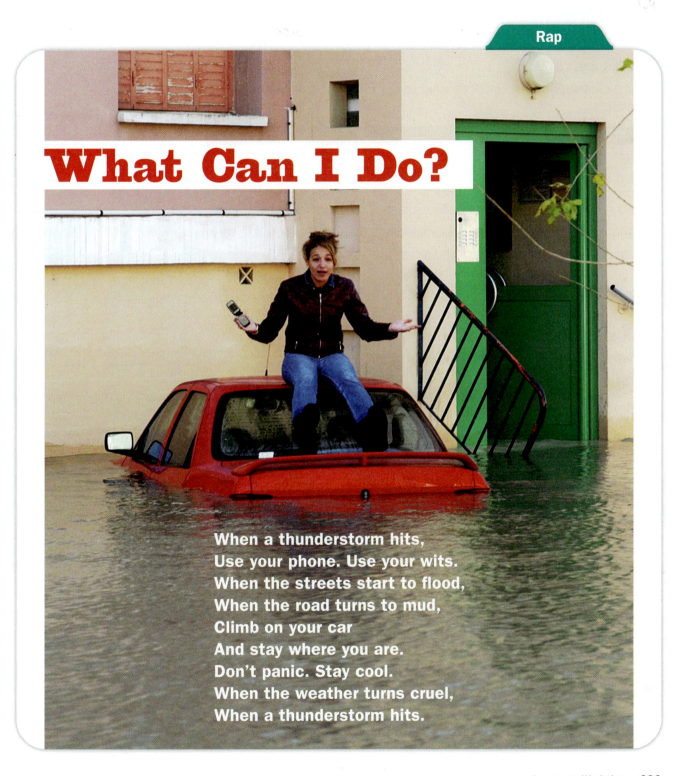

What Can I Do?

When a thunderstorm hits,
Use your phone. Use your wits.
When the streets start to flood,
When the road turns to mud,
Climb on your car
And stay where you are.
Don't panic. Stay cool.
When the weather turns cruel,
When a thunderstorm hits.

1 TRY OUT LANGUAGE
2 LEARN GRAMMAR
3 APPLY ON YOUR OWN

Use Commands

Use a **statement** to tell something. End the statement with a period.

> **Water floods the streets.**

Ask a **question** to find out something. End the question with a question mark.

> **What can I do?**

Give a **command** to tell someone what to do. End most commands with a period.

COMMANDS WITH ACTION VERBS	COMMANDS WITH *BE*
Climb up the wall.	**Be** calm.
Don't fall!	**Don't be** scared.

- A command begins with a verb. The subject (you) is understood.
- When you tell someone not to do something, use **don't** before the verb.
- Use the main verb form, don't add an -s.

Say It

Work with a partner. Say each sentence. Your partner says what kind of sentence it is.

1. This is a problem.

2. How can I get help?

3. Call someone.

4. Don't worry.

5. Be strong.

Write It

6–10. Write five commands. Use a different verb in each command.

close   open   underline   work   write

Don't panic!

Role-Play a Phone Call

With a partner, role-play a telephone conversation between two teens. In the conversation, you and your partner will tell each other to do (or not to do) certain things.

Remember these tips for commands:

HOW TO GIVE AND CARRY OUT COMMANDS

1. When you want to tell someone to do something, use a command.

> Hi, Mike. This is Dan. **Hurry**. **Meet** me at the bus stop. The buses stop running in ten minutes. We can't miss our bus!

Start a **command** with a verb.

2. Respond to the command with words such as "OK" and "I'll _____ right away."

> OK. **Don't** worry. I'll be there right away.

Use **don't** before the verb when you tell someone not to do something.

After you practice, present your role-play to the class.

"Don't let me down! Please get here soon."

PREPARE TO READ

▶ **Fight or Flight? What Your Body Knows About Survival**
▶ **Survivor Rulon Gardner: Hardheaded**

EQ **What Does It Take to Survive?**
Explore how the body and mind work together for survival.

Learn Key Vocabulary

Pronounce each word and learn its meaning.

Key Words

blood vessel (**blud ve**-sul) *noun*
▶ pages 298, 301

A **blood vessel** is a small tube in your body that carries blood from place to place.

circumstances (**sur**-kum-stans-uz) *noun*
▶ pages 308, 310, 311, 316

Circumstances are the facts or details of a situation. These people live in difficult **circumstances**.

danger (**dān**-jur) *noun*
▶ pages 298, 300, 302, 305, 311

Danger is something that can harm you. Construction workers often face **danger** in their jobs.

energy (**e**-nur-jē) *noun*
▶ page 305

Energy is the ability to move or be active. The runners have a lot of **energy**.

escape (is-**kāp**) *verb*
▶ page 301

When you **escape** something, you get away from it. He **escapes** danger.

perspire (pur-**spīr**) *verb*
▶ page 305

To **perspire** is to sweat. The athlete **perspires** to cool his body.

physical (**fi**-zi-kul) *adjective*
▶ pages 307, 311

Physical means about the body. **Physical** training makes you stronger.

system (**sis**-tum) *noun*
▶ pages 298, 300, 305

A **system** is an organized group of parts that work together. Inside the clock is a **system** of metal parts.

Practice the Words Make a **Word Map** for each Key Vocabulary word. Then compare maps with a partner.

Definition	Characteristics
the possibility of harm	can be scary, people try to prevent
danger	
possible during an earthquake	possible in a safe place
Example	Non-example

Fight or Flight? What Your Body Knows About Survival

science article by James E. Porter

Monitor Your Reading

When you read, make sure you understand the words. If there is a word that confuses you, reread or read on to **clarify** it, or make it clear.

Plan and Monitor

HOW TO CLARIFY VOCABULARY.

1. Ask, "Have I seen the word before? What do I already know about it?" Look at the word parts.

2. If you still do not understand the word, reread the sentence. "Reread" means to look back and read again. Try to find clues to predict the word's meaning.

3. If you still do not understand, read on. The meaning may become clearer in the text you read later.

4. Confirm your predictions as you read by looking them up in a dictionary.

Read the text. See how one reader clarified vocabulary while reading.

Look Into the Text

Your heart pumps faster. It sends blood to your arms and legs. Tiny blood vessels, called <u>capillaries</u>, get smaller. This makes your blood pressure go up. Now you can get a surface wound and not bleed to death.

Your body is now <u>supercharged</u>. It helps you against your enemy. You escape death by jumping higher and running faster than you ever could before.

> I do not know the word "capillaries". I will look back.

> **"The sentence gives a clue. It means *tiny blood vessels*."**

Try It

Reread the passage. Follow the steps in the How-To box to figure out the meaning of the word *supercharged*.

As you read "Fight or Flight?" reread and read on to clarify words that you don't understand. Use a dictionary to help confirm the meanings of the words.

Genre: Science Article

A science article like "Fight or Flight?" is nonfiction. This science article focuses on biology. Biology is the study of living things, such as plants, animals, and insects.

Biologists are scientists who study how living things work. Some biologists study the human body. Some research a specific body **system**, such as the circulatory system. The circulatory system is made up of the heart, blood, and **blood vessels**. The article "Fight or Flight?" is about what our bodies' systems do when we sense, or feel, **danger**.

www.hbedge.net
- Learn more about the circulatory system.
- Learn biology terms.

Fight
or *Flight?*

What Your Body Knows
About Survival
by James E. Porter

Run Away!

Imagine you are a caveman. You're out picking berries. Suddenly you are facing a tiger. While you were gathering, the tiger was hunting. The sight of you makes **his mouth water**.

Luckily for you, your body has weapons that take over when you sense **danger**. When you see the tiger, **your hypothalamus** sends a message through the **circulatory** **system** to parts of your body. It tells your **adrenal glands** to release special chemicals. In seconds, your body changes. You can run faster and hit harder. You can see more. You can hear better. You can think faster and jump higher.

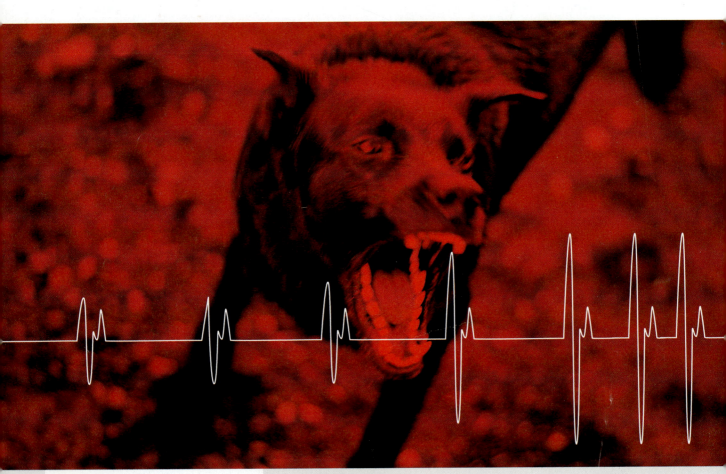

Key Vocabulary

danger *noun*, something that can harm you

system *noun*, an organized group of parts that work together

In Other Words

his mouth water him hungry
your hypothalamus the part of your brain that responds to fear
circulatory blood
adrenal glands organs that respond to fear or stress

Your heart pumps faster. It sends blood to your arms and legs. Tiny **blood vessels**, called capillaries, get smaller. This makes **your blood pressure** go up. Now you can get **a surface wound** and not bleed to death.

Your body is now **supercharged**. It helps you against your enemy. You **escape** death by jumping higher and running faster than you ever could before. The danger is now over. You find a safe place to rest your tired body.

Key Vocabulary
blood vessel *noun*, a small tube in your body that carries blood from place to place
escape *verb*, to get away from something

In Other Words
your blood pressure the rate at which blood moves through your body
a surface wound an injury that is not serious
supercharged very powerful

Monitor Comprehension

Explain
What are three things your body can do better in a survival situation?

Your Body Under Stress

You sense there is danger. What happens?

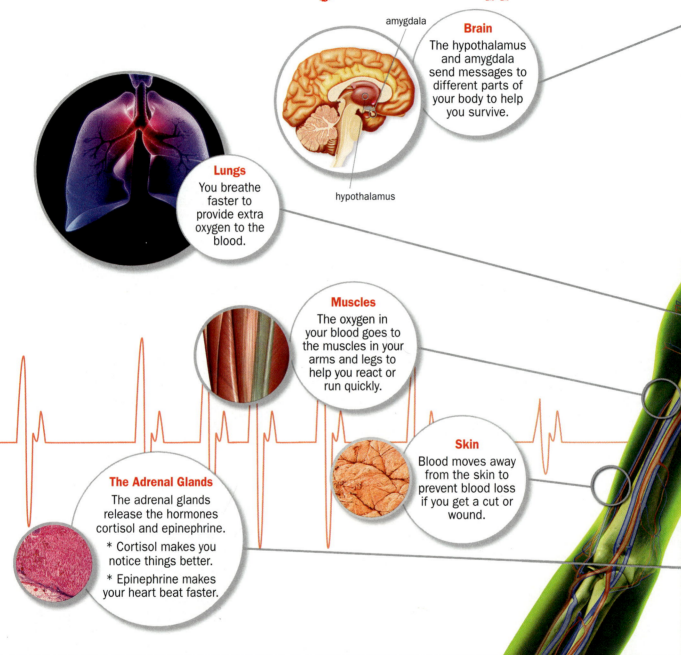

amygdala

Brain
The hypothalamus and amygdala send messages to different parts of your body to help you survive.

hypothalamus

Lungs
You breathe faster to provide extra oxygen to the blood.

Muscles
The oxygen in your blood goes to the muscles in your arms and legs to help you react or run quickly.

Skin
Blood moves away from the skin to prevent blood loss if you get a cut or wound.

The Adrenal Glands
The adrenal glands release the hormones cortisol and epinephrine.

* Cortisol makes you notice things better.

* Epinephrine makes your heart beat faster.

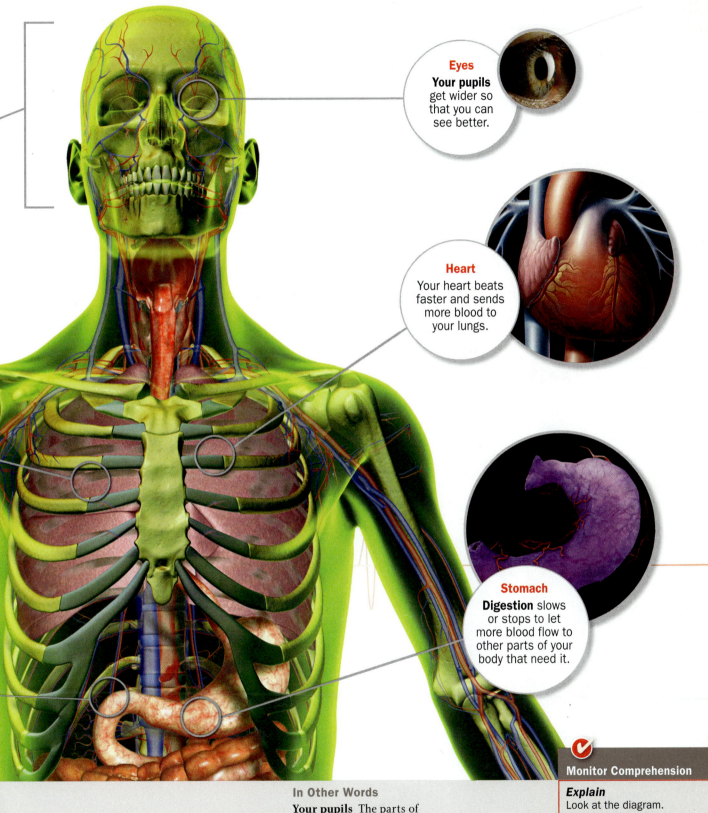

Eyes
Your pupils get wider so that you can see better.

Heart
Your heart beats faster and sends more blood to your lungs.

Stomach
Digestion slows or stops to let more blood flow to other parts of your body that need it.

In Other Words

Your pupils The parts of your eyes that let light in
Digestion The processing of food

Explain
Look at the diagram. What happens when your body senses danger?

Stand Your Ground!

Go forward to the present day. There have been a lot of changes in the past 25,000 years. **However**, you still have the same **internal** body parts as the caveman. Now you're in the lunchroom at school. You're hunting for food, but your teacher is out hunting, too. Guess what? He's hunting for you.

You hear terrifying words from your teacher. "Could I see you in my room, please?" When you see the tiger, uh, your teacher, your body reacts. Your hypothalamus sends a message to your adrenal glands. Your body turns on all the same powers that the caveman used to escape the tiger.

In Other Words
Stand Your Ground! Don't Move!
However Although this is true
internal inside

You walk down the hall to your teacher's room. You can feel your blood pressure going up. Is it the last test you turned in? Now, your mind races. Your heart **pounds**. Your mouth dries up and your hands feel cold. Your forehead <mark>perspires</mark>. You imagine **getting in trouble**. The caveman inside of you wants to come out. Maybe you'd like to run and hide. You can't. Welcome to the modern era.

Your teacher closes the door. Your body is ready **for fight or flight**. But you can't fight and you can't flee. All of that <mark>energy</mark> is inside of you with no place to go. You feel like you're going to explode. Your teacher begins to speak. "Here it comes," you think. But you're shocked by what you hear. "What did you say?" you ask your teacher.

"You have the top grade in your class," he repeats. ❖

ANALYZE Fight or Flight?

1. **Explain** Why does the author use the words "your teacher is out hunting"?

2. **Vocabulary** What does your circulatory <mark>system</mark> do when you sense <mark>danger</mark>?

3. **Reading Strategy** **Plan and Monitor** Find two or three words in the text that you needed to clarify. Talk with a partner about how you clarified the words' meanings.

Return to the Text

Reread and Retell Restate in your own words one example of your body's reaction to danger. How could this reaction help you survive a dangerous situation? Use facts from the text to support your ideas.

Key Vocabulary
<mark>perspire</mark> *verb*, to sweat
<mark>energy</mark> *noun*, the ability to move or
   be active

In Other Words
pounds beats very fast
getting in trouble your teacher is
   angry
for fight or flight to stay and
   defend itself or to run away

Text Structure: Sequence

When you know how a text is organized, it is easier to understand and remember. Some writers tell about events in the sequence, or order in which the events happened.

HOW TO IDENTIFY SEQUENCE

1. Read the text. Look for words related to time, such as *when*, *first*, *next*, and *later*.

2. Write the events in a **Sequence Chart**.

3. Use your Sequence Chart to keep track of the order of events.

Read the text and the Sequence Chart.

Look Into the Text

Accept your circumstances. "When I got to shore, I thought, 'If this isn't a dream, then I'll feel the sand. I'll feel the sun's warmth. I'll feel the heat.' I lay there for a while. But after everything I've been through, I knew I had to make myself act . . ."

* * * * * * * * *

Sit tight. "We were miles away from anyone and anything. We realized the best thing to do was prepare for the night . . ."

Time words help you keep track of the order of events.

Sequence Chart

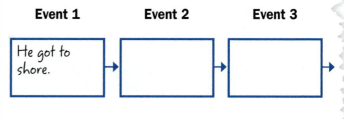

Event 1	Event 2	Event 3
He got to shore.		

Try It

Copy the Sequence Chart. Reread the text above and fill in events 2 and 3 in your chart.

As you read "Survivor Rulon Gardner: Hardheaded," record additional events in a Sequence Chart.

Connect Across Texts

In "Fight or Flight?" you learned what your body does automatically to survive. In this magazine profile, an Olympic champion tells what he has learned about survival.

Survivor Rulon Gardner: Hardheaded

by Andrea Minarcek
National Geographic Adventure

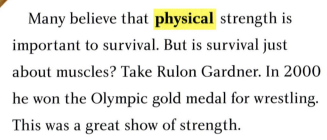

Many believe that **physical** strength is important to survival. But is survival just about muscles? Take Rulon Gardner. In 2000 he won the Olympic gold medal for wrestling. This was a great show of strength.

But in 2002, Gardner was stranded in the freezing **wilderness**. His physical strength could not help him. He lost a toe, but he survived. Then, in the winter of 2007, Gardner's plane crashed into a lake. How did he and his friends survive? Gardner explains.

Key Vocabulary
physical *adjective*, about the body

In Other Words
wilderness place far from people and things people build

Lake Powell, Utah

Take it one step at a time. "When the plane struck Lake Powell, the water was freezing. My two friends and I were two miles from shore. I'm not a great swimmer. I started **doing the backstroke**, slowly. I kept telling myself, 'Just make it to land.' That was my goal. Anything beyond that, I couldn't think about. It was too much."

Accept your circumstances. "When I got to shore, I thought, 'If this isn't a dream, then I'll feel the sand. I'll feel the sun's warmth. I'll feel the heat.' I lay there for a while. But after everything I've been through, I knew I had to make myself act. I couldn't get paralyzed by fear."

Key Vocabulary
circumstances *noun*, facts or details of a situation

In Other Words
doing the backstroke
swimming on my back

Make a game plan. "When I was wrestling, I'd work through what was about to happen. Having **positive mental imagery** beforehand gives you a plot to follow. That's what I did as soon as I got to shore."

Sit tight. "We were miles from anyone and anything. We realized the best thing to do was prepare for the night. It was **twenty-five degrees**. We tried to bask in the sun and dry our clothes. The last thing we could do was fall asleep. So we did anything and everything to keep awake."

Hypothermia

When Rulon Gardner was fighting for his life in Lake Powell, the water was freezing. His body temperature dropped below normal (**98.6° F**). This is called hypothermia.

What are the signs of hypothermia?

- Intense **shivering**
- Slow movement and confusion
- Lips, ears, fingers, and toes can turn blue

How can hypothermia be prevented?

Wearing the right clothing can help prevent hypothermia. In the water, wear a wet suit or dry suit to keep heat in your body. On land, wear a hat to keep your head warm. Since most heat is lost through your head, this is a very important step.

In Other Words

positive mental imagery pictures in your head about good things that can happen
Sit tight. Don't move.
shivering uncontrolled body shaking

twenty-five degrees –3° Celsius
98.6°F 37° Celsius

Monitor Comprehension

Explain
How did Rulon Gardner and his friends survive the plane crash?

Be glad for what you've got.

"If I started with nine lives, I think I have about two left. But, hey, that'll be enough to get me through." ❖

ANALYZE Survivor Rulon Gardner: Hardheaded

1. **Explain** Why is Rulon Gardner called a survivor?

2. **Vocabulary** What **circumstances** did Gardner decide to accept?

3. **Text Structure: Sequence** Review your **Sequence Chart** with a partner. Did you write down the same events? How did the chart improve your understanding of the text?

↩ Return to the Text

Reread and Retell What did Gardner decide to do after he swam to shore?

REFLECT AND ASSESS

▶ **Fight or Flight? What Your Body Knows About Survival**
▶ **Survivor Rulon Gardner: Hardheaded**

EQ What Does It Take to Survive?

Fluency

Listen to a reading. Practice fluency. Use the Reading Handbook, page 539.

Reading

Talk About Literature

1. Apply In what **circumstances** do people have a fight-or-flight response?

   People have a fight-or-flight response when _____ .

2. Describe How can you tell if someone has hypothermia? Describe the signs.

   A person with hypothermia _____ .

EQ 3. Speculate "Fight or Flight?" describes people's **physical** reactions to **danger**. How do you think Rulon Gardner's body reacted when his plane crashed? How did it help him survive?

Vocabulary

Review Key Vocabulary

Choose the correct vocabulary word to complete each sentence.

1. The growling dog stood ready to attack. Ana could not _____ .
2. The _____ was serious.
3. Ana wanted to run, but she was tired and had no _____ .
4. Her _____ strength went away, leaving her weak.
5. Sweat dripped down her face, and her hands began to _____ .
6. Blood raced through her circulatory _____ .
7. Her arms grew cold as the _____ in them got smaller.
8. Under the _____ , it was best for her to stay calm.

Vocabulary
- blood vessels
- circumstances
- danger
- energy
- escape
- perspire
- physical
- system

Writing

Write About Literature

EQ Opinion Statement Which is more important for survival: physical strength or mental strength? Why? Give examples from the selections to support your opinion. Use a chart to organize your thoughts.

1. State Opinion	2. Support Opinion
I think _____ is more important.	I think this because I read . . .

Grammar

Use Adverbs

An **adverb** often describes a verb. An adverb can tell how, when, or where.

Will it rain **soon**? (when)

We looked **carefully** at the clouds. (how)

Suddenly, the rain started to pour! (when)

We looked **down** at the water. (where)

Go **quickly**! (how)

Adverbs add details and bring life to your writing.

We ran. The rain poured on us.
(without adverbs)

We ran **quickly** and **effortlessly**. The rain poured **heavily** on us. (with adverbs)

Oral Practice Work with a partner. Choose a word from the box and say the sentence.

quickly	slowly	suddenly	truly	warmly

1. We ran _____ to the top of a hill.
2. I _____ thought the rain would never stop.
3. The clouds moved _____ across the sky.
4. _____, the rain stopped.
5. Then the sun started to shine _____.

Written Practice Expand these sentences. Add details with adverbs.

6. If we sense danger, we think _____.
7. We jump _____.
8. We look at things _____ from our usual way.
9. We digest our food _____.
10. We react _____ to danger.

Language Development

Give and Carry Out Commands

Learn to Survive a Power Failure Work with a partner. Use the Internet to find out what to do when the power fails. Then talk with your partner.

www.hbedge.net
- View pictures of some things that can cause a power failure.
- Learn how to prepare for a power failure.

Talk with your partner. Use commands to tell your partner what to do and what not to do during a power failure. You can start your commands like this:

- Be sure to _____.
- Call _____.
- Don't _____.
- Go _____.
- Keep _____.
- Take _____.
- Unplug _____.

> Keep a flashlight with new batteries. Don't panic. Call the power company.

Vocabulary Study

Multiple-Meaning Words

Remember, many English words have more than one meaning. The meanings are numbered in the dictionary. The entries often show different parts of speech.

> **gather** (ga-_thur_) _n._ **1** : a meeting
> _v._ **2** : to pick up or collect

The word _gather_ has more than one meaning. Read the dictionary entry above. Think about what _gather_ means in this sentence and what part of speech it is:

"While you were gathering, the tiger was hunting."

In this sentence, **gathering** is a verb. It means "collecting."

Tell which dictionary meaning fits the sentence.

1. "Luckily for you, your body has weapons that take over when you <u>sense</u> danger."

> **sense** (sens) _n._ **1** : the characteristic of having good judgment
> _v._ **2** : to be aware of something without being able to explain exactly why

2. "_What are the signs of hypothermia?_
   • Slow <u>movement</u> and confusion."

> **movement** (müv-munt) _n._ **1** : the act or process of moving **2** : a group of people with a particular set of goals **3** : one of the main parts of a piece of classical music

3. "Your <u>pupils</u> get wider so that you can see better."

> **pupil** (pyū-pul) _n._ **1** : a student **2** : part of the iris of an eye

Listening/Speaking

Act It Out

Work with a partner to act out Rulon's survival story.

www.hbedge.net
• Print the scripts of Rulon Gardner's survival story.

1. **Choose a topic.** Choose one of the scripts about Rulon Gardner's survival. Or you can write your own script.

2. **Practice the script.** Decide who will play each role. Each partner should take a part.

3. **Act out the play.** You may read your dialogue from the script.

   • **Read.** Read with expression. Think about how Rulon and his friends felt.

   • **Rehearse.** Practice your part alone and with the other actors. Try to read your part smoothly.

   • **Perform.** It's showtime! Have fun. Make the play enjoyable for your classmates, too.

1

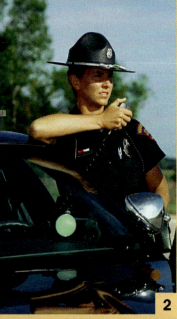

2

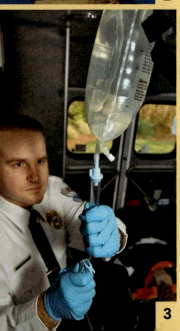

3

Public Safety Careers

Is a public safety job right for you? Take this career quiz to find out.

Career Quiz

1. In times of stress, I

ⓐ make decisions quickly.

ⓑ stay calm and try to think clearly.

ⓒ worry about what to do.

2. When things do not go well, I

ⓐ find a new solution quickly.

ⓑ take a break and try again later.

ⓒ feel frustrated.

3. Helping people in need

ⓐ interests me.

ⓑ is somewhat interesting to me.

ⓒ does not interest me very much.

Add up your points.

ⓐ = 3 points

ⓑ = 2 points

ⓒ = 1 point

What's your score?

9 points: Wow!
A public safety job seems perfect for you!

6–8 points: Maybe
A public safety job may be right for you.

3 points: No thanks
A public safety job may not be right for you. Do you know someone who would like this kind of work?

Public Safety Jobs

Here are some public safety jobs. Each job has different responsibilities and needs different education and training.

Job	Responsibilities	Education/Training Needed
Firefighter 1	· Fights and prevents fires · Helps people during fires and other accidents	· High school diploma · Associate's degree · Continuous on-the-job training
Police Officer 2	· Monitors public places for crimes or accidents · Investigates crimes	· High school diploma · Associate's degree
Emergency Medical Technician (EMT) 3	· Treats people hurt in accidents · Takes hurt people to the hospital	· High school diploma · Special training · Certificates

An EMT

Tran Nguyen takes people to the hospital in an ambulance.

Tran Nguyen is an emergency medical technician, or EMT. He describes his work in this interview.

Question: What is your workday like?

Answer: It can be stressful. We get calls about accidents. Then we rush to the scene. We work fast to help people who are hurt.

Question: What types of injuries do you treat?

Answer: Some injuries are not serious. Sometimes people suffer heart attacks. We may see people who swallowed dangerous things.

Question: What is the training like for an EMT?

Answer: Basic training teaches how to use standard equipment. There are two other levels of certification. They train EMTs on special equipment for complex injuries.

Question: What do you like most about your work?

Answer: I help people when they need it most. I save lives!

Research Public Safety Jobs

Learn more about a public safety job in the United States.

1. Choose a job from the chart on page 314.
2. Go online to **www.hbedge.net**. Read about the job you chose.
3. Complete this chart.

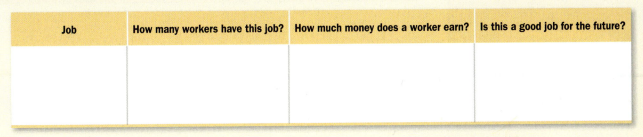

Job	How many workers have this job?	How much money does a worker earn?	Is this a good job for the future?

SURVIVAL

EQ **ESSENTIAL QUESTION:**
What Does It Take To Survive?

EDGE LIBRARY

Reflect on the Essential Question

With a group, discuss the Essential Question: What does it take to survive?

As you answer the questions, think about what you read in the selections and your choice of *Edge* Library books.

- What do we need to **survive** a dangerous situation?
- What are some ways people help others in an **emergency**?
- How can your body's survival **instincts** help you when you are in danger?

Do You Know?

1 point	**1** point	**1** point	**1** point
5 points	**5** points	**5** points	**5** points
10 points	**10** points	**10** points	**10** points
15 points	**15** points	**15** points	**15** points

Unit Review Game

You will need:

- 2, 3, or 4 players
- 1 **Do You Know?** board
- question cards
- paper to keep score
- pencil, pen, or marker

Objective: Be the player with the most points.

1. Download a **Do You Know?** board and question cards from **www.hbedge.net**. Print out and cut apart the question cards. Stack cards in four piles, according to their points.

2. **Player A** chooses a square, takes a card, and answers the question.

   - If the answer is correct, player A gets the points for that square. (If you can't agree on the answer, ask your teacher.)

   - If the answer is incorrect, every other player gets player A's points.

3. Cross out the square with an **X**.

4. **Player B** takes a turn. Then the other players take turns.

5. When all the squares are crossed out, the player with the most points is the winner.

Some events in nature can cause problems for people. For this project, you will write a paragraph to tell about a disaster in nature.

Write an Expository Paragraph

You can give information about a topic in a paragraph. Use facts, examples, and other details to explain your ideas.

1 Connect Writing to Your Life

You give people information all the time. You've probably told a friend what happened to you over the weekend. Or, maybe you've explained what a family custom or holiday is like to someone who doesn't know much about it.

2 Understand the Form

A paragraph

- starts with a topic sentence. The topic sentence tells what the paragraph is mostly about.
- presents facts, examples, and details that tell more about the topic.

Study the paragraph below. What does it explain?

Tornado Strikes Southeast
by John Martin

indent ▷ On April 28, 2008, ten tornadoes in Virginia left behind miles of destruction. The tornadoes ripped off roofs. They smashed houses. Strong winds knocked over trees. The force tossed cars around. Power lines came down. The Virginia tornadoes caused so much damage that the governor declared a state of emergency.

The **topic sentence** tells what the paragraph is mostly about.

Facts and details tell more about the topic stated in the topic sentence.

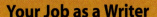

Your Job as a Writer

▶ **Prompt** Write a paragraph for an article for your classmates. Describe a disaster and what it took to survive. Be sure your paragraph has

- • a topic sentence
- • supporting facts and details.

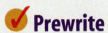

Prewrite

You've read many paragraphs. Now you can plan your own.

❶ Research and Choose a Topic

What things happen in nature and cause problems? Brainstorm a list. Do some research and find out about three disasters. List the disasters you researched. Choose one to write about.

Disasters
• flood
• fire
• earthquake

❷ Gather Details

List everything you know about the disaster. Read or talk to others to find out more. Go back to the information sources you used in step 1. Take notes. Gather any photos or images of the disaster. Think about how the details go together.

❸ Write a Topic Sentence

Look through all your details. Ask yourself:

- • Who will read my paragraph?
- • What is the most important thing I want my readers to know?

Use the answers to help you write a topic sentence.

❹ Organize Ideas

Use a **Paragraph Frame** to set up your paragraph. Add your topic sentence. Write the details that give more information about the topic.

Reflect on Your Plan

▶ Do you have enough information about your topic? Is your Paragraph Frame clearly organized?

✔ Write a Draft

Now you're ready to write! Don't worry about making mistakes. Just get down the ideas in your Paragraph Frame.

1 Start with Your Topic Sentence

Begin your paragraph with the topic sentence from your Paragraph Frame. Indent your paragraph.

Paragraph Frame

> **Topic Sentence**
> In October 1989, a powerful earthquake caused a lot of damage in San Francisco, California.

Paragraph

In October 1989, a powerful earthquake caused a lot of damage in San Francisco, California.

2 Add the Facts and Details

Turn each detail into a sentence. Add it to your paragraph. Add more facts and details from your research.

Paragraph Frame

> **Topic Sentence**
> In October 1989, a powerful earthquake caused a lot of damage in San Francisco, California.

Detail	**Detail**	**Detail**
destroyed hundreds of homes and businesses	made highways collapse	injured thousands

Paragraph

In October 1989, a powerful earthquake caused a lot of damage in San Francisco, California. The shaking destroyed hundreds of homes and businesses.

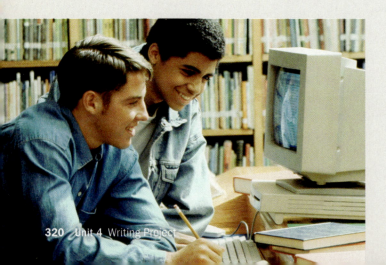

Reflect on Your Draft

▶ Did you include enough details?

✔ Revise Your Draft

A first draft isn't perfect. Make it better by revising it, or making changes to it.

1 Read Your Paragraph to a Partner

Find out what a reader thinks of your work. You can use your partner's ideas to decide how to make your writing better.

Look at this part of Emily's draft. What does her partner say about it?

> In October 1989, a powerful earthquake caused a lot of damage in San Francisco, California. The shaking destroyed hundreds of homes and businesses. ==Golden Gate Bridge is in San Francisco.== The top part of a busy freeway collapsed. Walls came apart. Windows shattered.

"Why did you talk about the **Golden Gate Bridge**?"

"Are these **sentences** in the right place?"

2 Decide What to Change

Think about your partner's comments. Then decide what you want to change.

3 Mark Your Changes

If you need to take out text, use this mark: ℓ

If you need to move text, use this mark: ↶⟲

> In October 1989, a powerful earthquake caused a lot of damage in San Francisco, California. The shaking destroyed hundreds of homes and businesses. ~~Golden Gate Bridge is in San Francisco.~~ The top part of a busy freeway collapsed. Walls came apart. Windows shattered. Cars were crushed underneath it. Thousands of people in the city were injured. The San Francisco earthquake was a disaster, but survivors began rebuilding right away.

Emily took out the detail about the Golden Gate Bridge.

Emily moved sentences so they are closer to the idea they are about.

Reflect on Your Revisions

▶ Think about your review. What are some of your strengths as a writer? What are some things that are giving you trouble?

✓ Edit and Proofread

Your revision is complete. Now it's time to proofread it to find and fix any mistakes that you made. Use these tips to make your paragraph perfect.

1 Use the Correct Verb Tense

Remember that to show that an action happened in the past, you use past tense verbs. With regular past tense verbs, add **-ed** to talk about the past. Irregular verbs use special forms.

When you write, keep your verbs in the same tense so your reader won't get confused about when things happen.

> The earthquake happened during the 1989 World Series. Most fans were in their seats when it ~~starts~~ started. They ~~feel~~ felt the stadium move.

2 Check Your Spelling

Circle each word that may not be spelled right. Look it up in the dictionary or ask for help. Fix the spelling if you need to.

3 Check for Capital Letters

When you use a proper noun, always capitalize it.

Proper Nouns	Examples
Proper nouns include the following:	
• months, days, special days, and holidays	**October Sunday Thanksgiving**
• names of places	**Pacific Garden Mall Santa Cruz**

4 Mark Your Changes

∧	ℛ	⌐	◯	≡	╱	¶
Add.	Take out.	Replace with this.	Check spelling.	Capitalize.	Make lowercase.	Make new paragraph.

Reflect on Your Corrections

▶ Note any errors you made. Make a list. Remember them the next time you write something.

Publish, Share, and Reflect

Publish and Share

You are now ready to publish your paragraph. Print or write a clean copy. Add photos and captions. Collect the class paragraphs to publish a disaster magazine.

Read your paragraph aloud to your class.

> ## HOW TO READ YOUR WORK ALOUD
>
> 1. **Practice Your Presentation** Try reading your paragraph to yourself in front of a mirror. Then you can see how you look and what you sound like. Or read it aloud to a friend or family member. Ask how you can make the presentation better.
>
> 2. **Look at Your Audience** As you read, don't hide your face behind your paper. Look up from time to time as you read.
>
> 3. **Speak at the Right Pace** Don't rush. Speak at a steady pace so your audience has time to think about what you are saying. That way they'll be able to better understand the facts and details you are sharing about your topic.
>
> 4. **Use the Right Volume** Speak loudly enough for everyone to hear. Talk to the people in the middle or the back of the room, not just the people in the front row.

Reflect on Your Work

▶ Think about your writing.

- What did you learn about writing that you didn't know before?

- What did you like best about writing a paragraph?

☑ **Save a copy of your work in your portfolio.**

FITTING IN

EQ **ESSENTIAL QUESTION:**

How Important Is It To Fit In?

Better to be wrong with everyone
than right by yourself.

—Moorish Proverb

Dance alone and you can jump
as much as you want to.

—Greek Proverb

How Important Is It to Fit In?

Study the Graph

What does it tell you about fitting in?

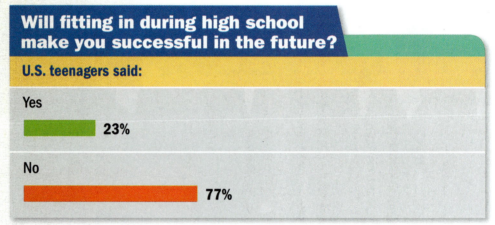

Will fitting in during high school make you successful in the future?

U.S. teenagers said:

Yes

23%

No

77%

Source: Teen Ink, March 2005

EQ **ESSENTIAL QUESTION**

In this unit, you will explore the **Essential Question** in class. Think about the question outside of school, too.

1 Study the Concept

At school, I try hard to **belong**. I think it's important to fit in.

I **believe** that most people worry about fitting in.

People make **judgments** about you based on how you look. I believe that is wrong.

—Jenna, 15

1. Do you **believe** it is normal to try to fit in?

2. What do some people do to **belong**?

3. How do you feel about making **judgments** about others based on their looks?

2 Choose More to Read

Choose something to read during this unit.

Frankenstein
by Mary Shelley
adapted by Larry Weinberg

A scientist creates a terrifying monster. No one knows that the monster just wants to fit in.

▶ **FICTION**

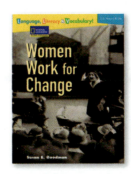

Women Work for Change
by Susan E. Goodman

In early America, women had few rights. And they could not vote for laws to gain rights. They believed that getting their rights was more important than fitting in. Find out how women finally won the right to vote.

▶ **NONFICTION**

www.hbedge.net
- Read how teens feel about fitting in.
- Read a cartoon about fitting in.

Use Context Clues

Context clues are words on the page that can help you figure out the meaning
of a word. There are different kinds of context clues.

Type of Clue	Description	Signal Words	Example
Definition clue	Explains what the word means	*is, are, was, refers to, means*	To **survive** *means* to live.
Restatement clue	Gives the meaning in a different way, usually after a comma	*or*	High school can be **overwhelming**, *or* stressful.
Example clue	Gives an example of what the word means	*such as, for example, including*	Deaf people have their own **culture**. *For example*, they have their own language.
Synonym clue	Gives a word or phrase that means almost the same thing	*like, also*	Cochlear implants, *like* other **devices**, have a special purpose.
Antonym clue	Gives a word or phrase that means the opposite	*but, unlike*	I am **popular** at school, *but* I get no attention at home.

When you read, you may find a word you do not know. Use context clues to
figure out the word's meaning.

• Read the words nearby. Look for signal words.

• Predict what the word means.

• Try out the predicted meaning to see if it makes sense.

Practice Using Context Clues

Use context clues to figure out the meaning of each underlined word.

1. Lori was <u>puzzled</u>, or very confused.

2. Like his other <u>talkative</u> friends, Mike usually talked a lot.

3. But he was <u>silent</u> today. For example, he didn't even speak at lunch.

4. Lori was <u>concerned</u>, but her other friends didn't seem to care.

Put the Strategy to Use

Work with a partner. Figure out the meaning of each underlined word.

5. For Lori, <u>friendship</u> meant caring about others.

6. "I feel <u>excluded</u>," Mike said. "You never invite me to spend time with you."

7. Lori was sorry, but she didn't know how to <u>apologize</u>.

8. "How about this?" she <u>inquired</u>. "Let's walk home together right now!"

Express Intentions

Listen to the chant. What will this person do?

1 TRY OUT LANGUAGE
2 LEARN GRAMMAR
3 APPLY ON YOUR OWN

Chant

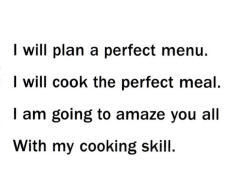

What Will I Do for You?

I will plan a perfect menu.
I will cook the perfect meal.
I am going to amaze you all
With my cooking skill.

I will make a special smoothie
That is better than ice cream.
I promise it will taste so good
You will not think it's real!

Language Workshop, continued

1 TRY OUT LANGUAGE
2 LEARN GRAMMAR
3 APPLY ON YOUR OWN

Use Verbs in the Future Tense

The tense, or time, of a verb shows when an action happens.

PAST — PRESENT — FUTURE

(before now) — (now) — (after now)

Use the **future tense** to tell about something that will happen later. To form the future tense, add **will** before the main verb.

Tomorrow I **will fix** dinner for my parents.

I **will be** careful.

Everything **will taste** great.

Say It

Work with a partner. Say the sentence. Then have your partner say the sentence in the future tense.

1. I take cooking lessons.

2. I become a better cook.

3. I invite my friend to my house for dinner.

4. She finds a big surprise at my house.

5. She loves my cooking.

Write It

Change the verb in parentheses to tell about the future. Write the sentence.

6. I _____ some black bean soup. (make)

7. I _____ a pie for dessert. (bake)

8. Elena _____ everything I make. (like)

9. She _____ a fine meal. (enjoy)

10. She _____ so happy! (be)

Talk About Plans

Work with a partner. Imagine that the two of you are preparing the food for a big party or picnic. Make your plans and report them to the class.

Follow these tips when you tell someone what you plan to do:

HOW TO EXPRESS INTENTIONS

1. Decide what you will do.

> We **will divide** the work.
> I **will go** to the store.
> What **will** you **do**?

You can use **future tense** to express intentions.

2. Give facts and details.

> I **will get** some ice. I **will find** bags of ice that fit in the cooler. We **will need** about six bags of ice.

To make your plans, talk to your partner and decide

- how you will work together
- what each of you will do
- how you will do the task

Then report your plans to the class.

They plan what they will do.

EQ How Important Is It to Fit In?
Think about when it is worth it to try to fit in.

Learn Key Vocabulary

Pronounce each word and learn its meaning.

Key Words

agreement (u-**grē**-munt) *noun*
▶ pages 339, 341

When you are in **agreement**, you have the same opinion, ideas, or beliefs. They are in **agreement** about the dress.

alone (u-**lōn**) *adverb*
▶ page 346

When you are **alone**, no one is with you. He does homework **alone**.

arrive (u-**rīv**) *verb*
▶ page 340

To **arrive** means to reach a place. She **arrives** home.

exotic (ig-**zah**-tik) *adjective*
▶ page 343

If something is **exotic**, you do not see, hear, or do it often. This fish's fins make it look **exotic**.

jealous (**je**-lus) *adjective*
▶ page 345

When you are **jealous**, you are unhappy because you want something that someone else has.

ordinary (**or**-du-nair-ē) *adjective*
▶ page 343

Something you see, hear, or do often is **ordinary**. On an **ordinary** Monday, these students go to school.

prepare (pri-**pair**) *verb*
▶ page 336

To **prepare** means to make ready. These sisters **prepare** a meal. *Synonym:* make

suggest (sug-**jest**) *verb*
▶ page 339

When you **suggest** something, you say it is possible. She **suggests** a place to go.

Practice the Words Use each word in a **Vocabulary Example Chart**. Write a definition and a sentence that give an example from your life.

Vocabulary Example Chart

Word	Definition	Example
alone	by yourself	I go to the park to be alone.

BEFORE READING Frijoles

novel excerpt by Gary Soto

Make Connections

Sometimes, what you read reminds you of something in your own life. When you **make connections**, you relate things from your own experience to ideas and information in the text. This improves your understanding of the text.

HOW TO MAKE CONNECTIONS

1. Read the text. Look for ideas that remind you of past experiences.

2. Ask, "Have I ever lived through anything like this?"

3. Write your connection on a self-stick note. Place it next to the text you are making a connection to.

4. Think about how the connection improves your understanding of the text.

Read the text and the self-stick note.

Look Into the Text

For the past three hours, Lincoln and Tony had been preparing the food. They cooked the beans and smashed them into *frijoles.* They chopped chilies, onions, and tomatoes for salsa. They made dough into tortillas. Now they brought the rest of the food to the table and joined their host family.

> I cooked for my family once. I wanted it to taste good. They probably feel the same way.

Try It

Reread the text above and make your own connection. Work with a partner. Compare your connections.

As you read "Frijoles," make connections. Think about how they help you understand Lincoln and Tony's experience.

Build Background

In "Frijoles," two teenage boys are discovering what it is like to live in a completely different culture. They are living in Japan.

The boys are taking part in a foreign **exchange program**. These "foreign exchange" students travel to other countries where they live with local families. The families are called "host families." They agree to take care of the students for a certain period of time, usually for several months. They help the students learn a new language and culture.

Every year, high school students around the world take part in foreign exchange programs. They are a small but important way that people of the world can share their lives with each other.

www.hbedge.net
- Learn about the author.
- Read about Japanese culture.

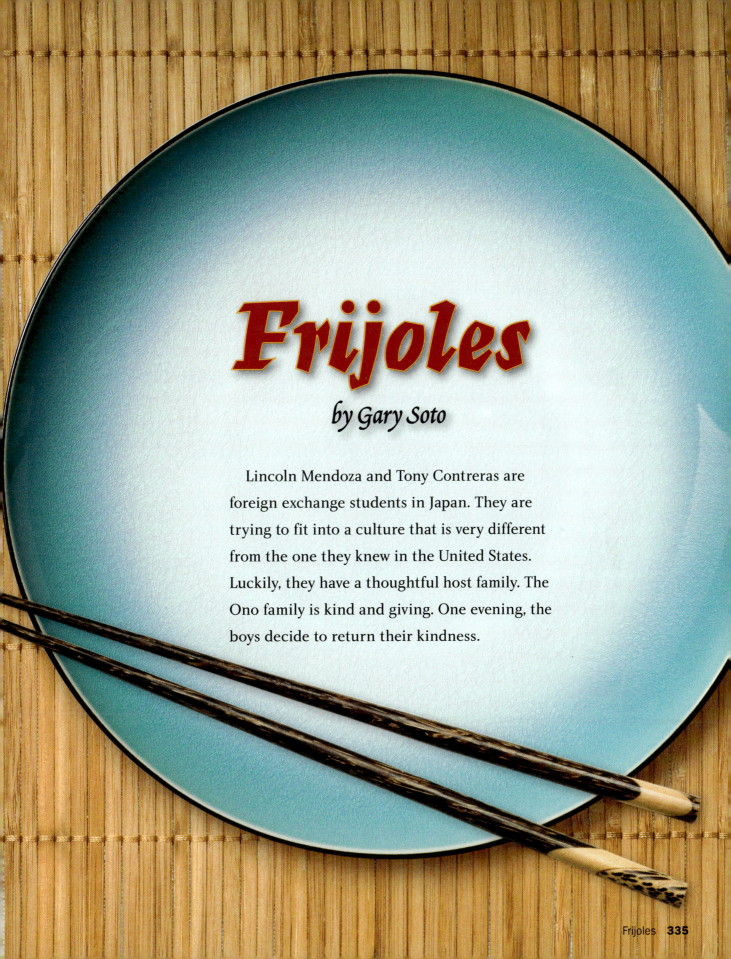

Frijoles

by Gary Soto

Lincoln Mendoza and Tony Contreras are foreign exchange students in Japan. They are trying to fit into a culture that is very different from the one they knew in the United States. Luckily, they have a thoughtful host family. The Ono family is kind and giving. One evening, the boys decide to return their kindness.

Lincoln and Tony are making a special meal for their hosts, the Ono family. Find out if the Onos like it.

Mr. Ono **raised** his dinner plate to his face and studied the *frijoles* curiously. "I know this smell," he said. He moved a **chopstick** across the plate. Then he sucked on the end. "I know this taste," he concluded.

"How can you know?" Mrs. Ono said.

"I just *know*," he answered. "I am an international eater." Mrs. Ono **rolled her eyes**. She got up to check on the boys in the kitchen.

For the past three hours, Lincoln and Tony had been **preparing** the food. They cooked the beans and smashed them into *frijoles*. They **chopped** chilies, onions, and tomatoes for salsa. They made dough into tortillas. Now they brought the rest of the food to the table and joined their host family.

Key Vocabulary
prepare *verb*, to make ready

In Other Words
raised lifted
frijoles cooked beans (in Spanish)
chopstick small stick used for eating
rolled her eyes moved her eyes to show that she didn't believe him
chopped cut

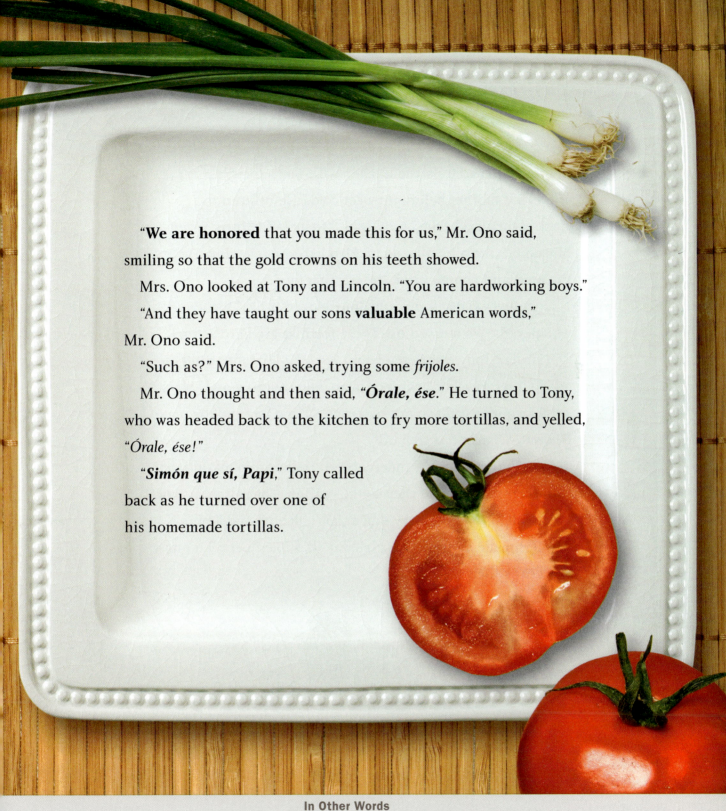

"**We are honored** that you made this for us," Mr. Ono said, smiling so that the gold crowns on his teeth showed.

Mrs. Ono looked at Tony and Lincoln. "You are hardworking boys."

"And they have taught our sons **valuable** American words," Mr. Ono said.

"Such as?" Mrs. Ono asked, trying some *frijoles*.

Mr. Ono thought and then said, *"Órale, ése."* He turned to Tony, who was headed back to the kitchen to fry more tortillas, and yelled, *"Órale, ése!"*

"Simón que sí, Papi," Tony called back as he turned over one of his homemade tortillas.

In Other Words

We are honored We feel good
valuable important
Órale, ése. Come on, man. (Spanish slang)
Simón que sí, Papi Yeah, for sure, Dad
(Spanish slang)

Tony returned from the kitchen with warm tortillas. "Here, try another before they get cold." He **offered** the stack of tortillas to the Onos' sons, Mitsuo and Toshi. When Mitsuo bit into a tortilla, it crackled like a potato chip. He **grunted and commented**, "Interesting food."

Lincoln looked at Tony, and Tony looked back. Lincoln **whispered**, "We **messed up**. These tortillas are hard as rocks."

"Harder," Tony whispered back. "And the avocados **ain't** any good either. Five bucks **apiece**, man, and they're mostly black."

"**No wonder** you two are so strong," Mrs. Ono said, trying to be kind. "The food is so hard."

Even the *frijoles* were undercooked. They had to mash them with their teeth before they could **swallow**. The salsa was more like ketchup than the fiery sauce that Lincoln's and Tony's mothers made. But the Onos tried it all, smiled between bites, and drank their tea.

In Other Words

offered gave
grunted and commented made a noise and said
whispered said very quietly
messed up made a mistake (slang)

ain't are not (slang)
apiece each
No wonder It is not a surprise that
swallow eat them

Monitor Comprehension

Describe
In your own words, describe how the food looks, smells, and tastes.

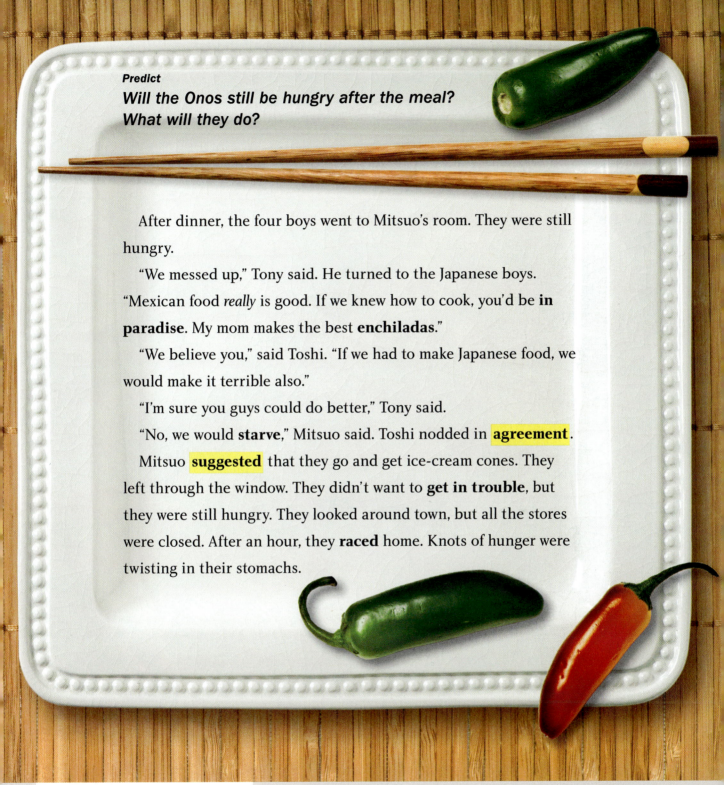

Predict
***Will the Onos still be hungry after the meal?
What will they do?***

After dinner, the four boys went to Mitsuo's room. They were still hungry.

"We messed up," Tony said. He turned to the Japanese boys. "Mexican food *really* is good. If we knew how to cook, you'd be **in paradise**. My mom makes the best **enchiladas**."

"We believe you," said Toshi. "If we had to make Japanese food, we would make it terrible also."

"I'm sure you guys could do better," Tony said.

"No, we would **starve**," Mitsuo said. Toshi nodded in <mark>agreement</mark>. Mitsuo <mark>suggested</mark> that they go and get ice-cream cones. They left through the window. They didn't want to **get in trouble**, but they were still hungry. They looked around town, but all the stores were closed. After an hour, they **raced** home. Knots of hunger were twisting in their stomachs.

Key Vocabulary

<mark>agreement</mark> *noun*, having the same opinion, ideas, or beliefs

<mark>suggest</mark> *verb*, to say something is possible

In Other Words

in paradise so happy
enchiladas corn tortillas stuffed with cheese, meat, or beans
starve not eat at all
get in trouble cause problems
raced hurried

They **arrived** just in time. Mr. and Mrs. Ono were frying a fish that was nearly as large as a guitar. A new pot of rice was steaming. The tea was simmering, and icy bottles of *ramune* were waiting. Then, at a quarter to ten, with the moon hanging like a **sickle** in the sky, the *fiesta* really began. ❖

In Other Words
ramune carbonated lemon-lime drink (in Japan)
sickle curved farming tool
fiesta party (in Spanish)

ANALYZE Frijoles

1. **Confirm Prediction** Did the Onos do what you predicted they would do? If so, what clues helped you predict correctly?

2. **Vocabulary** Do you think that Lincoln and Tony were in **agreement** about how their food tasted? How do you know?

3. **Reading Strategy Make Connections** Think about a time when you did something nice for someone. How did you feel? How do you think Lincoln felt as they cooked dinner for the Onos? Describe how you think the boys felt. Use examples from your own life.

Return to the Text

Reread and Retell In what ways do Lincoln and Tony try to fit into the Ono family? Reread the story to find details to support your answer.

Genre: Fable

A **fable** is a fictional story that teaches a moral, or a lesson. A fable often has animals as characters. A fable is different from most stories because it tells readers the moral it is trying to teach. As you read, make connections between how the characters behave and how people in real life behave.

> ### HOW TO INTERPRET FABLES
>
> **1.** As you read the story, think about how the characters act like people you know.
>
> **2.** Read the moral and think about how it connects to the story.
>
> **3.** Decide how the story and its moral connects to your experiences.

Read the text. See how one reader interprets the fable.

Look Into the Text

The jay decided to go back to his own kind. He flew across the field to his old home. But when he got there, the other jays were angry.

"We saw what you did," they said. "You wanted to be a peacock. Well, this is no home for you!" They chased him away, too.

The jay spent his life alone—without a friend and without a home.

MORAL: Be true to yourself or you may lose the respect of others. ❖

> Like the jays, people often get angry when others try to act superior.

> I lost respect for my friend when she started acting like she was better than everyone.

Try It

Read "The Jay and the Peacocks." Make connections to the main character and the moral. Then discuss the moral with a partner. Compare your connections.

Connect Across Texts

In "Frijoles," Tony and Lincoln do something special in order to fit in with the Ono family. In this fable, a bird does something special, too.

the Jay and the Peacocks

Based on the fable by Aesop • Illustrated by Keith Baker

One day, an <mark>ordinary</mark> jaybird flew by a farm. There he saw a **flock of peacocks**.

To the jay, the <mark>exotic</mark> peacocks seemed to have a perfect life. They had good food to eat from a birdfeeder. They had cool water to drink from a lovely **pond**. Their colorful feathers caught the sunlight like a rainbow. The peacocks seemed very **content**.

Key Vocabulary
<mark>ordinary</mark> *adjective*, something you see, hear, or do often
<mark>exotic</mark> *adjective*, something you do not see, hear, or do often

In Other Words
flock of peacocks group of birds with long, colorful feathers
pond small lake
content happy

The jay felt **jealous**. He looked at his own plain feathers. He thought of his own **boring** home. He wished he could live like a peacock.

Suddenly, the jay noticed something shiny lying along the path. The peacocks had dropped a few of their beautiful, long feathers. "I know what to do!" he said to himself. "I will make myself look like a peacock. Then I'll be as happy as they are." He tied the feathers to his tail. He practiced walking **as proudly as** a peacock.

The next day, the jay joined the flock. Because of his beautiful new feathers, he **fit right in**. He ate the good food from the birdfeeder. He drank the cool water from the pond. As long as he kept his secret, the jay belonged to the flock. He finally felt content with his life.

In Other Words

boring uninteresting
as proudly as like he felt good about himself as
fit right in seemed like the peacocks

Monitor Comprehension

Explain
Why does the jay pretend to be a peacock?

One day, a strong wind blew through the farm. As the peacocks watched, **the jay's false feathers** blew away. The peacocks were **furious**.

"You are not one of us!" they cried. "It takes more than fine feathers to make a fine bird!" They **pecked** the jay over and over.

The jay decided to go back to his own kind. He flew across the field to his old home. But when he got there, the other jays were angry.

"We saw what you did," they said. "You wanted to be a peacock. Well, this is no home for you!" They chased him away, too.

The jay spent his life **alone**—without a friend and without a home.

MORAL: Be true to yourself, or you may lose the respect of others. ❖

ANALYZE The Jay and the Peacocks

1. **Explain** How do the peacocks discover that the jay is not a peacock?

2. **Vocabulary** Why does the jay spend the rest of his life **alone**?

3. **Interpret Fables** What does this fable teach you about life? Do you agree with the lesson?

↩ **Return to the Text**

Reread and Retell The peacocks tell the jay, "It takes more than fine feathers to make a fine bird!" Retell what this means in your own words.

Key Vocabulary
alone *adverb*, by yourself

In Other Words
the jay's false feathers the feathers the jay had tied to his tail
furious very angry
pecked bit
MORAL: The lesson you can learn from the story is this:

EQ How Important Is It to Fit In?

Reading
Talk About Literature

1. Analyze In "Frijoles," Mrs. Ono bites the hard tortilla that Lincoln and Tony made. She says, "No wonder you two are so strong." What does she mean?

2. Interpret When the jay pretended to be a peacock, he "finally felt content with his life." What does this tell us about the jay? Explain.

> I think the jay felt _____. I think this because _____.

EQ 3. Explain Lincoln and Tony in "Frijoles" and the jay in "The Jay and the Peacocks" do different things to fit in. What do Lincoln and Tony do? What does the jay do? What do they learn about fitting in?

> In "Frijoles," Lincoln and Tony _____ to fit in with their host family. In "The Jay and the Peacocks," the jay _____ to fit in with the peacocks. They learn _____.

Fluency
Listen to a reading. Practice fluency. Use the Reading Handbook, page 540.

Vocabulary
Review Key Vocabulary

Choose the correct vocabulary word to complete each sentence.

1. Carmen sits in her room, _____, looking at herself in the mirror.
2. She decides that she is tired of her hairstyle. She thinks it is boring and _____.
3. Carmen often feels _____ of girls with interesting, stylish hair.
4. She wants her hair to be unusual and _____.
5. "What do you _____ I do about it?" Carmen asks her mom.
6. "_____ a list of ways we can change your hair," her mom says.
7. Carmen nods in _____. "Yes, then we can decide which way is best."
8. "Great! When I _____ home tomorrow night, we'll talk about your list."

Vocabulary
- agreement
- alone
- arrive
- exotic
- jealous
- ordinary
- prepare
- suggest

Writing
Write About Literature

Analysis What happens when you try to fit in? Use examples from the selections. Organize your thoughts in a **Cause-and-Effect Chain**. Then write a sentence to summarize your thoughts.

Cause-and-Effect Chain

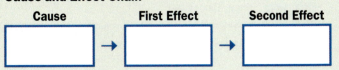

Cause	First Effect	Second Effect

Use Verb Tenses

PAST	PRESENT	FUTURE
(before now)	(now)	(after now)

The **tense** of a verb tells when an action happens. Use the correct form of a verb to show that the action is in **past**, **present**, or **future** time.

- Use the **past tense** for an action before now. Add **-ed** or use a special form.

  > The jay **wanted** to be like the peacocks.
  > He **made** a fake tail for himself.

- Use the **present tense** for an action that is happening now or that happens again and again. Add **-s** to the verb when you talk about one other person or one thing.

  > He just **wants** to fit in!
  > He **makes** trips to the river every day.

- Use the **future tense** to show that something is going to happen later. Use **will** before the main verb.

  > The jay **will want** the friendship of other jays.
  > He **will make** friends again someday.

Oral Practice Work with a partner. Say each sentence. Change the <u>verb</u> to the tense in parentheses.

1. Birds usually <u>lived</u> with others of their kind. (present)
2. The jay in the story <u>goes</u> with the peacocks. (past)
3. He <u>pretends</u> to be a peacock! (past)
4. One day, his fake tail feathers <u>fall</u> out. (past)
5. The peacocks <u>discover</u> his secret! (future)

Written Practice Fix the mistake in the <u>verb</u> and write the sentence.

6. My friend Mike <u>want</u> to be a professional writer.
7. Last week, he <u>writed</u> a story about animals.
8. The teacher <u>telled</u> him his story was excellent.
9. Yesterday, Mike <u>thinks</u> of another story.
10. My friend <u>become</u> famous a few years later!

Express Intentions

Make Plans for Summer What are you planning to do next summer? Work with a partner. Learn about different summer activities.

www.hbedge.net
- Watch a video about teen volunteers.
- Explore summer jobs for teens.

Choose an activity or job that interests you. Make a plan. Tell your partner what you plan to do this summer. Listen as your partner tells you his or her plans.

> I will work at my uncle's business next summer.

> Really? What kind of work will you do?

Use Synonym and Antonym Clues

When you come to an unfamiliar word in the text, look for context clues to explain the meaning. A synonym clue uses a word or phrase that is almost the same as the unfamiliar word. An antonym clue gives a word or phrase that means the opposite of the unfamiliar word.

"The salsa was more like ketchup than the fiery sauce that Lincoln's and Tony's mothers made."

> Salsa is a fiery sauce when the characters' mothers make it. Salsa must be a kind of sauce.

Use the context clues to help figure out the meaning of each underlined word.

1. Lincoln and Tony are trying to fit into a different culture, or way of life.

2. They want to show their gratitude, or thanks.

3. Their cooking experience is insufficient. It is not enough.

4. They leave the table still starving, not full and satisfied.

Country Profile

In "Frijoles," the characters travel to another country as part of a foreign exchange program. Think of countries that you would like to visit.

1. Choose a country to research.

2. Gather facts. 🍃 **Language and Learning Handbook**, page 510.

3. Make a poster to share what you learn. Include a map, drawings or pictures, and written information about the country.

4. Present your poster to your class. Explain what each piece of information tells about the country.

www.hbedge.net
- Gather information about different countries.
- See foods from different countries.

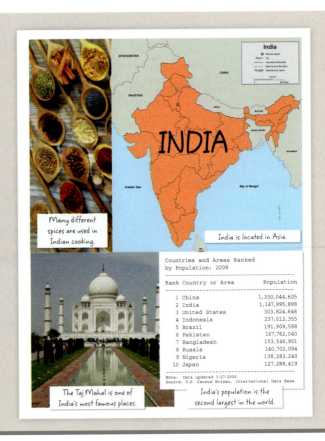

Many different spices are used in Indian cooking.

India is located in Asia.

The Taj Mahal is one of India's most famous places.

Countries and Areas Ranked by Population: 2008

Rank	Country or Area	Population
1	China	1,330,044,605
2	India	1,147,995,898
3	United States	303,824,646
4	Indonesia	237,512,355
5	Brazil	191,908,598
6	Pakistan	167,762,040
7	Bangladesh	153,546,901
8	Russia	140,702,094
9	Nigeria	138,283,240
10	Japan	127,288,419

Note: Data updated 3-27-2008.
Source: U.S. Census Bureau, International Data Base.

India's population is the second largest in the world.

Writing

Write a Letter to a Pen Pal

▶ **Prompt** The characters in "Frijoles" and "The Jay and the Peacocks" meet different people. Who would you like to meet? Write a letter to a pen pal, a friend that you write to.

1 Plan Find a pen pal, if you do not have one already. Think about what you will write. Read the model letter below.

www.hbedge.net
• Learn how you can find a pen pal.

> September 20, 2008 ◁ **date**
>
> Dear Gustavo,
>
>   I was so happy to receive your letter last week. I'm glad to hear that you're doing well.
>
>   School started two weeks ago. It's OK. I haven't made any friends yet. The kids here seem really different.
>
>   Next week I will try out for the basketball team. I remember your advice to get more involved. Maybe that will help me fit in. I'll let you know what happens.
>
>   Your pal,
>   Lani

Use a friendly greeting like "Dear" or "Hi."

A letter to a pen pal is friendly. It gives personal information and tells about recent events.

Use a friendly closing like "Your friend" or "Your pal."

2 Write If your pen pal is new, tell him or her about yourself. If you already have a pen pal, write about what is happening in your life. Be sure to use the correct verb tenses in your letter.

- Use the present tense to tell about an action that happens often.
- Use the past tense to tell about something that happened before now.
- Use the future tense to tell about an action that has not yet happened. Use **will** before the main verb to tell about an event in the future.

      I **will** try out for the basketball team.

3 Share Send the letter to your pen pal.

Use sentences like these:

- How are you? I am fine.

- Since I got your last letter, [Tell what you did].

- Next week, I will [Tell what you will do].

- By the time you read this, [Tell what will happen soon].

Express Opinions

Sandra and Hugo want to be class president. Listen to each student's speech.

Speech

VOTE FOR ME!

"I think my experience will help me be a great school president.

First, I am captain of the school dance team. Last May, I helped our team win a dance competition.

Second, I talk to many students about their problems and ideas.

Finally, I work with teachers to plan activities. For example, I helped organize Crazy Photo Day.

In my opinion, I am the best person for the job. "

"I think I will be a better school president than Sandra.

First, I have more student government experience. I am class treasurer this year.

Second, I started a new club for people with hearing problems.

Third, I have real-world work experience as a cashier.

I strongly believe that my school and work experience make me the better candidate. Thank you. "

1 TRY OUT LANGUAGE
2 LEARN GRAMMAR
3 APPLY ON YOUR OWN

Use Prepositions

Use **prepositions** to tell about the location of one thing compared to another. Some common prepositions are **in**, **on**, **over**, **under**, and **next to**.

The flag is **over** the white board.

Supplies are **in** the cabinet.

Her arm is **on** the desk.

Her backpack is **next to** the desk.

Her feet are **under** the desk.

Say It

Work with a partner. Look around the classroom. Say a sentence with each preposition about something you see in the classroom.

1. over   **2.** in   **3.** on   **4.** under   **5.** next to

Write It

Add a preposition from the box to complete each sentence. Then write the complete sentence.

| over | in | on | under | next to |

6. I see a book _____ the desk.

7. I have a pen _____ my pocket.

8. The poster is _____ the wall.

9. My friend is sitting _____ me.

10. There is a backpack _____ the floor.

Say What You Think

Think about three different clubs at your school. What are your opinions of these clubs? Discuss them with a partner. Prepare to report your opinions to the class.

Follow these tips to express your opinions clearly:

HOW TO EXPRESS OPINIONS

1. Say what you think. Use expressions like *I think*, *I believe*, and *in my opinion*.

> I like the Deaf Club a lot. I think it's the best club **in** the school.

Use a preposition to give a location.

2. Give reasons for your opinion.

> People **in** the club really understand me. I feel like I fit in there.

To get ready to present your opinions, work with a partner. Choose three clubs that you both know something about. For each club, discuss

- the things you like about the club
- why you like those things
- the things you don't like about the club
- why you don't like those things.

"I think the science club has the greatest value. We prepare for the science fair. Also, we have fun!"

How Important Is It to Fit In?
Learn what makes people feel good about themselves.

Learn Key Vocabulary

Pronounce each word and learn its meaning.

Key Words

attention (u-**ten**-shun) *noun*
▶ pages 369, 370

When you get **attention**, people notice you. The dancer has everyone's **attention**.

device (di-**vīs**) *noun*
▶ page 358

A **device** is a tool for a certain job. A calculator is a **device** that helps you do math.

disability (dis-u-**bi**-lu-tē) *noun*
▶ pages 356, 358, 364

A **disability** is a condition that stops you from doing something that most people can do.

disadvantage
(dis-ud-**van**-tij) *noun*
▶ page 362

A **disadvantage** is something that makes life more difficult for one person than it is for others.

identify (ī-**den**-tu-fī) *verb*
▶ pages 356, 368, 370

When you **identify** with a group or idea, you connect with it. The teammates **identify** with each other.

separate (**se**-pu-rāt) *verb*
▶ page 361

To **separate** means to keep things apart. We **separate** plastics, cans, and paper for recycling.

situation (si-chu-**wā**-shun) *noun*
▶ page 361

A **situation** is a set of events or circumstances. A traffic jam is a bad **situation**.

social (**sō**-shul) *adjective*
▶ pages 368, 370

Social means with other people. I love to spend time with my friends because I am **social**.

Practice the Words Make a **Definition Map** for three Key Vocabulary words.

Definition Map

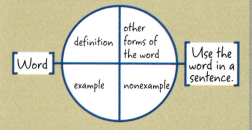

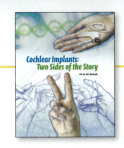

Make Connections

When you read a persuasive essay, it is important to **make connections** between your own experience and the opinions, or beliefs and ideas, of the writer. Making connections helps you understand the writer's opinions. It can also help you form your own opinions.

HOW TO MAKE CONNECTIONS

1. As you read, ask "What do the writer's ideas and experiences remind me of? Do they remind me of something I experienced or heard about?"

2. Compare the writer's opinion with your own experience. Write your connections on self-stick notes.

3. When you are done reading, use your connections to help you decide whether you agree with the writer.

Read the text and self-stick notes.

Look Into the Text

Good morning. My name is Caitlin Parton. I've had my cochlear implant for nine years, and I love it. It's helping me a lot.

I think it's important to have the implant as a choice for people who are deaf. It brings you into the hearing world, the world of sound. I wear this miracle of modern science. I'm a little different, but I'm a lot like everyone else, too.

> I remember when I had to make an important choice about . . .

> Right now I agree that people who are deaf should have a choice to hear or not.

Try It

As you read the following persuasive essays, use self-stick notes to make connections to the writers' ideas and opinions. Share your connections with a partner. Explain whether or not you agree with the writers.

Build Background

There are many different cultures in the world. People usually think that *culture* refers to the country or area you come from or the ethnic group you identify with. But many deaf people see deafness as part of their culture.

People of the same culture often speak the same language. Deaf people all over the world also have their own languages. They are called sign languages. In the United States, most deaf people use American Sign Language, or ASL, for short.

Like all cultures, deaf people have their own customs, or ways of doing things. People who **identify** with deaf culture may or may not be deaf. What they have in common is that they view deafness as a difference and not a **disability**.

These women are using American Sign Language to communicate.

www.hbedge.net
- Learn about deaf culture.
- View the American Sign Language alphabet.

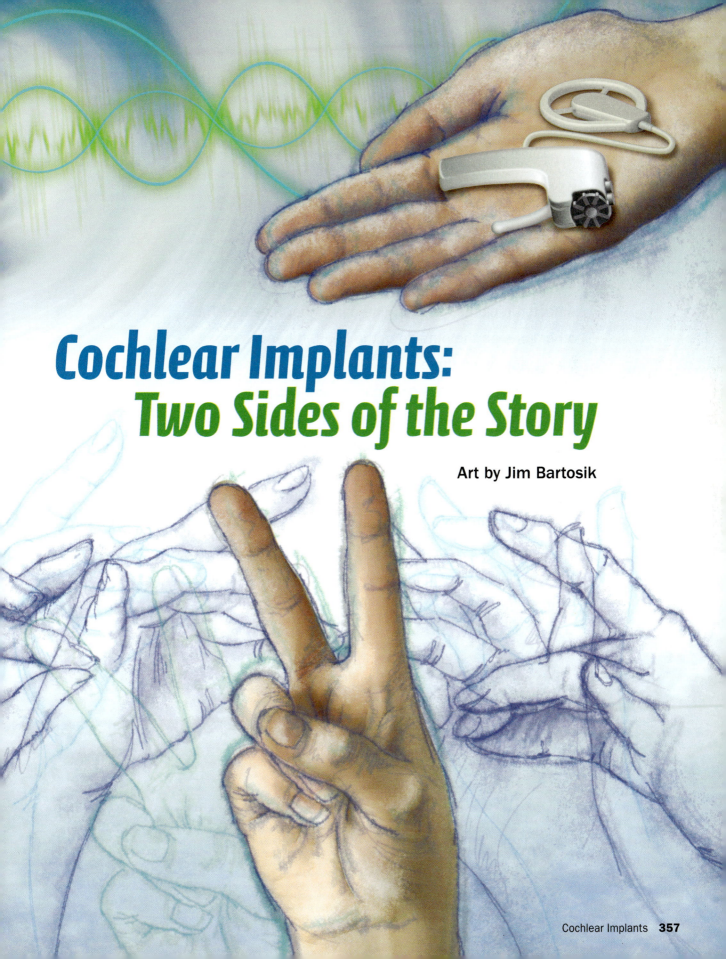

Cochlear Implants:
Two Sides of the Story

Art by Jim Bartosik

A cochlear implant (CI) is a **device** that helps **deaf people** to hear. Cochlear implants have two parts. A doctor implants, or puts, one part under the skin. The other goes on the outside of the head. It has a magnet that goes behind the ear.

To many people, the cochlear implant is a wonderful device. Children with a CI can learn to speak quickly. They can go to school with hearing children. Many never learn how to communicate using sign language.

Others disagree with the use of the cochlear implant. They don't believe that **deafness** is a **disability**. They don't think that surgery is necessary—especially for young children. They think cochlear implants are hurting deaf culture.

Key Vocabulary
device *noun*, tool for a certain job
disability *noun*, a problem that stops you from doing something that most people can do

In Other Words
deaf people people who cannot hear
deafness not being able to hear

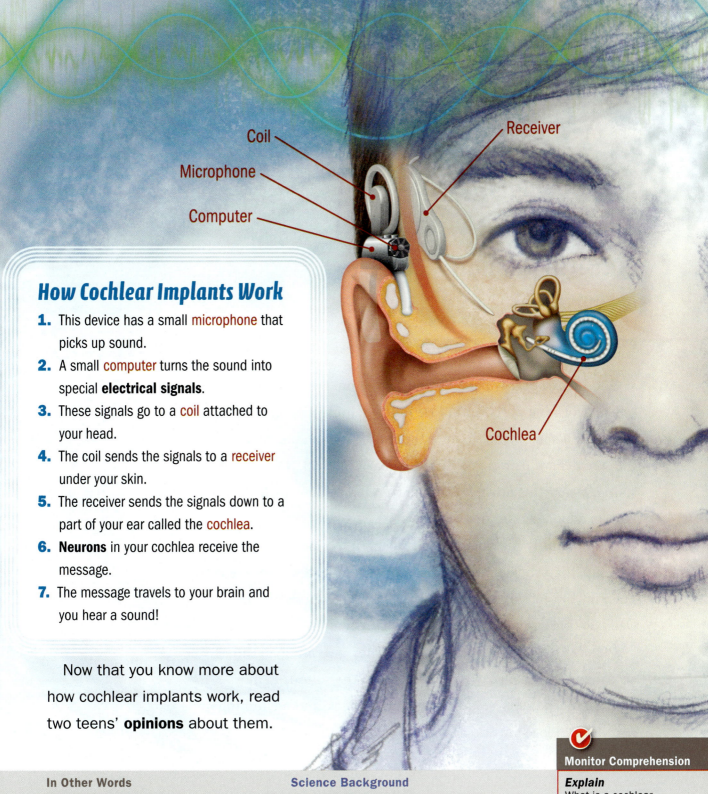

Coil

Microphone

Computer

Receiver

Cochlea

How Cochlear Implants Work

1. This device has a small microphone that picks up sound.
2. A small computer turns the sound into special **electrical signals**.
3. These signals go to a coil attached to your head.
4. The coil sends the signals to a receiver under your skin.
5. The receiver sends the signals down to a part of your ear called the cochlea.
6. **Neurons** in your cochlea receive the message.
7. The message travels to your brain and you hear a sound!

Now that you know more about how cochlear implants work, read two teens' **opinions** about them.

In Other Words
electrical signals messages
Neurons Nerve cells that carry messages
opinions ideas

Science Background
The cochlea is a part of the inner ear. It is shaped like a snail shell. It has three chambers, or parts, that are filled with liquid, and that help with hearing.

Monitor Comprehension

Explain
What is a cochlear implant?

Speaking for Myself: My Experience with the Cochlear Implant

BY CAITLIN PARTON

At age two and a half, Caitlin Parton was the youngest person in the U.S. to get a CI.

FDA SPEECH, MAY 21, 1997

Good morning. My name is Caitlin Parton. I've had my cochlear implant for nine years, and I love it. It's helping me a lot.

I think it's important to have the **implant** as a choice for people who are deaf. It brings you into the hearing world, the world of sound. I wear this **miracle** of modern science. I'm a little different, but I'm a lot like everyone else, too.

I don't wear the implant when I sleep. In the morning when I wake up, it's a shock to put it on. **Whoa!** All these sounds come in. Then my brain figures out what the different sounds are: the radio, Dad cooking, **traffic outdoors**.

Sounds are really important to me. They give me something exciting to experience every day. Some of the sounds I enjoy most are my parents' voices, my friends' voices, and me talking to everybody! I love music. I play the piano and the flute.

In Other Words

FDA Speech Speech to members of the Food and Drug Administration
implant tool
miracle wonderful product
Whoa! Wow!
traffic outdoors cars and trucks outside

I like talking on the phone. I can now use it without any special devices and **get** almost everything. I love the sound of thunder, the wind in the trees, the birds. I like being able to ask the store clerk where something is. I like hearing the "specials" at a restaurant and ordering for myself. I love reading to my little cousins.

This technology is not perfect. I don't hear everything. Some <mark>situations</mark> are hard for me. I have to ask people to help or repeat things. But I think implants will keep getting better. New kinds of implants are being developed. That will help all of us.

I don't wake up every day and say, "Oh, I'm deaf. Poor me." I like being deaf. I feel special.

I've read some of the articles against the implant. I know some people say that kids like me will grow up and not really belong to the **Deaf Culture world**. They think we won't belong to the hearing world either. They say implanted deaf kids don't fit in anywhere.

Instead of <mark>separating</mark> ourselves into little groups, we need to learn to respect our differences. Deep down we're all the same. I think we need to remember we have something **in common**. *We're all part of one community.*

Key Vocabulary
<mark>situation</mark> *noun*, a set of events or circumstances
<mark>separate</mark> *verb*, to keep things apart

In Other Words
get hear and understand
This technology How the CI works
Deaf Culture world community made up of people who cannot hear
in common that makes us all the same

Monitor Comprehension

Explain
List three reasons why Caitlin likes wearing the cochlear implant.

Being deaf can be a gift . . . a great gift

Dear Editor,

I am a girl who happens to be deaf. I don't have a cochlear implant (CI). I don't plan to get one, ever. I feel that deaf people don't need to be able to hear to be happy.

I have a lot of friends who have a CI. Many of them think being able to hear is better than being deaf. Some people don't realize that CIs don't help you hear much.

My friends say you can communicate better. But with a CI, you can only understand one person at a time. You still have to **lip-read**. Some of them tell me I am lucky to have two siblings and a mom who are deaf. This is the only point I can truly agree with them on.

It amazes me to see how far parents go **to implant their child**.

Once, someone even **begged** for money to fix his son's CI. If parents *do* want to put a CI on their child, they should wait until **s/he** is older. That way, the kid can decide what s/he really wants to do.

I used to long to be able to hear. I wanted to know what it is like to hear people talk. But then I realized that deafness is not a **disadvantage**. Now I love being deaf. And I will never stop treating my deafness as a gift.

Key Vocabulary
disadvantage *noun*, something that makes life more difficult for one person than it is for others

In Other Words
lip-read watch people's mouths to understand them
to implant their child to have doctors put a CI in their child's head
begged asked people
s/he she or he (abbreviation)

So, parents, please don't implant your child. Wait until they are older. Then they can make their own decisions. Please accept that they will never be fully hearing. Treat their deafness as if it was a gift, because it is.

If you grew up in a family like mine, you would understand why I think it is such a great gift to be deaf. I don't think that there are enough people who **prize their deafness**.

—Tanya S. ❖

This girl is signing the word, "play."

In Other Words

prize their deafness think of their deafness as something special

✔ **Monitor Comprehension**

Explain
Why doesn't Tanya want to get a cochlear implant?

ANALYZE Cochlear Implants

1. **Explain** What does Tanya S. mean when she says that not enough people prize their deafness?

2. **Vocabulary** Why do some people think deafness is a **disability**?

3. **Reading Strategy** **Make Connections** How do Caitlin's and Tanya's experiences relate to what you know or have read about a different culture? Tell a partner how it helped you understand the text better.

↩ Return to the Text

Reread and Retell Reread the last two paragraphs of Caitlin Parton's speech. Explain whether she shares Tanya S.'s opinion. Use facts from the text to support your ideas.

A *Different* Drummer

by Henry David Thoreau

Illustration by Jackdaw

If a man does not keep pace with his companions, perhaps it is because he hears a different drummer. Let him step to the music which he hears, however measured or far away.

In Other Words
keep pace with do the same thing as
companions friends

About the Writer

Henry David Thoreau (1817–1862) was a poet, writer, and philosopher. He believed that people should have a simple lifestyle. His book *Walden* describes the time he lived alone in a small house beside Walden Pond in the state of Massachusetts.

photo essay by Jona Frank

Make Connections

When you read, you learn how other people think and feel. Sometimes what you read reminds you of something in your own life. When you **make connections**, you relate things you believe or have experienced to the text.

Reading Strategy
Make Connections

HOW TO MAKE CONNECTIONS

1. Read the text. Look for words that explain how the writer thinks or feels.

2. Ask, "Have I ever thought or felt this way?"

3. Decide how your connection improves your understanding of the text.

Read the text. Then see how two readers explain their connections.

Look Into the Text

> You make friends quickest by joining sports. When you are in the newspaper, you feel famous.
>
> People come up to you from other schools—people you don't know. They are like, "Great game." It's awesome.

Being in a band makes me feel famous.

Last year when I joined the track team, I made many friends.

Try It

As you read "High School," make connections. Think about how each connection helps you understand the text.

Connect Across Texts

In "Cochlear Implants," Caitlin and Tanya have different ideas about what it means to fit in. Find out what the high school students in this photo essay say about fitting in.

High School

by Jona Frank

Our **generation** fears someone knowing who you really are. Everybody is **a faker**. Everybody **fronts**. They act like they are somebody different. When somebody finds out who they really are, that's when they get scared.

—New Jersey high school student

In Other Words

generation age group
a faker different from how they act (slang)
fronts pretends to be someone he or she is not (slang)

Fitting in is having a lot of people who are okay with who you are. You just want to belong to something. Then people start to **identify** you with it.

It's all one big **social** party. You see people try to **climb the social ladder.** You try to hang out with people to get higher socially.

—Lydia

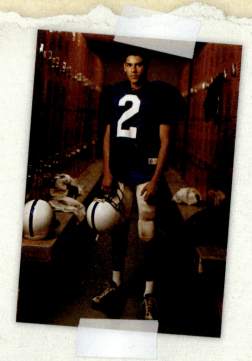

I will be honest. I think we rule the school. We're not scared of anyone. No one can tell us what to do.

You are either **a jock**, a **bookworm**, or **an alternative person**. You make friends quickest by joining sports. When you are in the newspaper, you feel famous. People come up to you from other schools—people you don't know. They are like, 'Great game.' It's awesome.

—Roberto

Key Vocabulary

identify *verb*, to connect with a group or idea

social *adjective*, with other people

In Other Words

climb the social ladder make friends with the popular kids

a jock an athlete

bookworm person who reads and studies a lot

an alternative person a person who dresses and acts in a different way

Monitor Comprehension

Describe
According to Roberto, what are the three main groups in high school?

The club started when I found out anything could be a club. I thought, why not have a club where you could have a lot of fun with no **structure**? Why not call it the Chris Blair Club? Now it's the second biggest club in the school, right behind the Debate Club. We once had sixty-five people at a meeting.

I love the **attention**. I'm just bored without the attention. If I'm not getting attention, I make something happen to get attention.

If I was wearing what you would consider all normal clothes, people wouldn't pay attention. If I'm wearing all black or makeup or the top hat, then people don't say anything to me, but they look. I get their eyes.

— Chris ❖

Key Vocabulary
attention *noun*, being noticed

In Other Words
structure rules

ANALYZE High School

1. **Explain** How does Chris try to get **attention**? What does Roberto say is the best way to make friends?

2. **Vocabulary** What **social** group in your school do you **identify** with?

3. **Reading Strategy** **Make Connections** Does Lydia remind you of anyone in your own life? Explain how relating things you believe or experienced added to your understanding of the text.

↩ **Return to the Text**

Reread and Retell Explain how each high school student tries to fit in. Use ideas from the text to support your answer.

EQ How Important Is It to Fit In?

Fluency

Listen to a reading. Practice fluency. Use the Reading Handbook, page 541.

Reading

Talk About Literature

EQ 1. Analyze In "Cochlear Implants," Tanya S. says that being different is a gift. Do you agree? Support your answer.

> I (agree/disagree) with Tanya S. because _____.

2. Compare In "High School," Roberto describes different groups. Compare Roberto's group to a group you belong to or know about. How are they similar and different?

> Roberto belongs to _____. I belong to _____. My group is similar to Roberto's because _____. My group is different from Roberto's because _____.

3. Interpret Do you think that Caitlin from "Cochlear Implants" and Chris Blair from "High School" would get along? Explain.

> Caitlin is _____. Chris Blair is _____. I think that Caitlin and Chris would (get along/not get along) because _____.

Vocabulary

Review Key Vocabulary

Choose the correct vocabulary word to complete each sentence.

1. My friend Lisa is deaf. She is at a _____ because she can't hear.

2. She doesn't believe that deafness is a _____, however.

3. Instead, she feels that being deaf is a positive _____.

4. It helps her _____ with other people who are different.

5. Lisa is very _____ and loves to meet new people.

6. When she talks to someone, she gives her full _____ to the person.

7. Sometimes she wears a _____ to help her hear.

8. It doesn't _____ her from others, though. It brings her closer to them.

Vocabulary

- attention
- device
- disability
- disadvantage
- identify
- separate
- situation
- social

Writing

Write About Literature

Opinion Statement In "High School," Roberto says, "You are either a jock, a bookworm, or an alternative person." Do you agree? Support your opinion. Use a chart to organize your thoughts.

1. State Opinion	2. Support Opinion
I agree with Roberto's statement. I disagree with Roberto's statement.	I agree because . . . I disagree because . . .

Use Prepositional Phrases

Prepositions show different things. Some prepositions show **location**.

> There were many students **in** the room.
> But I felt alone, like I was floating **above** them.

Some prepositions show **direction**.

> I walked alone **through** the crowd.
> I went **into** my classroom, but I didn't fit in.

Some prepositions have many uses.

> Making friends is hard **for** me.
> I am happy **with** my friend, Ana.

A **prepositional phrase** is a group of words that starts with a preposition and ends with a noun or pronoun. You can use a prepositional phrase to add details.

Study these sentences. Notice that they are plain:

> I had just one friend. I took off running.

These sentences are more interesting:

> I had just one friend **in the whole school**.
> I took off running **down the stairs**.

Oral Practice Work with a partner. Add a prepositional phrase to each sentence. Choose a different preposition from the box. Say the new sentence.

about	at	for	from	in	through	with

1. Some of the kids were sad.
2. Roberto plays sports.
3. Lydia looks worried.
4. Chris has a hat.
5. Kids don't always welcome other kids.

Written Practice For each sentence, add a prepositional phrase that gives more details. Write the new sentence.

6. Some kids have problems.
7. Parents sometimes don't help.
8. Kids move.
9. I see a lot of kids.
10. Everybody gets along somehow.

Express Opinions

Learn About Student Government Most high schools in the United States have student governments. Work with a partner. Find out more about student government, and discuss your opinions.

www.hbedge.net
• Learn about student government.

Do you think student government really works?

Do you think the students really decide who gets to be in student government?

Talk to your partner. Discuss the questions. Give your opinions.

• Say what you think.

• Give reasons for your opinion.

> I think the elections are fair. The students choose their leaders.

Use Context Clues for Multiple-Meaning Words

Some words are spelled the same but have more than one meaning. If you are not sure which meaning fits, try looking at the context. Pick the meaning that makes sense in the sentence.

> **issue** (i-shü) *n.* **1:** a disagreement between people **2:** a publication

The school newspaper published an entire issue about fitting in.

> The word **issue** is in the context of a statement about the school newspaper. It must mean "publication."

Explain which meaning fits the context of each sentence.

1. Fitting in is a big <u>issue</u> in our school.
2. Some people <u>monitor</u> how many friends they have online.
3. Lydia has so many friends that her list does not fit on her computer <u>monitor</u>.

> **monitor** (mah-nu-tur) *n.* **1:** a screen used to display electronic images *v.* **2:** to watch or keep track of something

4. She <u>stressed</u> that cochlear implants are not perfect.
5. Extremely loud noises can put <u>stress</u> on a cochlear implant.

> **stress** (stres) *n.* **1:** a force that acts on an object *v.* **2:** to give emphasis or special importance to something

Distinguish Fact and Opinion

Facts are statements that can be proved as true or false. Opinions are statements that tell what people think, feel, or believe. When you read, keep track of which statements are facts and which are opinions.

1. Read a statement. Ask, "Can this be proved as true or false?"
2. Look for words like *think* and *feel*. These words usually signal opinions.

Reread "Cochlear Implants: Two Sides of the Story." Look for different facts and opinions. Record them in a **Fact-and-Opinion Chart**.

Fact-and-Opinion Chart

Fact	Opinion
"I don't have a cochlear implant."	"I feel that deaf people don't need to be able to hear to be happy."

Writing

Write a Blog

▶ **Prompt** Is it more important to fit in or to stand out—to make people notice you? Give your opinion. Write it as a blog. A blog, or Web log, is like a journal. Writers publish their blogs on the Internet.

1 Plan State your opinion. Use phrases like "I think," "I believe," or "In my opinion." Then gather reasons and examples that support your opinion.

Opinion Chart

> Opinion: In my opinion, it is more important to fit in than to stand out.

> Reason: You feel more secure.

> Examples:
> • Kids join social clubs.
> • Kids at school fit into categories (nerds, bookworms).

Post a Comment

Emilio's Blog

October 27, 2008

⬤⬤

In my opinion, it is more important to fit in than to stand out. When kids are new in town, for example, they often join clubs where they can meet people. People feel more comfortable and secure when they fit in. . . .

Uses of Prepositions

USE	EXAMPLE
To show direction	*across, down, toward*
To show time	*after, before, during*
To show location	*behind, near, over*
Other uses	*at, from, with*

2 Write Use your notes. Organize your ideas into a paragraph. Use phrases like "I think" and "I believe" to express your opinion. Use prepositional phrases to add details.

3 Share Post your blog for others to read.

Express Ideas and Feelings

1 TRY OUT LANGUAGE
2 LEARN GRAMMAR
3 APPLY ON YOUR OWN

Listen to the conversation. Do you agree with what Rahima and Julia say about friendship?

Conversation

New Class

Rahima: What do you think of our new ballet teacher? Do you like her?

Julia: She's hard! I don't think she likes me. I'm glad you're here with me!

Rahima: I am, too! Everything is better when you have a friend with you.

Julia: You're right. Things that are difficult are less difficult with a friend.

Rahima: And things that are fun are more fun!

Julia: Yeah! Rahima, you know what? This class is going to be okay. The new teacher will like us! And you know what else? I'm really glad you're my friend.

Rahima: I'm glad too, Julia.

Use Object Pronouns

In English, sentences often follow the **S-V-O** pattern. There is a **subject (S)**, a **verb (V)**, and an **object (O)**.

Aisha already **knew** the **steps** of the dances.
subject   verb   object

Aisha then **trained** **Mike**.
subject   verb   object

Special forms of pronouns are used to replace nouns that are the objects of verbs. These are called **object pronouns**.

The **friends** **performed** the **dances** together.
    subject   verb   object

They really **performed** **them** beautifully.
subject   verb   object
pronoun   pronoun

Study the subject and object pronouns. Remember to use an object pronoun to replace an object noun in a sentence.

SUBJECT PRONOUN	OBJECT PRONOUN
I	me
you	you
he	him
she	her
it	it
we	us
they	them

Say It

Work with a partner. Say the sentence with the <u>object noun</u>. Then have your partner say the sentence with an object pronoun.

1. Aisha liked <u>Mike</u> a lot.

2. Mike knew <u>Aisha</u> for a long time.

3. No one saw <u>Aisha and Mike</u> dance together before.

4. Aisha and Mike both liked <u>the show</u>.

5. Aisha's mother said, "I think people loved <u>Aisha and Mike</u>."

Write It

Choose the correct object pronoun and write the new sentences.

6. Mike and Aisha work hard at their dance. They usually practice (it/them) every day.

7. Aisha's mother usually picks Mike up. She picks (him/them) up outside his school.

8. Then she goes by Aisha's school to pick (him/her) up.

9. She drives (it/them) to their dance class.

10. Aisha's mother does a lot for them. Aisha and Mike really appreciate (her/them).

Pass It On

Share with your classmates what you think and feel about a special friend.

Follow these tips to express your thoughts and feelings clearly:

HOW TO EXPRESS IDEAS AND FEELINGS

1. Say what you think.

> My best friend is Ricardo. I met **him** a long time ago.

Use **object pronouns** when your listener already knows who or what you are talking about.

2. Explain how you feel.

> Ricardo supports **me** in everything I do. I have a lot of respect for that guy.

Here are the steps to carry out the activity:

- Tell a partner about a special friendship you have and your feelings about it.
- Listen to your partner talk about his or her special friend.
- Then change partners. Tell your new partner about what your first partner told you.

She tells her partner how she feels about her best friend.

EQ

How Important Is It to Fit In?
Talk about how people can create their own space.

Learn Key Vocabulary

Pronounce each word and learn its meaning.

Key Words

nervous (**nur**-vus) *adjective*
▶ page 384

When you are **nervous**, you feel worried or afraid of doing something. The runners are **nervous** before the race.

nobody (**nō**-bu-dē) *pronoun; noun*
▶ pages 389, 392

A **nobody** is a person who others think is not important. When they didn't talk to her, she felt like a **nobody**.

participate (par-**ti**-su-pāt) *verb*
▶ pages 380, 383, 393

When you **participate**, you join in an activity. The whole family **participates** in washing the car.

perform (pur-**form**) *verb*
▶ pages 380, 386, 389

When you **perform**, you show a talent to a group of people. The singers **perform** a song.

somebody
(**sum**-bu-dē) *pronoun; noun*
▶ pages 389, 392

A **somebody** is a person who others think is important. When she gets attention, she feels like a **somebody**.

sponsor (**spon**-sur) *verb*
▶ page 382

When you **sponsor** an activity, you help make it happen. The senior class **sponsored** the race.

support (su-**port**) *noun*
▶ pages 380, 386, 387

Support is an action that shows you care. They show **support** for their team by cheering and clapping.

tension (**ten**-shun) *noun*
▶ page 384

Tension is a feeling of worry and stress. The students are filled with **tension** while taking the test.

Practice the Words Make a **Vocabulary Chart** for each Key Vocabulary word.

Vocabulary Chart

Word	support
Synonym	approval
Definition	help or encouragement
Sentence or Picture	My friends support me when I feel sad.

short story by Yeemay Chan

Make Connections

As you read a story, think about how it connects to the world around you. Then decide how the connections improve your understanding of the story.

> ### HOW TO MAKE CONNECTIONS
>
> 1. As you read, stop occasionally and think about how the story connects to something in the world.
>
> 2. Ask, "Does the connection help me understand the events? If so, write it in a **Connections Chart**.
>
> 3. Tell how it helps you better understand the text you are reading.

Read another part of the text. Then read the Connections Chart.

Look Into the Text

Sometimes, it was embarrassing to be around Lola. People said rude things about her hair, clothes, glasses—even about the fact that she got really good grades.

Connections Chart

The text says . . .	My connection . . .	This helps me because . . .
"People said rude things about her hair . . ."	People often say rude things at my high school.	I know how Lola might respond to what people are saying.

Try It

As you read "The Right Moves," **make connections**. Decide how each connection improves your understanding of the story.

Build Background

Talent shows are performances that allow people to share their talent, or artistic skill, with others. Talent shows are annual events in many high schools throughout the United States. Some schools have talent shows just for fun. Others have them to raise money and provide **support** for various causes.

Students often **perform** songs or dances in talent shows, but any talent is welcome. Sometimes students perform unusual skills, like juggling. Others **participate** in short funny plays, called skits.

Some of today's popular television shows are talent shows. People compete by singing or dancing. Judges and audience members vote for their favorite performers.

www.hbedge.net
- Learn more about talent shows.
- View photos of a dance team.

The Right Moves

by Yeemay Chan

"Lena, are you listening?"

I *was* listening. I just couldn't believe my ears.

"W-what did you say?" I **stammered**.

"Do you want to join our dance team?" the girl asked **impatiently**. "We win the talent show every year, and we need a new dancer."

I still couldn't believe it. The teachers **sponsored** a talent show each spring. It would be a huge night, and Maya Herrera wanted me to be on her dance team.

"Sure," I said.

Maya **glared** at someone behind me, her pretty face looking like she had tasted something sour. "Not *her*, though," Maya said loudly. "Just you."

I didn't have to turn around—I knew who she meant. "Uh, sure," I mumbled again. Maya was already heading back to the "popular table" when I felt someone **tap** on my shoulder.

"What happened?" Lola asked. When I saw her confused face, it was like waking up from a dream.

Lola Reyes and I had been friends since we were little kids. Lola was a smart, funny friend.

Key Vocabulary
sponsor *verb*, to help make something happen

In Other Words
stammered said with surprise
impatiently sounding angry and hurried
glared looked angrily
tap hit me lightly

But at school, Lola just didn't fit in. I had never noticed when we were alone, but it was obvious to all the kids at school. Lola's hair was **frizzy** and her thick glasses made her look a little like a fish. Kids in grade school could be mean.

Eight years later, Lola was as strange as ever. Girls in our school wore **trendy, brand-name clothes**, but Lola sewed hers. Most kids talked about TV shows and movies, but Lola didn't even have a TV. She **stood out like a sore thumb**.

Sometimes, it was **embarrassing** to be around Lola. People said rude things about her hair, clothes, glasses—even about the fact that she got really good grades. Lola was always able to ignore what other people thought. I wasn't.

"You're going to be in the talent show?" Lola asked. "That's great, Lena! I'm going to **participate** this year, too!"

"You are? What are you going to do?" I asked.

Lola smiled. "Oh, I'll think of something."

I pictured Lola in front of a huge crowd. I was worried already.

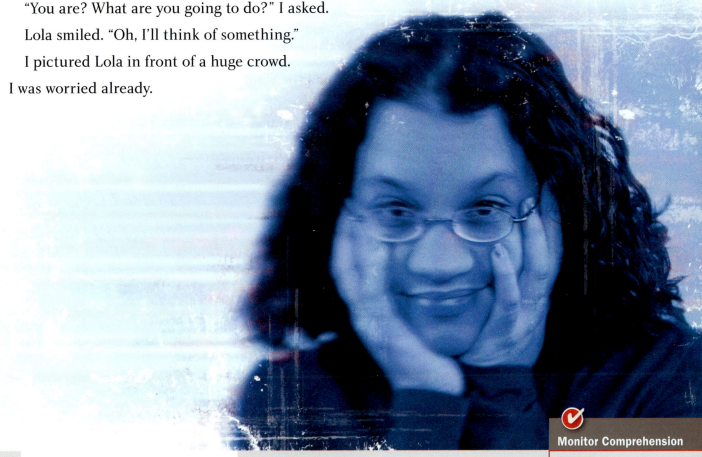

Key Vocabulary
participate *verb*, to join in an activity

In Other Words
frizzy really curly
trendy, brand-name clothes expensive clothing
stood out like a sore thumb was so different that everyone noticed
embarrassing uncomfortable

Lena is worried that she will make a mistake at the talent show. What do you think will happen?

The weeks passed quickly, and I barely saw Lola because I practiced every day with Maya and the team. The other dancers already knew the steps, so I worked hard to keep up. It wasn't as fun as I thought it would be. The other girls were **picky and critical**.

As the day of the talent show came closer, I felt more and more **nervous**. I didn't want to **stand out** from the rest of the group, so I worked day and night to learn all the right moves.

Finally, the talent show came. Backstage, excitement and nervous **tension** filled the air as groups practiced one last time.

Lola found me and gave me a big hug.

"You'll do great!" she said.

"I don't know," I whispered. "The other girls think I'm not good enough."

I didn't want to stand out from the rest of the group.

Key Vocabulary
nervous *adjective*, worried or afraid of doing something
tension *noun*, a feeling of worry and stress

In Other Words
picky and critical not very patient or friendly
stand out be different

Lola stopped smiling. "Lena, you care too much about what other people think," she said. "You're a great person and a wonderful dancer. Just be yourself."

Soon, I was taking my place on the stage.

"Don't mess this up," Maya **hissed** as the music began.

Surprisingly, I didn't. I remembered every step and every move. Before the music was over, the crowd was cheering. Maya's team had won another talent show.

In Other Words
hissed said in a low, mean voice

Monitor Comprehension

Confirm Prediction
How well did Lena perform at the talent show? Was your prediction correct?

Lola was the last singer to **perform**. As the music started, I recognized the song from an old movie we had seen together a million times. It was hard to hear because the crowd was whispering and moving around. I heard some giggles. For once, Lola didn't look like she was **ignoring** their comments. She looked scared.

"This ought to be good," Maya whispered loudly next to me.

I looked at Lola. She was standing alone, her homemade dress **shimmering** in the light. Her eyes were shimmering, too. At last, I made a decision. For years, I had counted on Lola's encouragement and **support**. Now it was my turn.

Key Vocabulary
perform *verb*, to show a talent to a group of people
support *noun*, help or action that shows you care

In Other Words
ignoring not noticing
shimmering shining

I stepped onto the stage. Behind me, Maya **gasped**, but Lola saw me and smiled. Together, we faced the audience and sang our favorite song. We weren't very good. In fact, we were terrible—and the crowd let us know it! When we finished, there was a little applause and a lot of comments that I didn't try too hard to hear.

As we walked off the stage, I knew that Lola wanted to say something, but I just laughed. Soon, Lola was laughing, too. I was done with the talent show. I was done with Maya and her dance group. And I was done trying to find all the right moves. ❖

ANALYZE The Right Moves

1. **Explain** Why were Lola and Lena laughing at the end of the talent show?

2. **Vocabulary** How does Lena show her <mark>support</mark> for Lola?

3. **Reading Strategy Make Connections** What connections did you make between "The Right Moves" and your own life? Tell a partner about them. How were these connections useful for understanding the story?

Return to the Text
Reread and Retell Reread page 383. Why does Lena think that sometimes it was embarrassing to be around Lola?

In Other Words
gasped made a sound of surprise

BEFORE READING **I'm Nobody**

poem by Emily Dickinson

Compare Genres

Poets write to express ideas and feelings. One way they do this is by using patterns of words, called stanzas. Like a paragraph a stanza separates one idea, image, or message from another. As you read a poem, think about the feelings that the poet is expressing in each stanza.

Writers create other kinds of texts, like biographies, to inform. These texts are organized into sentences and paragraphs. This divides the information logically. When you read a text that informs, notice the facts and details the author includes.

HOW TO COMPARE GENRES

1. Look at how the text is organized.

2. Decide what kind of text you are reading.

3. Ask, "What does the author want me to understand from this text?"

Read the different texts. Then see what one reader noticed about each one.

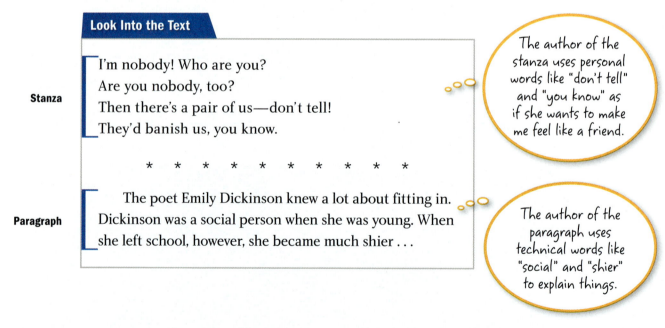

Look Into the Text

Stanza

I'm nobody! Who are you?
Are you nobody, too?
Then there's a pair of us—don't tell!
They'd banish us, you know.

*   *   *   *   *   *   *   *   *   *

Paragraph

The poet Emily Dickinson knew a lot about fitting in. Dickinson was a social person when she was young. When she left school, however, she became much shier . . .

> The author of the stanza uses personal words like "don't tell" and "you know" as if she wants to make me feel like a friend.

> The author of the paragraph uses technical words like "social" and "shier" to explain things.

Try It

As you read "I'm Nobody" and the biography of Emily Dickinson, look for key words and phrases. Use them to help you understand each kind of text.

Connect Across Texts

In *"The Right Moves,"* Lena gets attention when she **performs**. How does the speaker in this poem feel about getting attention?

I'm Nobody

by Emily Dickinson
Art by Sara Beazley

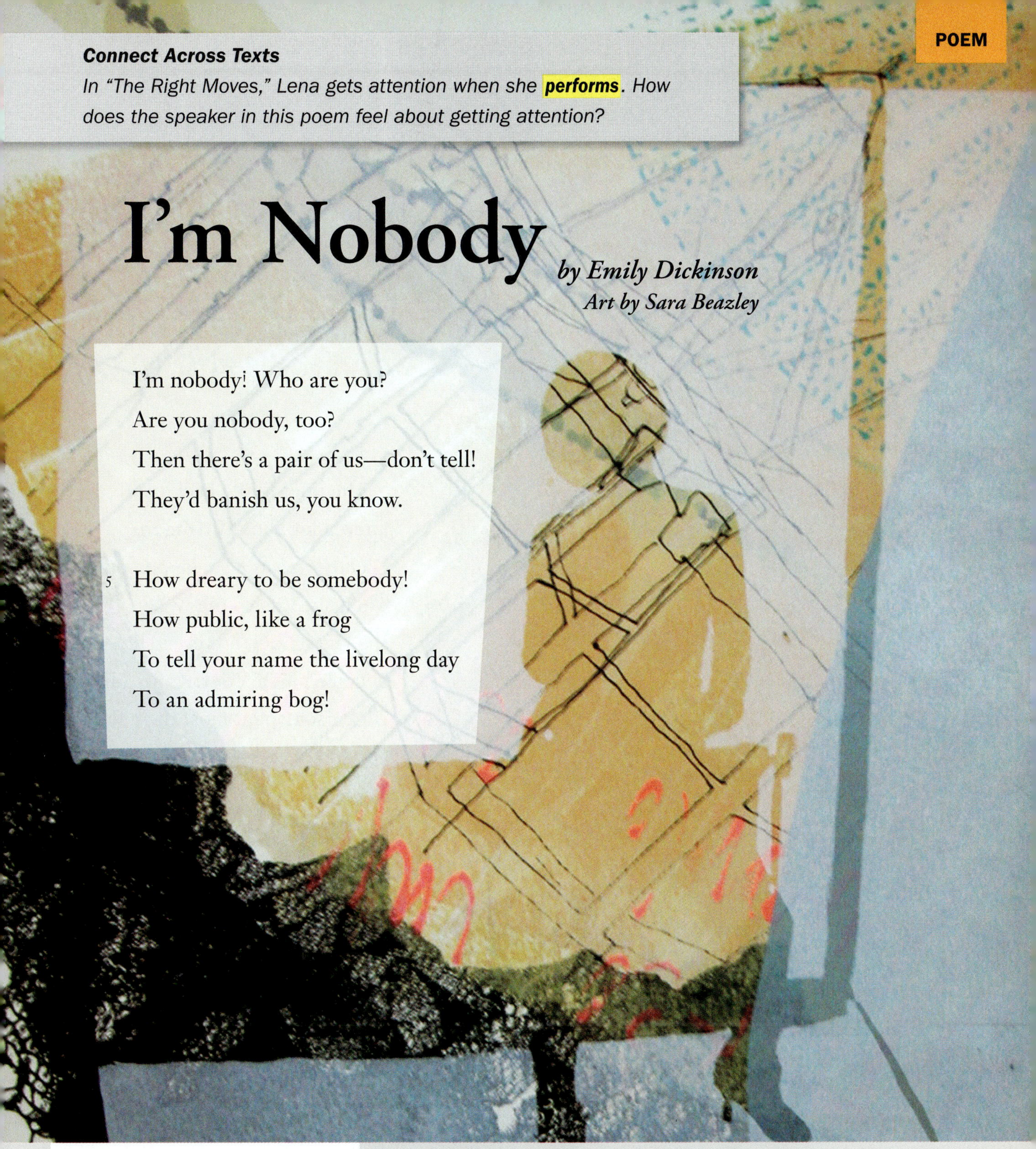

I'm nobody! Who are you?
Are you nobody, too?
Then there's a pair of us—don't tell!
They'd banish us, you know.

5   How dreary to be somebody!
How public, like a frog
To tell your name the livelong day
To an admiring bog!

Key Vocabulary

perform *verb*, to show a talent to a group of people

nobody *noun*, a person who others think is not important

somebody *noun*, a person who others think is important

In Other Words

banish us make us go away
dreary boring
tell your name the livelong day talk about the same things all the time
an admiring bog a group of people who only pretend to admire you

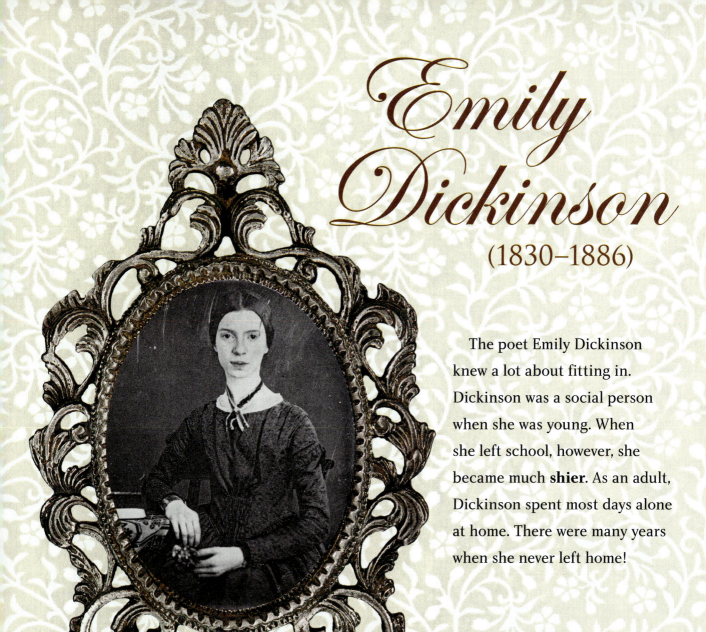

Emily Dickinson
(1830–1886)

The poet Emily Dickinson knew a lot about fitting in. Dickinson was a social person when she was young. When she left school, however, she became much **shier**. As an adult, Dickinson spent most days alone at home. There were many years when she never left home!

Emily Dickinson at about age 16.

In Other Words
shier more shy

Dickinson spent much of her time writing poetry. She wrote about nature, love, and death. She wrote more than one thousand poems. But Dickinson published fewer than ten poems when she was alive. Many of her **most famous** poems were **discovered** after her death.

Dickinson often wrote about being lonely. She did not have many **visitors**. But Dickinson was not all alone. She spent time at her home with a few close friends and family members. She also wrote many letters to friends. ❖

Dickinson probably wrote many of her poems in her quiet, plain bedroom.

Dickinson lived in this house almost her entire life. Her brother and his family lived next door.

In Other Words
most famous best known
discovered found
visitors people who came to her house to see her

Monitor Comprehension

Describe
In your own words, describe how Emily Dickinson lived her life.

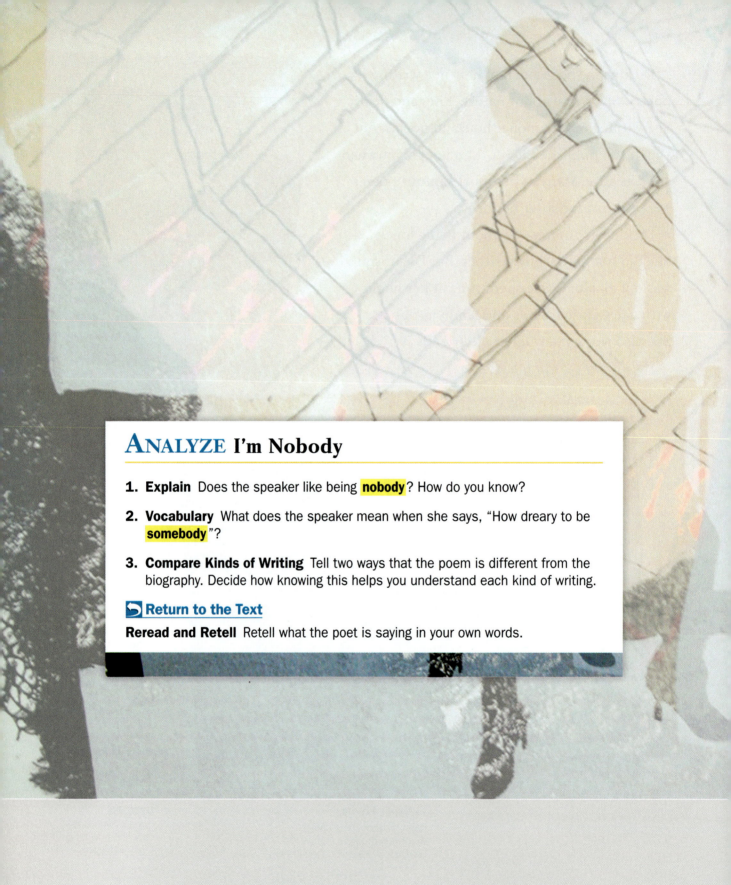

ANALYZE I'm Nobody

1. **Explain** Does the speaker like being <mark>nobody</mark>? How do you know?

2. **Vocabulary** What does the speaker mean when she says, "How dreary to be <mark>somebody</mark>"?

3. **Compare Kinds of Writing** Tell two ways that the poem is different from the biography. Decide how knowing this helps you understand each kind of writing.

Return to the Text

Reread and Retell Retell what the poet is saying in your own words.

EQ ## How Important Is It to Fit In?

Fluency

Listen to a reading. Practice fluency. Use the Reading Handbook, page 542.

Reading

Talk About Literature

EQ 1. Compare Reread "The Right Moves." Describe Lola's and Lena's attitudes about fitting in. How do their words and actions show their attitudes?

> *Lola thinks that fitting in is _____. For example, Lola _____. Lena thinks that fitting in is _____. For example, Lena _____.*

2. Speculate Do you think the speaker in "I'm Nobody" would **participate** in a high school talent show, such as the one in "The Right Moves"? Why or why not?

EQ 3. Analyze "The Right Moves" and "I'm Nobody" compare the difference between being popular and not being popular. How important is it to be popular? Explain.

> *It is important to _____ because _____.*

Vocabulary

Review Key Vocabulary

Choose the correct vocabulary word to complete each sentence.

1. Every year, our school likes to _____ a talent show.

2. Rico planned to _____ a song in the talent show.

3. He said, "One day, I'll be famous. I'll be _____."

4. Juan was a great guitar player. He wanted to _____ in the talent show, too.

5. On the day of the talent show, Juan was _____. He was afraid to play.

6. Juan was timid and felt like a _____, a person that no one wants to listen to.

7. Rico knew Juan was afraid. He said, "We'll _____ each other. I'll sing, and you can play the guitar."

8. Juan liked the idea. As he shook Rico's hand in agreement, all the _____ left his body. He relaxed and enjoyed the show.

Vocabulary

nervous
nobody
participate
perform
somebody
sponsor
support
tension

Writing

Write About Literature

Explanation Reread the selections. If someone asked you to **perform** in a talent show at your school, would you do it? Write a short explanation.

> *If someone asked me to perform, I would say yes because I am a good singer and I like to sing in front of people.*

Grammar

Use Subject and Object Pronouns

Review the forms of subject and object pronouns.

SUBJECT PRONOUN	I	you	he	she	it	we	they
OBJECT PRONOUN	me	you	him	her	it	us	them

Use a **subject pronoun** to replace a noun that is in the subject position in a sentence.

> Emily Dickinson was born in 1830. **She** is a famous American poet.

Use an **object pronoun** to replace a noun that is used as the object of a verb.

> Emily Dickinson wrote many poems. But she usually did not publish **them**.

Also use an **object pronoun** after a **preposition**.

> All of her poems are beautiful. Many **of them** are hard to understand.

Oral Practice Work with a partner. Use the correct pronoun and say the sentence.

1. Emily Dickinson lived in Amherst. _____ is a small town in New England.

2. _____ wrote more than two thousand poems!

3. Many of _____ are written on little scraps of paper.

4. Emily Dickinson did not publish many poems. Publishing was not important for _____.

5. I love Dickinson's poetry. Her poems really move _____.

6. _____ are the best poems I have ever read.

Written Practice Choose the correct pronoun and write the sentence.

7. Many of Dickinson's poems are about nature. She loves to write about (it/him).

8. Some of (it/them) are about death.

9. Dickinson wrote a letter to an editor. (Her/She) wanted to ask his advice.

10. The editor's name was Thomas Higginson. Dickinson respected (him/he).

11. Higginson published Dickinson's poems after her death, but he changed (it/them) a lot.

12. We now have Dickinson's poems just as she wrote them. They are her gift to (we/us).

Language Development

Express Ideas and Feelings

Poetry and Feelings Find out more about Emily Dickinson and listen to some of her poetry.

www.hbedge.net
- **Learn more about Emily Dickinson.**
- **Listen to a poem by Emily Dickinson.**

What do you like about her writing? How do the poems or writing make you feel?

Work with a partner. Discuss Emily Dickinson.

- Tell your partner what you know about her.

- Explain your feelings when you read her work.

> I felt joy when I read Emily Dickinson's nature poems.

> I felt sad when I read her poems about death.

Use Example Clues

Examples can give clues to a word's meaning. To figure out the meaning of an unknown word, look for an example in a sentence nearby. Then think about how the example makes the text clear.

> I was feeling more and more nervous. For example, I started to sweat and shake.

Sweating and shaking are examples of things people do when they are worried. Nervous must mean "worried."

Use example clues to figure out the meaning of the underlined word in each sentence.

1. Amalia was full of anticipation. Her heart was beating with excitement. She could not wait for the show to begin.

2. She had many goals for the performance. She wanted to remember every move. She wanted to jump high. She wanted to make the audience happy.

3. Her friends always said she was talented. She could paint, sing, and even juggle. But could she dance?

4. When Amalia finished her performance, the audience cheered with delight. They looked so happy and excited!

Compare Characters

Authors sometimes create characters that are very different. These differences can help you understand the story. Compare the characters in "The Right Moves."

Make a **Character Description Chart** for the main characters in "The Right Moves."

1. Draw a Character Description Chart.

2. Reread the story. Think about Lola's actions. List them in the second column. What do Lola's actions show about her? In the third column, write words to describe Lola.

3. Repeat step 2 for Lena and Maya.

4. In the last column, write a summary to compare the characters. Explain how their differences help you understand the story.

Character Description Chart

Character	What the Character Does	What This Shows About the Character	Summary Comparison
Lola			
Lena			

Integrate the Language Arts **395**

1

2

3

Technology Careers

Is a technology job right for you? Take this career quiz to find out.

Career Quiz

1. I think math and science classes are
  ⓐ easy.
  ⓑ not too difficult.
  ⓒ very difficult.

2. I think electronics and computers are
  ⓐ very interesting.
  ⓑ just OK.
  ⓒ boring.

3. I use computers and software
  ⓐ as often as I can.
  ⓑ sometimes.
  ⓒ almost never.

Add up your points.
  ⓐ = 3 points
  ⓑ = 2 points
  ⓒ = 1 point

What's your score?

9 points: Wow!
A technology job seems perfect for you!

6–8 points: Maybe
A technology job may be right for you.

3 points: No thanks
A technology job may not be right for you. Do you know someone who would like this kind of work?

Jobs in Technology

Here are some technology jobs. They have different responsibilities and need different education and training.

Job	Responsibilities	Education/Training Needed
Help Desk Technician 1	· Installs computer software and hardware · Solves people's computer problems	· High school diploma, with a lot of math and science classes · Associate's degree
Digital Artist 2	· Uses computers to make images · Creates animations for Web sites, games, and films	· Associate's, bachelor's, or master's degree · Knowledge of design programs
Information Systems Manager 3	· Manages computer systems · Keeps information on computers safe from hackers · Finds ways to do tasks more efficiently	· Bachelor's degree or master's degree

A Digital Artist

My name is Rosie Martín. I'm a digital artist. I make three-dimensional (3D) animation for television.

Rosie Martín adds details to a digital image.

I create objects such as tornadoes, helicopters, and volcanoes. I use one type of software to create digital images. Then I use other software to add movement. For example, I can make lava look like it's boiling! I save the images and send them to other professionals who put them on film.

I enjoy my job because I like both technology and art. It is interesting to make realistic images. It is exciting to see my work on television!

Research Technology Jobs

Learn more about a technology job in the United States.

1. Choose a job from the chart on page 396.
2. Go online to **www.hbedge.net**. Read about the job you chose.
3. Complete this chart.

Job	How many workers have this job?	How much money does a worker earn?	Is this a good job for the future?

FITTING IN

EQ   **ESSENTIAL QUESTION:**
**How Important Is It
to Fit In?**

EDGE LIBRARY

Reflect on the Essential Question

With a group, discuss the Essential Question: How important is it to fit in?

As you answer the questions, think about what you read in the selections and your choice of *Edge* Library books.

- How can people fit in with or **belong** to a group or a place? Is it possible to fit in to more than one group?
- In your **judgment**, is it more important to be popular or to be yourself? Is it okay to be different?
- How important is it for most people to **believe** that they fit in? What does "to fit in" mean to you?

Unit Review Game

You will need:

- 2, 3, or 4 players
- 1 **aMAZE!** board
- question cards
- 1 coin
- a marker for each player

Objective: Be the first player to get to FINISH.

1. Download an **aMAZE!** board and question cards from **www.hbedge.net**. Print out and cut apart the question cards. Mix them up.

2. **Player A** flips the coin.

   - For "heads" , go forward 2 spaces.

   - For "tails" , go forward 1 space.

3. Player A chooses a question card and answers it.

   - If the answer is correct, player A takes one more turn. (If you can't agree on the answer, ask your teacher.)

4. **Player B** takes a turn. Then the other players take turns.

5. The first player to reach **FINISH** is the winner.

People have different opinions about fitting in. For this project, you will write a paragraph to present your ideas about fitting in.

Write a Fact-and-Opinion Paragraph

For some paragraphs, like those for editorials, you can combine true information with your own thoughts or feelings about a topic.

❶ Connect Writing to Your Life

You probably express your opinion about something every day. Maybe you tell a friend how you feel about a new movie or restaurant and why you feel that way. You explain the reasons for your opinion so your friend understands.

❷ Understand the Form

In a fact-and-opinion paragraph, you try to express your ideas about a topic. Each fact-and-opinion paragraph

- begins with a topic sentence that states an opinion
- presents reasons, or arguments, to support the opinion
- ends with a closing sentence that restates the opinion.

Study this fact-and-opinion paragraph.

No More Dress Codes!

I think high schools should get rid of dress codes. Why can't teens have tattoos or earrings? What's wrong with orange hair? Are these things dangerous? No. They're just ways for us to express our identities. Thousands of kids who dress this way have gone to college. They are good students and good people. Don't judge us by what we wear. We should stop the dress codes and just trust teens to make their own decisions.

The **topic sentence** gives the writer's opinion about an issue.

The writer uses a **fact** and details to give reasons for her opinion.

The **closing sentence** reminds readers about the writer's opinion.

Your Job as a Writer

▶ **Prompt** Tell your classmates what you think. Write a fact-and-opinion paragraph to express your ideas about fitting in with a group at school. Be sure your paragraph has

- a topic sentence that states your opinion
- facts or examples to support your opinion
- a conclusion that reminds readers how you feel.

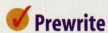 **Prewrite**

Follow these steps to make a plan for your paragraph.

1 Decide How You Feel

Think about the different groups at your school. Do you belong to a group? What is it like? Maybe there are other groups you want to be a part of or those you don't. Choose a group. Then form your opinion about fitting in or belonging to that group.

2 Gather Your Support

Why do you feel the way you do? Jot down facts, examples, or details that give reasons for your opinion. Do some research if you need to.

3 Write a Topic Sentence

A topic sentence in a fact-and-opinion paragraph states your opinion. Use opinion words like *must*, *should*, *think*, or *believe*.

4 Organize Your Ideas

Use an **Opinion Chart** to get organized. Add your topic sentence. Jot down your reasons and supporting facts or examples. Then remind readers about your opinion.

Opinion Chart

> **Opinion**
> Every school should have a culture club like ours at South High.

> **Reason**
> Some students with different backgrounds feel left out. A culture club helps them fit in.

> **Support**
> — we practice English
> — we learn songs and music
> — everyone is different, but everyone fits in

Reflect on Your Plan

▶ Is your opinion clear? Do you have enough facts or examples to support it?

✔ Write a Draft

Now you are ready to start writing your draft. Don't worry about making mistakes. Just get down the ideas you gathered in your Opinion Chart.

1 Start with Your Topic Sentence

Begin your paragraph with the topic sentence from your Opinion Chart.

Opinion Chart

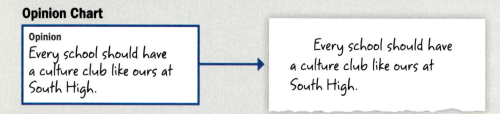

Opinion
Every school should have a culture club like ours at South High.

> Every school should have a culture club like ours at South High.

2 Add the Facts and Examples

Add facts or examples to support your opinion. Start with the ideas in your Opinion Chart. Then add more as you think of them.

Opinion Chart

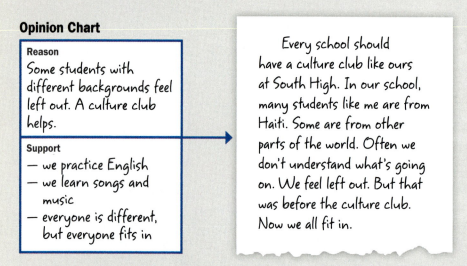

Reason
Some students with different backgrounds feel left out. A culture club helps.

Support
— we practice English — we learn songs and music — everyone is different, but everyone fits in

> Every school should have a culture club like ours at South High. In our school, many students like me are from Haiti. Some are from other parts of the world. Often we don't understand what's going on. We feel left out. But that was before the culture club. Now we all fit in.

3 End with Your Closing Sentence

Look back at your topic sentence. Use different words to remind your readers about your opinion.

> Having a culture club to go to is a must for every school.

Reflect on Your Draft

▶ Did you include enough facts and examples to support your opinion?

✓ Revise Your Draft

A first draft is not perfect. Now you can make it better by revising it, or making changes to it.

1 Read Your Paragraph to a Partner

Find out what a reader thinks of your work. You can use your partner's ideas to decide how to make your writing better.

Look at this part of Marten's draft. What does his partner say about it?

> Every school should have a culture club like ours at South High. In our school, many students like me are from Haiti. Some are from other parts of the world. Often we don't understand what's going on. We feel left out. But that was before the culture club. Now we all fit in.

"These ideas are very similar. Maybe you can combine them."

"Can you change any sentences so they don't all sound the same?"

2 Decide What to Change

Think about your partner's comments. Then decide what you want to change.

3 Mark Your Changes

Use these marks to make your changes:

∧ Add text.

✗ Take out text.

> Every school should have a culture club like ours at South High. In our school, many students like me are from Haiti. Some are from other parts of the world. Often we don't understand what's going on∧ **and** We feel left out. But that was before the culture club. Now we all fit in∧ **!** At our meetings, we practice English. Sometimes we teach each other songs∧ **and play music** ~~from our home~~ countries. ~~We play music from our home countries.~~ Twice a year, we have a party with foods, games, and clothing from each country. In our club, everyone is different∧ **But** everyone fits in. Having a culture club to go to is a must for every school.

Marten took out some repeated words and combined sentences.

Marten changed a sentence to an exclamation to make his writing more interesting.

Reflect on Your Revisions

▶ Think about your review. What are some of your strengths as a writer? What are some things that are giving you trouble?

✓ Edit and Proofread

After you've revised your draft, edit and proofread it to check for mistakes.

1 Check Your Prepositions

A preposition comes at the beginning of a prepositional phrase. Be sure your prepositions show what you want them to.

> Our book club meets **after** school. The group uses the library **next to** Room 5.

Some Prepositions		
Location		
by	in	next to
Time		
before	after	during
Direction		
across	into	up
Multiple Uses		
about	for	with

2 Check Your Spelling

Circle each word that may not be spelled right. Look it up in the dictionary or ask for help. Fix the spelling if you need to.

3 Check Your Punctuation

When you make a list of more than two things, separate them with commas.

Use a comma	Example
• to separate three or more items in a list	Please bring a pencil, a notebook, and a calendar to the next meeting.

4 Mark Your Changes

Now edit your own paper. Use these marks to show your changes.

∧	℘	⌐	◯	≡	╱	⁋
Add.	Take out.	Replace with this.	Check spelling.	Capitalize.	Make lowercase.	Make new paragraph.

Reflect on Your Corrections

▶ Note any errors you made. Make a list. Remember them the next time you write something.

✔ Publish, Share, and Reflect

Publish and Share

Now you are ready to publish your fact-and-opinion paragraph. Print or write a clean copy on a large sheet of paper. Collect the class paragraphs to post on a bulletin board.

Read at least one paragraph by a classmate. Compare your classmate's opinion to your own. Was your classmate's opinion about fitting in the same or different?

Here are some other ideas for sharing your work:

- Share the paragraph with a family member.
- Send it in an e-mail to a friend.
- Discuss it with a teacher, mentor, class, or group.

HOW TO PARTICIPATE IN A DISCUSSION

1. **Use Good Listening Skills** Sit quietly while the speaker shares his or her paragraph. Pay attention. Give the speaker time to finish before you respond.

2. **Ask Questions and Clarify Ideas** If you are the speaker, ask if there are any questions about your ideas. Answer any questions politely and respectfully.

3. **Respect Everyone's Opinion** Remember that not everyone has the same opinion about things. Be open to a different idea about fitting in. Talk to both those who agree with you and those who don't.

Reflect on Your Work

▶ Think about your writing.

- What did you learn about writing that you didn't know before?
- What did you like best about writing a fact-and-opinion paragraph?

☑ **Save a copy of your work in your portfolio.**

WHAT MATTERS MOST

What Is Most Important in Life?

Dumplings are better than flowers.
—**Japanese Proverb**

Wisdom is better than money.
—**American Proverb**

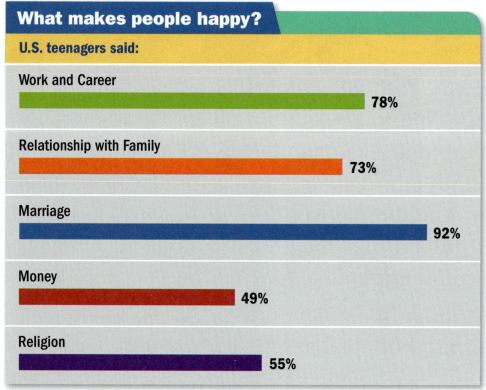

EQ ESSENTIAL QUESTION:

What Matters Most in Life?

Study the Graph

What do you learn about happiness?

What makes people happy?

U.S. teenagers said:

Work and Career
78%

Relationship with Family
73%

Marriage
92%

Money
49%

Religion
55%

Source: The Associated Press—MTV Poll; April 16–23, 2007

EQ ESSENTIAL QUESTION

In this unit, you will explore the **Essential Question** in class. Think about the question outside of school, too.

1 Study the Concept

What do you want most in life?

A career?

Wealth?

Family?

1. If you have **success** in life, it means you have done something well. What does success mean to you?

2. **Wealth** can mean having plenty of money. It can also mean having plenty of something else. What makes you wealthy?

3. Your **attitude** is how you feel about life and how this makes you behave. What kind of attitude does a person need to be happy?

2 Choose More to Read

Choose something to read during this unit.

Maasai Dreamer
by Adrienne Frater

When rain comes to a dry village in Kenya, everybody is happy. But one young woman worries about the problem of drought. She thinks of a plan to save what matters most.

▶ FICTION

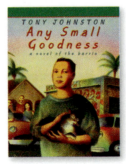

Any Small Goodness
by Tony Johnston

Meet Arturo Rodriguez. He lives with his family in Los Angeles. He knows about the hard life. He also knows about how to make good things happen, because he knows what matters most.

▶ FICTION

www.hbedge.net
- Read about a successful person.
- Take a quiz.

Interpret Figurative Language

Sometimes words mean exactly what they say. That exact meaning is called the **literal** meaning. **Figurative language** goes beyond the literal meaning. There are different types of figurative language.

Definition	Example	Explanation
An **idiom** is a group of words that does not match the literal, or exact meaning, of its words.	She worked **around the clock** to finish the project.	"Around the clock" means "all the time."
A **simile** uses words such as *like*, *as*, and *than* to compare two unlike things.	The project **was like a steep mountain**. She climbed it step by step.	The simile compares the project to a steep mountain.

Use different strategies to interpret figurative language.

- Use context clues. Look for words that suggest a comparison.
- Form a mental picture from the language. Decide what feeling or image the writer is trying to create.

Practice Interpreting Figurative Language

Identify each underlined phrase as an idiom or a simile. Figure out the meaning.

1. When Mr. Briggs announced the history test, Lotta was as quiet as a mouse.
2. She was unprepared because she was as sick as a dog last night.
3. Now Lotta was quaking in her boots.
4. She racked her brain as she tried to remember all the history dates.
5. As Mr. Briggs distributed the tests, Lotta made up her mind.
6. She decided to put her best foot forward.

Put the Strategy to Use

Work with a partner. Figure out the meaning of each underlined phrase.

7. Lotta opened the test booklet and was knocked off her feet.
8. The test questions were a piece of cake!
9. The facts were sitting in her memory like objects on a shelf.
10. When she turned in the test, she was as happy as a clown.
11. Lotta learned not to sell herself short.
12. Her regular study habits had saved her skin!

Give and Follow Directions

Look at the map and listen to the telephone conversation.

1 TRY OUT LANGUAGE
2 LEARN GRAMMAR
3 APPLY ON YOUR OWN

Conversation

Maya: Hello?

Ernesto: Hi, Maya. It's Ernesto.

Maya: Oh, hi, Ernesto. What's up?

Ernesto: I'm going to see a play at the Riverside Theater tonight. I don't know how to get there. Can you help me?

Maya: Sure! Are you leaving from your house?

Ernesto: Yes. I live at 223 Pine Street.

Maya: Okay. First, you need to go east on Pine Street and cross Third Avenue. Keep going on Pine Street to Fourth Avenue.

Ernesto: Fourth Avenue is just after the new pizza restaurant. Is that correct?

Maya: Yes. Turn right when you get to Fourth Avenue. Go past Riverside High School, and then you'll come to Elm Street. Turn left on Elm Street. Riverside Park will be on your right.

Ernesto: Is the theater in the park?

Maya: Yes. Keep going on Elm Street to Sixth Avenue. Turn right on Sixth Avenue. The theater is at the end of the street.

Ernesto: Great! Thanks, Maya.

Maya: No problem! Enjoy the play. Tell me what you think of it tomorrow.

Use Different Kinds of Sentences

There are four kinds of sentences. Each kind of sentence has a different purpose. Use the end mark that fits the purpose. Start every sentence with a capital letter.

KIND OF SENTENCE	EXAMPLE
• **Statement** Make a statement to tell something. End with a period.	We are going to see a play. The play is *Our Town* by Thornton Wilder.
• **Question** Ask a question to find out something. End with a question mark.	Where will you see the play? Where are your seats?
• **Command** Give a command to tell someone what to do. End with a period.	Go to the next aisle. Turn left at Row D.
• **Exclamation** Use an exclamation to express a strong feeling. End with an exclamation point.	I thought the play was wonderful! Ernesto thought it was terrible!

Say It

Say each sentence. Then say the kind of sentence it is and which mark goes at the end of it.

1. Do you want to go to the theater tonight ____

2. I'd love to go with you ____

3. Meet me in the lobby at 7:30 ____

4. Which theater is it ____

5. It's the Rialto Theater ____

This theater holds more than one thousand people.

Write It

Write each sentence and add the end mark. Then write the kind of sentence it is.

6. I want to have dinner before the play ____ _____

7. Do you know a good restaurant ____ _____

8. Luigi's Restaurant is amazing ____ _____

9. How do I get there ____ _____

10. Go south on Broad Street for three blocks ____ _____

Draw a Map

Draw a map of your neighborhood. Exchange maps with a partner. Give directions to a place while your partner follows on the map.

Follow these tips to give clear directions:

HOW TO GIVE AND FOLLOW DIRECTIONS

1. Give information about the location.

2. Give step-by-step directions.

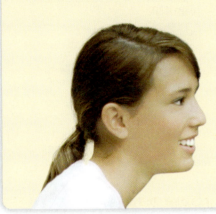

The theater is about a mile away from school. **Turn** left on Oak Street and **go** three blocks. Then **turn** right on Fifth Avenue and **go** two blocks.

Use commands when you give directions. A command often begins with a **verb**.

Here are the steps to carry out the activity:

- Draw your map. Remember to include street names, building names, and a compass rose with an arrow pointing north.

- Pick two different places on your map. Practice giving directions to go from one place to the other. Use these words: *go, turn, right, left, blocks, street, stop.*

- Then give your map to a partner. Tell your partner how to get from one place to the other. Ask your partner to follow the directions on the map with his or her finger.

"Walk several blocks. Look for the theater."

What Is Most Important in Life?
Think about how your attitude affects your life.

Learn Key Vocabulary

Pronounce each word and learn its meaning.

Key Words

exchange (iks-**chānj**) verb
▶ pages 420, 422, 423, 426

When you **exchange** something, you trade it for something else. People **exchange** money for food at the market.

fair (**fair**) adjective
▶ page 419

When something is **fair**, it is equal for everyone. Sports officials try to be **fair** when they make calls.

inspire (in-**spīr**) verb
▶ page 430

When something **inspires** you, it makes you want to do something. The scene **inspired** her to paint.

luck (**luk**) noun
▶ pages 419, 433

Luck means good fortune. The woman is having good **luck** playing the game.

offer (**ah**-fur) noun
▶ pages 420, 427

An **offer** is the price you want to pay for something. She will make an **offer** to buy the basket.

refuse (ri-**fyüz**) verb
▶ pages 420, 433

To **refuse** something means to say no to it. She **refuses** to eat this fruit.

reveal (ri-**vēl**) verb
▶ pages 429, 431, 433

To **reveal** is to show or tell something that was hidden. She took off the paper to **reveal** a great gift.

spirit (**spir**-ut) noun
▶ pages 429, 433

Your **spirit** is the way you act, think, and feel. This girl has a joyful **spirit**.

Practice the Words Work with a partner to write three sentences. Use at least two Key Vocabulary words in each sentence.

Sentence 1:
I think your <u>offer</u> to pay me $25 for my bike is <u>fair</u>.

BEFORE READING Luck

play by Elena Castedo

Make Inferences

Writers often give clues about characters and events instead of telling readers the information directly. When this happens, readers have to **make inferences**. When you make an inference, you combine what you know with what the writer says.

HOW TO MAKE INFERENCES

1. As you read, look for clues and details the author gives you about the characters and events.

2. Use what you know about people to make sense of the story. Connect your own experience to the details.

3. Track your thoughts on an **Inference Chart** like the one below.

Read the text and the Inference Chart to see how one reader made inferences about the play.

Look Into the Text

ACTOR 1. We are in shadows here already. Look, the mountain back there still has sunshine.

ACTOR 2. That's why I hate living down here in the valley. It's dark in the morning and dark in the evening. . . .

ACTOR 4. Up there on the mountain, they get all the summer breezes.

ACTOR 5. Why should they get all the luck? It's not fair.

Inference Chart

I read . . .	I know . . .	And so . . .
"Why should they get all the luck? It's not fair."	Some people are jealous when others have things they want.	These characters are jealous of the people on the mountain.

Try It

Create an Inference Chart. Make inferences as you read "Luck."

Genre: Drama

Drama is a type of literature that uses actors to tell a story. A play is an example of drama. Plays are usually divided into acts, or separate parts. Each act is a separate part of the play. Each act starts by describing the **setting**. The setting gives information about where and when the action happens.

Plays have characters. People called actors act out each character. **Stage directions** tell the actors how to perform. The words that actors say are also called **dialogue**.

A **script** tells people what to say and do when they perform the play. The script also gives information about the characters, the setting, and the acts. Read this script from "Luck."

ACT 1

> **SETTING:** An imaginary village in a valley. The time is the present.
>
> * * * * * * * * *
>
> **Character** [**ACTOR 1.** We are in the shadows here already. Look, the mountain back there still has sunshine.] **Dialogue**
>
> **Stage directions** [[ACTOR 1 *points to the* ACTORS *standing on the chairs.*]

www.hbedge.net
- Read an excerpt of a story by Elena Castedo.
- Watch a video clip of another play.

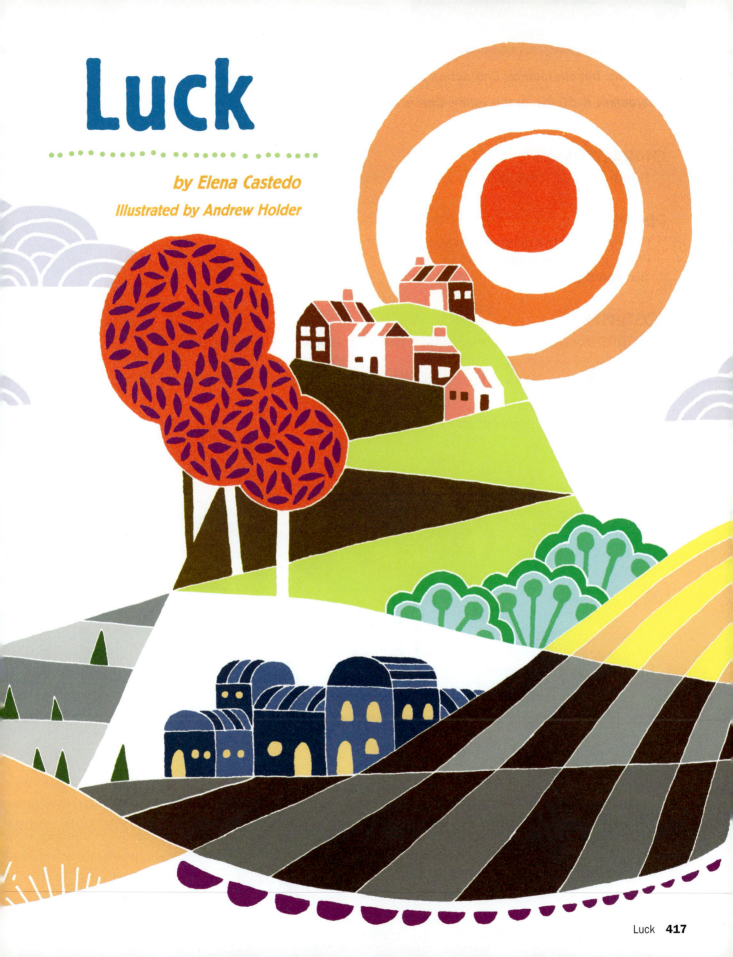

Luck

by Elena Castedo

Illustrated by Andrew Holder

There are ten characters. Characters 1–5 live in the mountains.

Characters 6–10 live in the valley. Chairs represent mountains.

CHARACTERS

Two or more ACTORS. ACTORS are always divided into two groups.

PROPS

Chairs for half the number of characters
Paper that **represents** money
Two **spotlights**

COSTUMES

ACTORS from each group wear **similar colors**. This will help identify the two groups.

Note: This version is written for ten characters. Use five chairs and about ten pieces of paper money.

In Other Words

Props Objects that the ACTORS use
represents we will pretend is
spotlights lights to shine on people
Costumes Clothes that the ACTORS wear
similar colors colors that are alike

One group of people lives in the mountains. Another group lives in the valley. Read to find out which group has more good <mark>luck</mark>.

ACT 1

SETTING: An imaginary village in a valley. The time is the present.

[*As the play opens, five chairs are in a row toward the back left side of the stage. ACTORS 6 to 10 stand on the chairs. They **are making motions as if** talking, but in silence. A spotlight shines on the front right side of the stage. ACTORS 1 to 5 enter. They stand at the front right area of the stage. They also talk silently. Then the light dims.*]

ACTOR 1. We **are in shadows** here already. Look, the mountain back there still has sunshine.

[ACTOR 1 *points to the* ACTORS *standing on the chairs.*]

ACTOR 2. That's why I hate living down here in the valley. It's dark in the morning and dark in the evening.

ACTOR 3. And we don't get any **views** down here.

ACTOR 4. Up there on the mountain, they get all the **summer breezes**.

[ACTOR 4 *moves arms to show breezes.*]

ACTOR 5. Why should they get all the luck? It's not <mark>fair</mark>.

ACTOR 1. There must be something we can do.

Key Vocabulary
<mark>luck</mark> *noun*, good fortune
<mark>fair</mark> *adjective*, equal for everyone

In Other Words
are making motions as if pretend to be
are in shadows have no sunshine
views beautiful things to look at
summer breezes gentle warm winds

ACTOR 2. Why don't we move to the mountain?

ACTOR 3. Because there are only five houses up there, and they took them all.

[ACTOR 3 *motions to the* ACTORS *on the chairs.*]

ACTOR 4. Maybe we can **exchange** our houses for theirs.

[ACTOR 4 *moves arms to make a motion of exchange.*]

ACTOR 5. What a great idea!

[ACTOR 5 *lifts up arms.*]

ACTOR 3. Naw. They probably won't want to do that.

ACTOR 4. Maybe we should pay them some extra money.

ACTOR 2. How much money do we have?

[*They take out money from their pockets, count, and share.*]

ACTOR 1. We'll make them an **offer** they can't **refuse**.

[ACTORS 1 *to 5 stir. Some leap, some push one another, and they all move toward the chairs.*]

ACTORS 1 to 5. Yes, yes, what a great idea. Let's go. Let's go ask them!

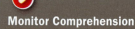

Monitor Comprehension

Summarize
How do the people in the valley feel about their home? What do they decide to do?

Key Vocabulary
exchange *verb*, to trade
offer *noun*, the price you want to pay for something
refuse *verb*, to say no to something

ACT 2

SETTING: An imaginary village in the mountains. The time is later that day.

[ACTORS 1 *to 5 stand in front of the* ACTORS *on the chairs and greet them.*]

ACTOR 1. Hi. We are the people from the valley. We are interested in exchanging houses. Our houses are very nice.

[ACTORS 1 *to 5 nod and make* **noises of agreement**.]

[ACTORS 6 *to 10 look at one another with surprise.*]

ACTOR 6. Hi. Thank you for your offer, but we don't want to exchange houses.

ACTOR 7. We like it up here on the mountain. We get a lot of sunshine.

ACTOR 8. And breezes in the summer.

ACTOR 9. And we like the beautiful view of the valley.

ACTOR 10. The air is very clean up here.

ACTOR 7. We **are so lucky** to be here on the mountain.

ACTOR 6. We are sorry you got the idea we wanted to exchange houses.

In Other Words
noises of agreement sounds that show they think the same way
are so lucky have such good luck

[ACTORS 1 *to 5 whisper to one another, search their pockets, and give bills to* ACTOR 1. *Then they face the* ACTORS *on the chairs.*]

ACTOR 2. Our houses are **in better shape** than yours. It would be a very good **deal** for you.

ACTOR 1. And we are prepared to pay you extra.

[ACTOR 1 *hands the* **wad of bills** *to* ACTOR 6.]

[ACTOR 6 *takes the bills and counts them.* ACTOR 6 *is* **impressed.** ACTOR 6 *passes them on to the other* ACTORS *on the chairs, who count them and are also impressed. They whisper to one another. They finally nod to one another and* **distribute the bills**.]

ACTOR 6. Okay. We'll exchange houses.

[ACTORS 6 *to 10 step down from the chairs. They move toward the front right area of the stage, which represents the valley.*]

[ACTORS 1 *to 5* **congratulate** *one another. They smile and* **make winning gestures** *as they climb onto the chairs.*]

In Other Words

in better shape much nicer
deal contract
wad of bills money
impressed pleased with the amount of money
distribute the bills give some of the money to each mountain person

congratulate say they are happy to
make winning gestures signal with their arms that they are happy

Monitor Comprehension

Confirm Prediction
How do the mountain people feel about the offer? Was your prediction correct? What clues helped you predict?

ACT 3

SETTING: The imaginary village in a valley. The time is a few days later.

[ACTORS 1 *to 5 stand on the chairs talking silently. They act cold and tired.*]

[ACTORS 6 *to 10 talk in the area that represents the valley.*]

ACTOR 6. I had no idea that life was so **pleasant** down here in the valley.

[ACTORS 1 *to 5 stop "talking" to one another. They* **urge** *one another to listen to the other group.*]

ACTOR 7. Me, too. These wells are full of delicious water.

ACTOR 8. It doesn't cost much to keep houses warm in the valley.

ACTOR 9. It's **lovely** not to have so much wind.

ACTOR 10. Have you noticed how easy it is to plant a garden?

ACTOR 6. The view of the mountains is beautiful.

ACTOR 8. Everything is so much easier than going up and down hills.

ACTOR 7. We are so lucky to be here in the valley.

In Other Words
pleasant nice
urge tell
lovely nice

[ACTORS 1 *to 5 make more* **gestures of discontent**. *They make gestures of being tired and cold. They whisper to one another and nod. They search their pockets and give bills to ACTOR 1. Then they step down from the chairs and move toward the group in the valley.*]

ACTOR 1. We would like to get our houses back.

ACTOR 6. These are our houses now, and we like them.

ACTOR 2. You said before that you liked living on the mountain.

ACTOR 3. We are prepared to pay you extra.

In Other Words
gestures of discontent movements that
show they are unhappy

ACTOR 1. We think you'll find this very **attractive**.

[ACTOR 1 *hands the wad of bills to* ACTOR 6.]

[ACTOR 6 *takes the bills and counts them.* ACTOR 6 *is impressed.* ACTOR 6 *passes them on to* ACTORS 7 *to 10, who are equally impressed. They whisper and nod to each other. They distribute the bills.*]

ACTOR 6. Okay. We'll exchange houses.

[ACTORS 6 *to 10 move toward the chairs and climb up.*]

[ACTORS 1 *to 5 shake hands to congratulate one another. They don't look as* **enthusiastic** *as before. The light now shines on the* ACTORS *on the chairs.*]

ACTOR 6. How nice! We still have sunshine! Look! Down in the valley it's all in shadows already.

[ACTOR 6 *points to the* ACTORS *in the valley.*]

ACTOR 9. The air is so fresh here.

ACTOR 10. What a beautiful view!

ACTOR 8. We have lots of money that the people from the valley gave us.

ACTOR 7. The main thing is that we are so lucky to be here on the mountain. ❖

In Other Words
attractive interesting
enthusiastic happy

ANALYZE Luck

1. **Explain** How do the mountain people feel about their new home in the valley? Why do they decide to move back to the mountain?

2. **Vocabulary** Why are the people who live on the mountain impressed by both the **offers** they received?

3. **Reading Strategy** **Make Inferences** Look again at the **Inference Chart** you began on page 415. Compare your inferences with a partner's. How are they the same? How are they different?

Return to the Text

Reread and Retell Reread Act 3. What makes the mountain people feel lucky? Discuss the play with a partner. Which group do you think has better luck at the end of the play? Why?

memoir by Huynh Quang Nhuong

Genre: Memoir

Sometimes authors tell stories about their own experiences and memories. These stories are called **memoirs**. Authors write memoirs about important people and events in their lives. A memoir is usually about how these people and events influenced, or changed, the author's personality or beliefs.

A memoir tells a story about something that really happened. Because authors of memoirs write about their own lives, they usually use the words *I*, *me*, and *my*.

HOW TO READ A MEMOIR

1. Read the text. Find important details about people and events. Write them on self-stick notes.

2. Decide which important things the author is describing. Ask, "Why did the author choose these details?"

3. Connect the details to the author's message about what influenced his personality or beliefs.

Read the text and the self-stick notes. See how one reader connects the details to what influenced the author.

Look Into the Text

My grandmother was quite old. But traces of her beauty were still there. Her hands, her feet, her face revealed that she had been an attractive young woman. Time didn't damage her youthful spirit.

"traces of her beauty were still there"

"Time didn't damage her youthful spirit."

The grandmother had a youthful spirit. The writer probably has a youthful spirit, too.

Try It

Read the memoir "Young at Heart." Connect the details to the author's message as you read.

Connect Across Texts

*In "Luck," the characters' view of what's important changes. In the following memoir, the writer tells about his grandmother's lifelong love of **theater**.*

YOUNG AT HEART

BY HUYNH QUANG NHUONG

When she was eighty years old, my grandmother was still quite strong. Every two days, she walked for more than an hour to reach the marketplace. She carried **a heavy load** of food. Then she spent another hour walking home.

My grandmother was quite old. But **traces** of her beauty were still there. Her hands, her feet, her face **revealed** that she had been **an attractive** young woman. Time didn't damage her youthful **spirit**.

Key Vocabulary
reveal *verb*, to show something that was hidden
spirit *noun*, the way you act, think, and feel

In Other Words
theater plays
a heavy load heavy bags
traces signs
an attractive a pretty

One of my grandmother's great **passions** was theater. This passion **never diminished** with age. She never missed a show when there were actors in town. If no actors came for several months, she would **organize** her own show. She was the manager, the producer, and the young **heroine**, all at the same time.

My grandmother's own plays were always dramas. They were **inspired** by books she had read and by what she had seen on the stage. She always chose her favorite grandson to play the role of the hero. He would always marry the heroine at the end. And they lived happily **ever after**.

In Other Words
passions loves
never diminished did not get less powerful
organize create
heroine female actor with the most important role
ever after for the rest of their lives

Monitor Comprehension

Describe
Describe the grandmother in this story.

My sisters told her that she was too old to play the young heroine. But my grandmother merely replied: "Anybody can play this role if she's young at heart." ❖

ANALYZE Young at Heart

1. **Describe** What do the author's sisters tell their grandmother?

2. **Vocabulary** What did the grandmother's actions **reveal** about her?

3. **Genre: Memoir** Reread the self-stick notes you wrote as you read "Young at Heart." Which details did you find? How did they help you understand what was important to the author?

⮌ Return to the Text

Reread and Retell The grandmother in the story says, "'Anyone can play this role if she's young at heart.'" Explain what this means in your own words. Use facts from the text to support your ideas.

The Marketplace

The grandmother in the memoir traveled a long distance to visit the market every day. In fact, the marketplace is a central part of life in Vietnam. Every day, **merchants** sell fruit, vegetables, rice, fish, medicine, clothing, and other important items.

Vietnamese women carry their goods to the market in baskets. They arrange and sell fresh food.

People do more than shop at the marketplace. People see friends and share news. The marketplace connects the community.

In Other Words
merchants people who sell things

Geography Background
Vietnam is a country in Southeast Asia. It is bordered by Cambodia, China, and Laos.

EQ **What Is Most Important in Life?**

Reading

Talk About Literature

1. **Draw Conclusions** The play "Luck" has two groups of people. Which group has the best **luck**? Why do you think so?

2. **Infer** How did the grandmother in "Young at Heart" keep her youthful **spirit**?

   She kept her youthful spirit by _____ .

EQ 3. **Compare** Each selection **reveals** a secret to a happy life. How do these ideas compare?

   According to "Luck," the secret to a happy life is _____ . According to "Young at Heart," the secret is _____ .

Fluency

Listen to a reading. Practice fluency. Use the Reading Handbook, page 543.

Vocabulary

Review Key Vocabulary

Choose the correct vocabulary word to complete each sentence.

1. Julio's family made an _____ to pay for his sister Janet's college.

2. They could not pay for Julio, too. "It's not _____!" Julio thought.

3. "My sister has all the good _____!" he said to himself.

4. Julio was not normally unhappy. In general, he had a joyful _____.

5. Even though Julio was unhappy, he did not _____ his feelings.

6. He _____ to get upset.

7. He read a book about ways to pay for college. The book _____ him.

8. Julio talked to his parents. They _____ ideas. Julio felt happy again.

Vocabulary

exchanged
fair
inspired
luck
offer
refused
reveal
spirit

Writing

Write About Literature

EQ **Explanation** Explain what makes people happy. Use examples from the selections and from your own life in your answer. Make a chart to organize your paragraph.

"Luck"	"Young at Heart"	My Life	Topic Statement
The people on the mountain are happy because . . .	The grandmother is happy because . . .	I am happy because . . .	People are happy with their lives because . . .

Grammar

Use Complete Sentences

A complete sentence has a subject and a predicate.

The subject always has a **noun** or **pronoun**.

The predicate always has one or more **verbs**.

SUBJECT	PREDICATE
The **people**	**move** to the mountain.
They	**feel** tired and cold.
The other **people**	**should give** their houses back.

A sentence fragment is a group of words that does not have a subject or a predicate. This fragment is missing a subject:

Offering money for the mountain homes.

This fragment is missing a verb:

The people money for the mountain homes.

A complete sentence has a **subject** and a predicate:

The **people** **offer** money for the mountain homes.

Oral Practice Say whether each group of words is a complete sentence. If it is not complete, add a subject or a predicate. Say the sentence.

1. The grandmother walks to the marketplace.
2. Is still a great beauty.
3. Is her greatest passion.
4. Her favorite grandson plays the hero.
5. The manager, the producer, and the heroine.

Written Practice (6–10) Now talk with a partner about the grandmother in "Young at Heart." Work together to write five complete sentences about her.

Language Development

Give and Follow Directions

Role-Play With a partner, play the roles of a valley person and a mountain person from the play "Luck."

Draw a map that shows the mountains and the valley. Add roads, rivers, and other details. Add the directions north, south, east, and west.

Exchange maps with your partner. Give each other directions to your character's home. Tell each other how to get up the mountain or go down into the valley.

Use these direction words to help you:

north	go
south	right
east	turn
west	left
up	miles
down	yards

Review Similes

Remember, a simile is one kind of figurative language. Similes use words such as *like*, *as*, and *than* to compare two unlike things. Writers use similes to create certain feelings or images in readers' minds.

SIMILE Aldo yells more loudly than a jet engine.

What is being compared?

Aldo's yelling is being compared to the sound of a jet engine. He yells really loudly.

Read each simile. What two things are being compared? What feeling or image is the writer trying to create?

1. Grandpa is old, but he is as playful as a puppy.
2. Grandma says he's as silly as a clown.
3. I think he's as sweet as honey!
4. He says that I'm clever, like a coyote.

Literary Element: Setting

The setting of a story is when and where it takes place. Look back at some stories you have read. Think about the settings of stories like "Growing Together" and "Alphabet City Ballet."

In many stories, the setting affects how characters act and feel. The setting of "Growing Together" is Carmita's new home in Georgia. The cold weather makes Carmita feel sad for her old home in Cuba.

Think about the setting in "Luck." Copy the **Setting Chart**. Look for words in the play that tell about the setting. Add these clues to the chart. Then analyze the clues.

How does the valley affect the characters that live there? How do the mountains affect the characters that live there? Discuss these questions in a group.

Setting Chart

Setting	How It Affects the Characters
Valley: – in the shadows – warmer	People felt . . .
Mountain:	People were . . .

Writing

Write a Skit

▶ **Prompt** People's attitudes, or ways of thinking, often reflect their values—what they think is important in life. Write a skit, or short play, that shows how attitudes reflect values. Include two characters. One character has a positive, or good, attitude. The other character has a negative, or bad, attitude.

1 Plan Review stage directions and dialogue. Then plan your skit. Visualize the action.

- Choose a setting and props.

- Choose a name for each of your characters.

- Decide what will happen in your skit.

- Decide what the characters will say and do.

Plan to write one scene. Make notes.

REMEMBER
• Stage directions tell the actors what to do. Use brackets, like this: [*She moves her arm.*]
• Dialogue is what the characters say. Begin each line of dialogue with the character's name.

Setting: A restaurant
Props:

Name of Character	What the Character Is Like	What the Character Says	What the Character Does
1.	positive attitude		
2.	negative attitude		

2 Write Use your notes to write your skit. Include stage directions and dialogue.

3 Share Ask two classmates to read and act out your skit. Can they follow your stage directions?

Engage in Discussion

Look at the picture and listen to the discussion.

Discussion

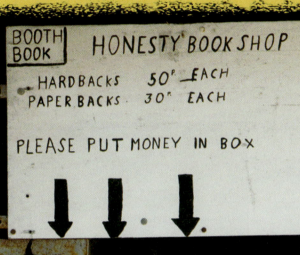

"**Honesty's the best policy.**"

—Miguel de Cervantes

Mrs. Lee: Think about what Cervantes said. Is honesty really always the best policy, or idea?

Angela: I definitely think so. If you cheat or lie, you only hurt yourself.

Charlie: I agree. Then you start to believe those lies. Soon you don't know the real truth anymore.

Mrs. Lee: So is honesty always the best policy?

Charlie: Always. You can only be true to yourself if you tell the truth.

Sari: I don't agree. What if you lie so you don't hurt someone's feelings? My sister got a new haircut last week, and she asked me if I liked it. I didn't like it, but I didn't want her to get mad. So I told her it looked great.

Angela: Did you feel guilty when you lied?

Sari: Well, at first I didn't. But then my sister offered to take me to get the same haircut. So I told her that I didn't really like it. Then she was mad, and I felt bad about lying.

Charlie: So lying to protect someone's feelings doesn't work out in the end.

Sari: I guess not.

1 TRY OUT LANGUAGE
2 LEARN GRAMMAR
3 APPLY ON YOUR OWN

Use Phrases and Clauses

A **phrase** is a group of words that work together. A sentence may have several phrases.

A sneaky **girl** / in my history class / **cheated** / on the final exam.
noun phrase   prepositional phrase   verb   prepositional phrase

This sentence is complete because it has a **subject** and a **verb**. A phrase never has both, so it does not express a complete thought.

A **clause** contains both a **subject** and a **verb**. A clause can stand alone as a sentence.

Our **teacher** **caught** her.

The **girl** **got** an automatic F on the test.

Say It

Work with a partner. Say each sentence. Then identify a phrase included in the sentence.

1. Someone cheated on the test.

2. He or she copied answers off this sheet of paper.

3. This is a serious matter.

4. The guilty person should admit it.

5. Everyone in the class may fail.

This girl is cheating on her exam.

Write It

Decide whether each group of words is a phrase or a clause.

If it is a phrase, use it in a sentence.

6. During the test.

7. At my paper.

8. The teacher saw it.

9. A two-hour detention.

10. Dishonesty doesn't pay.

Discuss Important Ideas

What is important to you? Discuss your views with your class or a small group. Follow these steps to discuss your ideas effectively:

HOW TO ENGAGE IN DISCUSSION

1. Tell people your ideas.
2. Take turns speaking.
3. Listen while others speak. Show respect for their ideas.
4. Use words and gestures to show that you are listening.
5. Focus on the topic of discussion.

> I think honesty is very important. If you are not honest, other people won't respect you.

> Hmmm. I disagree. Lots of famous people are not honest, and other people respect them.

Use a subject and a predicate in each of your sentences.

To prepare for your discussion, write four sentences about a belief that is important to you, such as honesty, truthfulness, or friendship. Use sentences like these:

- I think _____ is very important.
- To be _____, you have to _____.
- If you are not _____, you _____.
- If everyone is _____, the world will _____.

Then share your sentences. Discuss your ideas and those of the other members in the group. Do other members agree with your views? Do you agree with their views? Why or why not?

EQ What Is Most Important in Life?
Explore what it means to do the right thing.

Learn Key Vocabulary

Pronounce each word and learn its meaning.

Key Words

behavior (bi-**hā**-vyur) *noun*
▶ page 455

Your **behavior** is the way you act. His funny **behavior** made the students laugh.

cheat (**chēt**) *verb*
▶ pages 453, 458

To **cheat** is to do something that is unfair or against the rules. She **cheats** when she looks at my answers.

dignity (**dig**-nu-tē) *noun*
▶ pages 446, 451

Dignity is having pride in yourself. A person with **dignity** acts calmly and respectfully. My father has **dignity**.

honest (**ah**-nust) *adjective*
▶ pages 446, 459

An **honest** person tells the truth. In court, you must promise to be **honest**. *Synonym: truthful*

integrity (in-**te**-gru-tē) *noun*
▶ pages 453, 459

You have **integrity** when you do what you know is right. The scientist shows **integrity** with true test results.

recognize (**re**-kig-nīz) *verb*
▶ page 444

To **recognize** people or places is to know them when you hear or see them. She **recognizes** the voice on the phone.

standard (**stan**-durd) *noun*
▶ pages 455, 458

A **standard** is a measure of how good something is. The teacher has high **standards** for his students.

tradition (tru-**di**-shun) *noun*
▶ page 444

A **tradition** is a way of doing things. By **tradition**, students toss their hats in the air when they graduate.

Practice the Words Make an **Idea Web** for each of the three Key Vocabulary words. Write words that are related to each word you choose.

Idea Web

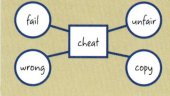

Make Inferences

A character's actions and behavior can show a lot about who he or she is. You can **make inferences** about characters based on their actions. This helps you understand the story better.

Reading Strategy
Make Inferences

HOW TO MAKE INFERENCES

1. Read the story. Notice details about how a character acts. Write them in the first column of an **Inference Chart**.

2. Think about what you already know. In the second column of your chart, write what you know about how people act.

3. Combine what you know with what you read to make an inference about the character. Write it in the third column of your chart.

This story is about a student who wins an honor called a scholarship jacket. She is talking to the principal. Read the text and the Inference Chart to see how one reader made inferences about the story.

Look Into the Text

> "Martha," he said, "as you know, the scholarship jacket has always been free. This year the Board decided to charge fifteen dollars."
>
> I stared at him in shock. I hadn't expected this. He still avoided looking in my eyes.

Inference Chart

I read . . .	I know . . .	And so . . .
"He still avoided looking in my eyes."	Sometimes when people avoid looking in your eyes, it means they do not want to tell you something.	The principal does not want to tell Marta about the scholarship jacket.

Try It

Make an Inference Chart. As you read "The Scholarship Jacket," make inferences about characters' actions.

Grandpa straightened up tiredly. He asked quietly, "What does a scholarship jacket mean?"

"It means you've earned it by having the highest grades and that's why they're giving it to you." Too late I realized the **significance** of my words. Grandpa knew that I understood it was not a matter of money. It wasn't that. He went back to pulling weeds. Finally he spoke again.

"Then if you pay for it, Marta, it's not a scholarship jacket, is it? Tell your principal I will not pay the fifteen dollars."

I walked back to the house. I was angry with Grandfather even though I knew he was right. I was angry with the Board, whoever they were. Why did they have to change the rules just when it was my turn to win the jacket?

In Other Words
significance meaning

Monitor Comprehension

Confirm Prediction
Was your prediction correct? Why didn't Marta's grandfather give her the money?

Predict
Marta is going to ask her grandfather for money.
What will he say?

"Grandpa," I said in Spanish, the only language he knew. He waited silently. "This year the principal said the scholarship jacket is going to cost fifteen dollars. I have to take the money in tomorrow, otherwise it'll be given to someone else."

Grandpa straightened up tiredly. He asked quietly, "What does a scholarship jacket mean?"

"It means you've earned it by having the highest grades and that's why they're giving it to you." Too late I realized the **significance** of my words. Grandpa knew that I understood it was not a matter of money. It wasn't that. He went back to pulling weeds. Finally he spoke again.

"Then if you pay for it, Marta, it's not a scholarship jacket, is it? Tell your principal I will not pay the fifteen dollars."

I walked back to the house. I was angry with Grandfather even though I knew he was right. I was angry with the Board, whoever they were. Why did they have to change the rules just when it was my turn to win the jacket?

In Other Words
significance meaning

Monitor Comprehension

Confirm Prediction
Was your prediction correct? Why didn't Marta's grandfather give her the money?

The next day the principal called me into his office. He looked uncomfortable and unhappy. I wasn't going to make it any easier for him. I looked him straight in the eye. He looked away.

"Martha," he said, "as you know, the scholarship jacket has always been free. This year the Board decided to charge fifteen dollars."

I stared at him in shock. I hadn't expected this. He still **avoided** looking in my eyes.

> *I wasn't going to make it any easier for him. I looked him straight in the eye.*

"So if you are unable to pay the fifteen dollars for the jacket, it will be given to the next one in line."

Standing with all the **dignity** I could **muster**, I said, "I'll speak to my grandfather about it, sir, and let you know tomorrow." I cried on the walk home from the bus stop.

Grandpa was out back working in the bean field. I walked slowly out to him, trying to think how I could best ask him for the money. I wanted that jacket so much. It was more than just being a valedictorian and giving a little speech on graduation night. It represented years of hard work and **expectation**. I knew I had to be **honest**.

Key Vocabulary
dignity *noun*, pride in oneself
honest *adjective*, truthful

In Other Words
avoided turned his head so he was not
muster find
expectation belief

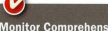

Monitor Comprehension

Explain
Why did the principal ask Marta to pay for the jacket?

Marta gets called to the principal's office. Find out why.

The small Texas school that I attended carried out a **tradition** every year during graduation; a beautiful gold and green jacket was awarded to the class valedictorian, the student who had maintained the highest grades. The scholarship jacket had a big gold S on the left front side and the winner's name was written in gold letters on the pocket.

I fully expected to win. I had been a straight-A student since the first grade. I looked forward to owning that jacket.

One day close to graduation, I was outside my classroom's door when I heard angry voices and arguing. I **recognized** the voices: Mr. Schmidt and Mr. Boone, two of my teachers. They seemed to be arguing about me. I couldn't believe it.

"I refuse to do it! I don't care who her father is, her grades don't even begin to compare to Martha's. I won't lie or falsify records. Martha has **a straight A-plus average** and you know it." That was Mr. Schmidt and he sounded very angry. Mr. Boone's voice sounded calm and quiet.

"Look, Joann's father is not only **on the Board**, he owns the only store in town. We could say **it was a close tie** and—"

Only a word here and there **filtered** through. " . . . Martha is Mexican. . . . resign. . . . won't do it. . . ." I don't remember how I made it through the afternoon. I went home and cried. It seemed a cruel **coincidence** that I had overheard that conversation.

Key Vocabulary
tradition *noun*, a way of doing things
recognize *verb*, to know people or places when you hear or see them

In Other Words
a straight A-plus average the best grades
on the Board part of the group that makes important decisions about the school
it was a close tie Joann had the same grades
filtered came
coincidence accident

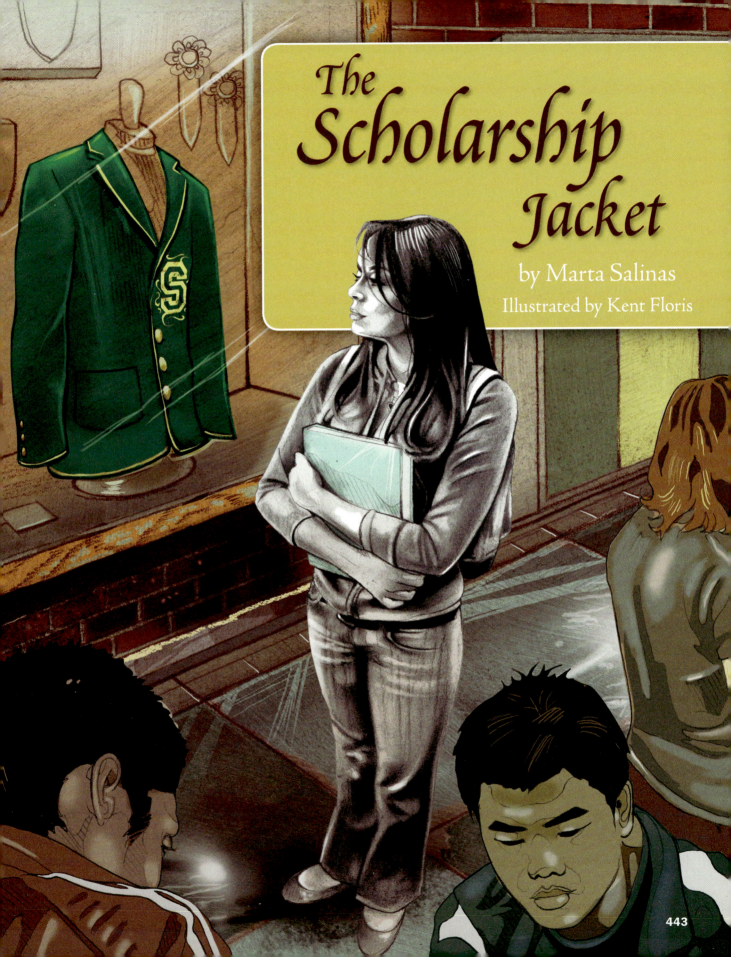

The Scholarship Jacket

by Marta Salinas

Illustrated by Kent Floris

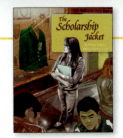

Make Inferences

A character's actions and behavior can show a lot about who he or she is. You can **make inferences** about characters based on their actions. This helps you understand the story better.

HOW TO MAKE INFERENCES

1. Read the story. Notice details about how a character acts. Write them in the first column of an **Inference Chart**.

2. Think about what you already know. In the second column of your chart, write what you know about how people act.

3. Combine what you know with what you read to make an inference about the character. Write it in the third column of your chart.

This story is about a student who wins an honor called a scholarship jacket. She is talking to the principal. Read the text and the Inference Chart to see how one reader made inferences about the story.

Look Into the Text

> "Martha," he said, "as you know, the scholarship jacket has always been free. This year the Board decided to charge fifteen dollars."
>
> I stared at him in shock. I hadn't expected this. He still avoided looking in my eyes.

Inference Chart

I read . . .	I know . . .	And so . . .
"He still avoided looking in my eyes."	Sometimes when people avoid looking in your eyes, it means they do not want to tell you something.	The principal does not want to tell Marta about the scholarship jacket.

Try It

Make an Inference Chart. As you read "The Scholarship Jacket," make inferences about characters' actions.

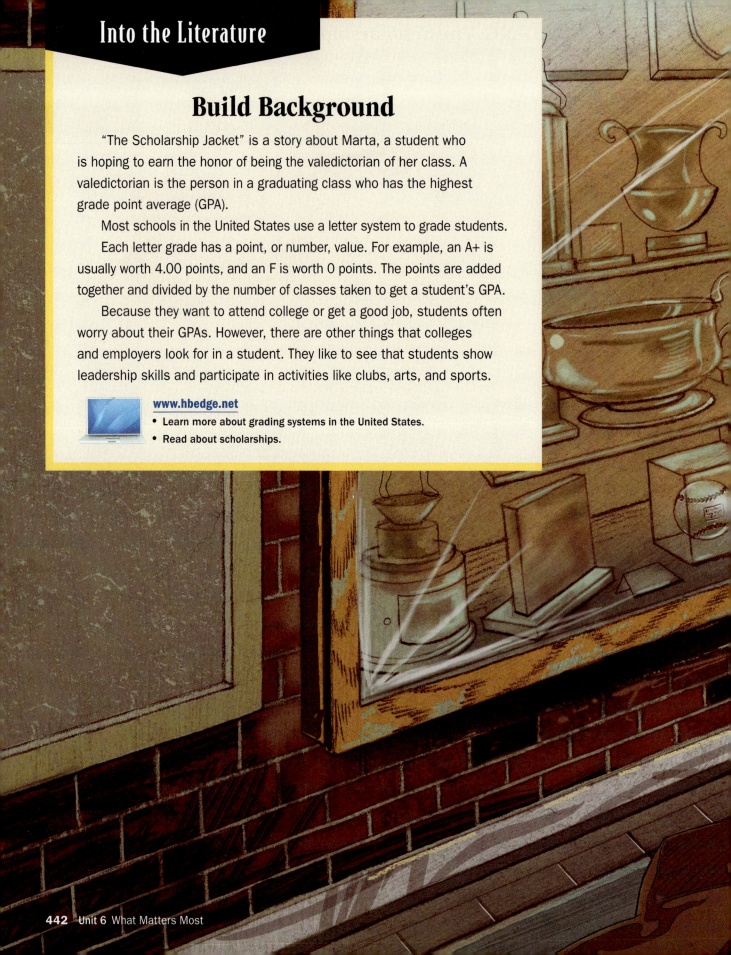

Build Background

"The Scholarship Jacket" is a story about Marta, a student who is hoping to earn the honor of being the valedictorian of her class. A valedictorian is the person in a graduating class who has the highest grade point average (GPA).

Most schools in the United States use a letter system to grade students. Each letter grade has a point, or number, value. For example, an A+ is usually worth 4.00 points, and an F is worth 0 points. The points are added together and divided by the number of classes taken to get a student's GPA.

Because they want to attend college or get a good job, students often worry about their GPAs. However, there are other things that colleges and employers look for in a student. They like to see that students show leadership skills and participate in activities like clubs, arts, and sports.

www.hbedge.net
- Learn more about grading systems in the United States.
- Read about scholarships.

I **dragged myself** into the principal's office the next day. This time he did look me in the eyes.

"What did your grandfather say?"

I sat very straight in my chair.

"He said to tell you he wouldn't pay the fifteen dollars."

The principal muttered something and walked over to the window.

"Why?" he finally asked. "Your grandfather has the money."

I forced my eyes to stay dry. "He said if I had to pay for it, then it wouldn't be a scholarship jacket." I stood up to leave. "I guess you'll just have to give it to Joann." I was almost to the door when he stopped me.

> *...if I had to pay for it, then it wouldn't be a scholarship jacket.*

"Martha—wait."

What did he want now? I could feel my heart pounding. **Something bitter and vile tasting** was coming up in my mouth. I was afraid I was going to **be sick**. I didn't need any sympathy speeches. He sighed loudly and looked at me.

In Other Words
dragged myself made myself go
Something bitter and vile tasting A very bad taste
be sick throw up

The Scholarship Jacket   **449**

"Okay, damn it. We'll **make an exception** in your case. I'll tell the Board, you'll get your jacket."

I could hardly believe it. "Oh, thank you, sir!" Suddenly I felt great. I wanted to yell, jump, run the mile, do something. At the end of the day, Mr. Schmidt winked at me and said, "I hear you're getting a scholarship jacket this year."

In Other Words
make an exception forget about the rule

His face looked as happy and **innocent** as a baby's, but I knew better. Without answering I gave him a quick hug. I cried on the walk home again, but this time because I was so happy. I ran straight to the field.

"The principal is making an exception for me, Grandpa. I'm getting the jacket **after all**. That's after I told him what you said."

Grandpa just gave me a pat on the shoulder and a smile. He pulled out his crumpled red handkerchief and wiped the sweat off his forehead.

"Better go see if your grandmother needs any help with supper."

I gave him a big **grin**. He didn't fool me. I skipped and ran back to the house whistling some silly tune. ❖

ANALYZE The Scholarship Jacket

1. **Confirm Prediction** Did you predict that Marta would get the jacket? If yes, what clues led you to your prediction? If no, why did you expect something different?

2. **Vocabulary** Why is it hard for Marta to keep her <mark>dignity</mark> when she hears about the cost of the jacket?

3. **Reading Strategy** **Make Inferences** Reread your **Inference Chart**. What inferences did you make about the characters? Compare your inferences with a partner. How did your inferences improve your understanding of the story?

⤴ Return to the Text

Reread and Retell Read pages 447–448. In your own words, explain how her grandfather's words help Marta resolve the conflict.

In Other Words
innocent unaware
after all even though I did not give him
    money for it
grin smile

from *Current Events*, January 9, 2004

Text Structure: Cause and Effect

Sometimes nonfiction is organized around **cause and effect**. A cause is the reason something happens. An effect is the result.

Magazine writers and news writers often use this text structure to explain why something happens. Texts often describe multiple causes and effects.

> ### HOW TO IDENTIFY CAUSES AND EFFECTS
>
> 1. Read the text.
>
> 2. Identify something that happens. Ask, "What happened?" "Why did it happen?" The reason it happened is the cause. The result is the effect.
>
> 3. Record the information in a **Cause-and-Effect Chart**.

Read this text about students cheating at school.

Look Into the Text

The effect is what is happening.

Why has the number of cheaters risen so much? Donald McCabe led the Rutgers University study about cheating. He says the Internet is partly to blame. "The Internet makes plagiarism very simple."

The cause is why it is happening.

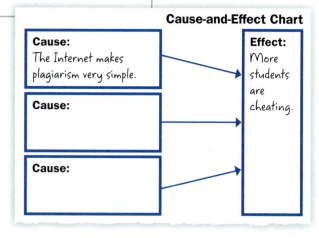

Cause-and-Effect Chart

Cause:
The Internet makes plagiarism very simple.

Cause:

Cause:

Effect:
More students are cheating.

Try It

Make a Cause-and-Effect Chart. As you read "Eye on Cheaters," look for additional reasons for the rise in cheating.

Connect Across Texts

In "The Scholarship Jacket," the characters learn that **integrity** is important. As you read this article, think about the value of integrity.

Eye on Cheaters

from *CURRENT EVENTS*, JAN. 9, 2004

THIS IS A TEST. Clear off your desks, and get your pencils.

1. A friend steals a copy of your social studies test. You

   (A) **high-five** him.

   (B) tell your teacher. **Cheating** is wrong.

2. You studied for your exam. Still, you just can't remember all those vocabulary words. You

   (A) look at the paper of the smart girl who sits next to you.

   (B) answer the questions you know. Next time you'll study harder.

3. You are doing research for a book report. You find a Web site that has essays already written. They're pretty good. You

   (A) **hit copy, then paste!**

   (B) write your own paper. Your ideas are better anyway.

Key Vocabulary

integrity *noun*, doing what you know is right

cheat *verb*, to do something that is unfair or against the rules

In Other Words

high-five show that you are proud of

hit copy, then paste! use the essay from the Internet instead of writing your own

DID YOU ANSWER "A" to any of the questions? If so, you're one of a growing number of students who cheat. If you answered "B," chances are the person next to you tried to copy your answers.

In 2002, the Josephson Institute of Ethics surveyed twelve thousand high-school students. It found that 74 percent cheated at least once that year. That's up from 61 percent ten years before.

Why has the number of cheaters risen so much? Donald McCabe led the Rutgers Unversity study about cheating. He says the Internet is partly to blame. "The Internet makes **plagiarism** very **simple**."

In Other Words
plagiarism copying the work of others
simple easy

Social Studies Background
Copyright laws protect ideas and words. Adults who plagiarize sometimes lose their jobs or have to pay money to the person they have stolen from.

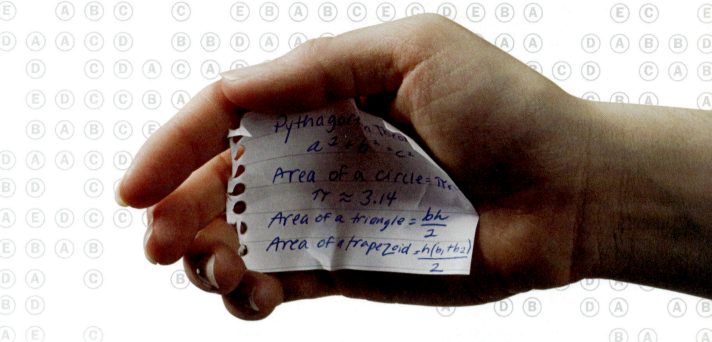

McCabe also thinks that cheating and **corruption** by famous adults are to blame. "I think kids today are looking to adults . . . for **a moral compass**. When they see the <mark>behavior</mark> occurring there, they don't understand why they should be held to a higher <mark>standard</mark>," he explained.

What do cheaters have to say for themselves? Half of students asked said that they didn't think copying answers was wrong.

"I think cheating has become . . . 'normal' in some cases," wrote one student.

Another responded, "You do what it takes to **succeed** in life. We're afraid **to fail**."

High-school senior Alice Newhall said: "What's important is getting ahead. . . . If you learn to **cut corners** to do that, you're going to be saving yourself time and energy. In the real world, that's what's going on. The better you do, that's what shows. It's not how moral you were in getting there."

Monitor Comprehension

Summarize
What does McCabe say about cheating?

Key Vocabulary
<mark>behavior</mark> *noun*, the way a person acts
<mark>standard</mark> *noun*, a measure of how good something is

In Other Words
corruption lying and stealing
a moral compass an understanding of what is right and what is wrong
succeed get what you want
to fail we will not get what we want
cut corners use work that isn't yours

TO FIGHT THE PROBLEM, some schools have a **secret weapon**—students. Marple Newtown High School in Philadelphia is one of a growing number of schools with student "academic integrity **committees**." At Marple, students on the committee visit classrooms to talk about cheating.

Committee leader Joey Borson, a senior, thinks the committee is useful. "Is there anything more important than your word? If you don't have your word or your honor, **what's the point**?"

In Other Words
secret weapon good solution
committees groups
what's the point? you have nothing.

THIS IS ANOTHER TEST. Take out your pencils and try again.

1. When you look at a friend's paper to get or check an answer, you

   Ⓐ lie about what you know.

   Ⓑ make it worse for yourself in the future. When questions get harder, you will not know the basics.

2. When you let a friend copy your work, you

   Ⓐ rob your friend of knowledge.

   Ⓑ make your own work **less valuable**.

3. When you copy something from a book or Web site, you

   Ⓐ **break the law** by stealing from someone.

   Ⓑ miss the chance to share information in your own voice.

ON THIS TEST, every answer shows the negative impact of cheating. What other ways does cheating **impact** you and others? ❖

In Other Words
less valuable worth less
break the law go against the law
impact affect

Monitor Comprehension

Explain
Who is Joey Borson? What does he say about cheating?

ANALYZE Eye on Cheaters

1. **Describe** What are some schools doing to help stop <mark>cheating</mark>?

2. **Vocabulary** What does McCabe mean when he talks about students being held to a higher <mark>standard</mark> than adults?

3. **Text Structure: Cause and Effect** Look again at the **Cause-and-Effect Chart** you began on page 452. Share the causes you added with a partner. Talk about how your Cause-and-Effect Chart affected your understanding of the text.

↩ Return to the Text

Reread and Retell What are the students at Marple Newtown High School doing to solve the problem of cheating?

EQ What Is Most Important in Life?

Reading

Talk About Literature

1. **Infer** Does the principal in "The Scholarship Jacket" act with **integrity**? Why do you think so?

   The principal (does/does not) act with integrity. I think this because _____ .

2. **Compare** Look again at the quiz on page 453. Would you answer the questions differently now that you know more about how cheating affects others? Why or why not?

   I would answer the questions _____ because I think _____ .

EQ 3. **Synthesize** Is it more important to be **honest** or successful? Use examples from both selections to explain your answer.

   I think it is more important to be _____ . As "The Scholarship Jacket" shows, _____ . As "Eye on Cheaters" shows, _____ .

Fluency

Listen to a reading. Practice fluency. Use the Reading Handbook, page 544.

Vocabulary

Review Key Vocabulary

Choose the correct vocabulary word to complete each sentence.

1. Every year the school has an essay contest. It's a _____ .

2. The school chooses only the best essays. The _____ are high.

3. Sara did not intend to _____ when she wrote her essay.

4. She took text from a Web page. That was not good _____ .

5. Sara did not _____ the problem until she read the contest rules.

6. She talked to her teacher. "Thank you for being _____ ," he said.

7. Sara felt ashamed. Her _____ was hurt.

8. But she had told the truth. She acted with _____ .

Vocabulary
- behavior
- cheat
- dignity
- honest
- integrity
- recognize
- standards
- tradition

Writing

Write About Literature

Position Statement In "Eye on Cheaters," Joey Borson asks, "Is there anything more important than your word?" Answer Joey's question. Support your opinion with two or three reasons. Make a chart to organize your writing.

Opinion	Reasons

Combine Sentences

You can put two short sentences together to make a **compound sentence**. Use a comma and the word **and**, **but**, or **or** to join the sentences.

- Use **and** to join similar ideas.
  Marta was first in the class. Joann was second.
  Marta was first in the class, **and** Joann was second.

- Use **but** to join different or contrasting ideas.
  Joann was second. She almost won the jacket.
  Joann was second, **but** she almost won the jacket.

- Use **or** to show a choice.
  Marta could say something. She could remain silent.
  Marta could say something, **or** she could remain silent.

Oral Practice Work with a partner. Say each pair of sentences. Combine sentences with **and**, **but**, or **or** to make a compound sentence. Then say the new sentence.

1. Marta won the jacket. She had to pay fifteen dollars for it.
2. She could pay the money. She could let Joann have the jacket.
3. Marta told her grandfather about the Board's decision. He would not pay the fifteen dollars.
4. Marta was angry with the Board. She was angry with her grandfather.
5. Marta talked to the principal. He changed his mind.

Written Practice (6–10) Rewrite the paragraph. Combine five pairs of sentences with **and**, **but**, or **or**.

You studied for your exam. You can't remember anything. You can see the paper of the girl next to you. Your teacher isn't looking. Should you copy her answers? Should you do the best you can on your own? Cheating is a serious offense. It can get you kicked out of school. You would love to get a good grade. You will not cheat.

Engage in Discussion

Think Like a Character Imagine that you are one of the characters in "The Scholarship Jacket." Get ready to discuss the character's beliefs. Prepare to say sentences like these:

- I think _____ is very important.
- To be _____, you have to _____.
- If you are not _____, you _____.
- If everyone is _____, the world will _____.

Form a group with students who chose the same character as you did. Discuss what is important to your character and why.

Review Idioms

Remember, an idiom is a kind of figurative language. Its meaning does not match the literal, or exact, meaning of its words. You can often use context to figure out the meaning.

IDIOM The walls have ears, so be careful what you say.

> Walls don't have ears! But "be careful what you say" gives a clue.

> This idiom must mean that people are listening.

Read each sentence. Figure out the meaning of the idiom. What feeling or image is the writer trying to create?

1. Nina and her sister Rosita do not always see eye to eye.
2. When Nina has a problem, she racks her brain and then jumps to a conclusion.
3. When Rosita has a problem, she prefers to sleep on it before she makes a decision.

🔖 **Reading Handbook**, page 555

Literary Element: Plot

Remember, the plot is the sequence, or order, of action in a story. It includes all the things that happen from the beginning to the end.

1. **Beginning** The plot begins with a **problem**.

2. **Middle**
   - **Events** make the problem worse.
   - When the problem is at its worst, something changes. This is called the **turning point**.

3. **End** The end of the story describes the **solution**.

Think back to the story "Two Were Left." The turning point happens when the plane finds the boy and his dog.

In "The Scholarship Jacket," the turning point is not as clear. Work with a partner. Make a **Plot Diagram** to show what happens in "The Scholarship Jacket."

Plot Diagram

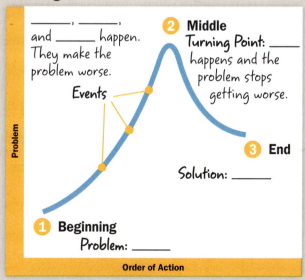

Writing

Write About Cheating

▶ **Prompt** What is the definition of cheating, according to your school? What happens if someone at your school cheats? Find out your school's rules about cheating. Then write a paragraph on the topic.

1 Plan Review the article "Eye on Cheaters." Ask about your school's rules about cheating.

- Brainstorm examples of cheating. Make a list.
- Then brainstorm ways to prevent cheating. How can students get better grades without cheating?

> Examples of Cheating
> 1. Stealing a copy of a test
> 2. Copying answers from a classmate's paper
> 3.

2 Write Use your notes to write your paragraph. You can express your ideas more completely when you use compound sentences. To make a compound sentence, join two sentences using **and**, **but**, or **or**.

REMEMBER
• Use **and** to join two ideas that are alike.
• Use **but** to join two ideas that are different.
• Use **or** to show a choice between two ideas.

Paragraph Organizer

The teachers and principal at [name of school] expect students to perform with integrity at all times. When students cheat, they lose the opportunity to show how much they really know. Cheating includes [example of cheating] , [another example] , and [another example] . If students are caught cheating, [Explain what happens.] . Students never need to cheat. If they do not feel that they can do well on a test or paper, they can [Explain how to get good grades without cheating.] .

3 Share Exchange papers with a partner. Read each other's paragraphs. Discuss your ideas. How do they compare?

Retell a Story

1 TRY OUT LANGUAGE
2 LEARN GRAMMAR
3 APPLY ON YOUR OWN

Listen to a folk tale from Vietnam. Then look at the pictures and listen to a retelling of the tale.

Folk Tale

There was a rooster who was all alone. He was very hungry and weak.

He walked around the countryside and looked for food everywhere. He didn't find anything to eat.

One day, the rooster found a shiny stone on the ground. He stared at it for a long time.

Finally, he said, "People will fight over this jewel. It will be valuable to them. But to me, the jewel is worthless because I cannot eat it. Shiny stones will not keep me alive." And the hungry rooster continued to look for food.

1 TRY OUT LANGUAGE
2 LEARN GRAMMAR
3 APPLY ON YOUR OWN

Use Complex Sentences

A **clause** has a **subject** and a **verb**.

- An **independent clause** can stand alone as a sentence.

  My photo album **is** valuable.

  independent clause

- A **dependent clause** also has a **subject** and a **verb**, but it cannot stand alone as a sentence. It begins with a **conjunction**. **Because**, **since**, **when**, **before**, and **after** are conjunctions.

  because **my grandmother** **gave** it to me

  dependent clause

You can use a conjunction to join a dependent clause to an independent clause. The new sentence is complete, and it is called a **complex sentence**.

My photo album **is** valuable **because** **my grandmother** **gave** it to me.

independent clause   dependent clause

Say It

Work with a partner. Match each independent clause on the left with a dependent clause on the right. Say the complex sentence.

1. I think of my best friend
2. She moved to Pittsburgh
3. I wear the locket to remind me of her
4. It is broken
5. I gave it to her

a. when I look at my broken locket.
b. because I gave my friend the other half.
c. since I never see her anymore.
d. before she moved away.
e. after her father got a new job there.

Write It

Match each independent clause on the left with a dependent clause on the right. Write the complex sentence.

6. Jamie put on her old green coat
7. She hardly wears it
8. She loves the coat
9. He got the coat
10. She found it in the attic

a. when he was in the army.
b. after he died.
c. before we went outside.
d. because it was her father's.
e. since it is so valuable to her.

Retell a Story

"The Rooster and the Jewel" is a folk tale that shows that the value of an object depends on who is looking at it. Think of a folk tale or story that you know. Retell it to your classmates.

Follow these steps as you tell your folk tale or story:

HOW TO RETELL A STORY

1. Remember the sequence of events.

2. Say the events in your own words. Use signal words like *first*, *second*, *next*, *then*, and *last*.

3. Speak clearly and show emotions in your voice.

4. Show emotions with your face and body.

A lost rooster was looking for food **because** he was hungry.

Join sentences with a **conjunction** to make your story clearer and more interesting.

To help you plan your retelling:

• Make a time line. It will help you remember what happens first, next, and so on.

A hungry rooster got lost.　　He looked for food.　　He saw a shiny stone.

• Look at the events on your time line. Think about how you can tell each part of the story in your own words.

• Practice telling the story. Say the events in the right order.

• As you retell the story to your classmates, show emotions with your face. Use gestures to show action.

EQ ## What Is Most Important in Life?
Consider how love matters.

Learn Key Vocabulary

Pronounce each word and learn its meaning.

Key Words

generosity (je-nu-**rah**-su-tē) *noun*
▶ pages 474, 487

When you share easily, you show **generosity**. Everyone knows about her **generosity**.

invent (in-**vent**) *verb*
▶ page 479

When you **invent**, you make something completely new. The student **invented** a robot.

precious (**pre**-shus) *adjective*
▶ pages 479, 481, 483

When something is **precious**, it has great value. Wedding rings are **precious** to people.

proud (prowd) *adjective*
▶ page 472

When you are **proud**, you feel happy about something. The students were **proud** of their grades.

reflect (ri-**flekt**) *verb*
▶ page 479

To **reflect** means to show or represent something. Her good grades **reflected** her hard work.

sacrifice (**sa**-kru-fīs) *verb*
▶ pages 480, 487

When you **sacrifice** something, you lose it, often for a reason. Members of the military often **sacrifice** their lives.

sensitive (**sen**-su-tiv) *adjective*
▶ pages 484, 486

A **sensitive** person or thing is easily affected, changed, or hurt. The **sensitive** boy cried when he fell.

wish (wish) *verb*
▶ page 478

To **wish** for something is to want it very much. The dog **wished** for the food.

Practice the Words Make a **Word Map** for three Key Vocabulary words. Compare maps with a partner.

Word Map

Definition	Characteristics
having great value	important, desirable
precious	
My ring is precious.	Something that no one cares for.
Example	**Non-example**

short story by O. Henry

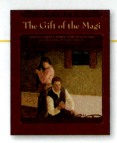

Make Inferences

Stories often have pictures or other visuals that relate to events in the text. You can use these visuals to **make inferences** about the story's characters and events. This can help with your understanding of the story.

> **Reading Strategy**
> **Make Inferences**

HOW TO MAKE INFERENCES

1. Look at a picture. Notice details about the picture. Write them in the first column of an **Inference Chart**.

2. Think about what you already know about the subject of the picture. Write it in the second column of your chart.

3. Combine what you know with what you see to make an inference about the characters or events. Write your inference in the third column.

Look at the picture and read the Inference Chart to see how one reader made inferences about the story.

Look Into the Text

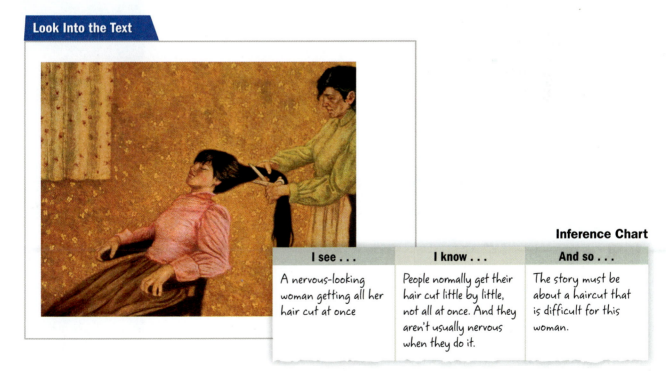

Inference Chart

I see . . .	I know . . .	And so . . .
A nervous-looking woman getting all her hair cut at once	People normally get their hair cut little by little, not all at once. And they aren't usually nervous when they do it.	The story must be about a haircut that is difficult for this woman.

Try It

As you read "The Gift of the Magi," use an Inference Chart to write inferences about the pictures.

Meet O. Henry
(1862–1910)

O. Henry is the author of a short story called "The Gift of the Magi."
O. Henry was a pen name, or false name, used by William Sydney Porter.
Porter worked at a drugstore, on a ranch, and as a teller at the First
National Bank in Austin, Texas. He began his writing career when he
started a small weekly magazine called the *Rolling Stone*. Then he worked
as a reporter for the *Houston Post*.

Porter went to prison in 1896 for embezzling, or stealing, bank funds.
He tried to escape to Honduras, but his wife was ill and he came home.
She died before he went to prison. In prison he began using the name
O. Henry. He wrote and sold stories to magazines to send money to his
daughter. After prison, O. Henry moved to New York City, where he wrote
numerous stories and books. Many of his stories are about the lives of
ordinary people in New York City. They often have surprise endings.

**William Sydney Porter (O. Henry) was born
in Greensboro, North Carolina.**

www.hbedge.net
- Learn more about O. Henry.
- Read another story by O. Henry.

The Gift of the Magi

ADAPTED FROM A SHORT STORY BY O. HENRY
ILLUSTRATIONS BY JAMES BENTLEY

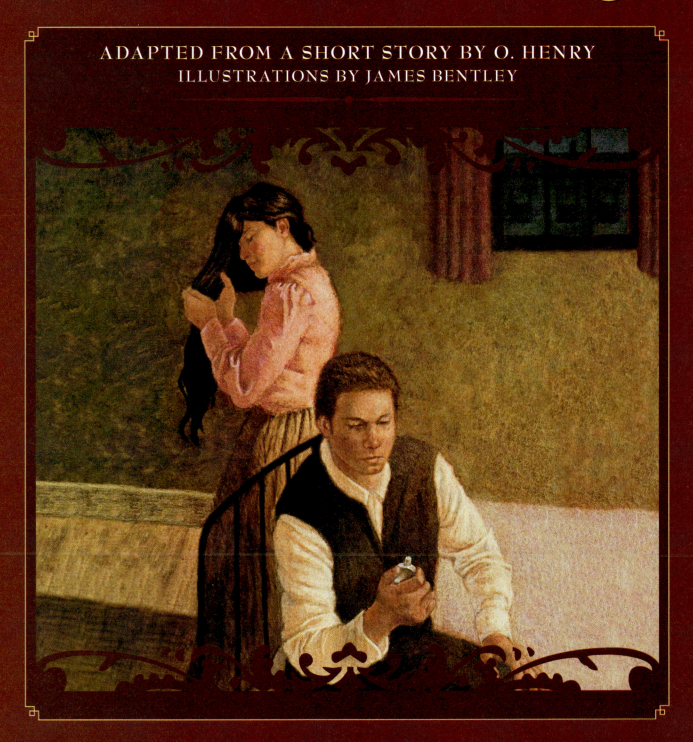

NEW YORK IN THE EARLY 1900s

In the 1900s, most large companies in the United States were **located** in New York City. Many rich people came to the city. Poor people also came looking for a better life. The rich **increased their wealth**, and the poor lived in crowded **slums**.

GATEWAY TO AMERICA

The Lower East Side, a slum, was the most crowded place in the city. It was five times as crowded as the rest of New York City. Although life was difficult, slums were **lively places**. Immigrants **kept alive traditions** from their countries.

TENEMENTS

Tenements were small, cheap buildings where people lived. They were very crowded. Air did not pass through them well. Disease spread quickly.

In Other Words

located found
increased their wealth got more money
slums neighborhoods
lively places neighborhoods full of activity
kept alive traditions practiced old customs

R. H. Macy & Co.

In 1902, Macy's opened its **flagship** store on Broadway. At one time it was the world's largest **department store**.

Fashion

In the 1900s, men and women wore formal clothing, if they could afford it. For parties and other celebrations, women wore jewelry and fancy dresses. Men wore pocket watches and suits made by tailors.

In Other Words

flagship biggest and most important
department store store that sells many different kinds of things
Fashion Style of clothes

It is almost Christmas, and Della does not have much money. What will she buy for Jim?

One dollar and eighty-seven cents. That was all. And sixty cents of it was in pennies. Della counted it three times: $1.87.

Tomorrow was Christmas Day, and that was all she had to buy Jim a present. She had wanted to give him something **fine and rare**—something **worthy of** a man like Jim.

Suddenly Della looked into her cheap mirror. She pulled down her hair and let it fall around her.

Now, the James Dillingham Youngs owned two things that they were **proud** of. One was Jim's gold watch. It had been his father's and his grandfather's. The other was Della's hair.

Della's beautiful hair fell around her, rippling and shining like a waterfall. Then she tied it up again nervously and quickly. A tear or two splashed on the **worn** red carpet.

With a bright **sparkle** still in her eyes, she **flew** out the door and down the street. She stopped at a sign that read: "Madame Sofronie. Hair Goods of All Kinds."

"Will you buy my hair?" asked Della.

"I buy hair," said Madame. "Let's look at it."

Della let her hair down.

"Twenty dollars," said Madame.

"Give me the money quickly," said Della.

Key Vocabulary
proud *adjective*, very happy about something

In Other Words
fine and rare very special
worthy of good enough for
worn old
sparkle shine
flew ran

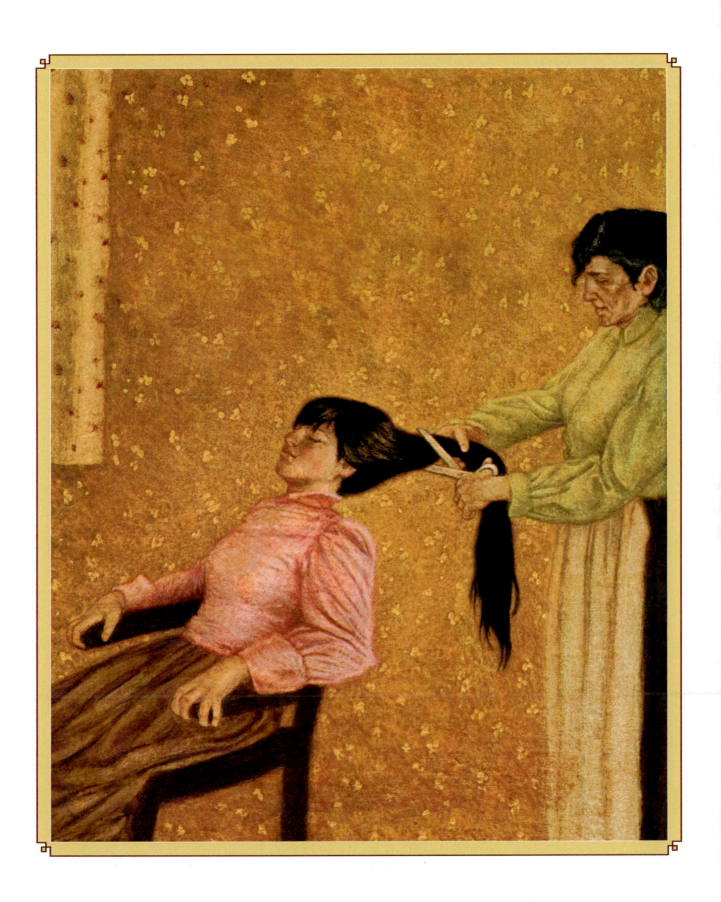

Oh, the next two hours were **like a rosy dream**. Della went through the stores, searching for Jim's present.

She found it at last. It was a platinum watch chain. It was **valuable** and simple. As soon as she saw it, she knew that Jim should have it. It was like him. The words "quietness" and "value" matched them both. She paid twenty-one dollars and hurried home with the eighty-seven cents.

She found it at last.

When Della reached home, she started to think **calmly**. She got out her curling irons and worked to repair the damage that happens when **generosity** is added to love. This is always a **huge task**, dear friends—a **mammoth** task.

Forty minutes later, Della's head was covered with tiny curls. She looked at her reflection in the mirror for a long time and whispered: "Please God, make him think I am still pretty."

Monitor Comprehension

Summarize
Retell the main events up to this point in the story.

The door opened and Jim came in. He looked thin and serious. Poor fellow! He was only twenty-two, but he had so much to worry about!

Jim froze inside the door. He stared at Della. She couldn't understand the expression in his eyes, and it terrified her. It was not anger, surprise, disapproval, or **horror**. It wasn't any of the feelings she expected. He just stared at her with that strange expression on his face.

"Jim, darling," she cried, "don't look at me that way. I had my hair cut off and sold. I couldn't live through Christmas without giving you a present. Let's be happy. You don't know what a beautiful, nice gift I've got for you."

"You cut off your hair?" asked Jim, slowly.

In Other Words
horror fear

"I cut it off and sold it," said Della. "Don't you like me just as well? I'm still me without my hair, right? It's Christmas Eve. Be good to me because the hair was sold for you," she said with a serious sweetness.

Don't you like me just as well?

Jim **wrapped** his Della in his arms. For ten seconds let us look carefully in the other direction. Eight dollars a week or a million a year—what is the difference? A **mathematician** would give you the wrong answer. The magi brought valuable gifts, but that was not one of them. This **mysterious** idea will be clear later. Jim took a package from his pocket.

"Don't make any mistake, Dell," he said, "about me. No haircut could ever make me like my girl any less. But once you unwrap this present, you may see why you surprised me at first."

In Other Words
wrapped held
mathematician person who knows math
mysterious strange and confusing

Cultural Background
In the Christian tradition, the Magi were the Three Wise Men who visited Jesus after he was born. They brought gifts of gold and perfumes.

Della quickly **tore** open the paper. She let out a cry of joy, but her joy soon turned to tears.

There lay The Combs—the hair combs that Della had wanted for so long in a store window. They were the perfect color for her hair. She knew that they were **expensive**. She had <mark>wished</mark> for them without any hope of ever owning them. And now, they were hers! But the long hair that should have gone with the lovely combs was gone.

Key Vocabulary
wish *verb*, to want something very
  much

Della looked up and smiled. "My hair grows so fast, Jim!" And then she jumped up and cried, "Oh, oh!"

Jim had not seen his beautiful present yet. She held it out to him **eagerly**. The **precious** metal **reflected** her bright, loving spirit.

"Isn't it **a dandy**, Jim? I looked for it all over town. Give me your watch. I want to see how the chain looks on it."

Jim didn't **obey**. Instead, he **tumbled** onto the couch and smiled.

"Dell," said he, "let's put our Christmas presents away for a while. I sold the watch to get the money to buy your combs."

As you know, the magi were wise men. They were the wonderful wise men who brought gifts to **the Babe in the manger**. They **invented** the art of giving Christmas presents. Since they were wise, their gifts must have been wise, too.

Monitor Comprehension

Confirm Prediction
Was your prediction correct? Did anything happen that you did not expect? Explain.

Key Vocabulary
precious *adjective*, valuable
reflect *verb*, to show or represent something
invent *verb*, to make something completely new

In Other Words
eagerly with excitement
a dandy wonderful (slang)
obey do what she said
tumbled let himself fall
the Babe in the manger Baby Jesus

And now I have told you an unimportant story about two **foolish** children who unwisely **sacrificed** their **treasures** for each other. But to all of today's wise men, I say that these two were the wisest of all. Of all people who give and receive gifts, they are wisest. Everywhere they are wisest. They are the magi. ❖

Key Vocabulary
sacrifice *verb*, to lose something, often
 for a reason

In Other Words
foolish silly
treasures important things

ANALYZE The Gift of the Magi

1. **Explain** The narrator calls Jim and Della "foolish," and then he calls them "wise." What does he mean?

2. **Vocabulary** Why were Della's hair and Jim's watch <mark>precious</mark>?

3. **Reading Strategy** **Make Inferences** Look at the picture on page 480. Make an inference about what the people in the picture are feeling. How do you know? Share your inference with a partner. Describe the details in the picture that led you to make your inference.

I See . . .	I Know . . .	And So . . .
Two people dancing in their house. They are smiling.		

↩ **Return to the Text**

Reread and Retell Reread page 476. In your own words, retell how Jim reacts when he sees Della.

poem by Naomi Shihab Nye

Elements of Poetry: Free Verse

Poets write to express ideas or feelings. Poems also create pictures in a reader's mind. Poetry comes in many forms. Some poems have a specific structure of rhythm and rhyme. **Free verse** poems do not follow any pattern. In free verse, the words and lines may be put together in any way.

> ### HOW TO READ FREE VERSE
>
> **1.** Read the poem.
>
> **2.** Note words that show feelings. Identify words and phrases that form pictures in your mind.
>
> **3.** Think about how the words and images affect you. Tell a partner.

Read this poem about a man carrying a baby. Then read what one reader told a partner about words that show feelings.

Look Into the Text

This man carries the world's most sensitive cargo
but he's not marked.
Nowhere does his jacket say FRAGILE,
HANDLE WITH CARE.

His ear fills up with breathing.
He hears the hum of a boy's dream
deep inside him.

> The words "most sensitive cargo" make me feel nervous. The man needs to be really careful with that baby!

Try It

Read the poem "Shoulders." Discuss the words and images with a partner. Compare the images in your mind and how the poem makes you feel.

Connect Across Texts

In "The Gift of the Magi," two young people give up **precious** things for something more valuable—love. As you read this poem, think about what is most important.

Shoulders

BY NAOMI SHIHAB NYE
ILLUSTRATED BY MURRAY KIMBER

A man crosses the street in rain,
stepping gently, looking two times north and south,
because his son is asleep on his shoulder.

No car must splash him.
5   No car drive too near to his shadow.

Key Vocabulary
precious *adjective*, having great value

In Other Words
crosses walks to the other side of
gently carefully
splash get water on

This man carries the world's most sensitive cargo
but he's not marked.
Nowhere does his jacket say FRAGILE,
HANDLE WITH CARE.

10 His ear fills up with breathing.
He hears the hum of a boy's dream
deep inside him.

Key Vocabulary
sensitive *adjective*, easily, affected,
changed, or hurt

In Other Words
he's not marked he doesn't come with
instructions

484 Unit 6 What Matters Most

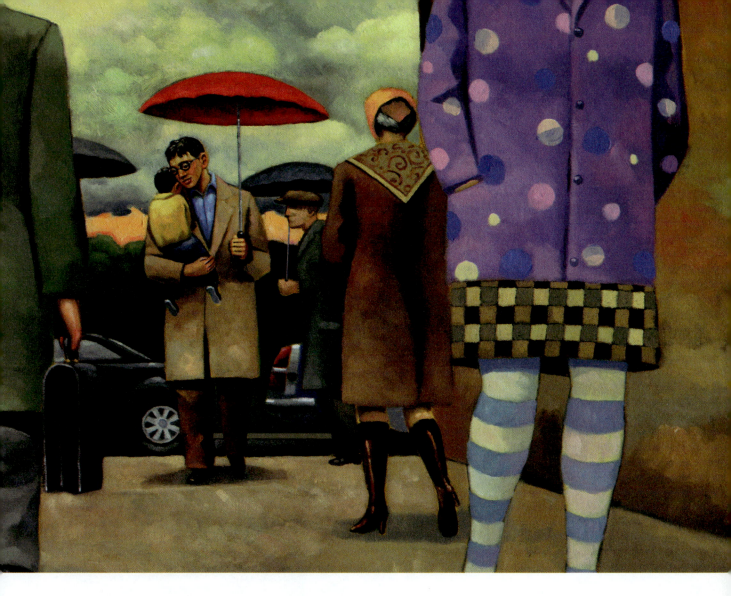

We're not going to be able
to live in this world

15 if we're not willing to do what he's doing
with one another.

The road will only be wide.
The rain will never stop falling.

ANALYZE Shoulders

1. **Explain** Why is the man trying to be careful?

2. **Vocabulary** Why does the poet call the man's cargo <mark>sensitive</mark>?

3. **Elements of Poetry** Think again about the words and images you discussed with a partner. Which words and images affected you most?

Return to the Text

Reread and Retell Reread the poem. Then look carefully at lines 13–16. What does the poet think we should be doing for each other? Explain what you think the poet means.

About the Poet

Naomi Shihab Nye (1952–) is a poet, songwriter, and author of children's books. She likes to write about the beautiful details in life. "We think in poetry. But some people pretend poetry is far away."

EQ What Is Most Important in Life?

Fluency

Listen to a reading. Practice fluency. Use the Reading Handbook, page 545.

Reading

Talk About Literature

1. **Summarize** In "The Gift of the Magi," both Della and Jim **sacrifice** things that are important to them. What do they sacrifice? What do their sacrifices tell us about the kind of people they are?

   Della sacrifices _____ because _____. Jim sacrifices _____ because _____.

2. **Interpret** The poem "Shoulders" describes what will happen if people are not willing to change. If they don't, the poet says, "the road will only be wide" and "the rain will never stop falling." What do these words mean?

EQ 3. **Compare** Both selections describe people who show **generosity**. How are the people alike in their generosity? How are they different?

   One way in which the people are similar is _____. They are different because _____.

Vocabulary

Review Key Vocabulary

Choose the correct vocabulary word to complete each sentence.

1. Esmeralda was _____ of her son Aldo.

2. He was the most _____ person in her life.

3. Aldo was shy, _____, and thoughtful.

4. He was also known for his _____.

5. Aldo _____ all of his free time to help Mr. Juarez.

6. "Mr. Juarez plans to _____ a flying machine. He needs my help."

7. Aldo's actions _____ his kindness.

8. "I _____ you would think about yourself sometimes!" Esmeralda said.

> **Vocabulary**
>
> generosity
> invent
> precious
> proud
> reflected
> sacrificed
> sensitive
> wish

Writing

Write About Literature

EQ **Freewrite** Look back at the selections. Think about what is important to you. What would you be willing to sacrifice for the people you love? Begin your response as shown. Once you begin writing, try not to stop for two minutes.

I would sacrifice . . .

Grammar

Combine Clauses

You can join a dependent clause to an independent clause to form a complex sentence. The clauses are joined by a conjunction. Different conjunctions have different meanings.

CONJUNCTION	MEANING	EXAMPLE
because	tells why	People came to New York City **because** they wanted a better life.
since		They wanted to find jobs **since** they didn't have any money.
after	tells the order of events	Many people lived in slums **after** they arrived.
before		Some thought life was better **before** they came to New York.
when	tells when	Life became easier **when** they began to earn money.

Oral Practice Join each pair of clauses. Choose a conjunction from the box. Say the complex sentence.

after	because	before	since	when

1. Della wanted to buy Jim a gift _____ she loved him so much.
2. She sold her hair _____ she needed some money.
3. She bought the watch chain _____ she sold her hair.
4. She quickly curled her short hair _____ Jim came home from work.
5. Jim looked shocked _____ he walked through the door.

Written Practice (6–10) Copy the paragraph and add details. Wherever you see a caret (^), add a dependent clause.

My grandfather gave me an old pocket watch after ∧. At first I was disappointed because ∧. His father gave him the watch beefore ∧. It saved his life when ∧. Then, I was honored to have it since ∧.

Language Development

Retell a Story

Retell "The Gift of the Magi" With a partner, take turns retelling the story. Speak clearly. Use gestures and facial expressions. Tell the events in the correct order.

Use sentences like these:
- At the beginning, _____.
- Next, _____.
- After that, _____.
- Then, _____.
- Finally, _____.

Review Idioms

Remember, an idiom is a kind of figurative language. Its meaning does not match the literal, or exact, meaning of its words. You can often use context to figure out the meaning.

IDIOM Della had only $1.87 to spend on a gift, but she <u>had something up her sleeve</u>.

> There's nothing in Della's sleeve. But if she did have something, it would be hidden.

> Della must have a hidden plan.

Explain each idiom in your own words.

1. Della took a <u>leap of faith</u> when she cut her hair.
2. She was so nervous that her <u>stomach was tied in knots</u>.
3. Jim was <u>blown out of the water</u> when he saw her.
4. Her actions <u>touched his heart</u>.

🔖 **Reading Handbook,** page 555.

Connect Characters and Theme

The theme is the main message of a story. Characters think, feel, say, and do things in a story that give you clues to the theme. Use these clues to identify the theme.

1. Make a **Character Chart**.
2. Reread "The Gift of the Magi." Fill in the chart.
3. With a partner, discuss the clues on your chart. State what you think the author is trying to tell you. Write a short paragraph about the theme. Be sure to include the clues that helped you find the theme.

Character Chart

Actions	Thoughts and Feelings	Words
Della buys a watch for Jim. Jim buys . . .	As soon as she saw it, she knew Jim should have it.	"I had my hair cut off and sold."

The theme of "The Gift of the Magi" is _____.
The clues that tell me this are _____.

Finance Careers

Is a finance job right for you? Take this career quiz to find out.

Career Quiz

1. I think math classes are
  a very interesting.
  b just OK.
  c boring.

2. Keeping track of the money I earn and spend is
  a fun.
  b something I do, but not very happily.
  c boring.

3. I think saving money and paying attention to prices of goods that go up or down is
  a interesting and important for the future.
  b something everyone needs to do.
  c not very interesting.

Add up your points.
  a = 3 points
  b = 2 points
  c = 1 point

What's your score?

9 points: Wow!
A finance job seems perfect for you!

6–8 points: Maybe
A finance job may be right for you.

3 points: No thanks
A finance job might not be right for you. Do you know someone who would enjoy this type of work?

Finance Jobs

Here are some finance jobs. They have different responsibilities and need different education and training.

Job	Responsibilities	Education/Training Needed
Stockbroker 1	• Takes orders from customers to buy and sell stocks • Communicates orders by telephone, in person, or by computer	• Bachelor's degree • Stockbroker's license
Accountant 2	• Tracks earnings and spending • Checks financial statements for accuracy • Prepares tax documents	• Bachelor's degree or master's degree • Certificate or license
Financial Manager 3	• Watches company spending and investments • Sets financial goals for a company	• Bachelor's degree or master's degree

An Accountant

Steve Munday checks financial records to make sure they are correct.

Steve Munday is an accountant. He works for a small company in Arlington, Virginia. In this interview, he describes his work.

Question: What is your workday like?

Answer: I search for, check, and calculate financial records.

Question: What types of records are they?

Answer: I make sure paychecks show the correct amount. I run computer reports to track how much money the company earns. I compare what the company earns and what it pays out.

Question: What do you like about your job?

Answer: I enjoy working with numbers. I like to keep track of money. Sometimes the records show the wrong amount. It is my job to find out what went wrong. I enjoy solving problems like this.

Research Finance Jobs

Learn more about a finance job in the United States.

1. Choose a job from the chart on page 490.
2. Go online to **www.hbedge.net**. Read about the job you chose.
3. Complete this chart.

Job	How many workers have this job?	How much money does a worker earn?	Is this a good job for the future?

WHAT MATTERS MOST

EQ **ESSENTIAL QUESTION:**

What Is Most Important in Life?

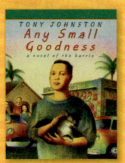
Reflect on the Essential Question

Discuss the Essential Question with a group: What is most important in life?

As you answer the questions, think about what you read in the selections and your choice of Edge Library books.

- How do people decide what **success** is? Is **wealth** a sign of success?
- How can certain **attitudes** help people in life?
- How should we take care of the people and things we value most?

Unit Review Game

You will need:

- 2, 3, or 4 players
- 1 **Lucky Wheel** board
- question cards
- note paper
- pencil, pen, or marker

Objective: Be the player with the most points.

1. Download a **Lucky Wheel** board and question cards from **www.hbedge.net**. Print out and cut apart the question cards. Mix them up.

2. **Player A** spins the spinner so that it lands on a wheel section.

3. Player A chooses a question card and answers it.

   - If the answer is correct, player A gets the points from the selected wheel section. (If you can't agree on the answer, ask your teacher.)

   - If the answer is incorrect, the player gets no points.

4. **Player B** takes a turn. Then the other players take turns.

5. The game ends when all question cards are used. The player with the most points wins.

Each new experience can change how you think and act. For this project, you will write a personal narrative to tell about an experience and what you learned from it.

Write a Personal Narrative

When you write a personal narrative, you tell a story about something that happened to you. You describe real people, places, and events from your own life.

1 Connect Writing to Your Life

You tell personal narratives all the time. You might tell your group about a weekend camping trip. Or you might tell a friend what happened when you tried out for a school play.

2 Understand the Form

A good personal narrative

- has a beginning, a middle, and an ending
- describes what things were like and how you felt
- explains what you learned from the experience.

Study this personal narrative.

Honesty
by Naomi Herrera

Last year, I learned a lesson about honesty. Everyone was studying for a math test. It was a hard class. No matter how much we studied, we never got good grades. But my friends and I studied morning, noon, and night.

The night before the test, we heard that many people were going to cheat. They thought it was the only way to get a good grade. My friends and I talked. Would we cheat, too?

In the end, we didn't cheat. We did our best, and our grades were not too bad. Some kids cheated and got higher grades, but that was OK. Some things are more important than grades, like being honest to your teacher—and yourself.

> The beginning sets up the story.

> Details in the middle help the reader understand the events and how the writer felt.

> The ending says what the writer learned and why the experience was important.

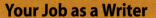

Your Job as a Writer

▶ **Prompt** Write a personal narrative for your classmates. Tell a story about an experience that happened to you and what you learned from it. Be sure your personal narrative

- has a beginning, a middle, and an ending
- shares your thoughts and feelings
- explains why the event is important to you.

 **Prewrite**

Follow these steps to plan your personal narrative.

1 Choose an Experience

What are some events you remember from your own life? Make a list. Think about each event on your list. Is each event important? Did you learn something from the experience? Choose the event that meant the most to you.

— Saturday's trip to the mall
— when Grandpa was sick
— fixing dinner for the family

2 Gather the Details

Jot down everything you remember about the event. Record details that tell where you were and what happened. Tell what you thought and how you felt, too.

3 Organize Your Ideas

Put your ideas in the order in which they happened. Use a **Sequence Chain**.

Sequence Chain

Beginning:	Middle:	End:
· I didn't like going to Grandpa's house. · I thought it was boring.	· Grandpa got sick. · He was in the hospital. · We worried about him.	· Grandpa got better. · I went to visit him. · I learned an important lesson.

Reflect on Your Plan

▶ Why was the event important to you? What details show this?

✓ Write a Draft

Now you're ready to start writing. Don't worry about making mistakes. Just start by writing the ideas you gathered in your Sequence Chain.

1 Write the Events in Order

Use your Sequence Chain to write the events of your narrative from the beginning to the end. Include details to help your readers understand your thoughts and feelings during each part.

Beginning:
· I didn't like going to Grandpa's house.
· I thought it was boring.

My Grandpa
I used to hate going to Grandpa's house. He lives at 513 W. Yale Street. It was so boring! We just sat, ate, and listened to his long stories all day. He had a really hot house. It was next to a bakery. I wanted to hang out with my friends. I didn't want to be there.

2 Add Transitions

Use transitions to help your ideas flow smoothly. <mark>Transition words</mark> can show when things happen.

Middle:
· Grandpa got sick.
· He was in the hospital.
· We worried about him.

<mark>Then one afternoon</mark>, Mom picked me up early from school. Something was wrong. Grandpa was in the hospital. We went there. He was very sick, and the doctors wanted to watch him for a few days. We stayed with Grandpa <mark>all night</mark>, but he didn't wake up. He was so quiet and still. Mom and I were very worried.

Transition Words that Say When
first, in the beginning
next, then, later
one day, last week
finally, in the end

3 Include Your Thoughts and Ideas

Write how you feel about the experience. Tell <mark>why it was important to you</mark>.

End:
· Grandpa got better.
· I went to visit him.
· I learned an important lesson.

A few days later, Grandpa was much better. What a relief! We visited him at home. This time, I listened to all his stories. He even listened to some of mine. We talked, laughed, and cried. <mark>That's when I saw how important family is. There are lots of great things, but family is the most important thing in my life.</mark>

Reflect on Your Draft

► Does your narrative include a clear beginning, middle, and end? Does it include how you feel about the events?

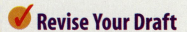

✔ Revise Your Draft

Your first draft won't be perfect. But you can make it better by revising it, or making changes to it.

1 Read Your Narrative to a Partner

Find out what a reader thinks of your work. You can use your partner's ideas to decide how to make your writing better.

Look at this part of the writer's draft. What does the partner say about it?

> I used to hate going to Grandpa's house. He lives at 513 W. Yale Street. It was so boring! We just ate and listened to his long stories all day. Grandpa's house was always hot. It was next to a bakery. I just wanted to hang out with my friends. I didn't want to be there.

"When did all this happen?"

"Is it important to know Grandpa's address or how hot it was? Maybe you should take out those details."

2 Decide What to Change

Think about your partner's comments. Then decide what you want to change.

3 Mark Your Changes

Use these marks to mark your changes:

∧ Add text.

✍ Take out text.

> When I was ten,
> ∧ I used to hate going to Grandpa's house. ~~He lives at 513 W. Yale Street.~~ It was so boring! We just ate and listened to his long stories all day. ~~Grandpa's house was always hot. It was next to a bakery.~~ I just wanted to hang out with my friends. I didn't want to be there.
>
> Then one afternoon, Mom picked me up early from school. Something was wrong. Grandpa was in the hospital. We went there. right away ∧

The writer added some transitions and sequence words to show when things happened.

The writer took out the details that weren't very important.

Reflect on Your Revisions

▶ Think about your review. What are some of your strengths as a writer? What things cause problems for you?

✔ Edit and Proofread

After you've revised your draft, edit and proofread it to check it for mistakes.

1 Check Your Sentences

Make sure that each sentence is complete with a subject and a predicate. Fix any sentence fragments you find.

Grandpa was better. ~~So~~ **We were** So relieved!

2 Check Your Spelling

Circle each word that may not be spelled right. Look it up in the dictionary or ask for help. Fix the spelling if you need to.

3 Check Your Commas

Whenever you combine sentences, use commas in the right place.

Use a comma	Example
• before **and**, **but**, or **or**	I listened, and I really enjoyed Grandpa's stories.

4 Mark Your Changes

Now edit your own paper. Use these marks to show your changes.

∧	✄	⌐	◯	≡	╱	⁋
Add.	Take out.	Replace with this.	Check spelling.	Capitalize.	Make lowercase.	Make new paragraph.

Reflect on Your Corrections

▶ Note any errors you made. Make a list. Remember them the next time you write something.

✓ Publish, Share, and Reflect

Publish and Share

Now you are ready to publish your personal narrative. Print or write a clean copy. Then collect the narratives in a class book called "The Important Things in Life."

Present your personal narrative to the class.

> ## How to SHARE EXPERIENCES
>
> 1. **Read Your Personal Narrative** Read the events of the story in order. Change your voice to tell about different people. Use your voice to express the feelings you wrote about.
>
> 2. **Share Experiences** Ask your listeners if they have any questions. Tell them more about the experience and what you learned. Then ask them to share any experiences that are similar to yours. Listen carefully as they speak.
>
> 3. **Discuss the Theme** What matters most in life? Form a small group. Talk together about what you learned from each other's stories. Discuss why people think some things are more important than others.

Reflect on Your Work

▶ Think about your writing.

- What did you learn about writing that you didn't know before?
- What did you like best about writing a personal narrative?

☑ **Save a copy of your work in your portfolio.**

RESOURCES

Language and Learning Handbook
Language, Learning, Communication

Reading Handbook
Reading, Fluency, Vocabulary

Writing Handbook
Writing Process, Traits, Conventions

Strategies for Learning and Developing Language

Technology and Media

Research

Learning and Developing Language

How Do I *Learn* Language?

There are many ways you can build your English language skills.

1 Listen and try out the language.

What to Do	Examples
Listen to others.	**You hear:** "When did our teacher say that the assignment is due?" **You say:** "Our teacher said that the assignment is due May 1."
Add new words into your speech.	**You hear:** "Send me an e-mail or a text message on my cell." **You think:** "My cell" means "my cell phone." I know what an e-mail is. A text message must be an e-mail that you send on a phone. **You say:** "I'll e-mail you. I do not think I can send text messages on my phone."
Use words you learn in one subject and apply them to another topic.	**You read this in science class:** Each person in the U.S. produces more than 4 pounds of garbage each day. There is not enough landfill space. We need to recycle. **You write this in your journal:** I will do my paper for English class on recycling. **At home, you might say:** Mom, did you recycle the empty bottles?
Try saying things in different ways.	**All of these sentences mean the same thing:** My teacher helps me with my English papers. My teacher tells me to improve my essays. Before I write an essay, my teacher helps me think of topics to write about.
Memorize new words.	Make vocabulary cards to help you remember new words and phrases.

2 Ask for help.

What to Do	Examples
Ask questions.	 "Did I say that right?" "Did I use that word the right way?" "Which is right: "brang" or "brought"?"
Ask for someone to explain something more clearly.	**You say:** "Wait! Could you go over that phrase again, a little more slowly?" **Other examples:** "Is 'paper' another word for 'essay'?" "Does 'have a heart' mean 'to be kind'?"

3 Use clues that are not spoken.

What to Do	Examples
Use gestures to show an idea.	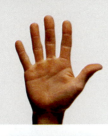 I will hold up five fingers to show that I need five minutes.
Look for clues that are not spoken.	 María wants me to go to a concert. It's her favorite band, but I think their music is vile! Vile must mean "bad." She looks unhappy!
Find and respond to clues that are not spoken.	Let's give him a hand. Everyone is clapping. "Give him a hand" must mean to clap. I should clap for him, too.

4 Prove how language works.

What to Do	Examples
Test guesses about how language works.	**You can try out what you learned:** I can add -ation to the verb observe to get the noun observation. So maybe I can make a noun by adding -ation to some verbs that end in -e. Let's see. Prepare and preparation. Yes, that is right! Preserve and preservation. That is correct, too! Compare and comparation. That does not sound correct. I will check the dictionary . . . Now I get it! It's comparison.
Use spell-check, the dictionary, and other reference books.	**You just finished your draft.** **You think:** *Now I'll use spell-check to see what words I need to fix.*
Use what you already know.	You can figure out new words by looking for words you do know. **Example:** I felt embarrassed for Tom when he behaved like a clown. I know the word "clown." Maybe "embarrassed" means the way I feel when my friend starts acting like a clown.
Compare how your language works to how English works.	**You hear:** **You think:** "She is a doctor." *In English, an article, such as a or an, is used before a job title. In my language, no article is used: "She is doctor."*
Use a word map to find the relationship between words.	jogging — tennis — football — exercising — weightlifting — water — swimming — goggles — pool **You think:** Where should I place the word ball? It can go with the word football or tennis because both sports use a kind of ball.
Use imagery.	Use describing words to make a picture in your mind. This will help you figure out the meaning of a word you don't know.

5 **Check your learning.**

What to Do	Examples
Check how well you are learning the language.	*Did I use the right verb form to tell what my plans are for the future?* *Was my speech formal enough? Did I use transitions correctly?*
Take notes.	**Active Voice Compared to Passive Voice** • I should write my sentences in active voice. The "doer," or actor, of the verb in the sentence should be the subject. **Incorrect**: The race was won by Jon. **Correct**: Jon won the race.
Use visuals to help understand the meaning.	*This paragraph is confusing. Maybe I can use a graphic organizer. It will help me organize the main ideas.*
Review.	*Do I understand everything? I should go over my notes and graphic organizers.*

How to Use Technology to Communicate

Technology helps you to communicate in school, in the workplace, and with friends and family.

Cell Phone

A **cell phone** can be used anywhere there is a wireless phone network. Cell phones can be used to send text messages, play music, take photos, and make phone calls.

Fax Machine

A **fax machine** uses phone lines to send or receive a copy of pages with pictures or text.

Personal Computer

A **personal computer** helps you to create, save, and use information. You can use a computer to send e-mails, surf the Internet, listen to music, or chat with friends.

A **desktop computer** stays in one place. It has several parts, including a monitor, a mouse, a keyboard, and a CD drive.

A **laptop computer** is small so you can take it anywhere. A laptop computer usually fits in a travel case.

The Computer Keyboard

Use the **keys** on the **keyboard** to write, do math, or give the computer commands. Keyboards may look different, but they all have keys like these:

escape key
Press here to stop loading a webpage.

tab
Press this key to indent for a new paragraph.

function keys
Press these keys to give the computer commands.

delete or **backspace key**
Press here to erase the character to the left of the flashing cursor. You can also erase text that you highlight.

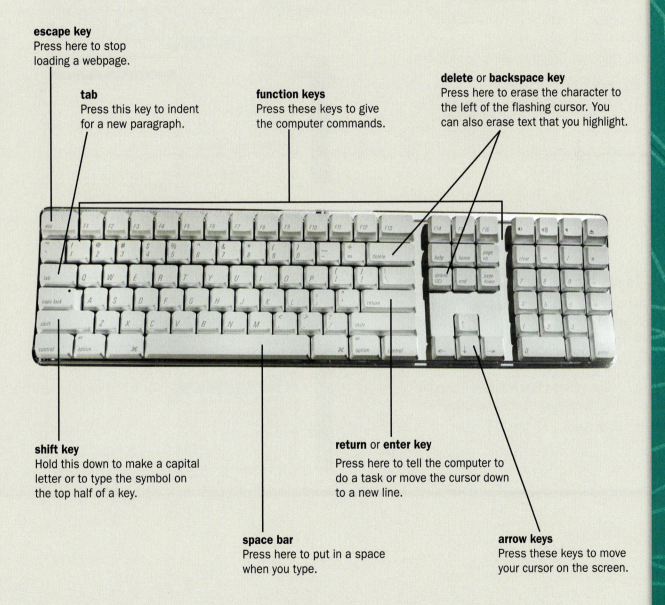

shift key
Hold this down to make a capital letter or to type the symbol on the top half of a key.

return or **enter key**
Press here to tell the computer to do a task or move the cursor down to a new line.

space bar
Press here to put in a space when you type.

arrow keys
Press these keys to move your cursor on the screen.

How to Use Technology to Create Final Products

Technology helps you to create interesting final products. To write using a computer, you will need to know how to create new documents, save documents, and open documents.

To create a new document

When you want to create a new piece of writing:

1. Open your word-processing program.
2. Click on the **File** menu.
3. Click on **New Blank Document**.

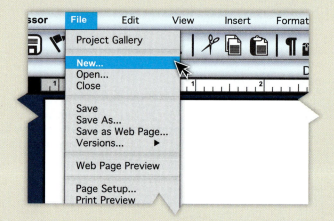

To save a document

When you are done writing and you are ready to save your work:

1. Click on the **File** menu.
2. Click on **Save As**.
3. A box labeled **File Name** will appear. In it, type a name for your document.
4. Click **Save**.

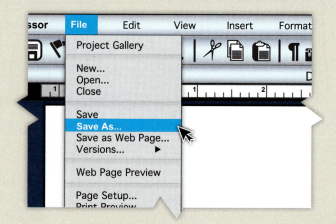

To open a document

When you want to open a document that you have already saved:

1. Click on the **File** menu.

2. Click **Open**.

3. Find the title of the document that you want.

4. Click on the title.

5. Click **Open**.

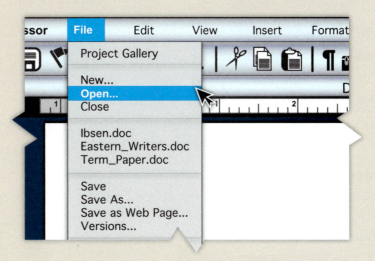

What Is Research?

Research is collecting information about a subject.

How to Use the Research Process

When you **research**, you look up information about a topic. You can use the information you find to write a story, article, book, or research report.

Choose Your Topic

Think of something you want to learn more about and something that interests you. That will be your research **topic**.

When choosing a topic, make sure

- your teacher approves your topic.
- you pick a topic that is not too general, or large. A smaller topic is much easier to write about.

Discover What Is Known and What Needs to Be Learned

Get to know your topic. Find recent articles or reports that relate to your topic.

Decide What to Look Up

What do you already know about your topic? What do you want to know about it? Write down some questions that you want to find the answers to. Look at the most important words in your questions. Those are key words you can look up when you start your research.

Is there life on Mars?
Can things live on the surface of Mars?
What have space missions to Mars discovered?

Find Resources

Now that you know what to research, you can use different **resources** to find information about your topic. Resources can be experts, or people who know a lot about a topic. Resources can also be nonfiction books, textbooks, magazines, newspapers, or the Internet. You can find resources all around you.

Nonfiction Books

Magazines and Newspapers

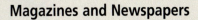

Expert

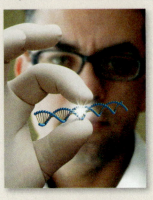

Encyclopedia

Internet

Dictionary

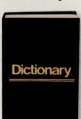

Almanac

Atlas

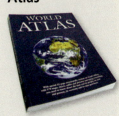

Think about your research questions. Some resources may be more helpful than others, depending on what kind of information you need.

- Do you need to look up facts or scientific data?
- Do you want to know about something that happened recently?
- Do you want to see pictures?

These questions will help you decide which resources to use. Whatever your topic is, try exploring the library first. There you will discover a whole world of information.

Finding Information on the World Wide Web

The **World Wide Web** allows you to find, read, and organize information. The Internet is like a giant library, and the World Wide Web is everything in the library including the books, the librarian, and the computer catalog.

The Internet is a fast way to get the most current information about your topic! You can find resources like encyclopedias and dictionaries. You can even find amazing pictures, movies, and sounds!

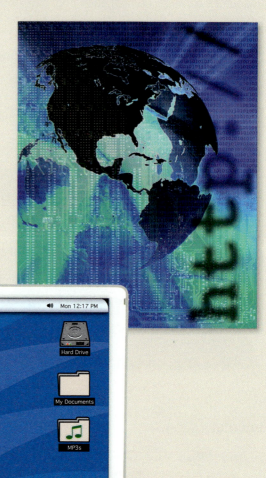

How to Get Started

Check with your teacher for how to access the Internet from your school. Usually you can just double click on the icon, or picture, to get access to the Internet and you're on your way!

Doing the Research

Once the search page comes up, you can begin the research process. Just follow these steps.

1 **Type your subject in the search box. Then, click on the Search button.**

If you already know the address of a Web site, you can type it in the address box.

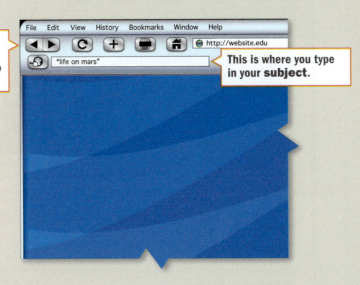

You'll always see a **toolbar** like this one at the top of the screen. Click on the pictures to do things like print the page.

This is where you type in your **subject**.

2 **Read the search results.**

All underlined, colored words are **links**, or connections, to other sites.

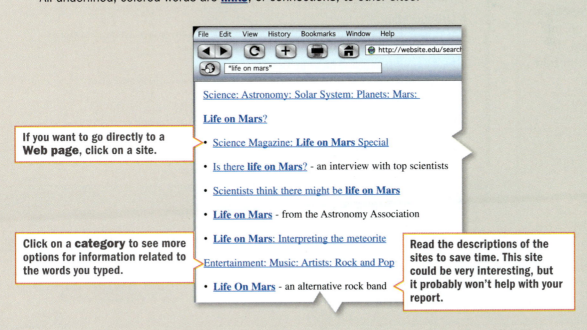

If you want to go directly to a **Web page**, click on a site.

Click on a **category** to see more options for information related to the words you typed.

Science: Astronomy: Solar System: Planets: Mars:

Life on Mars?

- Science Magazine: **Life on Mars** Special
- Is there **life on Mars**? - an interview with top scientists
- Scientists think there might be **life on Mars**
- **Life on Mars** - from the Astronomy Association
- **Life on Mars**: Interpreting the meteorite

Entertainment: Music: Artists: Rock and Pop

- **Life On Mars** - an alternative rock band

Read the descriptions of the sites to save time. This site could be very interesting, but it probably won't help with your report.

3 **Select a site, and read the article.**

You might want to pick a new site or start a new search. If so, click on the **back arrow** to go back a page to the search results.

If you want to go to another Web page, click on a **link**.

4 **You may choose to print the article if it is helpful for your research. Later on, you can use the article to take notes.**

File   Edit   View   History   Bookmarks   Window   Help

http://www.redplanet.edu/article_database

"life on mars"

Anything you ever wanted to know about the planet Mars is on this site! Is it really red? Does it really have water? Information about the appearance of the planet is only the beginning. Articles are about the planet's history, from its discovery to the most recent evidence scientists have gathered about this interesting planet. Search the list by title or by topic.

MORE ON MARS:

● **The Red Planet**
You can see the planet Mars from Earth. Seen from Earth, Mars appears red. But there is more to the planet than its famous red color. Mars is a planet with interesting surfaces—volcanoes, craters, deserts, polar ice caps, mountains, canyons.

● **Mariner 4**
In 1965, scientists thought Mars might be covered with liquid similar to our oceans. In recent years, scientists have been able to gather evidence about the liquid history of Mars.

● **Orbiting Mars**
Mars has many spacecraft circling it: Mars Odyssey, Mars Express, Mars Reconnaissance Orbiter and Phoenix Mars Lander. Mars also has two Exploration Rovers: *Spirit* and *Opportunity*.

● **Phobos and Deimos—Mars has Two Moons**
Some people think these moons may have originally been asteroids that were caught by Mars' gravity.

● **Life on Mars?**
What would life be like on Mars? Scientists thought they had the answer.

● **Models of Mars Missions**
Experience a mission to Mars! Click the link to watch video and read scientific analysis of the planet's properties.

Take Notes

Once you have found a lot of useful sources, you are ready to begin your research. **Notes** are important words, phrases, and ideas that you write while you are reading and researching. Your notes will help you remember details. They'll also help you remember the source. The source is where you got the information.

Write notes in your own words. Set up your notecards so that you can easily put your information in order when you write.

Remember to:

- Include your research question.
- Write down the source. List the title, author, and page number.
- List details and facts in your own words.
- If you copy exactly what you read, put quotation marks around the words.

What do we know about Mars?

Mars by Seymour Simon, page 27

−Viking spacecraft created to find out if there's life

−hard to prove there is life

−Maybe scientists looked in the wrong places?

READING HANDBOOK

Reading Strategies

Reading Fluency

Vocabulary

Reading Strategies

What Are Reading Strategies?

Reading strategies are hints or tips. You can use these tips to help you become a better reader. Reading strategies help you understand what you read. They can be used before, during, and after you read.

Plan and Monitor

What is this strategy about?

- previewing and planning
- asking questions and setting a purpose for reading
- making and checking predictions
- checking that you understand what you read

How do I PLAN?

Plan your reading *before* you read. To plan, **preview**, or look at what you will read. Previewing helps you learn what the text is about. After you preview, **think about the text**. What **questions** do you have? Use your questions to **set a purpose for reading**. Your purpose tells you **why** you will read the text.

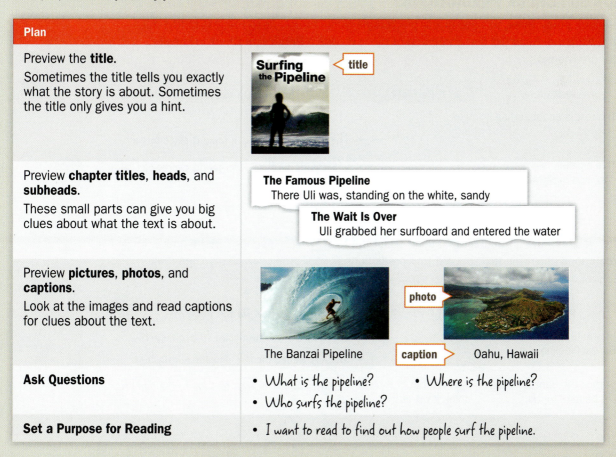

Plan	
Preview the **title**. Sometimes the title tells you exactly what the story is about. Sometimes the title only gives you a hint.	**Surfing the Pipeline** — title
Preview **chapter titles**, **heads**, and **subheads**. These small parts can give you big clues about what the text is about.	**The Famous Pipeline** There Uli was, standing on the white, sandy **The Wait Is Over** Uli grabbed her surfboard and entered the water
Preview **pictures**, **photos**, and **captions**. Look at the images and read captions for clues about the text.	The Banzai Pipeline — caption — Oahu, Hawaii — photo
Ask Questions	• What is the pipeline? • Where is the pipeline? • Who surfs the pipeline?
Set a Purpose for Reading	• I want to read to find out how people surf the pipeline.

How do I MAKE PREDICTIONS?

A **prediction** is a careful guess about what will happen in the text. Making predictions about a text will help you understand what you read. To make a prediction:

- **preview** information
- ask **questions**
- think about what you **already know**

Predict	
Preview Information	• The word "Surfing" is in the title. • A picture shows Hawaii.
Ask Questions	• What is this story about? • What is the pipeline?
I Already Know . . .	• I know many people surf in the ocean. • I've seen a movie about people surfing on big waves.
Make Predictions	• The text is about surfing. • This pipeline is a place to surf. It is in Hawaii.

How do I CHECK PREDICTIONS?

To **check predictions**, you see if your predictions were correct. Read the text to find out what happens. Read the first paragraph of the text. Use a **Prediction Chart** to check your predictions.

Prediction	Is It Correct?	How Do You Know?
The text is about surfing.	yes	• title is "Surfing the Pipeline" • The Banzai Pipeline is a famous place to surf.
This pipeline is a place to surf. It is in Hawaii.	yes	• Uli stands on the white, sandy shores of Oahu, Hawaii. • The famous Banzai Pipeline is right in front of her.

After you read the first paragraph, think about the text. What happened? **Make new predictions** about the text. Record your predictions in your prediction chart. Then read the rest of "Surfing the Pipeline" to see if your predictions are correct.

Prediction	Is It Correct?	How Do You Know?
Uli wants to surf the Banzai Pipeline.	yes	• She is at the starting point to begin surfing. • She has waited for this day for a long time.
Surfing the Banzai Pipeline will be hard for Uli.	Not yet, but I think it will be.	• Uli uses all her energy to swim to the starting point.

Surfing the Pipeline

Prediction: Uli wants to surf the Banzai Pipeline.

Uli stands on the white, sandy shores of Oahu, Hawaii. The famous Banzai Pipeline is right in front of her. The Banzai Pipeline is a special place. It is one of the most difficult places to surf in the world. It is also a dangerous place to surf. Uli looks out and sees twelve-foot waves. She watches the tall waves crash loudly.

==Uli had been waiting for this day for a long time. She is ready.==

Check Prediction: This part of the text shows my prediction is correct.

Prediction: Surfing the Banzai Pipeline will be hard for Uli.

Uli grabs her surfboard and enters the water. The waves are strong. ==Uli uses all of her energy to swim.== She swims to the surfing location. She sees rocks sticking up in the water. Uli finally finds the perfect starting point. She waits anxiously to begin surfing.

Check: This part of the text shows my prediction is correct.

The Banzai Pipeline

Oahu, Hawaii

How do I MONITOR MY READING?

When you **monitor your reading**, you are making sure that you understand what you read. Use these monitoring strategies to help you.

Strategy	How to Use It
Reread	Reread means read again. Reread the text that you don't understand. First, reread it silently. Then reread it aloud. Continue reading until you understand the text better.
Use Vocabulary Resources	Find a word that you do not know in a dictionary or thesaurus. You can also ask a classmate what the word means. ". . . dangerous places to surf . . ." I'm not sure what "surf" means. I'll look in a dictionary.
Read On and Use Context Clues	Find the text that you don't understand. Then keep reading. What does the rest of the text tell you? Are there words or phrases that help you understand? ". . . looks out and sees twelve-foot waves . . ." Maybe "surf" means riding ocean waves.
Change Your Reading Speed	Read slowly when something is confusing or difficult. Reading Speed — SLOW ← → FAST — Easier Text / Confusing or Difficult Text
Change Your Purpose for Reading	Think of your purpose for reading. Do you have a new reason for reading? I wanted to find out how people surf the pipeline. Now I want to read to see if Uli actually surfs it!

How Do I Organize Information?

Graphic organizers are tools. Use graphic organizers to **record your ideas**. They can also help you **remember information**. Choose an organizer that matches the type of information you need to organize. For examples of graphic organizers, see pages 637–640.

Visualize

What is this strategy about?

- creating mental images
- using all your senses

How do I VISUALIZE?

When you **visualize,** you use your imagination to help you understand what you read. You can use the writer's words to create pictures in your mind.

My Favorite Car Is a Truck

My name is Steven. I've been working hard and saving money all summer. I finally have enough money for a down payment on a new car. My father took me to the dealership to pick out a new car. I found my favorite vehicle. It was a <mark>red, shiny</mark> truck with <mark>gleaming</mark> wheels. I climbed inside and looked around. The <mark>brown seats</mark> were <mark>sparkling clean</mark>, and the truck still had that new car smell. I put the key in the ignition and turned it on. The <mark>quiet hum of the engine</mark> made me so happy.

Sensory words help you visualize.

How to Visualize Using Sketches

- **Before Reading** Look at any illustrations or graphics.
- **Read the Text** Pay attention to descriptive words that help you imagine events, places, and people.
- **Draw the Events** Sketch pictures to show what is happening.

How to Visualize Using Your Senses

- **Look for Words** Find words that tell how things look, sound, smell, taste, and feel.
- **Add What You Know** As you read, think about your own experiences. Add what you know to the information in the text.
- **Create a Picture in Your Mind** What do you hear, feel, see, smell, and taste?

I smell: new-car smell

I see: red, shiny truck

I hear: engine humming

I feel: texture of the seats, the key

Determine Importance

What is this strategy about?

- finding the most important ideas in the text
- putting the ideas in your own words

How do I DETERMINE IMPORTANCE?

When you **determine importance**, you find the most important details or ideas in the text. Then you state the main idea in your own words.

Look at the picture below. What is the most important idea in this picture? Use an Idea Web to help you organize information. Write details about the picture in the circles. Then use the details to find the most important idea.

Detail: the people are playing soccer

Detail: the ball is in the net

What is the picture about?

The player for the red team makes a goal.

Detail: one player stands by the net

Detail: some players wear blue; other players wear red

Make Connections

What is this strategy about?

- thinking about what you know
- thinking about what you have experienced

How do I MAKE CONNECTIONS?

When you **make connections**, you think about how the text connects to other things. As you read, think about what the text says, what you already know, and how it connects.

Look at the picture below. What connections can you make to **yourself**?

The picture shows: A person speaking

I already know: Speaking in front of people can be scary.

I have experienced: In class, I had to give a speech. I was so nervous!

Picture-to-self connection: I was nervous during my speech. But this person is smiling. Maybe I should try to smile more during speeches.

Look at the picture below. What connections can you make to the **picture** above?

The picture shows: A person speaking

I already know: The speaker in the picture above is smiling.

I have experienced: When I smile, I feel less nervous.

Picture-to-picture connection: This speaker is not smiling. He does not look happy. But he does not look nervous. Each speaker has a different way of speaking.

What connections can you make to the **world**?

Picture-to-world connection: Speaking is important. A lot f people have to speak in their jobs. On TV, I see people running for president speaking. They have to be good speakers to get the votes that they need.

Make Inferences

What is this strategy about?

This strategy is about making guesses using

- what you already know
- what you have experienced
- facts and details from the text

How do I MAKE INFERENCES?

When you **make inferences**, you guess what the text is about. To make guesses, you use what is in the text. You use what you already know. You also use your own experiences.

Look at the picture below. Make inferences about the people in the picture. Use what you know, what you have experienced, and what you see in the picture.

Inferences		
I see . . .	**I know . . .**	**So I think . . .**
a woman, man, and two children	My parents used to take me outside when I was younger. We went to the park.	This is a family playing in the snow park.
they are laughing	I laugh a lot when I play with my younger brother.	The family is happy. They would not laugh if they were unhappy.

Ask Questions

What is this strategy about?

- learning new information
- figuring out what is important
- checking that you understand what you read

How do I ASK QUESTIONS?

Asking questions helps you find information that you might have missed. Use **a question word** such as *Who, What, When, Where, Why,* or *How*. Use the **text**, **photographs**, or other **visuals** to answer your questions.

Look at the picture below. Ask questions about the picture. Use question words. Then find the answers. You can find the answers in the picture or using what you already know.

Question Words	Questions	Answers
Who	**Who** is in the picture?	There are many people in the picture. Some people look like children. Some people are adults.
What	**What** is happening in the picture?	The people are laughing. They are eating food.
When	**When** did this take place?	I don't know when the party took place. But there is a cake. The picture might have been taken on someone's birthday.
Where	**Where** are they?	It looks like they are at a party. The party is at someone's house.
Why	**Why** are the people together?	The people are celebrating someone's birthday.

Questions to Yourself

Asking **yourself** questions can help you learn new information. Asking questions can also help you understand what is happening in the text. There are many ways that asking questions can help you take control of your reading.

Ask Yourself Questions to . . .	Example Questions
understand something that is confusing.	• What are the people in the story doing? • Why is this detail important? • Who is this person? • How can I figure out what this word means?
keep track of what is happening.	• What happened after the character went to school? • Where did this event take place?
think about what you know.	• Do I agree with what the text is saying? • Have I ever experienced something like this before? • What do I already know about this topic?

Questions to the Author

Sometimes, you may have questions about what the **author** is trying to tell you in a text. Ask questions, and then try to answer them by reading the text.

Ask the Author Questions to . . .	Example Questions
understand what the author is trying to tell you.	• What is the author trying to say in this part of the text? • Does the author explain his or her ideas clearly? • What is the author talking about? • Can I find facts that support the author's ideas?

Asking questions is a good way to make sure you're actively thinking—before, during, and after reading.

Reading Fluency

What Is Reading Fluency?

When you read fluently, you read smoothly and expressively. It is easy to understand a fluent reader. Fluent readers understand what they read better. Fluent readers enjoy what they read more. Build your fluency in four areas:

- accuracy and rate
- phrasing
- intonation
- expression

How to Improve Accuracy and Rate

Accuracy is the correctness of your reading. Rate is the speed of your reading.

How to read accurately:

- Pronounce words correctly.
- Emphasize the correct syllables.

How to read at the right rate:

- Match your speed to what you are reading.
- Recognize and use punctuation.

Practice Accuracy and Rate

Choose a text you know. Listen to a friend read the text or listen to a reading on a CD-ROM. Learn how to pronounce difficult words.

Practice reading the text aloud. Practice reading it silently. Read the text multiple times.

Read the text to a partner. Ask your partner to circle words or phrases that were not accurate. Review those words and phrases. Practice reading and try again.

Ask your partner to use a watch or clock to time you while you read a passage aloud. Record the times. See how your reading rate improves.

How to Improve Phrasing

Use your voice to group words together.

When you read, follow these steps:

1. Read at an even pace. Do not read too quickly or too slowly.
2. Pause for key words.
3. Use punctuation to tell you when to stop, pause, or emphasize.

Mark	Name	What to Do
.	Period	Pause at the end of a sentence.
,	Comma	Take a short pause within the sentence.
!	Exclamation point	Emphasize the end of the sentence. Then pause.
?	Question mark	Emphasize the end of the sentence. Then pause.

Practice Phrasing

Put a slash mark (/) within a sentence where you will pause.

/ = short pause
// = long pause

Read aloud. The slash marks will help you remember to pause.

There are many ways / to get involved in your school / and community. // Join a club. // Join a sports team. // You can play basketball, / soccer, / or tennis. //

Practice reading with a partner. Use the rubric to score yourself and your partner.

Phrasing Rubric		
1	**2**	**3**
Very choppy	Mostly smooth	Very smooth
No pauses for punctuation	Some pauses for punctuation	Correct pauses for punctuation

How to Improve Intonation

Intonation is the rise and fall of your voice. Intonation involves pitch and tone.

Pitch:
Quiet or Soft   Loud

Tone:
Low   High

When you read, follow these steps.

1. Change your voice to match what you read.
2. Raise your voice to emphasize words.
3. Use visual clues.

Visual Clue	Example	Meaning	What to Do
Italics	She is *smart*.	Draw attention to the word.	Emphasize "smart."
Exclamation point (!)	She is smart!	Shows energy, excitement, or anger.	Make your voice louder at the end of the sentence.
Question mark (?)	She is smart?	Shows curiosity or confusion.	Raise the pitch of your voice slightly at the end of the sentence.
Quotation marks (" ")	"Smart" means intelligent.	Refers to the word, not the meaning of the word.	Emphasize "smart."
Dash (—)	She is—smart.	Shows a quick break in a sentence.	Pause before saying "smart."

Practice Intonation

Pick a sentence to read. Change your intonation.

- This is *fun*.
- This is fun.
- This is fun!
- This is fun?
- This is—fun.

Use the rubric to score yourself and your partner.

Intonation Rubric		
1	**2**	**3**
The reader's voice sounds the same. There are **no changes** in pitch or tone.	There are **some changes** in pitch or tone.	The reader's tone **changes to match what is read**.

How to Improve Expression

Use your voice to show feelings.

slow, quiet

fast, loud

sad
serious

excited
angry

Use your voice to bring characters to life.

Use different voices for different texts.

GENRE	VOICE
Funny story	Happy voice
Sad story	Sad voice
Information text	Serious voice

Practice Expression

Read aloud with a partner. Read each sentence twice.

First, read with no expression.

Next, read with expression.

- I am very sad.
- That was a boring movie.
- We won the game.

Use the rubric to score yourself and your partner.

Expression Rubric

1	2	3
The reader's voice **does not have feeling**.	The reader's voice has **some feeling**.	The voice reader's voice has feeling. The **feeling matches the text**.

Reading Fluency Practice

Practice Phrasing: "First Names"

Use your voice to group words together. Use the rubric on page 528.

> We have the same first name—Amy. Amy means "loved."
> We are loved. There are other Amys. But we are all different.

Practice Intonation: "Growing Together"

Raise and lower your voice as you read. Use the rubric on page 529.

> I tell Papi how I feel.
>
> "I hate it here! I am not like them. They are not like me!" I say.
>
> He asks, "Carmita, do you know what it means to graft a tree?"
>
> I nod. "You take a branch from one tree. You add it to another tree. Then they grow together."

Practice Intonation: "Ways to Know You"

Raise and lower your voice as you read. Use the rubric on page 529.

> Everyone has different fingerprints. These triplets look similar. But they have different fingerprints. Can you see the differences?
>
> Fingerprints are unique in more than ten different ways. Each fingerprint has a pattern. Study your right thumb. Which patterns do you see? No one else has your fingerprints.

Practice Phrasing: "How Ananse Gave Wisdom to the World"

Use your voice to group words together. Use the rubric on page 528.

> Ananse planned to hide it at the top of a big, tall tree. Ananse's wife got him a large pot. Ananse put all the wisdom in the pot. He didn't tell anyone.
>
> Then Ananse got a rope. He tied one end around the pot and tied the other around his neck. That night, he sneaked out of the house. He walked slowly into the forest.

Practice Expression: "Be Water, My Friend"

Use your voice to show feelings. Use the rubric on page 530.

At Yip Man's school, Bruce didn't have to be still. He had to use his body. He loved it. But one day Bruce used his skills to fight. Yip Man was not happy.

"Then what are martial arts for?" Bruce Lee asked.

Yip Man explained. "Heavy snow sometimes breaks big branches. But smaller plants that look weak bend and survive. Calm your mind. Do not fight the flow of nature. There is gentleness in martial arts."

"How can I be gentle when I am fighting?" Bruce asked.

Practice Expression: "Mathematics"

Use your voice to show feelings. Use the rubric on page 530.

Visitors never came with empty hands. Mina received their presents with a smile. She was pleased by the wildflowers. She was just as pleased by a set of towels. She would then point to her closet. "On the second shelf is a can of peaches. In the drawer are new handkerchiefs."

One poor granddaughter gave a few oranges. She went home happily with new socks. A tired daughter brought jelly. She left excitedly with money for rent. The rich son received an orange. All were given with joy.

Practice Phrasing: "If the World Were a Village"

Use your voice to group words together. Use the rubric on page 528.

These numbers are big. They can be hard to understand. Instead, think of them differently. Imagine the world as a village of 100 people. Each person in this village stands for 67 million people from the real world. We can learn about these villagers. They can teach us about people in the real world. They also teach us about world problems.

Practice Expression: "Behind the Veil"

Use your voice to show feelings. Use the rubric on page 530.

When everyone finished speaking, Nadia rose slowly from the corner. She walked to the middle of the room. "This has been a memorable week," she said. "But it has also been one of my most uncomfortable."

"All of you have been wonderful to me," she said. "But I realize that some of you are afraid of me and my beliefs. I understand. You only know the Islam that you hear about in the media. You don't know the truth of our religion."

What she said was true. We knew about the beliefs of Islamic terrorists. But we knew nothing about the beliefs of nonviolent Muslims. I didn't know anything about her religion.

Practice Expression: "Alphabet City Ballet"

Use your voice to show feelings. Use the rubric on page 530.

She heard a key in the lock. Then Luis was in the kitchen in front of her.

She bit her lip. "I want to wear your sweatband Wednesday. I wanted to try it on. For ballet."

"You don't raise no sweat in 'ballet.'" He said "ballet" so that it sounded like "sweat."

Marisol was suddenly angry. "You don't know anything about it! It's *all* sweat!"

"Whoa. What're you mad for?" Luis asked.

"You think you're so smart! It's tougher than soccer!" she yelled.

"Okay. All right."

Practice Expression: "Two Were Left"

Use your voice to show feelings. Use the rubric on page 530.

Now! Now was the time to strike!

A terrible feeling came over Noni as he started to cry. He could not hurt Nimuk. He cursed the knife and threw it far from him. He fell.

Now the dog growled. He circled the boy's body. Noni was sick with fear. Without the knife, he was defenseless. He was too weak to go get it now. And Nimuk was hungry.

The dog circled him. Noni heard this breathing from behind and knew Nimuk was getting close. He prayed for the attack to be fast. He felt the dog's breath against his neck. He knew this was the end.

Then he felt the dog's hot tongue. Nimuk was licking his face.

Noni's eyes opened. He did not believe it. He pulled the dog into his arms. Then he began to cry.

The plane came out of the south. The pilot looked down. He saw something flashing. He turned his plane. He saw a shape. It looked human. Or were there two shapes?

Practice Phrasing: "Surviving Katrina"

Use your voice to group words together. Use the rubric on page 528.

In 2005, Courtney was living in New Orleans. His father had moved across the country. His mother was in jail. Courtney stayed with his grandmother, but she moved away, too. The teenager was on his own, with no food or money. Life was hard.

"I was trying to go down a straight street, but I had all these obstacles," Courtney said. Neighbors offered to help, but he usually refused. He worked to take care of himself.

Then Hurricane Katrina struck. Courtney's neighborhood was flooded. There was no electricity. People had no food or clean water. The flood waters were knee high. "Man, we have to do something to get out of here," Courtney told his friends.

What Courtney did next makes some people call him a hero. Others call him a criminal. But Courtney and his friends knew what they had to do. One night, they broke into a bus station. Courtney didn't have a driver's license, but he took a bus anyway. He drove back to his neighborhood and picked up his neighbors. Then he brought them to safety.

Practice Intonation: "Fight or Flight?"

Raise and lower your voice as you read. Use the visual cues. Use the rubric on page 529.

Go forward to the present day. There have been a lot of changes in the past 25,000 years. However, you still have the same internal body parts as the caveman. Now you're in the lunchroom at school. You're hunting for food, but your teacher is hunting too. Guess what? He's hunting for you.

You hear terrifying words from your teacher. "Could I see you in my room, please?" When you see the tiger, uh, your teacher, your body reacts. Your hypothalamus sends a message to your adrenal glands. Your body turns on all the same powers that the caveman used to escape the tiger.

You walk down the hall to your teacher's room. You can feel your blood pressure going up. Is it the last test you turned in? Now your mind races. Your heart pounds. Your mouth dries up and your hands feel cold. Your forehead perspires. You imagine getting in trouble. The caveman inside of you wants to come out. Maybe you'd like to run and hide. You can't. Welcome to the modern era.

Practice Expression: "Frijoles"

Use your voice to show feelings. Use the rubric on page 530.

Mr. Ono raised his dinner plate to his face and studied the *frijoles* curiously. "I know this smell," he said. He moved a chopstick across the plate. Then he sucked on the end. "I know this taste," he concluded.

"How can you know?" Mrs. Ono said.

"I just *know*," he answered. "I am an international eater." Mrs. Ono rolled her eyes. She got up to check on the boys in the kitchen.

For the past three hours, Lincoln and Tony had been preparing the food. They cooked the beans and smashed them into *frijoles*. They chopped chilies, onions, and tomatoes for salsa. They made dough into tortillas. Now they brought the rest of the food to the table and joined their host family.

"We are honored that you made this for us," Mr. Ono said, smiling so that the gold crowns on his teeth showed.

Mrs. Ono looked at Tony and Lincoln. "You are hard-working boys."

"And they have taught our sons valuable American words," Mr. Ono said.

"Such as?" Mrs. Ono asked, trying some *frijoles*.

Mr. Ono thought and then said, "*Órale, ése*." He turned to Tony, who was headed back to the kitchen to fry more tortillas, and yelled, "*¡Órale, ése!*"

"*Simón que sí, Papi*," Tony called back as he turned over one of his homemade tortillas.

Practice Phrasing: "Cochlear Implants: Two Sides of the Story"

Use your voice to group words together. Use the rubric on page 528.

Good morning. My name is Caitlin Parton. I've had my cochlear implant for nine years, and I love it. It's helping me a lot.

I think it's important to have the implant as a choice for people who are deaf. It brings you into the hearing world, the world of sound. I wear this miracle of modern science. I'm a little different, but I'm a lot like everyone else, too.

I don't wear the implant when I sleep. In the morning when I wake up, it's a shock to put it on. Whoa! All these sounds come in. Then my brain figures out what the different sounds are: the radio, Dad cooking, traffic outdoors.

Sounds are really important to me. They give me something exciting to experience every day. Some of the sounds I enjoy most are my parents' voices, my friends' voices, and me talking to everybody! I love music. I play the piano and the flute.

I like talking on the phone. I can now use it without any special devices and get almost everything. I love the sound of thunder, the wind in the trees, the birds. I like asking a store clerk where something is. I like hearing the "specials" at a restaurant and ordering for myself. I love reading to my little cousins.

Practice Expression: "The Right Moves"

Use your voice to show feelings. Use the rubric on page 530.

"Lena, are you listening?"

I *was* listening. I just couldn't believe my ears.

"W-what did you say?" I stammered.

"Do you want to join our dance team?" the girl asked impatiently. "We win the talent show every year, and we need a new dancer."

I still couldn't believe it. The teachers sponsored a talent show each spring. It would be a huge night, and Maya Herrera wanted me to be on her dance team.

"Sure," I said.

Maya glared at someone behind me, her pretty face looking like she had tasted something sour. "Not *her,* though," Maya said loudly. "Just you."

I didn't have to turn around—I knew who she meant. "Uh, sure," I mumbled again. Maya was already heading back to the "popular table" when I felt someone tap my shoulder.

"What happened?" Lola asked. When I saw her confused face, it was like waking up from a dream.

Lola Reyes and I had been friends since we were little kids. Lola was a smart, funny friend.

But at school, Lola just didn't fit in. I had never noticed when we were alone, but it was obvious to all the kids at school. Lola's hair was frizzy and her thick glasses made her look a little like a fish. Kids in grade school could be mean.

Practice Expression: "Luck"

Use your voice to show feelings. Show the different characters from this play with your voice. Use the rubric on page 530.

ACTOR 1. We are in shadows here already. Look, the mountain back there still has sunshine.

ACTOR 2. That's why I hate living down here in the valley. It's dark in the morning and dark in the evening.

ACTOR 3. And we don't get any views down here.

ACTOR 4. Up there on the mountain, they get all the summer breezes.

ACTOR 5. Why should they get all the luck? It's not fair.

ACTOR 1. There must be something we can do.

ACTOR 2. Why don't we move to the mountain?

ACTOR 3. Because there are only five houses up there, and they took them all.

ACTOR 4. Maybe we can exchange our houses for theirs.

ACTOR 5. What a great idea!

ACTOR 3. Naw. They probably won't want to do that.

ACTOR 4. Maybe we should pay them some extra money.

ACTOR 2. How much money do we have?

ACTOR 1. We'll make them an offer they can't refuse.

ACTOR 1 to 5. Yes, yes, what a great idea. Let's go. Let's go ask them!

Practice Intonation: "The Scholarship Jacket"

Raise and lower your voice as you read. Use the visual cues. Use the rubric on page 529.

The small Texas school that I attended carried out a tradition every year during graduation; a beautiful gold and green jacket was awarded to the class valedictorian, the student who had maintained the highest grades. The scholarship jacket had a big gold *S* on the left front side and the winner's name was written in gold letters on the pocket.

I fully expected to win. I had been a straight-A student since the first grade. I looked forward to owning that jacket.

One day close to graduation, I was outside my classroom's door when I heard angry voices arguing. I recognized the voices: Mr. Schmidt and Mr. Boone, two of my teachers. They seemed to be arguing about me. I couldn't believe it.

"I refuse to do it! I don't care who her father is, her grades don't even begin to compare to Martha's. I won't lie or falsify records. Martha has a straight A plus average and you know it." That was Mr. Schmidt and he sounded very angry. Mr. Boone's voice sounded calm and quiet.

"Look, Joann's father is not only on the Board, he owns the only store in town. We could say it was a close tie and—"

Only a word here and there filtered through. ". . . Martha is Mexican . . . resign . . . won't do it . . ." I don't remember how I made it through the afternoon. I went home and cried. It seemed a cruel coincidence that I had overheard that conversation.

Practice Phrasing: "The Gift of the Magi"

Use your voice to group words together. Use the rubric on page 528.

One dollar and eighy-seven cents. That was all. And sixty cents of it was in pennies. Della counted it three times: $1.87.

Tomorrow was Christmas Day, and that was all she had to buy Jim a present. She wanted to give him something fine and rare—something worthy of a man like Jim.

Suddenly Della looked into her cheap mirror. She pulled down her hair and let it fall around her.

Now, the James Dillingham Youngs owned two things that they were proud of. One was Jim's gold watch. It had been his father's and his grandfather's. The other was Della's hair.

Della's beautiful hair fell around her, rippling and shining like a waterfall. Then she tied it up again nervously and quickly. A tear or two splashed on the worn red carpet.

With a bright sparkle still in her eyes, she flew out the door and down the street. She stopped at a sign that read: "Madame Sofronie. Hair Goods of All Kinds."

"Will you buy my hair?" asked Della.

"I buy hair," said Madame. "Let's look at it."

Della let her hair down.

"Twenty dollars," said Madame.

"Give me the money quickly," said Della.

Vocabulary

How to Make a Word Your Own

When you cook, you follow the steps of a recipe. This helps you make food correctly. When you read, there are also steps you can follow to learn new words. The following steps will help you practice words in different ways and make the words your own.

Learning a Word

Follow these steps to add new words to your vocabulary.

1. **Say the Word** Write and say the word one syllable at a time.

re-a-lize

Think about what looks familiar in the word. For example, *real* is part of *realize*.

2. **Study Examples** When you are given examples, read them carefully and think about how and why the word is being used.

   - **Example**: *Marietta did not **realize** that Lupe was so busy.* What does this sentence tell you about Marietta and Lupe?

   Look for more examples to study in books or magazines.

3. **Elaborate** Make new sentences to check your understanding of the word.

   - Finish these sentence frames for practice:
     - I **realized** I was happy when _____.
     - Steve's mom **realized** he was growing up when _____.
     - How did your teacher **realize** that you _____?

4. **Practice the Word** Use the word in many different ways.

"I can use the new word to help me remember and understand its meaning."

How to Relate Words

A good way to build your vocabulary is to **relate new words** to words or concepts you already know. Think about how the new word is similar to or different from words you are already familiar with.

Related Word Map

You can create a map with **related words** to help you study the new word.

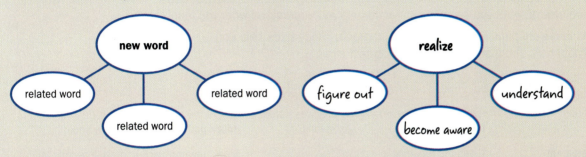

Definition Map

You can create a **definition** map to put all the information about a word in one place.

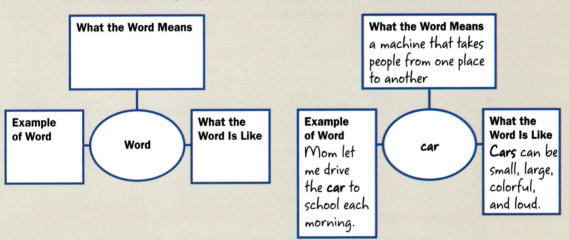

Five-Senses Map

You can create a **Five-Senses Map** that describes the word using the five senses.

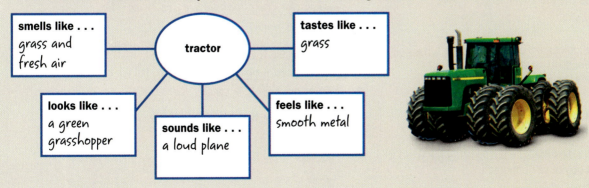

How to Use Context to Understand Words

Context Clues

Context is the text near a word or phrase. This text can help explain the meaning of the word or phrase. The underlined words below are context for the word *slugs*.

Slugs are unusual animals. They have soft bodies and live places where it is wet.

There are several ways you can use context to help you understand what you read.

Context clues are hints in a sentence or paragraph. These hints help define words that you do not know. There are many types of context clues.

Type of Context Clue	Description	Signal Words	Example
Definition	Explains what the word means	*is, are, was, refers to, means*	*Slug* is the common name for a **gastropod mollusk** without a shell.
Restatement	Gives the meaning in a different way, usually after a comma	*or*	Slugs have **tentacles**, or feelers, on their heads.
Example	Gives an example of what the word means	*such as, for example, including*	There are many **predators** that eat slugs, such as frogs, snakes, and toads.
Synonym	Gives a word or phrase that means almost the same thing	*like, also*	Also **destructive** animals, slugs can be harmful to your garden.
Antonym	Gives a word or phrase that means the opposite of the word	*but, unlike*	Slugs are mainly **nocturnal**, unlike other animals that are awake during the day.

Look at the chart below to see how to use different context clues.

Example	Unknown Words	Context Clues
The universe means "outer space."	universe	Definition: I see what the word means. I know that universe means "outer space."
A telescope magnifies, or makes the stars look larger.	magnifies	Restatement: I see the word or and a comma. The words makes the stars look larger are clues. They tell me magnifies means "make larger."
I love looking at celestial bodies, such as stars, planets, and moons.	celestial bodies	Example: I see the words such as. The words stars, planets, and moons are clues. They tell me celestial bodies are objects in space.
Like Earth, Jupiter is a planet.	Jupiter	Synonym: I see the word like. Jupiter must be a planet.
Earth orbits the sun, but stars do not circle the sun.	orbit	Antonym: I see the word but. The word orbit means "circle."

How to Understand Words with Different Meanings

Multiple-Meaning Words

Some words have **different meanings** depending on how they are used in a sentence. Use the context to find which meaning is correct. Replace the word or words with each meaning until you find the use that makes the best sense.

Example	Please **park** in the lot behind the school.
Meaning 1	Park can mean "stop and leave your car."
Meaning 2	Park can mean "a public place for people to enjoy."
Replace the Word	Please **stop and leave your car** in the lot behind the school. Please **a public place for people to enjoy** in the lot behind the school.
Which meaning is correct?	In this sentence, park means "stop and leave your car."

Vocabulary

There are many examples of words with more than one meaning. Here are some to remember.

Word	Sample Sentence	Part of Speech	Possible Meanings
approach	Emma had a creative **approach** to the problem.	noun	a way to do something
	It's wise to **approach** dogs with caution.	verb	to go near
	I will **approach** Joe about helping with the party.	verb	to go to with a request
	How should we **approach** this assignment?	verb	to begin to work
area	I have never been to that **area** of town.	noun	a place or region
	The doctor's **area** of expertise is pediatrics.	noun	a field of study
	The **area** of the room is 200 square feet.	noun	measurement of space
brief	His meeting will be very **brief**.	adjective	taking a short time
	He kept his speech very **brief**.	adjective	using few words
	I will **brief** you on what happened in today's meeting.	verb	to give a short explanation
challenge	It's a real **challenge** to train for the ten-mile race.	noun	something difficult that tests your skills
	Yolanda likes to **challenge** me to chess.	verb	to invite into a contest or fight
	I **challenge** their authority to ban those books.	verb	to question the right of
	That movie will **challenge** your thinking.	verb	to make active

A chess challenge

Word	Sample Sentence	Part of Speech	Possible Meanings
code	Our school has a strict dress **code**.	noun	a set of rules
	During the war, messages were written in a secret **code**.	noun	a system of signs and symbols
	She used a different **code** for the new software.	noun	instructions for a computer program
conduct	At work it's important to **conduct** yourself professionally.	verb	to behave
	Who will **conduct** the tour of the museum?	verb	to lead or guide
	The wires **conduct** electricity in the house.	verb	to carry or allow passage through
	Miguel will **conduct** the orchestra.	verb	to direct in a performance
document	A birth certificate is a legal **document**.	noun	a written paper that gives information
	I will carefully **document** all my research.	verb	to give evidence for
draft	The final **draft** of the story was exciting to read.	noun	a version of a piece of writing
	At age 18, men used to register for the military **draft**.	noun	selection for a person for a specific duty
	The **draft** from the window feels cold.	noun	a current of air in a room
	My lawyer will **draft** the contract.	verb	to write something that will probably change
file	He keeps all the stories he writes in a special **file**.	noun	a box or folder for storing papers
	I named the **file** "historyreport.doc."	noun	electronic information stored on a computer
	The school has a **file** on every student.	noun	a collection of personal information about a person or topic
	He used a **file** to shape his nails.	noun	a tool used to smooth and shape something that is rough

Word	Sample Sentence	Part of Speech	Possible Meanings
issue	The first **issue** of the magazine goes out today.	noun	edition of a newspaper or magazine
	Stem cell research is a big **issue**.	noun	a point or subject that people are discussing
	The team will **issue** new uniforms tomorrow.	verb	to give out or distribute
link	There is a definite **link** between smoking and cancer.	noun	a logical connection between two things
	The bridge **links** the two towns.	verb	to join or connect
minor	A 17-year-old is still a **minor**.	noun	a person under the age of 18
	That point is just a **minor** detail.	adjective	less important or serious
	In college I think I'll **minor** in Spanish.	verb	to study as a secondary course in college
monitor	My new computer has a big **monitor**.	noun	computer screen
	The **monitor** measured the amount of air pollution.	noun	a tool for collecting data
	The nurse will **monitor** the patient's breathing throughout the night.	verb	to observe or check
odd	My younger brother looks **odd** in his blue suit.	adjective	strange or unusual
	The basket is full of **odd** socks.	adjective	mismatched
	We used **odd** scraps of fabric to make a quilt.	adjective	leftover
	One and three are examples of **odd** numbers.	adjective	not able to be divided by two
prime	Clothing is a **prime** export of China.	adjective	first in importance
	We had **prime** seats at the play.	adjective	great, wonderful
	At age 34, Joon was in his **prime**.	noun	the time of life when a person is at his or her best
	I **primed** the group for the mission.	verb	to make ready or prepare

Word	Sample Sentence	Part of Speech	Possible Meanings
quote	I **quoted** a line from my favorite poem.	verb	to repeat information from a text or person
	The plumber **quoted** the repairs at $110.	verb	to give an estimation
range	These shoes come in a **range** of colors.	noun	variety, or number of different things in the same category
	The age **range** of students is from 15 to 18 years old.	noun	complete group included between the two points on a scale
	The radar has a **range** of ten miles.	noun	maximum distance that something can reach
	The Himalayas are the tallest **range** in Asia.	noun	a series of connected mountains
	The cows grazed on the **range**.	noun	a large area of open land
source	We did not know the **source** of the problems.	noun	the cause of something
	My **source** for the article was reliable.	noun	a person who provides information
	The **source** of the river is farther north.	noun	the spring or lake where a river begins
stress	She's under a lot of **stress** to make the swim team.	noun	suffering from worries and tension
	The skater's ankle bone broke from too much **stress**.	noun	pressure that pushes on an object
	I want to **stress** the importance of daily exercise.	verb	to emphasize an important point
volume	The can has a smaller **volume** than the box.	noun	amount of space that something occupies
	I need to find the first **volume** of the encyclopedia.	noun	one of the books in a set of books
	Turn down the **volume** of the radio.	noun	loudness

Figurative Language

Figurative language is a tool that writers use. This tool helps you visualize or relate to what is happening in the text. Figurative language uses words that do not mean exactly what they say. You can use pictures in your mind or context clues to figure out the meaning.

Similes and Metaphors

Similes use *like* or *as* to compare two things. **Metaphors** also compare two things, but they do not use *like* or *as*. Find what is being compared. Then use context clues or what you already know to figure out the meaning.

Example	Simile—What is being compared?	Context Clues/What I Already Know
The willow tree's branches are like silken thread.	This simile is comparing a tree's branches to silk thread.	Silk is very soft and smooth. The simile means the willow's branches are also very soft and smooth.

Example	Metaphor—What is being compared?	Context Clues/What I Already Know
The night sky is a black curtain.	This metaphor compares the night sky to a black curtain.	A black curtain would block out light from coming in a window. This metaphor means the night sky is very dark.

Idioms

An **idiom** is a colorful way to say something. Usually a few words work together to create a new meaning. In an idiom the words mean something different from what they say. Look for words or phrases that give clues about its meaning.

Example	Idiom	Context Clues
Don't bite off more than you can chew or you will never finish the job.	*"bite off more than you can chew"* I know that people don't really bite things when they work on a job. This must be an idiom. So it does not really mean biting or chewing.	I can use clues in the sentence to figure out the meaning: The sentence says you will never finish the job. Bite off more than you can chew must have something to do about work. It can mean people should not agaree to do more work than they can do.

Common Idioms

Here are some common idioms.

Idiom	Meaning	Sample Sentence
all ears	very eager to hear	If you have a good idea, then I am **all ears**.
around the clock	open 24 hours a day	The store is **open around the clock**.
beat around the bush	to avoid the question or point	He **beat around the bush** before finally asking me to go to the movies.
blown out of the water	to destroy or defeat completely	The other team was so good, they totally **blew us out of the water**.
cut corners	to not do something completely	We will have to **cut corners** in order to finish our project on time.
give your word	to promise	I **gave my word** that I would finish my homework before going to the movies.
get cold feet	to feel hesitant or afraid	She wanted to ask him to dance but **got cold feet** and didn't.
jump to a conclusion	to guess without knowing all the information	I **jumped to a conclusion** without knowing all the facts.
keep one's eyes peeled	to watch out for	The police **kept their eyes peeled** for the robber.
knocked off one's feet	to cause great surprise	She was **knocked off her feet** after hearing that rumor.
let the cat out of the bag	to reveal a piece of information	She **let the cat out of the bag** about Delisa's surprise party.
make ends meet	to have enough money to pay bills	Mrs. Charles works hard **to make ends meet**.
piece of cake	easy to do	My math test was a **piece of cake**.
pop the question	to ask someone to get married	Mike loves Amy and wants to **pop the question**.
pull one's leg	to joke or kid	My brother told me that he was fired, but he was just **pulling my leg**.
quake in one's boots	to be very scared	I was **quaking in my boots** after watching that scary movie.

Idiom	Meaning	Sample Sentence
save one's own skin	to protect oneself from danger or difficulty	He **saved his own skin** by admitting the truth to his parents.
see eye to eye	to agree with someone completely	My cousin and I **see eye to eye** on everything.
sleep on it	to think something over before making a decision	I had a job offer, but I wanted to **sleep on it** before I accepted it.
something up one's sleeve	a secret plan to be used at the right time	The coach always seems to have **something up her sleeve** when the team is in trouble.
steal the spotlight	to take attention away from someone else	My friend likes to **steal the spotlight** from others.
take five	to take a break during work	The workers **take five** every few hours.
think outside the box	to think in a new, creative way	To solve this problem, I am going to have to **think outside the box**.
tie in knots	to make someone nervous	The thought of going to the dentist **tied him in knots**.
turn up one's nose	to not accept something	Carlos felt bad when Linda **turned up her nose** at his birthday gift.
24-seven	constantly; all the time	Kaysar and Will are together **24-seven**.
under the weather	feeling ill or tired	The flu made Danielle feel **under the weather**.
up the creek	in trouble	Lupe was **up the creek** when he lost his ID.
the walls have ears	people might be listening secretly	Don't say too much because **the walls have ears**.
wrack one's brain	to think hard to solve a problem	I **wracked my brain** for a way to save more money.
young at heart	to feel young or youthful	My grandpa is 82 years old, but he is very **young at heart**.
zip it	to keep quiet	John wanted to tell his secret, but decided to **zip it**.

How to Analyze Word Parts

Each piece in a puzzle fits together to make a picture or an image. Words have pieces that come together, too. You can analyze, or look at, the parts of words to help you learn the meaning of entire words.

Compound Words

Compound words are made when two words are put together to make a new word.

Example	Word Parts	Analyze Word Parts
doghouse	• dog • house	I know that dog is an animal and house is a place where people live. Doghouse means a small house for a dog.

Remember these rules when analyzing compound words:

- Sometimes the compound word has a space between each part, such as *ice cream* or *cell phone.*
- Sometimes the new word's meaning is different from what the other two words mean alone. For example, *butterfly* is an insect, not butter that flies.

Prefixes

A **prefix** is a word part that comes at the beginning of a word. It changes the meaning of the word. The chart below shows common prefixes.

Prefix	Meaning	Sample Sentence
dis-	opposite	If I say I like raw fish, I would be **dishonest**.
im-, in-	not	It's **impossible** to walk to the moon.
pre-	before	I like to **preview** movies before I buy them.
mis-	wrongly	I **misspell** words, so I always proofread my work.

Suffixes

A **suffix** is a word part that comes at the end of a word. It changes a word's meaning and its part of speech. The chart below shows common suffixes.

Suffix	Meaning	Sample Sentence
-able	can be done	I wasn't surprised by the **predictable** ending.
-ful	full of	The **resourceful** boy survived in the desert.
-less	without	I try to avoid **careless** mistakes.
-ment	action or process	The landlord expects **payment** by Tuesday.
-ness	state of	The baby squealed with **happiness**.

Inflected Forms

An **inflection** is a change in the form of a word to show how it is used. Different inflections have different meanings. An inflection changes the meaning of a word. You can learn new words by analyzing what type of inflection is being used.

Inflection	Meaning	Examples
-er	more	cold**er**, fast**er**
-ed	in the past	call**ed**, talk**ed**
-s	plural	pen**s**, dog**s**

Cognates and False Cognates

Cognates are words that come from two different languages but have the same root origins. Cognates have similar spelling and meanings.

Cognates	Meaning
artist (English) *artista* (Spanish)	"a person who creates art"

False cognates seem like they share a meaning but they do not.

False Cognates	Meaning
rope (English)	"a cord to tie things with"
ropa (Spanish)	"clothing"

How to Use Cognates to Determine Word Meaning

- Think about what the words mean in the language you are most familiar with.
- Substitute the meaning of the word with your language's definition.
- If your language's definition does not make sense, you may be using a false cognate. Try to learn the word using a different resource.

How to Use a Reference

Dictionary

A **dictionary** lists words. Use the dictionary to learn

- how to spell a word
- how to say a word
- what a word means
- how to use a word
- where a word comes from

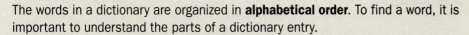

The words in a dictionary are organized in **alphabetical order**. To find a word, it is important to understand the parts of a dictionary entry.

> **sur•vive** \sər-'vīv\ *v.* to continue to live after an illness or accident [M.E., to out-live, from L. *supervivere,* from *super- + vivere* to live]

Use the dictionary's key to understand any abbreviations or symbols.

Key	
ME	Middle English (an old version of English)
L.	Latin
ə	pronounced like *uh*
'	accented syllable
v.	verb
n.	noun

To use a dictionary to find the meaning of a word, follow these steps:

1. Read all the definitions of the new word to find the use and meaning you need.

2. Go back to the text and reread it.

3. Replace the meaning you found for the original word.

4. Check to make sure it is the correct use of the word.

> *"Conduct can mean either to guide or to behave."*

> **con•duct** \kon-duhkt\ **1:** *n.* way of acting, to behave. **2:** *v.* to lead or guide.

> I work for my town's Natural History Museum. On the weekends, I **conduct** tours of the museum. I guide visitors through our many exhibits.

> *"I can see that the correct meaning of the word in the text is to lead, or guide."*

Practice Your Vocabulary

When you are trying to learn something new, like a musical instrument, you **practice**. The more you practice, the better you become. Practicing vocabulary words is an important step in learning new words.

Memorize New Words

1. Read the word and its definition silently and aloud.

2. Cover the definition and try to restate the word's meaning.

3. Write words on one side of index cards and their meanings on the opposite sides to make flashcards. Have someone show you the words, and try to recite their definitions from memory.

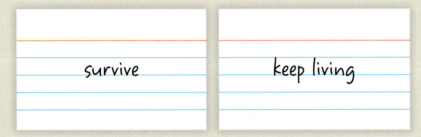

4. Ask yourself questions using the definition and the word.
How would I survive, or keep living, in the desert?

5. Think of clues or mental images to associate with the new word to help you better remember its definition.

Review New Words

1. Reread the definition of each word.

2. Create sentences expressing the correct meaning of each word.

I **survived** the hurricane.

Miguel and John **survived** the ten-mile race.

3. Make lists of new words with their definitions in a notebook to review on a regular schedule.

4. Study each word until you are confident you understand its meaning and how to use the word.

The Writing Process

Writing Forms

Grammar, Usage, Mechanics, and Spelling

Writing Process

What Are the Steps of the Writing Process?

Writing is like playing music or a sport. If you want to be good at it, you have to work on it. There are steps to follow. Some things you do first. Some things you do later.

Writers follow steps to make their writing the best it can be. The writing process usually has five stages. These stages are: **prewriting**, **drafting**, **revising**, **editing and proofreading**, and **publishing**.

1 Prewrite—Get Ready to Write

Prewriting is what you do before you write. You choose a topic. You think about what to say. You make a plan. What plan is best for you? You can write notes. You can make an outline. Or you can even make drawings.

2 Draft—Get It Down on Paper

Drafting is the next step. Writing down the first draft is sometimes the hardest part. But it can also be the most fun. Remember, your first draft doesn't have to be perfect. You can go back and make changes later, so relax and enjoy the work.

3 Revise—Get It to Sing

After your draft is done, put it away for awhile. Later, when you come back to it, you might make major changes! You might move sentences or add new ideas. You can show your work to someone else, too, and ask for ideas.

4 Edit and Proofread—Get It Right

Once you are done making the big changes, start to work on the details. This is when you fix any mistakes in grammar, spelling, or punctuation.

5 Publish, Share, and Reflect—Get It Out There

Do you want other people to read your work? Then publish it! Writer's share their work in newspapers, magazines, and books. Many writers are publishing on the Internet, too.

Sharing your writing with your family, friends, and classmates is another form of publishing. Also, think back to reflect on what you have created.

Prewrite

Prewriting is what you do before you write. During this step, you gather ideas, choose your topic, make a plan, gather details, and organize your ideas.

❶ Gather Ideas

Writing ideas are everywhere! Think about things you've done, things you have read, or things you have seen. You can talk about these ideas with your classmates, friends, and family. Keep the best ideas in a computer file, or a notebook. Then you will have many ideas to choose from when you are ready to write.

❷ Choose Your Topic

Sometimes there are a lot of ideas that you want to write about. Other times, your teacher can give you a writing prompt, or a writing assignment. But it is still up to you to decide what to write about. To help you decide, make a list of your best writing ideas. Circle the one you like best of all. That idea will be your topic.

> I could write about...
>
> a concert my friends and I went to
>
> when my grandparents arrived in the U.S.
>
> why we need more school dances
>
> why the eagle is a popular symbol

❸ Plan Your Writing

An **FATP** chart can help you to put your thoughts in order. A chart can also help you to see the important details you'll need for your writing.

FATP Chart

The **form** tells you the type of writing. Study examples of the form to help you decide how to craft your writing.

A specific **topic** will help you collect only those details you need.

HOW TO UNLOCK A PROMPT
Form: personal narrative
Audience: my teacher and classmates
Topic: when my grandparents arrived in the U.S.
Purpose: to describe a personal experience

If you know your **audience**, you can choose the appropriate style and tone. For example, if you are writing for your friends, you can use friendly, informal language.

The **purpose** is why you are writing. Your purpose can be to describe, to inform or explain, to persuade, or to express personal thoughts or feelings.

④ Gather Details

To write about something that happened to you, try making a list of the things you remember about the event. For other kinds of writing, you can talk about your topic with others. Or you can do research to gather information.

There are many ways to show the details you've gathered. You can:

- make charts, lists, or webs
- draw and label pictures
- take notes on notecards
- make a story map
- use a gathering grid to write down answers to your questions

Show your details in a way that works best for you and for your topic.

Gathering Grid

Topic: Vietnam	Get to Know Vietnam (book)	Internet
What is the population?		
What fuels the economy?		

⑤ Research

Some writing forms and topics may need to be researched. Use these resources to find out more about your topic:

- **Internet** Develop a list of terms, or words, to enter into a search engine. Use sites that end in .edu or .gov for the best information.
- **Library** Search the library's catalog and databases for books and articles about your topic. Ask a librarian for help.
- **Interview** You could talk to a person who knows a lot about your topic. Make your questions ahead of time and write down the person's answers.

⑥ Get Organized

Review your details and plan an interesting way to write about your topic. Put the details in the best order for your writing.

- Sometimes you can organize the details as you write them down.
- Other times, you can use numbers to order events in time sequence or to order the details from the most to least important.
- You could also make an outline to show main ideas and supporting details.

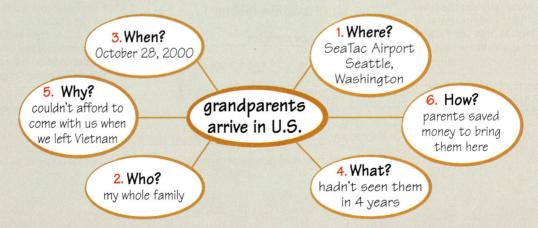

Draft

Now you are ready to start writing. At this stage, don't worry about making mistakes. Just get your ideas on the paper! Turn your ideas and details into sentences and paragraphs. As you write, you may think of new ideas. Add those to your draft.

Trang Bui's Draft

My family stood by the windows and watched the plane land at SeaTac Airport in Seattle on October 28, 2000. We were so excited to see the plane. The people started coming though the door. We lined up so we could see. I had to lift my little sister up so she could see.

Suddenly everyone was hugging and crying. "I see them," my mother cried. My little sister tried to hide. My sister didn't know my grandparents. She was feeling shy.

Remember Purpose, Form, and Audience Remember, you made many important choices about your work during the prewriting stage. Return to your writing plan often. Remind yourself of your purpose, form, and controlling idea as you organize your paragraphs. Think carefully about your audience, voice, and tone as you choose words and write sentences.

Work Collaboratively When you are writing your draft, remember to ask other people for their help. Teachers, classmates, and family members can help you see what needs to be changed to make your work better. Listen carefully to what they have to say. Take notes on their ideas.

Revise A first draft can always be improved. When you revise a draft, you make changes to it.

Read Your Draft As you read your draft, ask yourself questions about the most important ideas. Make sure your ideas are clear, and complete. Make sure they are presented in the best way.

Revise

Mark Your Changes What changes do you want to make to your draft? Use the Revising Marks or special features in your computer's word-processing program to show the changes.

Trang Bui's Revisions

My family stood by the ^big, glass^ windows and watched the plane land at SeaTac Airport in Seattle on October 28, 2000. We were so excited, ~~to see the plane.~~ ^When the passengers^ ~~The people~~ started coming though the door. We lined up so we could see. I had to lift my little sister up so she could ^look over the heads of the people in front^ ~~see.~~

Suddenly everyone was hugging and crying. "I see them," my mother cried. My little sister tried to hide! ^because she^ ~~My sister~~ didn't know my grandparents. ^and^ ~~She~~ was feeling shy. ^It took four long years but my grandparents finally arrived.^

Revising Marks	
^	Add
↪	Move to here
⌄	Replace with this
و	Take out

Hold a Peer Conference Share your draft during a peer conference. As you hear ideas, take notes. You might not be able to do everything your reader suggested. That's OK, but think about *why* your reader suggested the change.

How to Have a Peer Conference

GETTING FEEDBACK

- Don't explain your paper before you begin. Let it speak for itself.
- Ask for your reader's overall opinion. What were the strongest points? What were the weakest points? Was anything confusing?
- Ask for suggestions. What does your reader want to know more about?

GIVING FEEDBACK

- As you read, look for the main idea. Do all the details relate to the main idea?
- Give your overall opinion. Did you understand every part? Which parts did you like the most or least?
- Give suggestions for improvement. Which parts need more detail? Can anything be cut?
- Be polite, but honest. Help your partner improve your work.
- Don't focus just on problems.

Edit and Proofread

After you revise your draft for content, it's time to check it for mistakes.

Take Your Time Good editing and proofreading need attention to detail. The following hints will help you do your best work:

- Use a printed copy of your work. Text looks different on paper than on a computer screen. Many people catch more mistakes when they look at a printed version of their work.

- Set your work aside for awhile. You may see more mistakes if you are rested.

- Read line by line. Use a ruler or a piece of paper to cover the lines below the one you are reading. This will help you see only the words in front of you.

Check Your Sentences When you edit, check that your sentences are clear. Make sure they are complete and correct. Ask yourself does each sentence have a subject and a predicate?

Check for Mistakes Proofread to find errors in capitalization, punctuation, grammar, and spelling. Look especially for:

- capital letters, end marks, apostrophes, and quotation marks
- subject-verb agreement
- misspelled words
- use of pronouns

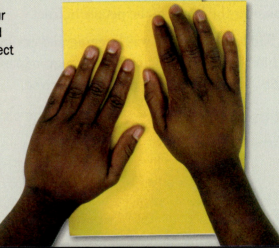

Getting there in time was essential, but I hesitated for a moment. Outside, the wind blew feircely. It

Trang Bui's Proofread Draft

When we left vietnam, my grandparents had to stay behind. "We are too old to go someplace new," my grandfather said. My grandmother cooked a special dinner for us before we left, but we could not eat. We didn't know how long it would be before we would see each other again.

Proofreader's Marks		
	℘	Delete
	∧	Add text
	⟳→	Move to here
	⊙	Add period
	⁁	Add comma
	≡	Capitalize
	/	Make lowercase
	¶	Start new paragraph

Publish

❶ Print Your Work

The final version of your work should be neat. It should be easy to read. It should be nice to look at.

The Best Day of My Life
by Trang Bui

My family stood by the big, glass, windows and watched the plane land at SeaTac Airport in Seattle on October 28, 2000. We were so excited! When the passengers started coming through the door, we lined up so we could see. I had to lift up my little sister so she could look over the heads of the people in front.

Suddenly everyone was hugging and crying. My little sister tried to hide because she didn't know my grandparents. It took four long years, but my grandparents finally arrived!

❷ Publish Your Work

Take your work beyond the classroom and share it in new ways.

- Save examples of your writing in a folder, also called a portfolio. This will allow you to see how your writing has improved over time. Organize your portfolio by date or by form. Each time you add something to your portfolio, take some time to compare the new piece to your older work.

Portfolio Review

☑ How does this writing compare to other work I've done?

☑ What makes me a super writer?

- Think about making your work into a poster, a video, or a Web site. What images best show your ideas? How should the text appear?

- Many newspapers and Web sites publish teen writing. Ask a teacher or librarian for examples.

Evaluate Your Work

Now that your work is done, look to see what you could make better.

- Discuss your work with your teacher and classmates, then ask yourself:

What did I do well?

I added some description. My details were in order.

What are some weaknesses that I could improve on easily?

I need to make my sure that my sentence structures are not all the same.

How will I make sure I improve on those weaker areas?

I could pick topics that I feel strongly about. When I revise I can check my sentence structures.

What are some weaknesses that may take time to improve?

Getting better ideas, and making my voice sound older.

- Set goals based on what you want to improve. Make a list of goals.

Share Your Work

Sharing It with Friends

If you want to keep your writing "among friends," try these ideas:

- Write a letter to a friend or family member asking him or her to read your writing.
- Send your writing attached to an email.

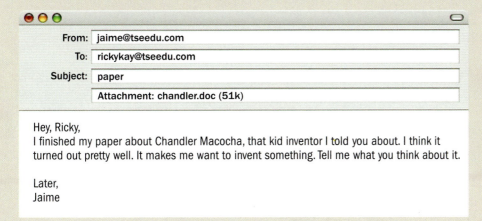

From: jaime@tseedu.com
To: rickykay@tseedu.com
Subject: paper
Attachment: chandler.doc (51k)

Hey, Ricky,
I finished my paper about Chandler Macocha, that kid inventor I told you about. I think it turned out pretty well. It makes me want to invent something. Tell me what you think about it.

Later,
Jaime

Making It Public

The advice you get from others will help you become a better writer. Here are some ways to make your writing public.

- Turn in your work to your school newspaper or magazine.
- Read your writing to another class—perhaps to kids in a younger grade.
- Look for writing contests in your local newspaper or online.

Writing Organization: Paragraphs

Paragraphs

A **paragraph** is a group of sentences that tell about the same idea.

Paragraph Organization

Writers put sentences together in an organized way to create paragraphs. Most paragraphs begin with a <mark>topic sentence</mark>. It tells the main idea. Other sentences give details. Details tell more about the main idea.

The first sentence of a paragraph is indented.

<mark>Stamps are little works of art that show something about a country.</mark> Some stamps from Australia show the country's shape. <mark>Others show native Australian animals like a fish and a wombat.</mark> In Brazil, there are stamps of festivals, like Carnival. Stamps from Botswana may have pictures of birds. People in colorful clothing are on some stamps from Ecuador.

The topic sentence states the main idea.

The details tell more about main idea.

Different Kinds of Paragraphs

Cause-and-Effect Paragraphs

A **cause-and-effect** paragraph states the main idea and then uses the details to explain why something happened. A **cause** is a reason something happened. An **effect** is the result of a cause.

Depending on your topic, you can choose different ways to organize your cause-and-effect papers. Try using a graphic organizer like the one below.

Event 1
My brother Miguel was born.

Event 2
I was nervous. I was used to being the baby in the family.

Event 3
My dad talked to me about being an older sister.

Event 4
It made me feel important.

Cause-and-Effect Paragraph

The birth of my brother Miguel had many effects on my life. Before Miguel was born, I was the only child in my family. I was not sure how things would change with another baby around. Since I was nervous, my father had a talk with me. After the talk, I felt a lot better.

Compare-and-Contrast Paragraphs

A **compare-and-contrast** paragraph tells how two things are alike and different. When you **compare**, you write about how two things are similar. When you **contrast**, you write to show how two things are different.

You can use a **Venn Diagram** to show how two things are alike and how they are different.

Venn Diagram

Alligator
heavier than a crocodile
has a round snout

Both
live in swamps
have large eyes
tough skin
long tails

Crocodile
snout is pointy
has 2 large teeth you can see when its mouth is closed

It is easy to confuse a crocodile and an alligator. Both live in marshes and swamps. They look alike. Both have tough skin, long tails, and large eyes. But, they are different in other ways. An alligator is heavier than a crocodile. The crocodile's snout comes to a point at the end, while an alligator's snout is rounded.

Descriptive Paragraphs

A **descriptive paragraph** gives the reader a strong idea of a place, event, person, animal, or object. Use words that help the reader to "see" and "feel" what you are writing about. Try using a Five-Senses Chart to help you organize your ideas.

Five-Senses Chart

I saw . . .	• stars and planets in the planetarium
I heard . . .	• the voice of our tour guide • the buzzing sound of the projector
I smelled . . .	• the clean smell of the museum
I tasted . . .	• the cafeteria food
I touched . . .	• the soft, comfy chair • the cold surface of the telescope

Descriptive Paragraphs

I sat down in my seat. I could not believe how comfortable I was. I was almost lying down! The chairs were dark blue with a red stripe across them. They looked very new.

In the middle of the chairs was the projector. It looked like a spaceship and made a soft buzzing noise. It was white and ended in a huge ball covered in small lenses. The images of stars and planets come through those lenses.

Literary Responses

A **literary response** describes your personal opinion about a poem, story, or essay. Explain what you liked. You can also explain what you did not like. Write your opinion.

Use a graphic organizer like the one below to organize your ideas.

> **Opinion**
> I really liked this book. The characters felt real, as if they were my friends. I learned how important it is to get to know people.
>
> ───────────────────────
>
> **Supporting Examples**
> —Raymond is laughed at because he is "different."
> —He always sits alone at lunch.
> —Olga becomes Raymond's friend. Raymond learns to "fly like a bird" because of their friendship.

Book Review

Fly Like a Bird, by Darren Knowles, is a great book with interesting characters. The author makes you feel that the characters are real people. It is a book that teens will enjoy reading.

The book tells the story of a boy named Raymond. He is "different," because he likes to talk to birds. The other kids at school laugh at him. He always sits alone at lunch and watches the other kids eat together and play.

The only one who does not laugh at him is Olga. She becomes his friend. The book really shows how hard things can be for someone who is different. Olga gets to know Raymond really well—so did I! Through his friendship with Olga, Raymond learns to "fly like a bird" emotionally.

Fly Like a Bird taught me the importance of getting to know people, not just judging them. I also learned that people do better when other people support them.

Narratives

Narratives tell a story. Narratives can be real or made-up. Made-up narratives, or fiction, tell stories that have characters, settings, and plots.

Personal Narrative

When you tell about something that happened to you, you are telling a **personal narrative**. Because the story is about you, you use the words *I, me,* and *my* a lot.

Personal Narrative Overview

Beginning
Introduce the people, setting, and situation. State why the event or experience was important.

Middle
Give details about what happened in the order that it happened. Share your thoughts and feelings. Use lively details and dialogue.

End
Explain how the action came to an end or how the problem was solved. Summarize why the event or experience was important.

Personal Narrative

A Hard Lesson Learned

When Marie invited me to her birthday party, I was thrilled. She was the most popular girl in school. My best friend said, "Why do you want to go? Marie is not nice. She does not know how to be a friend." I wish I had listened, because my friend was right. The best I can say about my time with Marie is that it taught me a hard but valuable lesson about friendship.

Journal Entry

Journal entries record daily events or personal feelings. They can also be used for learning, too.

Journal Entry Model

> January 4, 2008
>   I went to the library today to research my paper about hip-hop music. I was worried that I wouldn't find anything. Then I remembered to ask a librarian! He was very helpful. We found three books and six magazine articles. I am glad I thought to ask. It definitely made the work easier for me.

Biography

When you write a **biography**, you tell the story of someone else's life. A good biography gives information about the person and tells about events in the person's life.

Biography

> ### Satchel Paige
> by Lawrence Paddock
>
>   Pitcher Leroy "Satchel" Paige was born in Alabama in 1906. His childhood was difficult. At 12, he was sent to reform school for truancy and shoplifting. But there he learned how to pitch from his supervisor, Eddie Byrd. After finishing school in 1923, he joined the Mobile Tigers, a semi-pro baseball team.

Short Story

Short stories entertain. Every story happens in a place at some time. That place and time are called the **setting**. The people or animals in the story are called the **characters**. The things that happen in a story are the **events**. The order, or sequence of events, is called the **plot**.

Plot Diagram for Fiction

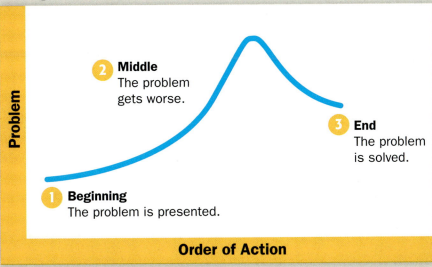

Realistic Fiction

Some stories have characters that seem like people you know. They happen in a place that seems real. These stories are called **realistic fiction**. They tell you about something that could happen in real life.

Realistic Fiction

Another Saturday Morning

Mom and I were eating breakfast Saturday morning when a woman knocked on the door to our apartment.

"Hello," she said. "I'm from Bikes and Stuff. We're having a drawing for a mountain bike. Would you be interested in signing up?" Mom agreed and filled out a form for me.

"Come by this afternoon to see if you have won," the woman said.

Historical Fiction

Historical Fiction is a story that takes place in the past during a certain time in history. Some of the characters may be real people. Some of the events really happened, too. However, the story is fiction because the writer made it up.

Fairy Tale

A **fairy tale** is a special kind of folk tale. It often has royal characters, like princesses and princes, and fun creatures like elves and ogres.

Fairy Tale

Cinderella

Once upon a time, there was a sweet, gentle girl name Cinderella who wanted to go to the royal ball. Her mean stepmother told her to stay home and scrub the floor while she and her daughters went to the ball. Cinderella wept.

Suddenly, Cinderella's fairy godmother appeared. She waved her wand and turned Cinderella's ragged clothes into a sparkling gown and her shoes into glass slippers. She also turned a pumpkin into a coach and mice into horses. Now Cinderella could go to the ball!

Persuasive Paragraphs

In a **persuasive paragraph** you tell your opinion about something. You try to persuade your readers. That means you try to get them to agree with you. TV commercials, newspaper editorials, and speeches are kinds of persuasive writing.

The **topic sentence** gives your opinion. The detail sentences give reasons for your opinion. Here are some words you can use to show your opinion:

I think

I believe

We should

We must

When you change the oil in your car, I think you should recycle the used oil. If you poor the used oil onto the ground, it harms the soil where plants are trying to grow. If you dump the used oil down a storm drain, it will end up in the ocean where it could kill a lot of fish. If you recycle used oil, however, it can be cleaned and reused. Please, you must help our planet! Just take your used oil to a gas station or other place where it can be recycled.

Use **facts** to support your argument.

Use **persuasive words** to get your readers to take action.

Problem-and-Solution Paragraphs

A **problem-and-solution** paragraph tells readers about a problem and gives ways to solve it. A good problem-and-solution paper states a problem and explains it clearly. Then it gives a solution.

You can use a Problem-and-Solution chart to help organize your thoughts.

Problem-and-Solution Chart

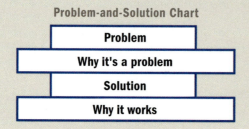

Problem
Why it's a problem
Solution
Why it works

Describe the problem.

The Surprise Party
by Serena Jones

Belinda decided to throw a surprise birthday party for her friend Alicia. After she had already sent the invitations, she found out that Alicia's family was leaving town for the weekend. Belinda used her cell phone and e-mail to contact everyone on her list. Luckily, she was able to change the party date to the following weekend.

Show the solution.

Problem
Alicia's Family is going out of town.

Why it's a problem
Belinda had already sent out invitations for a surprise birthday party.

Solution
Belinda contacts everyone by phone and e-mail.

Why it works
She is able to change the party to the next weekend.

Summary

In a **summary**, you tell about something you have read or seen. You write the most important ideas. You might write a summary when you do research or when you study for an exam.

Article

Corn Pops Up Everywhere!

What plant is used to make food, medicine, and fuel? What plant grows all over the world? The answer is corn!

Scientists think that thousands of years ago, native people of the Americas grew a corn plant that was good to eat. Explorers took the plant back to Europe. Corn farming spread quickly around the world after that.

One reason corn became so popular is that it grows well almost anywhere. It can grow in the mountains or by the sea. It can grow in rainy places and in dry places.

Corn is an important food. People eat a lot of corn, too! Most of the corn grown in the U.S. is for cows, pigs, and other farm animals.

Corn is also used to make products such as glue, ink, and some medicines. There is even a fuel for cars made from corn. It helps gasoline burn better so there is less pollution.

Corn is very helpful!

Here are some tips for planning your summary.

1. **Keep Track of the Important Details**

   Read carefully and take notes. Make a list of the most important ideas. These are the **main ideas**.

2. **Organize Your Notes**

   Read through your list. Cross out details. Keep only the main ideas.

3. **Turn Your Notes Into Sentences**

   Use your own words. This is a good way to make sure you understand what you're saying.

> People have been growing corn for thousands of years. It is very useful, and it can grow almost anywhere. A lot of food is made from corn. Corn is used to make other products, too. Corn is very important!

> Corn is everywhere!
> Useful
> has been around for
>   thousands of years
> grows almost anywhere
> ~~can grow in the mountains~~
> A lot of food comes from corn.
> ~~Pigs eat corn.~~
> used for other things
>   besides food

Career and Workplace Communication

The following writing forms will help you at your workplace.

Business Letter

Business letters have many purposes. You might need to write a business letter to

- ask for information about an item you want to buy
- complain about a product that left you unhappy
- thank someone for very good service.

A good business letter states the situation clearly and uses a polite tone. It follows the standard business-letter format. Business letters should be typed. Check your letters carefully for errors.

Letter of Request

Heading

> 2397 Casanova Street
> Neptune Shores, FL 34744
> February 6, 2008

Inside Address

Electronic Games, Inc.
57821 Sutter Blvd.
New York, NY 10017

Greeting

Dear Sir or Madam:

Body

Please send me your latest catalogue of electronic video games. I am especially interested in your latest version of Ultimate Hockey. Thank you for your prompt attention.

Closing
Your Signature
Your Name

Respectfully,
Ann Gardner
Ann Gardner

Job Application

When you apply for a job, you may be asked to fill out a **job application**. Make sure that the information is clear and easy to read.

Please type or print neatly.

Today's Date: _5_ / _1_ / _08_

First Name: _____Adam_____   Last Name: _____Russell_____

Address: _____1297 Newport Ave._____

City: _Chicago_   State: _IL_   Zip: _79910_

Phone: _(555) 212-9402_   Birth date: _7_ / _20_ / _92_

Sex: M ☑ F ☐

Follow Instructions.

Education

High School Name: _Currently attending Julius Jones High School._

Employment History (List each job, starting with most recent.)

1. Employer: _____The Grainery Foods_____   Phone: _(555) 436-0090_

   Dates: _5/07 – 9/07_   Position: _Full-time checkout and stock clerk_

   Duties: _Check out orders and stock inventory._

Provide correct information.

References

1. Name: _Consuela Ybarra_   Relationship: _supervisor_

   Company: _The Grainery Foods_

   Address: _123 Main Street, Chicago_   Phone: _(555) 436-0092_

2. Name: _Roman Hrbanski_   Relationship: _teacher/coach_

   Company: _Julius Jones High School_

   Address: _321 N. Elm Street, Chicago_   Phone: _(555) 233-0765_

Give contact information for people who can tell the employer that you are a good worker.

Advertisements

Advertisements are a powerful form of persuasion. They can be used to "sell" almost anything—food, clothes, vacations, even political candidates.

Print Ad

Print ads appeal to readers by combining text with visual pictures.

Attract readers' attention with images

Use **descriptive words** to appeal to consumers

THE SOFT DRINK WITH THE BIG TASTE

ORANGE FIZZ

One sip, and you'll never go back to those other soft drinks. We've added real orange juice, and some surprises, too. Together, these flavors produce a taste that is sparkling smooth. The flavor is so big, we could hardly fit it into a glass!

Employment Advertisements

Employers place advertisements for workers they need to hire. You can find this information in the Classified section of your local newspaper. By reading an **employment advertisement**, you can find out details about the job.

Retail Sales

Out of This World gift shop seeks (P/T) person (eves and weekends) to assist customers as they browse and buy. Our one-of-a-kind shop offers a wide range of space-oriented items, and we seek someone who is enthusiastic about our products. Good math skills, friendly personality, and dependability required. Min. wage with attractive sales bonus. Apply in person at City Mall, Saturdays (9:00 a.m.–noon).

Most advertisers use standard abbreviations. *P/T* stands for *part-time*.

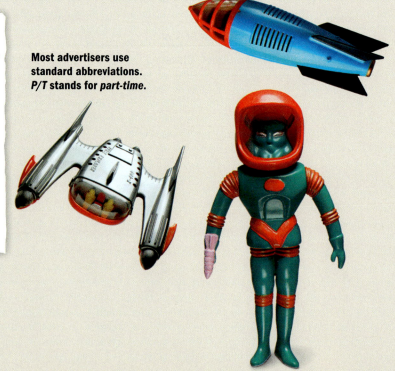

Creative Writing

Creative writing allows to you describe people, things, and events in new and interesting ways!

Poetry

A **poem** uses words in a special way to give the reader a special feeling. There are different kinds of poetry. In a rhyming poem, some of the words rhyme, or have the same ending sound. Other poems have a style all their own. These are called free verse poems.

Free Verse Poem

Friendship

To never judge

To accept your true self

Through all your faults

Still loyal and caring.

That is the making,

An act of giving and taking,

Of what we call a true friend.

Play

A **play** is a story that is acted onstage. Real people, or actors, pretend to be characters in the story. The script for a play tells what the actors will say and do during the performance.

James. You mean I won? [*grabbing Paula's hands*]

Paula. Yes, you did. You won the Battle of the Singers competition!

James. [*shocked, then jumps screaming and hooting*] I can't believe it!

Poster

A **poster** is used to get people's attention. It can give information. A large title often tells what the poster is about. They should also have a purpose and give just enough details to get your message across. Often, posters use colors and pictures to grab attention.

Electronic Communication

Today many people write to each other using electronic communication.

E-mail

People write **e-mail** messages for many reasons. They can chat with friends and family, talk with coworkers, sometimes even apply for a job.

Keep the following in mind when writing e-mail:

- Carefully check the address of your recipient.
- Include the subject line of the e-mail.
- Include a greeting.
- Unless you are writing to a friend or family member, use a formal tone and proper grammar.
- Include a closing, and give your name.

From: student@studentweb.edu
To: n.patterson@njc.library.org
Subject: Library Books

Dear Mrs. Patterson:

I have returned the books that you asked me about. I put the books in the return box. Please let me know if you don't get them.

Thank you,
Jamie

Instant Messaging

Instant messaging, or **IM**, allows you to talk with your friends over the Internet. Like e-mail, it requires you to have an account. IM is used most often by friends, so the style is very casual.

Blogs

Blogs are like Internet newsletters. Many people use blogs to share their ideas. Some blogs are much like a newspaper or magazine. Other blogs are more like journals where people write about their lives and interests.

Media Writing

Media writing forms are used in newspapers, magazines, radio, and television programs.

Editorial

An **editorial** is a newspaper or magazine article that is written to persuade people to believe the same things you do. When you write an editorial, you tell how you feel about something. That's your opinion. Give facts to support your opinion.

February 6, 2008

Save the Gentle Manatees

Our manatees need protection from speeding boats. If we don't keep boat speeds slow, more of these gentle beasts will die.

A few members of the City Council want to pass a law that will increase boat speeds in some waterways where manatees live. When boats go fast, the manatees can't get out of the way of the dangerous boat propellers in time. We need to tell the City Council that saving the manatees is important to us!

News Article

A **news article** tells about an event that really happened. It includes only facts. Most news stories tell about current events, or things that happened recently.

Kids Rescue Puffins—Again

By Evelyn Davis

VESTMANNAEYJAR, Iceland—Last night many of the children in Vestmannaeyjar were out rescuing birds. Pufflings, or young puffins, have wandered into town again this year. The children stayed awake to capture them and take them back to the ocean where they belong.

Pufflings were everywhere. They were under bushes and cars, in the streets, and on the grass. The birds aren't old enough to fly very well. The birds went looking for open water but ended up in the city.

Critique or Review

A **critique**, or **review**, gives your opinion of a book, movie, or other creative work. A review usually includes a quick summary and says how you feel about the work.

Happy Feet

Reviewed by Brittany Howe

"Happy Feet" is one of my favorite movies! It's is a tale about a young penguin named Mumble. He has an unusual gift. He loves tap dancing! Many of the other penguins don't understand why Mumble is so different. But after many adventures, Mumble finally shows the other penguins that being different can be a good thing.

This may seem like a children's movie, but I think it's also good for adults. This movie proves that being who you are can really make a difference in the world.

Social Communication

Social communications help you keep in touch with friends and family.

Friendly Letter

You can write a **friendly letter** to someone you know well. A good friendly letter includes details about recent events and shares your thoughts and feelings.

Friendly Letter

The greeting is how you say hello in a letter.

Molly included the date in the upper right corner.

December 29, 2008

Dear Anne,

How are you? I haven't heard from you in awhile. I hope you are doing well. Something terrible happened last week. Our house caught on fire! We had to leave fast—so fast that we left our dog Scruffy behind. We couldn't find him. We were very worried. But you will never guess who saved him—Jill!

Jill is very brave. She heard Scruffy barking in the kitchen and ran in to get him. He was scared, but thanks to Jill, he is safe! Jill is so cool! Now we're all OK, even if our house will need some repair.

I hope to hear from you soon. I also hope you will come and visit me!

Your friend,

Molly

Molly uses friendly, informal language.

Molly uses an affectionate closing before her signature.

Thank-You Letter

A **thank-you** letter is a brief letter you send when someone gives you a gift or does something nice for you.

September 4, 2008

Dear Janita,

Thank you so much for your help on the school newsletter. You hard work was a big part of our success!

Thanks again,

Mr. Hahn

Invitation

An **invitation** gives the date, time, and place of a special event. An invitation often includes an R.S.V.P. This means "please respond." It asks people to call or write and say if they will come.

Come One, Come All!

Come celebrate Crystal's sixteenth birthday!

Where: Elm Park
1900 Elm Park

When: Friday, May 25
6:00-8:30p.m.

RSVP: Please let Crystal know by Wednesday, May 23, whether you can attend.

Postcard

When you go on a trip, you may send a **postcard** to a friend. It usually tells about your trip. You can write your message on the back of the postcard. Make sure to put your friend's name and address on the back of the card as well. And don't forget to put a stamp in the upper right corner!

June 10, 2008

Dear Marc,

Chicago is amazing! O'Hare airport is huge—even bigger than the one in Los Angeles. Can you believe that the Sears Tower is 110 stories tall? I walked along Lake Michigan yesterday and found out why Chicago's nickname is "The Windy City."

I'm having a great time. I can't wait to show you my pictures when I get back.

Your friend,
Felipe

Marc Rountree
347 Driscoll Street
Los Angeles, CA 90064

Directions

Directions tell how to play a game, how to get somewhere, or how to make something. When you write directions, the most important thing to do is put the steps in order.

Directions to a place

When giving directions to a place, make sure you use direction words. They tell people which way to go. Add details to describe the place so that people can find it. You can even draw a map!

> To get to the theater, turn left out of the parking lot. Go four blocks past the school. Turn right on Citrus Street. The theater is on the left. It's a yellow building with a big, white sign.

Directions for Making Something

When giving directions for making something, make sure you include a list of materials. This will help the reader know what to use. Also include a list of steps that are in order.

What's Cooking

Shrimp and Vegetable Stir Fry

Ingredients
¾ pound of shrimp
2 tablespoons oil
½ sliced onion
½ cup sliced green pepper
¼ cup chopped cabbage
¼ cup teriyaki sauce
1 cup quick-cook brown rice
2 cups water

1. Boil water in a pot. Add the rice and cook for 20 minutes.
2. Heat oil in a large skillet.
3. Place vegetables in the skillet and cook for 5 minutes.
4. Remove vegetables from the skillet.
5. Place shrimp in the skillet and cook for 3 minutes.
6. Add vegetables back in with the shrimp.
7. Add teriyaki sauce and heat until the sauce is warm.
8. Spoon the stir fry over the rice.

Grammar, Usage, Mechanics, and Spelling

Sentences

A sentence is a group of words that expresses a complete thought.

Types of Sentences	Examples
A **statement** tells something. It ends with a period.	The football game was on Friday. The coach made an important announcement.
A **question** asks for information. It ends with a question mark.	What did the coach say?

Kinds of Questions

Questions That Ask for a "Yes" or "No" Answer	Answers
Can you tell me what he said?	Yes.
Does everyone know the news?	No.
Is it about the team?	Yes.
Did the team win the game?	Yes.
Are the players sad?	No.
Were the fans surprised?	Yes.
Questions That Ask for Specific Information	**Answers**
Who heard the announcement?	The team and the fans heard the announcement.
What did the coach say?	He said the team will play in a special game.
Where will the team play this game?	In Hawaii
When did the coach find out?	Right before the game
How did he feel?	He felt so happy!
Why was our team chosen?	Our team was chosen because we won a lot of games.
How many games has the team won this year?	All ten of them
How much will the tickets to the game cost?	Fifteen dollars

An **exclamation** shows surprise or strong feeling. It ends with an exclamation mark.	That's fantastic news! I can't believe it!

Types of Sentences, continued	Examples
A **command** tells you what to do or what not to do. It usually begins with a verb. It often ends with a period.	Give the team my congratulations. Buy a ticket for me, too.
If a command shows strong emotion, it ends with an exclamation mark.	Don't forget!

Negative Sentences	Examples
A **negative sentence** uses a **negative word** like *not*.	
• Add *not* after *am*, *is*, *are*, *was*, or *were*.	The game in Hawaii **was not** boring!
• Add *do not*, *does not*, or *did not* before all other verbs.	The other team **did not play** well.
• Combine the verb and *not* to make a **contraction**.	Our team **didn't make** any mistakes.

Contractions with *not*

To make a **contraction**, take out one or more letters and add an **apostrophe (')**.

are + not = aren't	The fans of the other team **aren't** happy.
is + not = isn't	Their coach **isn't** happy either.
can + not = can't	The other team **can't** believe they lost.
was + not = wasn't	The game **wasn't** fun for them.
were + not = weren't	The players **weren't** playing their best.
do + not = don't	They **don't** want to go to practice on Monday.
does + not = doesn't	The quarterback **doesn't** want to hear about his mistakes.
did + not = didn't	The other team **didn't** want to lose.

Capitalization in Sentences	Examples
Every sentence begins with a **capital letter**.	**O**ur team was very proud.
	What do you think of all this? **I**t's a wonderful story!

Complete Sentences	Examples
A **complete sentence** has a **subject** and a **predicate**. A complete sentence expresses a complete thought.	**Many people** visit our National Parks. Grand Canyon National Park, Arizona
A **fragment** is not a sentence. It is not a complete thought. You can add information to a fragment to turn it into a sentence.	**Fragment:** A fun vacation **Complete Sentences:** You can have a fun vacation. Will we have a fun vacation at the park? Go to a national park and have a fun vacation.

Subject-Verb Agreement	Examples

> **The verb must always agree with the subject of the sentence.**

A **singular subject** names one person or thing. Use a **singular verb** with a singular subject.	Another popular **park is** the Grand Canyon. **It has** a powerful river.
A **plural subject** tells about more than one person or thing. Use a **plural verb** with a plural subject.	The **cliffs are** beautiful. **We were amazed** by their colors.

Singular and Plural Verbs

Singular	Plural
The park **is** big.	The parks **are** big.
The park **was** beautiful.	The parks **were** beautiful.
The park **has** campsites.	The parks **have** campsites.
The park **does** not **open** until spring.	The parks **do** not **open** until spring.

Nouns

A noun names a person, place, or thing. There are different kinds of nouns.

Common and Proper Nouns	Examples
A **common noun** names any person, place, or thing.	A **teenager** sat by the **ocean** and read a **book**.
A **proper noun** names one particular person, place, or thing. The important words in a proper noun start with a capital letter.	**Daniel** sat by the **Atlantic Ocean** and read *Save the Manatee*.

Singular and Plural Nouns	Examples

> **A singular noun names one thing.**
> **A plural noun names more than one thing.**

Follow these rules to make a noun plural: • Add **-s** to most nouns.	desk book teacher apple line desk**s** book**s** teacher**s** apple**s** line**s**
• If the noun ends in **x**, **ch**, **sh**, **s**, or **z**, add **-es**.	box lunch dish glass waltz box**es** lunch**es** dish**es** glass**es** waltz**es**
• Some nouns change in different ways to show the plural.	child foot tooth man woman **children** **feet** **teeth** **men** **women**

Possessive Nouns	Examples
A **possessive noun** shows ownership. It often ends in **'s**.	Daniel**'s** book was very interesting.

Nouns that Name People

Family Words

Girls/Women	Boys/Men
great-grandmother	great-grandfather
grandmother	grandfather
mother	father
stepmother	stepfather
sister	brother
stepsister	stepbrother
half-sister	half-brother
daughter	son
granddaughter	grandson
aunt	uncle
cousin	cousin
niece	nephew

My family includes my grandmother, mother, father, sister, cousins, aunts, uncles, and me.

People at Work

architect

artist

astronaut

athlete

baker

bank teller

barber

bus driver

business person

cab driver

cashier

coach

construction worker

cook

custodian

dancer

dentist

designer

doctor

editor

eye doctor

farmer

firefighter

flight attendant

florist

gardener

guard

historian

lawyer

letter carrier

librarian

mechanic

messenger

model

mover

musician

nurse

office worker

painter

photographer

pilot

plumber

police officer

reporter

sailor

salesperson

scientist

stylist

teacher

veterinarian

writer

Nouns that Name Places

At Home

bathroom
bedroom
dining room
garage
garden

kitchen

living room

yard

In Town

airport
bank
basketball court
beauty shop
bookstore

bus stop

cafe
city hall
clothing store

fire station
flower shop
garage
gas station

hardware store

hospital
intersection
jewelry store
library

mall
market
motel
movie theater
museum
music store
nursing home
office building
park
parking garage
parking lot
pet shop
police station
pool

post office
restaurant

school

shoe store
sports stadium
supermarket
theater
toy store
train station

On the Earth

beach
canyon
desert
forest
hill
island
lake

mountains

ocean

plains
pond
rain forest
river
sea
seashore
valley
wetland

Singular and Plural Nouns	Examples
Noncount nouns are nouns that you cannot count. A noncount noun does not have a plural form.	My favorite museum has **furniture** and **art**. Sometimes I wonder how much **money** each item is worth.

Types of Noncount Nouns

Activities and Sports				Examples
baseball	camping	dancing	fishing	I love to play **soccer**.
golf	singing	soccer	swimming	

Category Nouns					Examples
clothing	equipment	furniture	hardware	jewelry	My **equipment** is in the car.
machinery	mail	money	time	weather	

Food					Examples
bread	cereal	cheese	corn	flour	I'll drink some **water** on my way to the game.
lettuce	meat	milk	rice	salt	
soup	sugar	tea	water		

	Examples
You can count some food items by using a measurement word like **cup**, **slice**, **glass**, or **head** plus the word **of**. To show the plural form, just make the measurement word plural.	I'll drink **two glasses of water** on my way to the game.

Ideas and Feelings					Examples
democracy	enthusiasm	freedom	fun	health	I'll also listen to the radio for **information** about the weather.
honesty	information	knowledge	luck	work	

Materials				Examples
air	fuel	gasoline	gold	The radio says the **air** is heavy. What does that mean?
metal	paper	water	wood	

Weather					Examples
fog	hail	heat	ice	lightning	Uh-oh! First came the **lightning** and the **thunder**. I want **sunshine** for my next soccer game!
rain	smog	snow	sunshine	thunder	

Some words have more than one meaning. Add **-s** for the plural only if the noun means something you can count.	Throw me those **baseballs**. I want to learn to play **baseball**.

Articles	Examples
An **article** is a word that helps identify a noun. An article often comes before a count noun.	After **the** game, we found **a** coat and **an** umbrella on **the** field.
Use **a** or **an** before **nouns** that are not specific. Use **the** before **nouns** that are specific.	A **boy** walked around the field. The coach's **son** walked around the field.
Use **a** before a word that starts with a consonant sound. Use **an** before a word that starts with a vowel sound.	a **b**all a **g**ate a **p**layer a **o**ne-way street (*o* is pronounced like *w*) a **c**ap a **k**ick a **n**et a **u**niform (*u* is pronounced like *y*) **a** **e** **i** **o** **u** **silent h** an **a**nt an **e**lbow an **i**nch an **o**live an **u**mbrella an **h**our an **a**pron an **e**el an **i**dea an **o**cean an **a**mount an **e**lection an **o**wl an **a**rtist an **or**ange
Do not use **a** or **an** before a noncount noun.	The soccer ball was made of ~~a~~ leather.
Do not use **the** before the name of: • a city or state • most countries • a language • a day, a month, or most holidays • a sport or activity • most businesses • a person	Our next game will be in **Dallas**. Games in **Texas** are always exciting. We will play a team from **Mexico**. People will be cheering in **Spanish** and **English**. The game will take place on **Monday**. Is that in **February**? Yes, on **President's Day**. That will be a good day to play **soccer**. The fans will have hot dogs to eat from **Sal's Market**. You may even see **Sal** himself.

Pronouns

A pronoun takes the place of a noun or refers to a noun.

Pronoun Agreement	Examples
Use the correct **pronoun** for a person or thing.	
• To tell about yourself, use **I**. • When you speak to another person, use **you**.	I want to find out about careers. What career are you interested in?
• To tell about a boy or man, use **he**. • For a girl or woman, use **she**. • For a thing, use **it**.	Scott likes art. **He** wants to be a photographer. Anna likes animals. **She** wants to be a veterinarian. What about music? Is **it** a good career?
• For yourself and other people, use **we**.	Sam, Jill, and I like music. We might be good musicians.
• When you speak to more than one other person, use **you**.	Joe and Maylin, what do you want to do?
• To tell about other people or things, use **they**.	Joe and Maylin love children. **They** want to be teachers.

Subject Pronouns	Examples
Some pronouns tell who or what does the action. They are called **subject pronouns**.	Anna likes animals. **She** works at a pet shop. Ernesto works there, too. **He** is in charge of the fish section. **It** is a big area in the store. Anna takes care of the birds. **They** are in cages.

Subject Pronouns

Singular	Plural
I	we
you	you
he, she, it	they

Object Pronouns	Examples
Some pronouns come after an action verb or after a word like *to, for,* or *with*. They are called **object pronouns**.	The parrots get hungry at 5 o'clock. Anna feeds **them** every day. The parrots are nice to **her**. One day, Ernesto fed the parrots. They didn't like **him**. The parrots took the food and threw **it** on the floor. Now only Anna can feed **them**.

Pronouns

Subject Pronouns	Object Pronouns
I	→ me
you	→ you
he	→ him
she	→ her
it	→ it
we	→ us
you	→ you
they	→ them

Adjectives

An adjective describes, or tells about, a noun. Many adjectives tell what something is like. An adjective can also tell "how many" or "which one".

Adjectives	Examples
Usually an **adjective** comes <u>before</u> the **noun** it describes.	You can buy **fresh food** at the market. You can buy **colorful fruit**. You can buy **delicious vegetables**.
An **adjective** can come <u>after</u> the noun in sentences with verbs like *is*, *are*, *was*, or *were*.	The **bananas** are **yellow**. The **tomato** is **round**. The **market** was **busy**. The **shoppers** were **happy**.
Some **adjectives** tell "how many." They always come before the **noun**.	This farmer has **six kinds** of tomatoes. My mom wants **three tomatoes**. She has **five dollars**.
Some **adjectives** tell the order of persons or things in a group. They usually come before the **noun**. They can come after the noun in sentences with verbs like *is*, *are*, *was*, and *were*.	Mom looks at the tomatoes in the **first basket**. Then she looks at the tomatoes in the **second basket**. My **mom** is **first** in line to buy them!
Never add -s or -es to an **adjective**, even if the **noun** it describes is plural.	Look at the **green cucumbers**. Mom wants **two cucumbers**. The **vegetables** tonight will be **delicious**!
A possessive **adjective** tells who or what owns something.	Anna's favorite parrot is a red-and-blue male. **His** name is Repeat. Repeat knows how to say **her** name. Repeat knows Ernesto's name, too. The bird says **their** names over and over again.

Sensory Adjectives

An adjective can tell how something looks, sounds, tastes, feels, or smells.

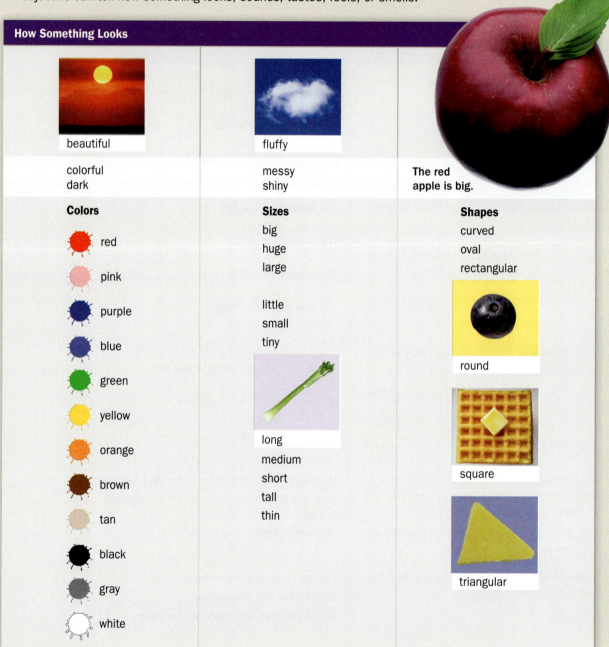

How Something Looks		
beautiful	fluffy	
colorful	messy	**The red**
dark	shiny	**apple is big.**
Colors	**Sizes**	**Shapes**
red	big	curved
pink	huge	oval
purple	large	rectangular
blue	little	
green	small	round
yellow	tiny	
orange	long	square
brown	medium	
tan	short	triangular
black	tall	
gray	thin	
white		

How Something Sounds

blaring
crunchy
loud
noisy
quiet
soft
rattling

I like crunchy apples.

How Something Feels

bumpy
dry
hard
hot
rough
sharp
slimy
smooth
soft
sticky
warm

The outside of a pickle feels bumpy.

These cinnamon rolls are very sticky!

How Something Tastes

bitter
delicious
fresh
juicy
salty
sour
spicy
sweet
tasty

These vegetables will taste fresh.

Chili can be very spicy.

How Something Smells

fishy
fragrant
fresh
rotten
sweet

It smells very fragrant here!

Feelings

An adjective can tell how someone feels.

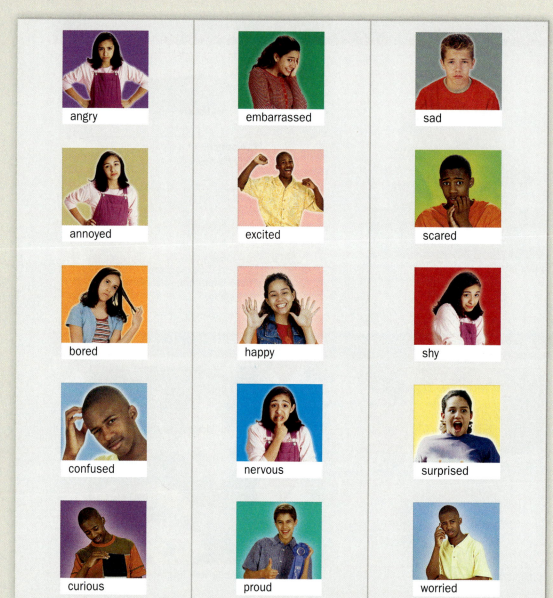

angry	embarrassed	sad
annoyed	excited	scared
bored	happy	shy
confused	nervous	surprised
curious	proud	worried

Numbers

Numbers are a special kind of adjective. They can tell how many. They can also tell the order of things in a sequence.

Number Words				Order Words	
0	zero	30	thirty	1st	first
1	one	40	forty	2nd	second
2	two	50	fifty	3rd	third
3	three	60	sixty	4th	fourth
4	four	70	seventy	5th	fifth
5	five	80	eighty	6th	sixth
6	six	90	ninety	7th	seventh
7	seven	100	one hundred	8th	eighth
8	eight	500	five hundred	9th	ninth
9	nine	1,000	one thousand	10th	tenth
10	ten	5,000	five thousand	11th	eleventh
11	eleven	10,000	ten thousand	12th	twelfth
12	twelve	100,000	one hundred thousand	13th	thirteenth
13	thirteen	500,000	five hundred thousand	14th	fourteenth
14	fourteen	1,000,000	one million	15th	fifteenth
15	fifteen			16th	sixteenth
16	sixteen			17th	seventeenth
17	seventeen			18th	eighteenth
18	eighteen			19th	nineteenth
19	nineteen			20th	twentieth
20	twenty				

This woman is the first customer. She buys two heads of broccoli for $1.98.

Verbs

Every complete sentence has a verb.

The Forms of *be*	Examples
The words **am, is,** and **are** are **verbs**. They are forms of the verb **be**. They tell about something that is happening now, or in the present.	I **am** in New York with my mom. She **is** here for the first time. We **are** excited to see the buildings. They **are** amazing!
The **verbs** **was** and **were** are also forms of the verb **be**. They tell about something that happened in the past.	I **was** in Central Park yesterday. It **was** beautiful. We **were** with some friends. They **were** very helpful.

Forms of the Verb *be*

Present	Past
I **am**	I **was**
you **are**	you **were**
he, she, it **is**	he, she, it **was**
we **are**	we **were**
you **are**	you **were**
they **are**	they **were**

Contractions with Verbs	Examples
You can shorten the verbs *am*, *is*, and *are* to make a **contraction**.	Today **we're** going to Lincoln Center.

Contractions with Verbs

To make a **contraction**, take out one or more letters and add an **apostrophe (')**.

I + am = I'm	**I'm** glad to be in New York.
you + are = you're	**You're** going to meet my brother.
he + is = he's	**He's** staying with my aunt.
she + is = she's	**She's** in a performance at Lincoln Center.
it + is = it's	**It's** a ballet.
we + are = we're	**We're** going to watch a ballet practice.
they + are = they're	**They're** coming to our hotel at 3:00.

Action Verbs	Examples
Most verbs are **action verbs**. They tell what a person or thing does.	The dancers **hop** and **spin**.
When you tell what another person or thing does, use **-s** or **-es** at the end of the **verb**.	The spotlight **shines** on them. One dancer **twirls** around and around. Then she **stretches** a leg and **leaps** gracefully.

Action Verbs

act
add
answer
arrive
ask
bake
bathe
boil
bounce
brush
burn
call

carry

change
check
chop
circle
clap

clean

climb
close
comb
cook
copy
count
cross
cry

dance

deliver
discuss
drop
dry
enter
erase

exercise

fill
finish
fix
fold
hammer
help
introduce
invite
jog
join

jump

kick
laugh
artist

learn
listen
look

mail

mark
mix
mop
move

open

paint
plant
play
point
pour
pull
push
raise
rake
repair
repeat
skate
slice
spell
start
stir
stop
stretch

talk

tie
turn
type
underline
use
vote

walk

wash
watch
water
wipe

work

The Verbs *Can, Could, May, Might*	Examples
You can use the verbs **can, could, may,** or **might** with an action verb to express: • the ability to do something • a possibility, or the chance that something may happen	A hurricane **can cause** a lot of damage. Several inches of rain **might fall** in just a few minutes. The wind **may blow** at high speeds. It **might knock** over trees. It **could break** windows.

Present Tense Verbs	Examples
The tense of a verb shows when an action happens.	
The **present tense** of a verb tells about an action that is happening now, or in the present.	My mom **looks** at her charts. She **checks** her computer screen. She **takes** notes.
The **present tense** of a verb can also tell about an action that happens regularly or all the time.	My mom **works** for the local TV station. She **is** a weather forecaster. She **reports** the weather every night at 5 p.m.
The **present progressive** form of a verb tells about an action as it is happening. It uses **am**, **is**, or **are** and a main verb. The main verb ends in **-ing**.	Right now, she **is getting** ready for the show. "I can't believe it!" she says. "I **am looking** at a terrible storm!" The high winds **are starting** to blow. Trees **are falling** down.

Wind damage from Hurricane Floyd, 1999

Past Tense Verbs	Examples
The **past tense** of a verb tells about an action that happened earlier, or in the past.	Yesterday, my mom **warned** everyone about the hurricane. The storm **moved** over the ocean toward land. We **did** not **know** exactly when it would hit.
The past tense form of a **regular verb** ends with **-ed**.	The shop owners in our town **covered** their windows with wood. We **closed** our shutters and **stayed** inside.
Irregular verbs have special forms to show the past tense. See page 339 for more examples.	The storm **hit** land. The sky **grew** very dark. It **began** to rain.

Some Irregular Verbs

Present Tense	Past Tense
hit	hit
grow	grew
begin	began

Future Tense Verbs	Examples
The **future tense** of a verb tells about an action that will happen later, or in the future. To show future tense, use one of the following: • **will** plus another verb	After the storm, people **will come** out of their houses. They **will inspect** the damage.
• a **contraction** with **will** plus another verb	**They'll uncover** their windows. **They'll clean** up their yards. Some people **won't have** as much work as other people.
• the phrase **am going** to, **is going** to, or **are going** to plus a verb.	I **am going to take** the tree branches out of my yard. The city **is** not **going to clean** every street. We **are** all **going to help** each other.

Contractions with *will*

I + will	=	I'll
you + will	=	you'll
he + will	=	he'll
she + will	=	she'll
it + will	=	it'll
we + will	=	we'll
they + will	=	they'll
will + not	=	won't

Irregular Verbs

These verbs have special forms to show the past tense.

Present	Past	Present	Past	Present	Past
become	became	find	found	put	put
begin	began	fly	flew	read	read
bend	bent	get	got		
blow	blew				
break	broke				
build	built				

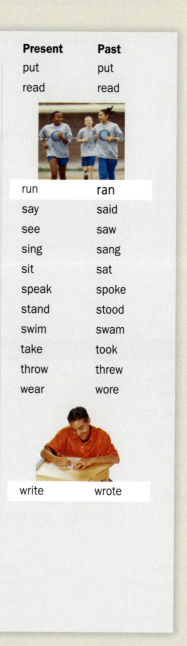

give	gave
grow	grew
go	went
have	had
hear	heard
hide	hid
hit	hit

buy	bought
catch	caught
come	came
cut	cut
do	did
draw	drew

drink	drank

hold	held
keep	kept
lead	led
leave	left

run	ran
say	said
see	saw
sing	sang
sit	sat
speak	spoke
stand	stood
swim	swam
take	took
throw	threw
wear	wore

write	wrote

eat	ate
fall	fell
feel	felt

make	made
pay	paid

Punctuation Marks

Punctuation marks make words and sentences easier to understand.

Period	Examples
Use a **period**: • at the end of a statement or a polite command	Georgia read the paper to her mom**.** Tell me if there are any interesting articles**.**

• after an abbreviation	There's a new restaurant on Stone St**.** near our house.
	 It opens at 10 a**.**m**.** today.
	 But: *Do not use a period in an acronym:*
	 National Aeronautics and Space Administration **NASA**
	 Do not use a period in the abbreviation of a state name written in a mailing address:
	
	     Massachusetts **MA** Illinois **IL** Texas **TX**
	     California **CA** Florida **FL** Virginia **VA**

• after an initial	The owner of J**.**J**.** Malone.
• to separate dollars and cents. The period is the decimal point.	The article says lunch today costs only $1**.**50.
• in an Internet address. The period is called a dot.	The restaurant has a Web site at www**.**jjmalone**.**org.

Question Mark	Examples
Use a **question mark**: • at the end of a question	What kind of food do they serve**?**
• after a question that comes at the end of a statement	The food is good, isn't it**?** **But:** *Use a period after an indirect question. In an indirect question, you tell about a question you asked.* I asked how good the food could be for only $1.50.

Exclamation Mark	Examples
Use an **exclamation mark**:	
• after an interjection	Wow**!**
• at the end of a sentence to show that you feel strongly about something	One-fifty is a really good price**!**

Comma	Examples
Use a **comma**:	
• to separate three or more items in a series	Articles about the school**,** a big sale**,** and a new movie were also in the newspaper.
	The school will buy a new bus**,** 10 computers**,** and books for the library.
• when you write a number with four or more digits.	There was $500**,**000 in the school budget.

Use a **comma** in these places in a letter:	
• between the city and the state	144 North Ave.
• between the date and the year	Milpas**,** AK
	July 3**,** 2008
• after the greeting	Dear Mr. Okada**,**
	I really like computers and am glad that we have them at school, but ours are out-of-date. As principal, can you ask the school board to buy us new ones for next year?
• after the closing	Sincerely**,**
	Patrick Green

Quotation Marks	Examples
Use **quotation marks** to show:	
• a speaker's exact words	"Listen to this!" Georgia said.
• the exact words quoted from a book or other printed material	The announcement in the paper was "The world-famous writer Josie Ramón will be at Milpas Library Friday night."
• the title of a song, poem, or short story	Her poem "Speaking" is famous.
• the title of a magazine article or newspaper article	It appeared in the magazine article "How to Talk to Your Teen."
• the title of a chapter from a book	On Friday night she'll be reading "Getting Along," a chapter from her new book.
• words used in a special way	We will be "all ears" at the reading.
Always put **periods** and **commas** inside quotation marks.	"She is such a great writer," Georgia said. "I'd love to meet her."

Colon	Examples
Use a **colon**:	356 Oak St. Milpas, AK Sept. 24, 2008 Features Editor *Milpas Post* 78 Main St. Milpas, AK
• after the greeting in a business letter	Dear Sir or Madam**:**
• to separate hours and minutes • to start a list	Please place this announcement in the calendar section of your paper. Friday at 7**:**15 p.m., the writer Josie Ramón will be speaking at Milpas Library. When people come, they should bring**:** 1. Questions for Ms. Ramón. 2. Money to purchase her new book. 3. A cushion to sit on! Thank you. Sincerely, Hector Quintana

Capital Letters

A reader can tell that a word is special in some way if it begins with a capital letter.

Proper Nouns	Examples

A common noun names any person, place, thing, or idea.
A proper noun names one particular person, place, thing, or idea.

All the important words in a **proper noun** start with a capital letter.

	Common Noun	Proper Noun
Person	captain	Captain Meriwether Lewis
Place	land	Louisiana Territory
Thing	team	Corps of Discovery
Idea	destiny	Manifest Destiny

Proper nouns include:

• names of people and their titles

Laura Roberts
Captain Merriwether Lewis

But: *Do not capitalize a title if it is used without a name:*

The captain's co-leader on the expedition was William Clark.

• abbreviations of titles

Mr. Ramos
Mrs. Ramos
Dr. Schuyler
Ms. Nguyen

Abbreviations of Titles

Capt.	for the captain of a boat or in the armed forces
Pres.	for the president of a country, a company, a club, or an organization
Sen.	for a member of the U.S. Senate
Rep.	for a member of the U.S. House of Representatives

• words like ***Mom*** and ***Dad*** when they are used as names

"**Mom** can you tell me more about the expedition?" said Laura.

But: *Do not capitalize names if they follow a word like* my.

I ask my **mom** a lot of questions.

• organizations

United Nations   Science Club   Wildlife Society   Lodi City Council

• names of languages, subject areas, and religions

Spanish   Mathematics   Buddhism

Vietnamese   Social Studies   Christianity

Proper Nouns, continued	Examples

- names of geographical places

Cities and States

Dallas, Texas

Miami, Florida

St. Louis, Missouri

Countries

Iran

Ecuador

Cambodia

Continents

Asia

South America

Africa

Streets and Roads

King Boulevard

Main Avenue

First Street

Landforms

Rocky Mountains

Sahara Desert

Grand Canyon

Public Spaces

Hemisfair Plaza

Central Park

Muir Camp

Bodies of Water

Yellow Stone River

Pacific Ocean

Great Salt Lake

Gulf of Mexico

Buildings, Ships, and Monuments

Empire State Building

Titanic

Statue of Liberty

Planets and Heavenly Bodies

Earth

Jupiter

Milky Way

- abbreviations of geographic places

Words Used in Addresses

Avenue	Ave.	Highway	Hwy.	South	S.
Boulevard	Blvd.	Lane	Ln.	Square	Sq.
Court	Ct.	North	N.	Street	St.
Drive	Dr.	Place	Pl.	West	W.
East	E.	Road	Rd.		

Abbreviations for State Names in Mailing Addresses

Alabama	AL	Hawaii	HI	Massachusetts	MA	New Mexico	NM	South Dakota	SD
Alaska	AK	Idaho	ID	Michigan	MI	New York	NY	Tennessee	TN
Arizona	AZ	Illinois	IL	Minnesota	MN	North Carolina	NC	Texas	TX
Arkansas	AR	Indiana	IN	Mississippi	MS	North Dakota	ND	Utah	UT
California	CA	Iowa	IA	Missouri	MO	Ohio	OH	Vermont	VT
Colorado	CO	Kansas	KS	Montana	MT	Oklahoma	OK	Virginia	VA
Connecticut	CT	Kentucky	KY	Nebraska	NE	Oregon	OR	Washington	WA
Delaware	DE	Louisiana	LA	Nevada	NV	Pennsylvania	PA	West Virginia	WV
Florida	FL	Maine	ME	New Hampshire	NH	Rhode Island	RI	Wisconsin	WI
Georgia	GA	Maryland	MD	New Jersey	NJ	South Carolina	SC	Wyoming	WY

- months, days, special days and holidays

January	July	Sunday	New Year's Day
February	August	Monday	Mother's Day
March	September	Tuesday	Thanksgiving
April	October	Wednesday	Hanukkah
May	November	Thursday	Kwanzaa
June	December	Friday	
		Saturday	

In Letters	Examples
Capitalize the first word used in the **greeting** or in the **closing** of a letter. Street, city, and state names in the address, as well as their abbreviations, are also capitalized.	 **Dear Kim,** I wish you could explore the Academy of Natural Sciences with me. I've learned so much about the flora and fauna that Lewis and Clark found. The museum even has some of the original samples! I'll tell you about it when I get home. See you soon. **Your friend,** Jamal **Kim Messina** **10250 W. Fourth St.** **Las Vegas, NV 89015**

Vocabulary Glossary

The definitions in this glossary are for words as they are used in the selections in this book. Use the Pronunciation Key below to help you use each word's pronunciation. Then read about the parts of an entry.

Pronunciation Key

Symbols for Consonant Sounds

b	box	**p**	pan
ch	chick	**r**	ring
d	dog	**s**	bus
f	fish	**sh**	fish
g	girl	**t**	hat
h	hat	**th**	earth
j	jar	**th**	father
k	cake	**v**	vase
ks	box	**w**	window
kw	queen	**wh**	whale
l	bell	**y**	yarn
m	mouse	**z**	zipper
n	pan	**zh**	treasure
ng	ring		

Symbols for Short Vowel Sounds

a	hat
e	bell
i	chick
o	box
u	bus

Symbols for Long Vowel Sounds

ā	cake
ē	key
ī	bike
ō	goat
yū	mule

Symbols for R-controlled Sounds

ar	barn
air	chair
ear	ear
īr	fire
or	corn
ur	girl

Symbols for Variant Vowel Sounds

ah	father
aw	ball
oi	boy
ow	mouse
oo	book
ü	fruit

Miscellaneous Symbols

shun	fraction
chun	question
zhun	division

Parts of an Entry

The **entry** shows how the word is spelled and how it is broken into syllables.

The **pronunciation** shows you how to say the word.

The **part of speech** shows how the word functions in a sentence.

The **definition** gives the meaning of the word.

The **sample sentence** uses the word in a way that shows its meaning.

af·firm (u-**furm**) *verb*, showing, saying, or proving that something is true. *My decision to volunteer at the hospital was **affirmed** when I saw how happy the patients were because of my visit.*

A

advice (ud-vīs) *noun*

Advice is an opinion about what someone should do. My friends give me good **advice** when I am sad.

angry (ang-grē) *adjective*

If you feel **angry**, you are mad about something. The girls are **angry** with each other. *Synonym:* upset

agreement (u-grē-munt) *noun*

When you are in **agreement**, you have the same opinions, ideas, or beliefs. They are in **agreement** about the dress.

arrive (u-rīv) *verb*

To **arrive** means to reach a place. She **arrives** home.

alone (u-lōn) *adverb*

When you are **alone**, no one is with you. He does homework **alone**.

attention (u-ten-shun) *noun*

When you get **attention**, people notice you. The dancer has everyone's **attention**.

attitude (**a**-tu-tüd) *noun*

Attitude is a way of looking at the world. Her positive **attitude** helped her get a job as a camp counselor.

B

beautiful (**byū**-ti-ful) *adjective*

Something that is **beautiful** is pretty. The roses are **beautiful**.

become (bi-**kum**) *verb*

To **become** means to begin to be something. She is studying to **become** a doctor.

behavior (bi-**hā**-vyur) *noun*

Your **behavior** is the way you act. His funny **behavior** made the students laugh.

belief (bu-**lēf**) *noun*

A **belief** is an idea that you think is true. People sometimes fight for their **beliefs**.

believe (bu-**lēv**) *verb*

To **believe** means to think something is true. He **believed** that he did well on the test.

belong (bi-**long**) *verb*

When you feel like you **belong**, you feel happy in a situation. She feels like she **belongs** on stage.

blood vessel (**blud ve**-sul) *noun*

A **blood vessel** is a small tube in your body that carries blood from place to place.

break (**brāk**) *verb*

When you **break** something, you separate it into pieces or parts. He **breaks** the wood with his hand.

C

call (**cawl**) *verb*

To **call** means to use a name for someone or something. She is Rebecca. We **call** her Becky.

cheat (**chēt**) *verb*

To **cheat** is to do something that is unfair or against the rules. She **cheats** when she looks at my answers.

choice (**chois**) *noun*

You make a **choice** when you pick between two or more things. It is hard for him to make a **choice** between the sandwiches.

circumstances (**sur**-kum-stans-uz) *noun*

Circumstances are the facts or details of a situation. These people live in difficult **circumstances**.

connect (ku-**nekt**) *verb*

When you **connect** people or things, you join them together. Cables **connect** the computer to the wall.

country (**kun**-trē) noun

A **country** is an area of land that has its own government. Every **country** has its own flag.

crowded (**krow**-dud) adjective

A **crowded** place is full of people or things. The bus is **crowded**.

culture (**kul**-chur) noun

A country's **culture** includes the traditions and beliefs of its people. Football is part of American **culture**.

D

damage (**da**-mij) noun

Damage is harm or hurt. The storm did a lot of **damage** to the chair. *Synonym:* destruction

danger (**dān**-jur) noun

Danger is something that can harm you. Construction workers often face **danger** in their jobs.

decide (di-**sīd**) verb

When you **decide** to do something, you make a choice to do it. The signs help you **decide** where to go.

defenseless (di-**fens**-lus) adjective

You are **defenseless** when you cannot protect yourself from something that can hurt you. The diver is **defenseless**.

device (di-**vīs**) noun

A **device** is a tool for a certain job. A calculator is a **device** that helps you do math.

die (dī) *verb*

When a person, plant, or animal **dies**, it stops living. One of the flowers **died**.

different (**di**-frunt) *adjective*

Different means not like someone or something else. The two shoes are **different**.

difficult (**di**-fi-kult) *adjective*

Difficult means hard or not easy to do. Chin-ups can be **difficult**.

dignity (**dig**-nu-tē) *noun*

Dignity is having pride in yourself. A person with **dignity** acts calmly and respectfully. My grandfather has great **dignity**.

disability (dis-u-**bi**-lu-tē) *noun*

A **disability** is a condition that stops you from doing something that most people can do.

disadvantage (dis-ud-**van**-tij) *noun*

A **disadvantage** is something that makes life more difficult for one person than it is for others.

disaster (di-**zas**-tur) *noun*

A **disaster** is an event that harms a lot of people, animals, or things. A flood is a **disaster**.

dream (drēm) *noun*

A **dream** is something you hope for. Her **dream** is to be an engineer.

E

easy (ē-zē) adjective

When something is **easy**, it is not difficult. It is **easy** for some children to ride a tricycle. *Synonym:* simple

emergency (i-**mur**-gunt-sē) noun

An **emergency** is a dangerous situation that needs action. A fire is an example of an **emergency**.

energy (e-nur-jē) noun

Energy is the ability to move or be active. The runners have a lot of **energy**.

enough (i-**nuf**) adjective

When you have **enough** of something, you have as much as you need. There is **enough** food in the cart for everyone.

escape (is-**kāp**) verb

When you **escape** something, you get away from it. He **escapes** danger.

everyone (ev-rē-wun) pronoun

Everyone means all the people in a group. **Everyone** in the picture is smiling.

everywhere (ev-rē-wair) adverb

Everywhere means in all places. In the library, books are **everywhere**.

exchange (iks-**chānj**) verb

When you **exchange** something, you trade it for something else. People **exchange** money for food at the market.

exotic (ig-**zah**-tik) *adjective*

If something is **exotic**, you do not see, hear, or do it often. The fish's fins make it look **exotic**.

experience (ik-**spear**-ē-uns) *noun*

An **experience** is something that you did or saw. They helped many people during their **experiences** as volunteers.

explain (ik-**splān**) *verb*

To **explain** means to make something clear. The teacher is **explaining** the math problem.

F

fair (**fair**) *adjective*

When something is **fair**, it is equal for everyone. Sports officials try to be **fair** when they make calls.

family (**fam**-lē) *noun*

The people you are related to are your **family**. The whole **family** went to the zoo.

fear (**fear**) *noun*

Fear is the feeling you get when you are afraid. The man felt **fear** when he jumped from the plane.

fight (**fīt**) *verb*

To **fight** is to hurt or yell at someone. The children are **fighting** in the store.

find (**fīnd**) *verb*

When you **find** something, you learn where it is. She **finds** the book that she is looking for.

forget (fur-**get**) *verb*

When you **forget** something, you cannot think of it. He **forgets** how to solve the math problem.

friend (**frend**) *noun*

A **friend** is someone you care about. The **friends** play video games.

G

generosity (je-nu-**rah**-su-tē) *noun*

When you share easily, you show **generosity**. Everyone knows about her **generosity**.

grow (**grō**) *verb*

To **grow** is to make bigger or to cultivate. A lemon tree **grows** lemons.

H

hard (**hard**) *adjective*

When something is **hard**, it is not easy to do. Rock climbing is **hard**.

harm (**harm**) *verb*

To **harm** means to hurt. The boys are **harming** each other.

history (**his**-trē) *noun*

History is what happened in the past. The grandparents share the family **history** with their granddaughter.

home (**hōm**) *noun*

A **home** is where you live. The family is happy and comfortable at **home**.

honest (**ah**-nust) *adjective*

An **honest** person tells the truth. In court, you must promise to be **honest**. *Synonym:* truthful

hungry (**hung**-grē) *adjective*

When you are **hungry**, you need or want something to eat. The baby birds are **hungry**.

I

idea (ī-**dē**-u) *noun*

When you have an **idea**, you have a thought or a plan. She has an **idea** for a paper she will write.

identify (ī-**den**-tu-fī) *verb*

When you **identify** with a group or idea, you connect with it. The teammates **identify** with each other.

injured (**in**-jurd) *adjective*

When a part of your body is **injured**, it is hurt. He felt a lot of pain from his **injured** leg.

inspire (in-**spīr**) *verb*

When something **inspires** you, it makes you want to do something. The scene **inspired** her to paint.

instead (in-**sted**) *adverb*

Instead means in place of something else. She is buying carrots **instead** of broccoli.

instinct (**in**-stingkt) *noun*

Instinct means the way someone or something naturally reacts without having to think. Most people have an **instinct** to run from danger.

integrity (in-te-gru-tē) noun

You have **integrity** when you do what you know is right. The scientist shows **integrity** with true test results.

invent (in-**vent**) verb

When you **invent**, you make something completely new. The student **invented** a robot.

J

jealous (je-lus) adjective

When you are **jealous**, you are unhappy because you want something that someone else has. She gets **jealous** when he talks to others.

joy (**joi**) noun

When you feel **joy**, you are very happy. The soccer champions smile with **joy**.

judgment (juj-munt) noun

When you make a **judgment**, you form an opinion after examining and comparing information. It's important to do research before making a **judgment**.

L

learn (**lurn**) verb

When you **learn**, you understand something new. In this school, students **learn** how to cook.

leave (lēv) verb

To **leave** is to go away. She is happy to **leave** the group.

like (līk) verb

When you **like** people or things, you feel good about them. She **likes** pizza.

listen (lĭ-sun) *verb*

When you **listen** to someone, you hear what the person says. She **listens** to her friend's story.

lonely (lōn-lē) *adjective*

If you feel **lonely**, you are not happy because you are not with other people. He is **lonely** without his friends.

luck (luk) *noun*

Luck means good fortune. The woman is having good **luck** playing the game.

M

meal (mēl) *noun*

A **meal** is all the food you eat at one time. Breakfast, lunch, and dinner are **meals**.

miss (mis) *verb*

When you **miss** people or places, you are sad that you are not with them. She **misses** her little sister.

N

name (nām) *noun*

A **name** is what a person, place, or thing is known by. The **name** of this street is Broadway.

neighbor (nā-bur) *noun*

Your **neighbor** is someone who lives near you. The friends are also **neighbors**.

nervous (nur-vus) *adjective*

When you are **nervous**, you feel worried or afraid of doing something. The runners are **nervous** before the race.

no one (**nō**-wun) *pronoun*

No one means no person. When you are alone, **no one** is with you.

nobody (**nō**-bu-dē) *pronoun; noun*

A **nobody** is a person who others think is not important. When they didn't talk to her, she felt like a **nobody**.

O

obstacle (**ob**-sti-kul) *noun*

An **obstacle** is something that stops you from doing what you want to do. Lava is an **obstacle** on this road.

offer (**ah**-fur) *noun*

An **offer** is the price you want to pay for something. She will make an **offer** to buy the basket.

ordinary (**or**-du-nair-ē) *adjective*

Something you see, hear, or do often is **ordinary**. On an **ordinary** Monday, these students go to school.

other (**u**-thur) *adjective*

Other means someone or something else. Many apples are red. The **other** apple is green.

P

participate (par-**ti**-su-pāt) *verb*

When you **participate**, you join in an activity. The whole family **participates** in washing the car.

pattern (**pa**-turn) *noun*

A **pattern** is a design that repeats. There is a **pattern** on the bottom of these shoes.

perform (pur-**form**) *verb*

When you **perform**, you show a talent to a group of people. The singers **perform** a song.

personality (pur-su-**na**-lu-tē) *noun*

Your **personality** is the way you act and feel. These friends have different **personalities**.

perspire (pur-**spīr**) *verb*

To **perspire** is to sweat. The athlete **perspires** to cool his body.

physical (**fi**-zi-kul) *adjective*

Physical means about the body. **Physical** training makes you stronger.

poor (**por**) *adjective*

A **poor** person has little money. The **poor** man has no money in his wallet. *Antonym:* rich

popular (**pah**-pyu-lur) *adjective*

When something is **popular**, many people like it. Soccer is **popular**.

powerful (**pow**-ur-ful) *adjective*

Something that is **powerful** is very strong. A lion is a **powerful** animal. *Antonym:* weak

practice (**prak**-tus) *verb*

When you **practice** an activity, you do it regularly so you can improve. She **practices** tennis twice a week.

precious (**pre**-shus) *adjective*

When something is **precious**, it has great value. Wedding rings are **precious** to people.

prepare (pri-**pair**) *verb*

To **prepare** means to make ready. These sisters **prepare** a meal. *Synonym:* make

problem (**prah**-blum) *noun*

A **problem** is something that needs to be fixed. Her car has a **problem**. She needs help.

proud (**prowd**) *adjective*

When you are **proud**, you feel happy about something. The students were **proud** of their grades.

R

receive (ri-**sēv**) *verb*

When you **receive** something, you take what someone gives you. He **receives** the gift.

recognize (**re**-kig-nīz) *verb*

To **recognize** people or places is to know them when you hear or see them. She **recognizes** the voice on the phone.

recover (ri-**ku**-vur) *verb*

To **recover** means to get better after being hurt or sick. His mom helps him **recover**. *Synonym:* improve

reflect (ri-**flekt**) *verb*

To **reflect** means to show or represent something. Her good grades **reflected** her hard work.

refuse (ri-**fyüz**) *verb*

To **refuse** something means to say no to it. She **refuses** to eat this fruit.

religion (ri-**li**-jun) *noun*

Religion is a set of strong ideas about god or gods. Christianity, Judaism, and Islam are **religions**.

remember (ri-**mem**-bur) *verb*

When you **remember** something, you think of it again. Family pictures help them **remember** the past.

respect (ri-**spekt**) *noun*

When you show **respect**, you show that you value someone or something. A bow is a sign of **respect**.

rest (**rest**) *verb*

When you **rest**, you do not work. She stops to **rest** during a game.

reveal (ri-**vēl**) *verb*

To **reveal** is to show or tell something that was hidden. She took off the paper to **reveal** a great gift.

rich (**rich**) *adjective*

A **rich** person has a lot of money. *Antonym:* poor

S

sacrifice (**sa**-kru-fīs) *verb*

When you **sacrifice** something, you lose it, often for a reason. Members of the military often **sacrifice** their lives.

safe (sāf) *adjective*

If something is **safe**, it doesn't hurt you. It is important to have **safe** water to drink. *Antonym:* dangerous

safety (sāf-tē) *noun*

Safety is a place where you cannot be hurt. She wears a helmet and pads for **safety**.

save (sāv) *verb*

To **save** is to stop someone or something from being hurt or destroyed. A firefighter's job is to **save** people.

scientist (sī-un-tist) *noun*

A **scientist** studies plants, animals, chemicals, and other things in our world.

selfish (sel-fish) *adjective*

Selfish people do not help others. The **selfish** man does not care about others around him.

sensitive (sen-su-tiv) *adjective*

A **sensitive** person or thing is easily affected, changed, or hurt. The **sensitive** boy cried when he fell.

separate (se-pu-rāt) *verb*

To **separate** means to keep things apart. We **separate** plastics, cans, and paper for recycling.

share (shair) *verb*

To **share** is to give part of something to others. They **share** noodles. *Synonyms:* divide, split

similar (**si**-mu-lur) *adjective*

When things are **similar**, they are almost the same. The violins are **similar**.

simple (**sim**-pul) *adjective*

Simple means easy. Adding small numbers is **simple**. *Synonym:* clear

situation (si-chu-**wā**-shun) *noun*

A **situation** is a set of events or circumstances. A traffic jam is a bad **situation**.

social (**sō**-shul) *adjective*

Social means with other people. I love to spend time with my friends because I am **social**.

solution (su-**lü**-shun) *noun*

A **solution** is an answer. The mechanic explains his **solution**.

somebody (**sum**-bu-dē) *prounoun; noun*

A **somebody** is a person who others think is important. When she gets attention she feels like a **somebody**.

special (**spe**-shul) *adjective*

If something is **special**, it is not like the others. The gold egg is **special**.

spirit (**spir**-ut) *noun*

Your **spirit** is the way you act, think, and feel. This girl has a joyful **spirit**.

sponsor (spon-sur) *verb*

When you **sponsor** an activity, you help make it happen. The senior class **sponsored** the race.

sport (sport) *noun*

A **sport** is a game, such as baseball or basketball.

standard (stan-durd) *noun*

A **standard** is a measure of how good something is. The teacher has high **standards** for his students.

stranger (strān-jur) *noun*

A **stranger** is someone you do not know. **Strangers** often sit next to each other on the bus.

study (stu-dē) *verb*

When you **study** something, you look at it carefully. The boys **study** the map.

succeed (suk-sēd) *verb*

To **succeed** is to reach a goal. When you **succeed** at college, you graduate.

success (suk-ses) *noun*

When you have **success**, you have reached your goal. She had **success** in solving the problem.

suggest (sug-jest) *verb*

When you **suggest** something, you say it is possible. She **suggests** a place to go.

support (su-**port**) *noun*

Support is an action that shows you care. They show **support** for their team by cheering and clapping.

survive (sur-**vīv**) *verb*

When you **survive** a dangerous situation, you stay alive. Everyone needs water to **survive**.

system (**sis**-tum) *noun*

A **system** is an organized group of parts that work together. Inside the clock is a **system** of metal parts.

T

tension (**ten**-shun) *noun*

Tension is a feeling of worry and stress. The students are filled with **tension** while taking the test.

together (tu-**ge**-<u>th</u>ur) *adverb*

When you put things **together**, you combine them. She plants the flowers **together**.

touch (**tuch**) *verb*

When you **touch** something, you feel it. To read Braille, you must **touch** the bumps.

tough (**tuf**) *adjective*

Tough means strong and not easily hurt. The player looks **tough**.

tradition (tru-**di**-shun) *noun*

A **tradition** is a way of doing things. By **tradition**, students toss their hats in the air when they graduate.

truth (trüth) *noun*

Something that is a fact is the **truth**. People must tell the **truth** in court.

try (trī) *verb*

To **try** means to work hard. The runners all **try** to finish the race.

U

uncomfortable (un-**kumf**-tur-bul) *adjective*

Uncomfortable means not feeling easy. The new driver is **uncomfortable**.

understand (un-dur-**stand**) *verb*

When you **understand** something, you know how it works or what it means. The students **understand** the question.

unique (yū-**nēk**) *adjective*

Something is **unique** when it is the only one of its kind. The orange fish is **unique** in this school of blue fish.

V

victim (**vik**-tum) *noun*

A person who has been hurt by someone or something is a **victim**. The flood **victim's** home is ruined.

victory (**vik**-tu-rē) *noun*

When you have a **victory**, you win. The young man enjoys his **victory**.

village (**vi**-lij) *noun*

A **village** is a very small town. This **village** is by the ocean.

W

wait (wāt) *verb*

When you **wait**, you stay in one place until something happens. The people **wait** for the bus to stop.

weak (wēk) *adjective*

Weak means not strong. Baby animals are often too **weak** to stand. *Antonyms:* strong, powerful

wealth (welth) *noun*

Wealth means having a lot of something. It often refers to money. **Wealth** is important to many people.

wisdom (wiz-dum) *noun*

Wisdom is what you learn over a period of time. He shares **wisdom** with his granddaughter.

wish (wish) *verb*

To **wish** for something is to want it very much. The dog **wished** for the food.

world (wur-uld) *noun*

The **world** is the earth and all its people, places, and things. They are learning about the **world**.

Cycle Diagram

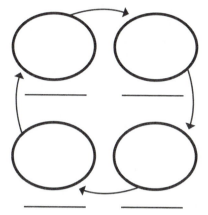

Sequence Chain

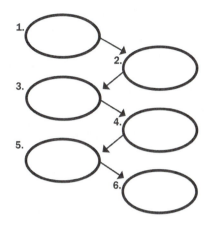

Time Line

Main-Idea Diagram

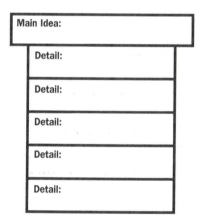

Idea Web

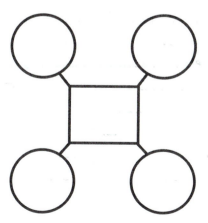

Topic Triangle

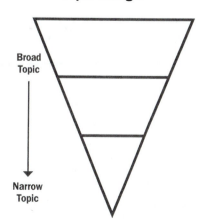

Beginning-Middle-End

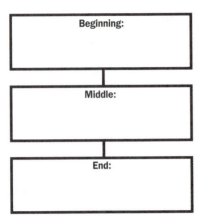

Beginning:

Middle:

End:

Character-Setting-Plot

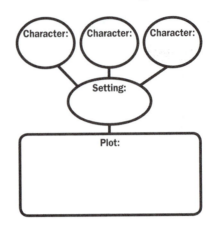

Character: Character: Character:

Setting:

Plot:

Character Description

Character	What the Character Does	What This Shows About the Character

Goal-and-Outcome

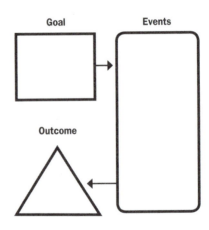

Goal   Events

Outcome

Problem-and-Solution

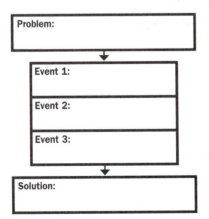

Problem:

Event 1:

Event 2:

Event 3:

Solution:

Cause-and-Effect Chart

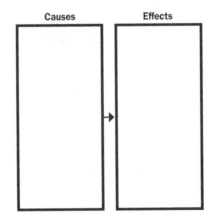

Causes   Effects

Venn Diagram

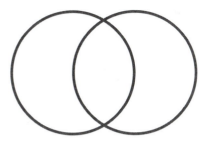

Classification Chart

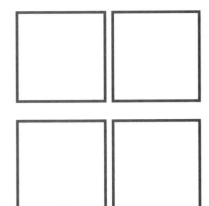

Five-Ws Chart

What?	
Who?	
Where?	
When?	
Why?	

KWL Chart

K What Do I Know?	W What Do I Want to Learn?	L What Did I Learn?

Table

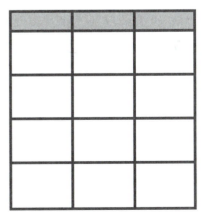

Outline

I. _____

   A. _____

   B. _____

II. _____

   A. _____

   B. _____

III. _____

   A. _____

   B. _____

Graph

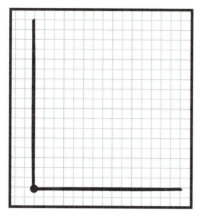

T Chart

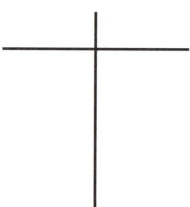

Word Map

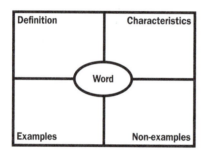

INDEX OF SKILLS

Listening & Speaking, continued

interview 48
listen actively and respectfully 405
presentation 239, 323, 349
poetry reading 79
read aloud 323, 499
report opinions 353
report plans 331
retell a story 465
role-play 295
share experiences 499
tell a story 247
tell about a friend 9
use a bar graph 185
weather report 273

Viewing & Representing

analyze visuals 2–3, 4, 13–18, 34, 53–61, 69, 80–81, 82, 89–97, 159, 160, 171, 172, 173, 185, 198–202, 241, 242, 243, 245, 249, 260, 266, 283, 302–303, 324–325, 326, 334, 359, 406–407, 408, 467, 481
  art 2–3, 80–81, 159, 241, 324–325, 406–407
  bar graph 171, 172, 185, 326, 408
  diagram 59, 302–303, 359
  illustrations 89–97, 249, 467, 481
  map 34, 283, 334
  map (globe) 198–202
  photos 4–5, 13–18, 82–83, 160, 173, 260, 266
  photos and diagrams 53–61
  poster 242–243
  storyboard 245
  time line 69
create visuals 28, 33, 45, 79, 126, 130, 186, 239, 247, 349, 413
  comic strip 126
  drawing 33, 130
  family picture 45
  illustration 28, 79
  map 413
  photo essay 186
  poster 239, 349
  storyboard 247
critical viewing 3, 81, 159, 241, 325, 407

Writing

Applications

advertisement 582
advice column 152
analysis 347
article 318
biography 575
blog 374, 584
book review 573
comic strip 126
critique 585
description 234
directions: process 588
directions to a place 588
editorial 585
e-mail 584
employment advertisement 582
explanation 67, 123, 393, 433
fairy tale 576
freewrite 487
historical fiction 576
instant messaging 584
invitation 203, 587
interview 48
job application 581
journal entry 145, 227, 575
letter, business 580
letter, friendly 350, 586
letter of request 580
letter, thank-you 586
literary response 573
news article 585
opinion statement 183, 289, 311, 371
paragraph
  cause-and-effect 571
  comparison-contrast 206, 571
  descriptive 104, 234, 318, 572
  fact-and-opinion 400
  persuasive 577
  problem-and-solution 101, 292, 462, 578
personal narrative 494, 574
photo essay 186
play 583

poem 48, 74, 331, 583
position statement 459
postcard 28, 587
print ad 582
poster 583
quickwrite 25
realistic fiction 576
reflection 45
review 585
short story 270, 575
skit 436
summary 579
survival guide 267
writing modes
  descriptive 234–239, 572
  expository 152–157, 318–323
  expressive 74–79, 400–405
  narrative 494–499, 574–576
  persuasive 577, 585
writing on demand 28, 48, 74, 104, 126, 152, 186, 206, 234, 270, 292, 318, 350, 374, 400, 436, 462, 494
  advice column 152
  article 318
  blog 374
  comic strip 126
  comparison-contrast paragraph 206
  descriptive paragraph 104, 234
  fact-and-opinion paragraph 400
  friendly letter 350
  interview 48
  personal narrative 494
  photo essay 186
  poem 74
  postcard 28
  problem-and-solution paragraph 292, 462
  short story ending 270
  skit 436

Writing Strategies

analyze a model 74, 152, 234, 318, 400, 490
draft 75, 77, 153, 155, 186, 237, 320, 402, 496, 562, 565
  add facts and details 320

INDEX OF AUTHORS AND TITLES

INDEX OF ART AND ARTISTS

Acknowledgments, continued from page ii

Audio Vision: "Fight or Flight: What Your Body Knows About Survival" is adapted from "Fight or Flight: The Evolution of Stress" by James E. Porter from www. StressStop.com. Used by permission of the author.

BOA Editions, Ltd.: Naomi Shihab Nye, "Shoulders" from RED SUITCASE. Copyright © 1994 by Naomi Shihab Nye. Used with the permission of BOA Editions, Ltd., www.boaeditions.org.

Boyds Mills Press: "Hands" from A STEP FROM HEAVEN by An Na. Copyright © 2001. Published by Front Street, an imprint of Boyds Mills Press. Reprinted by permission.

Cobblestone Publishing, Co.: "Test Your Survival Skills" by Nick D' Alto. Adapted from ODYSSEY's December 2005 issue: SURVIVAL! © 2005, Carus Publishing Company, published by Cobblestone Publishing, 30 Grove Street, Suite C, Peterborough, NH 03458. All rights reserved. Used by permission of the publisher.

Philip Devitt: "Behind the Veil" by Philip Devitt is adapted from "Behind the veil we are all alike" by Philip Devitt. Copyright Philip Devitt. Used by permission of the author.

Gannett Co., Inc.: "Tornado survivor called 'the luckiest man on earth'" is adapted from "Hurled through the raging blackness" by Wes Johnson from SPRINGFIELD NEWS-LEADER, March 19, 2006. Map (adapted) and photograph from SPRINGFIELD NEWS-LEADER, March 19, 2006. Copyright © 2006 by News-Leader. Used by permission of Gannett Co., Inc.

HarperCollins Publishers: "Luck" by Elena Castedo from YOU'RE ON!: SEVEN PLAYS IN ENGLISH AND SPANISH selected by Lori Marie Carlson. Copyright © 1999 by Lori M. Carlson and published by HarperCollins Publishers. "Young at Heart" is adapted from "Opera, Karate, and Bandits" from THE LAND I LOST by Huynh Quang Nhuong. Copyright © 1982 by Huynh Quang Nhuong. Used by permission of HarperCollins Publishers.

Houghton Mifflin Harcourt Publishing Company: "Frijoles" is an excerpt from PACIFIC CROSSING by Gary Soto. Copyright © 1992 by Gary Soto. Reprinted by permission of Houghton Mifflin Harcourt Publishing Company. All rights reserved.

Hugh B. Cave Irrevocable Trust: Adaptation of "Two Were Left" by Hugh B. Cave. Copyright 1942 by the Crowell Collier Publishing Co. Reprinted by permission of the Hugh B. Cave Irrevocable Trust.

Kids Can Press, Ltd.: Material from IF THE WORLD WERE A VILLAGE: A BOOK ABOUT THE WORLD'S PEOPLE written by David J. Smith is used by permission of Kids Can Press Ltd., Toronto. Text © 2002 David J. Smith.

Lee and Low Books, Inc.: BE WATER, MY FRIEND: THE EARLY YEARS OF BRUCE LEE text copyright © 2006 by Ken Mochizuki. Permission arranged with Lee & Low Books, Inc. New York, NY 10016. "The Same" from POEMS TO DREAM TOGETHER text copyright © 2005 by Francisco X. Alarcón. Permission arranged with Lee & Low Books, Inc. New York, NY 10016.

MSM Productions, Ltd.: "Being deaf can be a gift... a great gift" by Tanya S. was reprinted from www. CochlearWar.com by permission of MSM Productions, Ltd. / DEAF.com.

Nancy Shepherdson, Inc.: "Freaky Food" by Nancy Shepherdson. Used by permission of Nancy Shepherdson Inc. and Boy Scouts of America.

National Geographic Society: "Survivor Rulon Gardner: Hardheaded" by Andrea Minarcek from NATIONAL GEOGRAPHIC ADVENTURE MAGAZINE, August 2007. Copyright © 2007 by National Geographic Society. Used by permission of National Geographic Image Collection.

Kofi Asare Opoku: "How Ananse Gave Wisdom to the World" by Kofi Asare Opoku is adapted from "African Proverbs" by Kofi Asare Opoku. Copyright © by Kofi Asare Opoku. Used by permission of the author.

Caitlin Parton: "Speaking for Myself: My Experience with the Cochlear Implant" by Caitlin Parton. Copyright © 1997 by Caitlin Parton. Used by permission of the author. Photograph of Caitlin Parton also used by permission of the author.

Random House, Inc.: "My People," from THE COLLECTED POEMS OF LANGSTON HUGHES by Langston Hughes, edited by Arnold Rampersad with David Roessel, Associate Editor, copyright © 1994 by The Estate of Langston Hughes. Used by permission of Alfred A. Knopf, a division of Random House, Inc.

Marta Salinas: "The Scholarship Jacket" by Marta Salinas. Copyright © Marta Salinas.

Simon & Schuster: Adaptation of "Mathematics" by Alma Flor Ada. Reprinted with the permission of Atheneum Books for Young Readers, an imprint of Simon & Schuster Children's Publishing Divison from WHERE FLAME TREES BLOOM by Alma Flor Ada. Text copyright © 1994 Alma Flor Ada.

Erika Tamar: ALPHABET CITY BALLET by Erika Tamar. Copyright © 1996 by Erika Tamar. Used by permission of the author. Photograph of Erika Tamar also used by permission of the author.

Universal Music: "You Can Get It If You Really Want" by Jimmy Cliff © 1970 Island Music Ltd. (PRS). Copyright renewed. All Rights Administered in the U.S. and Canada by Universal - Songs Of PolyGram Int., Inc. (BMI). Used By Permission. All Rights Reserved.

Weekly Reader: "Eye on Cheaters" from CURRENT EVENTS, January 9, 2004, a Weekly Reader Publication. Special permission granted by Weekly Reader, published and copyrighted by Weekly Reader Corporation. All rights reserved.

W.W. Norton & Company, Inc.: "Remember," from SHE HAD SOME HORSES by Joy Harjo. Copyright © 1983, 1997, 2006 by Thunder's Mouth Press. Used by permission of W.W. Norton & Company, Inc.

PHOTOGRAPHS:

vii (tc) Alex Williamson/PhotoDisc/Getty Images. ix (tc) The Bridgeman Art Library/Getty Images. xi (tc) Stéphan Daigle/Images.com. xiii (tc) Antar Dayal/Illustration Works/CORBIS. xv (tc) Golconde, 1953 (oil on canvas), Magritte, Rene (1898-1967)/ Menil Collection, Houston, TX, USA, DACS/Lauros/ Giraudon/The Bridgeman Art Library. xvii (tc) Artkey/CORBIS. xxi (mr) Jackdaw 003 (UnitOp) Alex Williamson/PhotoDisc/Getty Images. 004 (tr) NASA Jet Propulsion Laboratory (NASA-JPL); (ml) DigitalStock; (mr) Getty Images; (br) DigitalStock; (tl) PhotoDisc; (ml) PictureQuest; (bc) Stockbyte; (tr) DigitalStock; (mr) Darrin Klimek/Digital Vision/Getty Images; (br) CORBIS; (mr) PhotoDisc; (c) Image Library; (bl) Image Library; (tc, tl) PhotoDisc; (bc) DigitalStock; (tr) Laura Dwight/PhotoEdit; (bl) moodboard/Alamy; (br) Image Source Black/Alamy; (ml) Heide Benser/zefa/CORBIS; (bl) Richard Ross/Photographer's Choice/Getty Images; (br) Rainer Eistermann/Stone/Getty Images; (tl) Peter Augustin/Getty Images; (c) Chris Thomidis/ Getty Images; (tl) Steve Dunwell/Getty Images. 005 (c) Photo Japan/Alamy; (tl) New Century Graphics. 007 (bc) Heide Benser/zefa/CORBIS; (bc) Heide Benser/zefa/CORBIS. 008 (mr) CORBIS. 009 (br) Masterfile; (ml) ImageState Royalty Free/Alamy; (ml) ROB & SAS/CORBIS. 010 (tl) Simon Jarratt/CORBIS; (tc) Cristina Fumi Premier Collection/Alamy; (tr) Stock Image/Jupiter Images; (ml) Superstudio/Getty Images; (mc) Comstock Images/Jupiter Images; (mr) Blend Images/Jupiter Images; (bl) Workbook Stock/Jupiter Images; (bc) Georgette Douwma/Photographer's Choice/Getty Images. 011 (ml) dk & dennie cody/ Masterfile; (mr) Creatas Images/Jupiter Images; (mc) Digital Stock; (mr) Creatas Images/Jupiter Images; (br)

Mazer. 013 (bl), (mr) Artville; (tc, br) Digital Stock; (bl) PhotoDisc; (mr) Artville; (mr) Creatas Images/ Jupiter Images; (ml) dk & dennie cody/Masterfile. 014 (c) Roy Morsch/zefa/CORBIS. 015 (c) Jose Luis Pelaez Inc./Getty Images. 016 (t) Image Source Black/ Getty Images; (b) StockTrek/ Getty Images. 017 (bl) Nancy Honey/Getty Images; (tr) Erich Lessing/ Art Resource, NY. 018 (tc) Hill Street Studios/Stock This Way/CORBIS. 021 (mr) Content Mine International/Alamy. 023 (c) ArenaPal/Topham/ The Image Works. 024 (bc) Classic Image/Alamy. 027 (br) Andrew Rich/Getty Images. 028 (tc) Digital Stock; (mr) Digital Stock. 029 (br) Mark Horn/Getty Images. 030 (br) Christian Kober/Getty Images. 031 (mr) David Young-Wolff/PhotoEdit. 032 (tl) David Lorenz Winston/Brand X/CORBIS; (tc) Inga Spence/Visuals Unlimited/Getty Images; (tr) Ablestock/Jupiter Images; (ml) JUPITERIMAGES/ Comstock Premium/Alamy; (mc) Radius Images/ Jupiter Images; (mr) Bubbles Photolibrary/Alamy; (bl) DK Limited/CORBIS; (bc) CORBIS/Jupiter Images. 033 (br) Mazer. 034 (mc) Mapping Specialists. 044 (bc) The Granger Collection, New York. 045 (br) Mazer. 046 (tl) David Sacks/Getty Images; (tmr) Steve Gorton/Getty Images; (tr) PBNJ Productions/ CORBIS; (tml) Kevin Dodge/CORBIS. 048 (mr) Kristy-Anne Glubish/Design Pics/CORBIS. 049 (tl) Ernest Washington/Getty Images; (ml) Cartesia. 050 (tc) David Young-Wolff/Getty Images; (tl) Jose Luis Pelaez, Inc./Blend Images/CORBIS; (ml) Michael Bann/Getty Images; (mc) Jose Luis Pelaez, Inc./ Getty Images. 051 (tr) Edgardo Contreras/Getty Images. 052 (tl) Andrea Chu/Taxi Japan/Getty Images; (tc) Workbook Stock/Jupiter Images; (tr) Blend Images/Jupiter Images; (ml) Photos.com/ Jupiter Images; (mc) Jamie Grill/Blend Images/ CORBIS; (mr) Roy McMahon/CORBIS; (bc) Philippe Chevreull/Jupiter Images; (bl) CORBIS/Jupiter Images. 053 (tr, ml) Colin Anderson/Brand X/CORBIS. 054 (tc) Photos.com/Jupiter Images. 054–055 (c) Colin Anderson/Brand X/CORBIS. 056 (m) Robert W. Ginn/PhotoEdit; (bl) Powered by Light RF/Alamy; (bc) AGB Photo/Alamy; (br) AbleStock.com/Jupiter Images. 056–057 (t) Colin Anderson/Brand X/ CORBIS. 057 (ml) NA/Alamy; (mc) iconsight/Alamy; (mr) WoodyStock/Alamy. 058 (tr) Blend Images/ Jupiter Images; (tr) CORBIS Premium RF/Alamy; (mr) Chloe Johnson/Alamy; (ml) Thinkstock/CORBIS. 058–059 (t) Colin Anderson/Brand X/CORBIS. 059 (mr) Ian McKinnell/Alamy; (mr) MedicalRF.com/ Jupiter Images. 060 (l) Blend Images Photography/ Veer. 060–061 (t) Colin Anderson/Brand X/CORBIS. 061 (c) Patrick Enge/Associated Press; (bc) Colin Anderson/Brand X/CORBIS. 062 (ml) Steve McCurry. 063 (l) Steve McCurry. 064 (tr, tl) Steve McCurry. 065 (c) Alexandra Boulat. 066 (tr) Steve McCurry. 070 (tl) Brand X Pictures/Jupiter Images; (ml) INSADCO Photography/Alamy; (bl) Masterfile. 071 (tl) Workbook Stock/Jupiter Images; (tc) Diane & Jordan/Riser/Getty Images; (tr) Masterfile. 072 (c) BananaStock/Jupiter Images. 075 (c) Photodisc/Alamy; (bl) Alloy Photography/Veer. "079 (bc) Masterfile. 081 (UnitOp) The Bridgeman Art Library/Getty Images. 082 (tc) Charlie Riedel/ Associated Press; (ml) Tim Pannell/CORBIS; (br) Michael Newman/PhotoEdit. 083 (tl) Mazer. 085 (bc) CORBIS/SuperStock. 086 (tr) Jeremy Maude/ Getty Images. 087 (ml) Jack Hollingsworth/CORBIS; (br) PhotoSpin, Inc./Fotosearch. 088 (tl) Ansgar Photography/zefa/CORBIS; (tc) Masterfile; (tr) Creatas Images/Jupiter Images; (ml) Thinkstock Images/Jupiter Images; (mc) John Lund/Paula Zacharias/Blend Images/Getty Images; (mr) Ken Seet/CORBIS; (bl) Tony Lilley/Alamy; (bc) Thinkstock Images/Jupiter Images. 090 (tl) David Fischer/Digital Vision/Getty Images. 105 (bc) Comstock Select/CORBIS. 106 (tr) Heide Benser/zefa/CORBIS; (mc) moodboard/ CORBIS; (mr) Mark Karrass/CORBIS; (br) Steve Baccon/Getty Images; (bc) Dennis MacDonald/

Alamy. **107** (bc) Lee Strickland/Getty Images. **108** (tl) Score./Jupiter Images; (tc) Blend Images/Jupiter Images; (tr) BananaStock/Jupiter Images; (ml) Ole Graf/zefa/CORBIS; (mc) Ligia Botero/The Image Bank/Getty Images; (mr) Harry Sieplinga/HMS Images/The Image Bank/Getty Images; (bc) Radius Images/Jupiter Images; (bl) Don Hammond/Design Pics/CORBIS. **110** (ml) Bettmann/CORBIS. **119** (b) Bruce Laurance/Taxi/Getty Images. **120** (b) Megan Wyeth/Aurora/Getty Images; **121** (t) Rob Howard/CORBIS. **122** (t) Chris Cheadle/The Image Bank/Getty Images. **127** (ml) Artville; (mr) Somos Images/CORBIS; (bl) Justin Dernier/epa/CORBIS; (bc) Imagemore Co., Ltd./CORBIS; (br) Alex von Dallwitz. **128** (tr) Roger Ressmeyer/CORBIS. **129** (bl) Ingram Publishing/Getty Images. **130** (tl) Comstock Images/Jupiter Images; (tc) ASIASTOCK/AGE Fotostock; (tr) moodboard/CORBIS; (ml) Image Source Pink/Alamy; (mc) Carol and Mike Werner/Alamy; (mr) Pixland/Jupiter Images; (bl) Image Source Pink/Getty Images; (bc) Alberto Fresco/Alamy. **140** (ml) George H. H. Huey/CORBIS; (mc) Marc Muench/CORBIS. **141** (bgl) Buddy Mays/CORBIS; (cl) Darrell Gulin/CORBIS; (cr) Raymond Gehman/CORBIS; (bgc) Scott T. Smith/CORBIS; (bgr) Sally A. Morgan/CORBIS. **142** (tl) Marc Muench/CORBIS; (bg) Robert & Lorri Franz/CORBIS; (c) George H. H. Huey/CORBIS. **143** (ml) David Muench/CORBIS; (c) Phil Schermeister/CORBIS; (mr) Mark Karrass/CORBIS; (bc) David Muench/CORBIS. **144** (tr) Mark Baigent/Alamy; (bc) Carlo Allegri/Getty Images; (bgr) Scott T. Smith/CORBIS; (bgl) Buddy Mays/CORBIS. **147** (br) David Young-Wolff/PhotoEdit. **148** (tl) Gideon Mendel/CORBIS; (ml) Creatas Images/Jupiter Images; (bl) Bob Daemmrich/PhotoEdit. **149** (tl) Somos Images LLC/Alamy; (tc) Ariel Skelley/CORBIS; (tr) Blend Images/Alamy.
150 (c) Flying Colours Ltd./Digital Vision/Getty Images. **153** (mc) PhotoDisc/Alamy; (ml) Peter Augustin/Riser/Getty Images. **154** (bl) CORBIS Premium RF/Alamy. **157** (bl) Polka Dot Images/Jupiter Images. **159** (c) Stéphan Daigle/Images.com. **160** (bg) Photomosaic ® by Robert Silvers, www.photomosaic.com; (tl) Jeff Greenberg/Alamy; (ml) Klaus Hackenbery/zefa/CORBIS; (c) ImageState/ Alamy; (mr) Blaine Harrington lll/Alamy; (bl) Robert Fried/Alamy; (bc) DAJ/Getty Images. **163** (c) Baerbel Schmidt/Getty Images. **164** (mr) Digital Vision/Getty Images. **165** (ml) PhotoDisc/Alamy; (br) Clive Limpkin/Alamy. **166** (tl) Digital Vision/Getty Images; (tc) Jana Renee Cruder/35mm film/CORBIS; (tr) Don Farrall/Getty Images; (ml) Tom Ulrich/Visuals Unlimited/Getty Images; (mc) Eric Glenn/DK Stock/Getty Images; (mr) Brian Tolbert/CORBIS; (bl) Japack Company/CORBIS; (bc) Bertrand Gardel/Hemis/CORBIS. **167** (tr) Image Source Black/Getty Images; (ml) Peter Adams/Getty Images. **168–169** (c) Image Source Black/Getty Images. **171, 172** (tc) Image Source Black/Getty Images. **173** (tl) Peter Adams/ Getty Images; (tr) Michael S. Yamashita/CORBIS; (ml) Randy Faris/CORBIS; (mr) Mohamed Zatari/AP Photo. **174, 175** (tc) Image Source Black/Getty Images. **177** (c, br) Hampton-Brown; (bc) Francisco Dominguez. **179** (tl, tr) Artville; (bl) Michael Freeman/CORBIS. **180** (br) Foodcollection/Getty Images. **181** (t) Artville; (b) Niall Benvie/CORBIS. **182** (t) Artville. **186** (bl) Yamini Chao/Getty Images. **187** (b) Picture Partners/Alamy. **188** (tr) Randy Faris/CORBIS. **190** (tl) Cindy Charles/PhotoEdit; (tc) Jeff Greenberg/PhotoEdit; (tr) Tetra Images/Getty Images; (ml) Pegaz/Alamy; (mc) Tomi Junger/Alamy; (mr) M Stock/Alamy; (bl) Jeff Cadge/Riser/Getty Images; (bc) Creatas Images/Jupiter Images. **191** (tr) Reza Abedini Studio/Reza Abedini. **193** (c) Reza Abedini Studio/Reza Abedini. **195** (t) Peter M. Wilson/Alamy; (c) Betsy Winchell. **196–197** (c) Betsy Winchell. **197** (bc) Peter M. Wilson/Alamy. **198** (c) Mapping Specialists. **199** (t) Score. By Alto/Jupiter Images. **200** (ml) Jeff J. Mitchell/Getty Images; (mc) Stockbyte/Getty Images; (mr) Mapping Specialists; (bl) John Van Hasselt/CORBIS; (bc) Stockbyte/Getty Images; (br) Mapping Specialists.
200–201 (t) Randy Faris/CORBIS.
201 (ml) Themba Hadebe/Associated Press; (mc) Stockbyte/Getty Images; (mr) Mapping Specialists; (bl) Fabio Polenghi/CORBIS; (bc) Stockbyte; (br) Mapping Specialists. **202** (t) Randy Faris/CORBIS; (ml) David Young-Wolff/PhotoEdit; (mc) Stockbyte; (mr) Mapping Specialists; (bc) Score. By Alto/Jupiter Images. **207** (bl) Yellow Dog Productions/Getty Images; (tr) Tony Freeman/PhotoEdit. **208** (tr) Mathew Sturtevant/Alamy. **209** (ml) Somos Images/CORBIS; (br) David Young-Wolff/PhotoEdit. **210** (tl) Paula Solloway/Alamy; (tc) Image Source; (tr) Bloom Works Inc./Alamy; (ml) Lori Adamski Peek/Getty Images; (mc) CORBIS RF/Alamy; (mr) Spencer Grant/PhotoEdit; (bc) Masterfile; (bl) Jeff Greenberg/Alamy. **212** (ml) David Turnley/CORBIS. **230** (tl) Michael Newman/PhotoEdit; (ml) Gary Conner/PhotoEdit; (bl) David Frazier/ PhotoEdit. **231** (tl) Susan Murcott; (mr) Mapping Specialists. **232** (c) Andersen Ross/Getty Images. **234** (bc) Visage/Alamy. **235** (ml) Inti St. Clair/Digital VIsion/Getty Images; (mc) David Katzenstein/CORBIS. **239** (bl) Floresco Productions/CORBIS.
241 (UnitOp) Antar Dayal/Illustration Works/CORBIS. **242** (tr) Sami Sarkis/Photographer's Choice/Getty Images; (mr) Artville; (br) MetaPhoto. **246** (br) Eric Nguyen/CORBIS. **247** (ml) Eric Raptosh Photography/Workbook Stock/Jupiter Images; (bl) plainpicture/Hoenig, T./Jupiter Images; (bc) O'Boyle, John/Star Ledger/CORBIS; (br) Hakes Alan/CORBIS Sygma. **248** (tl) Workbook Stock/Jupiter Images; (tc) Norbert Wu/Science Faction/Getty Images; (tr) AGB Photo/Alamy; (ml) David du Plessis/Gallo Images/Getty Images; (mc) Turba/zefa/CORBIS; (mr) DLILLC/CORBIS; (bl) Stockbyte/Getty Images; (bc) tbkmedia.de/Alamy. **250** (tr) Mapping Specialists; (ml) LMR Group/Alamy. **260** (ml) Springfield News-Leader.
261 (bg) Carsten Peter/Getty Images. **262–263** (c) Carsten Peter/Getty Images. **263** (c) Mapping Specialists. **264–265** (bg) Carsten Peter/Getty Images. **265** (t) Springfield News-Leader. **266** (b) Alan R. Moller/Getty Images; (bc) Carsten Peter/Getty Images. **271** (c) AP Photo/Eric Gay. **273** (ml) YANNICK FAGOT/Stock Image/Jupiter Images; (br) Reuters/CORBIS. **274** (tl) Michael Goldman/Photographer's Choice/Getty Images; (tc) Mike Goldwater/Alamy; (tr) John Henley/CORBIS; (ml) Design Pics Inc./Alamy; (mc) Chase Jarvis/CORBIS; (mr) ImageState/Alamy; (bl) Flint/CORBIS; (bc) Jim West/Alamy. **275** (tr, c) Warren Faidley/CORBIS.
276 (ml) Dave Martin/Associated Press. **276–277** (c) Warren Faidley/CORBIS. **278–279** (t) Smiley N. Pool/Dallas Morning News/CORBIS. **280** (bl) Dave Martin/AP Photos; (br) Mike Theiss/Ultimate Chase/CORBIS. **280–281** (bg) Jim Reed/CORBIS. **281** (t) Sylvia Pitcher Photolibrary/Alamy. **282** (c) Warren Faidley/CORBIS. **283** (ml, mr) Mapping Specialists. **286** (tr) Dustin Steller/Design Pics/CORBIS. **287** (br) C Squared Studios/Getty Images. **291** (ml) Masterfile. **293** (c) AP Photo/Claude Paris. **294** (mr) Kim Steele/Getty Images. **295** (bl) gulfimages/Getty Images; (br) BlueMoon Stock/Alamy. **296** (tl) Image Source; (tc) Gideon Mendel for Action Aid/CORBIS; (tr) Michael Doolittle/Alamy; (ml) Pixland/Jupiter Images; (mc) Patrick Ryan/Stone/Getty Images; (mr) Nick Dolding/zefa/CORBIS; (bl) Somos Images/CORBIS; (bc) Michael Melford/Riser/Getty Images. **297** (tr) Jed Share/Photonica/Getty Images. **298–299** (c) Jed Share/Photonica/Getty Images. **300** (c) Chris Carroll/CORBIS. **301** (c) Philip Corbluth/Illustration Works/CORBIS. **302** (tc) BSIP/Photo Researchers, Inc.; (ml) MedicalRF.com/CORBIS; (c) MedicalRF.com/CORBIS; (bl) Visuals Unlimited/CORBIS; (bc) Micro Discovery/CORBIS. **303** (tr) Don Hammond/Design Pics/CORBIS; (l) MedicalRF.com/CORBIS; (mr) Jane Hurd/MedNet/CORBIS; (br) Visuals Unlimited/CORBIS. **304** (c) Benjamin Lowy/CORBIS. **305** (bc) Don Hammond/Design Pics/CORBIS.
307 (bl) Billy Stickland/Getty Images. **308** (tl) Winston Luzier/Transtock/CORBIS; (tc) Buddy Mays/CORBIS; (tr) Mapping Specialists. **309** (mr) Dorling Kindersley. **310** (tl) Kevin Winter/Getty Images.
313 (ml) moodboard/CORBIS. **314** (tl) Workbook Stock/Jupiter Images; (ml) Brand X Pictures/Jupiter Images; (bl) Peter Casolino/Alamy. **315** (tl) PBNJ Productions/Blend Images/Getty Images; (mr) David R. Frazier Photolibrary, Inc./Alamy. **316** (c) Michael Blann/Digital Vision/Getty Images. **318** (b) Digital Vision. **320** (bl) Jose Luis Pelaez, Inc./CORBIS.
323 (bl) Charles Gupton/CORBIS. **325** (UnitOp) Golconde, 1953 (oil on canvas), Magritte, Rene (1898–1967)/Menil Collection, Houston, TX, USA, DACS/Lauros/Giraudon/The Bridgeman Art Library. **327** (ml) Heide Benser/zefa/CORBIS. **329** (c) Digital Vision/Alamy. **331** (br) Michael Newman/PhotoEdit. **332** (tl) CORBIS Photography/Veer; (tc) Erin Patrice O'Brien/Taxi/Getty Images; (tr) trbfoto/Brand X/CORBIS; (ml) Polka Dot Images/Jupiter Images; (mc) Fancy Photography/Veer; (mr) Matt Henry Gunther/Stone/Getty Images; (bl) Masterfile; (bc) David Young-Wolff/PhotoEdit. **333** (all) mazerstock. **334** (ml) Mapping Specialists. **334–339** (all) mazerstock. **340–341** (c) Studio Eye/CORBIS. **349** (mc) photocuisine/CORBIS; (mr) Cartesia; (bc) Steve Allen/Brand X/CORBIS. **351** (ml) Polka Dot Images/Jupiter Images; (mr) GoGo Images/Jupiter Images. **352** (tl) Michael Newman/PhotoEdit. **353** (br) Lis Pines/Getty Images. **354** (tl) Nonstock/Jupiter Images; (tc) Creatas Images/Jupiter Images; (tr) David Young-Wolff/PhotoEdit; (ml) Volker Moehrke/zefa/CORBIS; (mc) Tom Carter/PhotoEdit; (mr) Kim Karpeles/Alamy; (bl) A. Carrasco Ragel/epa/CORBIS; (bc) CORBIS/Jupiter Images. **356** (ml) Michael Newman/PhotoEdit. **360** (tc, tr) Caitlin Parton.
363 (bc) Barbara Stitzer/Photo. **365** (c) Jackdaw; (bc) Hulton Archive/Getty Images. **366** (ml) Michael Newman/PhotoEdit; (mc) David Young-Wolff/PhotoEdit. **367** (t) Thinkstock Images/Jupiter Images; (bl, bc, br) Arena Street Press. **368–369** (all) Arena Street Press. **370** (bg) Thinkstock Images/Jupiter Images. **373** (ml) Hola/SuperStock. **375** (bc) Manchan/Getty Images. **377** (br) Darius Ramazan/zefa/CORBIS. **378** (tl) David Young-Wolff/PhotoEdit; (tc) Denkou Images/Alamy; (tr) UpperCut Images/Getty Images; (ml) Jim West/Alamy; (mc) Masterfile; (mr) Marco Garcia/Getty Images; (bl) Jeff Greenberg/PhotoEdit; (bc) Malcolm Case-Green/Alamy. **379** (tr) Nonstock/Jupiter Images. **380–381** (c) Nonstock/Jupiter Images. **382** (tr) Allana Wesley White/CORBIS; (t) Nonstock/Jupiter Images. **383** (b) Novastock/Stock Connection. **384** (tr) CanStock Images/Alamy; (t) Nonstock/Jupiter Images. **385** (b) Design Pics/ImageState. **386–387** (c) Miguel A. Muñoz Pellicer/Alamy. **387** (bc) Nonstock/Jupiter Images. **389** (c) Sara Beazley. **390** (ml) The Granger Collection, New York; (b) PhotoSpin, Inc./Alamy. **390–391** (bg) mazerstock. **391** (tr) Dennis Vandal/Associated Press; (bc) Carol Lollis-The Daily Hampshire Gazette/AP Photo. **392** (bg) Sara Beazley. **395** (ml) Image Source/SuperStock. **396** (tl) Simon Potter/Image Source; (ml) Kim Kulish/CORBIS; (bl) Hitoshi Nishimura/Taxi Japan/Getty Images. **397** (tc) ImageState/Alamy; (ml) Digital Art/CORBIS. **398** (c) Michael Newman/PhotoEdit. **399** (mr) The United States Mint. **405** (bl) Steve Skjold/Alamy. **407** (UnitOp) Artkey/CORBIS. **409** (tl) CORBIS; (ml) Barbara Penoyar/Getty Images; (mr) D. Hurst/Alamy; **409** (br) Kayte M. Deioma/PhotoEdit. **412** (mr) altrendo images/Getty Images. **413** (ml) PhotoAlto/Laurence Mouton/Getty Images; (br) Redlink Producion/CORBIS. **414** (tl) Gary John Norman/The Image Bank/Getty Images; (tc) Andersen Ross/Digital Vision/Getty Images; (tr) Ruaridh Stewart/ZUMA/CORBIS; (ml) Radius Images/Jupiter Images; (mc) Jeff Greenberg/Alamy; (mr) fotovisage/Alamy; (bl) Stockbyte/Alamy; (bc) Steve Wisbauer/Digital Vision/Getty Images. **428** (ml) Digital Vision/Getty Images. **429** (ml) Bohemian Nomad Picturemakers/CORBIS; (mc) Digital Vision/Getty Images; (mr) Peter Adams/The Image Bank/Getty Images. **430** (ml) Richard I'Anson/Lonely Planet Images; (mc) Peter Adams/The Image Bank/Getty

Acknowledgments, continued

Images; (mr) Megapress/Alamy. **431** (ml) Natalie Fobes/CORBIS; (mc) Simone van den Berg/Alamy; (mr) Charles Peterson/The Image Bank/Getty Images. **432** (ml) Noboru Komine/Lonely Planet Images; (tr) John Sones/Lonely Planet Images; (br) Mapping Specialists. **437** (l) Homer Sykes/CORBIS. **438** (mr) Andy Sacks. **440** (tl) Somos Images LLC/Alamy; (tc) PhotoAlto/Alamy; (tr) Image Source Pink/Alamy; (ml) Tim Pannell/CORBIS; (mc) Keith Brofsky/UpperCut Images/Getty Images; (mr) Jose Luis Pelaez, Inc./Getty Images; (bl) ColorBlind Images/Iconica/Getty Images; (bc) Patrik Giardino/CORBIS. **453** (c) mazerstock. **454** (b) M. Thomsen/zefa/CORBIS.
455 (t) mazerstock. **456** (b) Keith Brofsky/UpperCut Images/Getty Images. **457** (c) Howard Shooter/Dorling Kindersley/Getty Images; (r) Image Club. **458** (bg) mazerstock. **464** (mr) Eye-Stock/Alamy.
465 (ml) ImageState Royalty Free/Alamy. **466** (tl) Sean Justice/Getty Images; (tc) Workbook Stock/Jupiter Images; (tr) James Worrell/Stone/Getty Images; (ml) Brand X Pictures/Jupiter Images; (mc) Patrick Lynch/Alamy; (mr) Visions of America, LLC/Alamy; (bl) Blend Images/Alamy; (bc) Digital Vision/Alamy. **468** (tl) Hulton Archive/Getty Images. **470** (tl, mr) Bettmann/CORBIS; (bl) Lambert/ Getty Images. **470–471** (b) The Mariner's Museum/CORBIS. **471** (tr) Bettmann/CORBIS; (ml) Christel Gerstenberg/CORBIS; (mc) Mansell/Time Life Pictures/Getty Images.
486 (bl) Ha Lam. **490** (tl) Ed Kashi/CORBIS; (ml) Spencer Grant/PhotoEdit; (bl) Chabruken/Taxi/Getty Images. **491** (tl) David Raymer/CORBIS; (mr) Joe Bator/CORBIS. **492** (c) David Young-Wolff/PhotoEdit. **499** (bl) Will Hart/PhotoEdit. **503** (c) Stockbyte/Punchstock; (b) Digital Stock/Punchstock. **507** (c) Spencer Jones/Photographer's Choice/Getty Images. **509** (br) F64/Getty Images. **510** (b) Jupiter Images/Brand X/Alamy. **511** (tc) Getty Images; (tr) Varie/Alt/CORBIS; (ml) White Packert/The Image Bank/Getty Images; (bl) Jupiter Images/Brand X/Alamy; (bc) Brand X Pictures/Jupiter Images; (br) Masterfile.
512 (tr) Getty Images. **514** (tc) Jupiter Images/Brand X/Alamy. **515** (br) NASA Hubble Space Telescope/epa/CORBIS. **517** (mc) Vince Cavataio/Pacific Stock; (bc) Tony Arruza/CORBIS; (br) Ron Dahlquist/Pacific Stock. **519** (bl) Tony Arruza/CORBIS; (br) Ron Dahlquist/Pacific Stock. **520** (tr) Brand X Pictures/Jupiter Images. **521** (tr) Transtock/CORBIS. **522** (ml) moodboard/CORBIS. **523** (ml) Digital Vision/Alamy; (bl) Comstock Images/Jupiter Images. **524** (ml) Alloy Photography/Veer. **525** (ml) Stockbyte Photography/Veer. **527** (mr) Tim Pannell/CORBIS; (bl) Image Club; (bc) Jack Hollingsworth/Getty Images. **547** (bc) Jack Michael/dmac/Alamy. **549** (bc) Michael Newman/PhotoEdit; (bc) DAVID NOBLE PHOTOGRAPHY/Alamy. **550** (bc) moodboard/Alamy. **553** (bl) PhotoObjects.net/Jupiter Images; (bc) Deco/Alamy; (br) David Michael. Zimmerman/CORBIS. **558** (c) Thomas Northcut/Riser/Getty Images; (bc) Alex Cao/Digital Vision/Getty Images. **559** (tr) Brand X Pictures/Jupiter Images. **560** (ml) Masterfile; (mc) Christophe Dupont Elise/Icon SMI/CORBIS. **565** (tr) PhotoDisc. **567** (mr) Scott Rosen/Bill Smith Studio. **570** (b) Lew Robertson/CORBIS. **571** (br) Martin Harvey; Gallo Images/CORBIS. **572** (b) Danita Delimont/Alamy. **577** (b) ImageZoo Stock Illustration/Getty Images. **580** (bc) PhotoDisc/Getty Images. **582** (tc) Edward Tamez; (mr, bc, br) CSA Plastock/Getty Images. **584** (bc) CORBIS. **587** (mr) Lake County Museum/CORBIS; (br) Sharon Swanson/Illustration Works/Getty Images. **588** (mr) Patrick LaCroix/Alamy. **590** (tr) M Stock/Alamy. **591** (tr) Tom Bean/Getty Images. **592** (tr) Corel. **593** (tr) PhotoDisc/Getty Images; (ml) Michael Newman/PhotoEdit; (mc) Skip Nall/Getty Images; (mr) Jonathan Nourok/PhotoEdit; (bc) Rudy Von Briel/PhotoEdit. **594** (tl, tc) Liz Garza Williams; (tr) David Young-Wolff/PhotoEdit; (ml) Phil McCarten/PhotoEdit; (mc) Courtesy of Brown Publishing Network; (mr) Liz Garza Williams; (bl) Schafer & Hill/Getty Images; (br) Digital Stock. **597** (all) Liz Garza Williams. **600** (tl) PhotoDisc/Getty Images; (tc) Ron Chapple/Thinkstock/Jupiter Images; (tr) PhotoDisc/

Getty Images; (mr, c) Artville; (mr) Tim Turner/FoodPix/Jupiter Images; (br) New Century Graphics. **601** (tl) Liz Garza Williams; (tr) Artville; (mr, ml, bl) John Paul Endress; (br) Spencer Grant/PhotoEdit. **602** (all) Liz Garza Williams. **603** (c) Liz Garza Williams. **604** (br) Corel. **605** (tl, tc, tr, ml, mc, mr, bl, bc) Liz Garza Williams; (br) David Young-Wolff/PhotoEdit. **606** (br) Mic Smith/CORBIS Sygma.
608 (all) Liz Garza Williams. **616** (tl) Masterfile; (tr) Ansgar Photography/zefa/CORBIS; (ml) CORBIS Photography/Veer; (mr) trbfoto/Brand X/CORBIS; (bl) Erin Patrice O'Brien/Taxi/Getty Images; (br) Nonstock/Jupiter Images. **617** (tl) Nancy R. Cohen/Digital Vision/Getty Images; (tr) Somos Images LLC/Alamy; (ml) David Lorenz Winston/Brand X/CORBIS; (mr) Cindy Charles/PhotoEdit; (bl) Paula Solloway/Alamy; (br) ImageShop/CORBIS. **618** Row 1: (l) Masterfile, (r) PhotoAlto/Alamy; Row 2: (l) Image Source, (r) Michael Goldman/Photographer's Choice/Getty Images; Row 3: (l) Score./Jupiter Images, (r) Gideon Mendel for Action Aid/CORBIS; Row 4: (l) Simon Jarratt/CORBIS, (r) Comstock Images/Jupiter Images. **619** Row 1: (l) Ian McKinnell/Taxi/Getty Images, (r) Michael Doolittle/Alamy; Row 2: (l) Digital VIsion/Getty Images, (r) Jana Renee ruder/35mm film/CORBIS; Row 3: (l) Masterfile, (r) Norbert Wu/Science Faction/Getty Images; Row 4: (l) Workbook Stock/Jupiter Images, (r) Creatas Images/Jupiter Images. **620** Row 1: (l) AGB Photo/Alamy, (r) David Young-Wolff/PhotoEdit; Row 2: (l) Cristina Fumi Premier Collection/Alamy, (r) Volker Moehrke/zefa/CORBIS; Row 3: (l) Masterfile, (r) Mike Goldwater/Alamy; Row 4: (l) Image Source Pink/Alamy, (r) Image Source. **621** Row 1: (l) Bloom Works Inc./Alamy, (r) Patrick Ryan/Stone/Getty Images; Row 2: (l) Bill Stormont/Bill Stormont/CORBIS, (r) Stock Image/Jupiter Images; Row 3: (l) Pixland/Jupiter Images, (r) Superstudio/Getty Images; Row 4: (l) Don Farrall/Getty Images, (r) Gary John Norman/The Image Bank/Getty Images. **622** Row 1: (l) Polka Dot Images/Jupiter Images, (r) JUPITERIMAGES/Alamy; Row 2: (l) Jeff Greenberg/PhotoEdit, (r) David du Plessis/Gallo Images/Getty Images; Row 3: (l) Blend Images/Jupiter Images, (r) BananaStock/Jupiter Images; Row 4: (l) Andersen Ross/Digital Vision/Getty Images, (r) Andrea Chu/Taxi Japan/Getty Images. **623** Row 1: (l) Tetra Images/Getty Images, (r) Ablestock.com/Jupiter Images; Row 2: (l) Comstock Images/Jupiter Images, (r) Ole Graf/zefa/CORBIS; Row 3: (l) Sean Justice/Getty Images, (r) ASIASTOCK/AGE Fotostock; Row 4: (l) Inga Spence/Visuals Unlimited/Getty Images, (r) JUPITERIMAGES/Comstock Premium/Alamy.
624 Row 1: (l) Tim Pannell/CORBIS, (r) Turba/zefa/CORBIS; Row 2: (l) Tom Ulrich/Visuals, (r) Ruaridh Stewart/ZUMA/CORBIS Unlimited/Getty Images; Row 3: (l) Workbook Stock/Jupiter Images, (r) Eric Glenn/DK Stock/Jupiter Images; Row 4: (l) Tom Carter/PhotoEdit, (r) Paul Chauncey/Alamy. **625** Row 1: (l) Keith Brofsky/UpperCut Images/Getty Images, (r) JUPITERIMAGES/Alamy; Row 2: (l) Workbook Stock/Jupiter Images, (r) Noel Hendrickson/Digital Vision/Getty Images; Row 3: (l) Fancy Photography/Veer, (r) Radius Images/Jupiter Images; Row 4: (l) moodboard/CORBIS, (r) Blend Images/Jupiter Images. **626** Row 1: (l) Image Source Pink/Alamy, (r) Bubbles Photolibrary/Alamy; Row 2: (l) Creatas Images/Jupiter Images, (r) James Hardy/PhotoAlto Agency/Getty Images; Row 3: (l) Radius Images/Jupiter Images, (r) John Henley/CORBIS; Row 4: (l) Brian Tolbert/CORBIS, (r) David Young-Wolff/PhotoEdit. **627** Row 1: (l) Blend Images/Jupiter Images, (r) Matt Henry Gunther/Stone/Getty Images; Row 2: (l) Denkou Images/Alamy, (r) Workbook Stock/Jupiter Images; Row 3: (l) Design Pics Inc./Alamy, (r) UpperCut Images/Getty Images; Row 4: (l) Jeff Greenberg/Alamy, (r) Photos.com/Jupiter Images. **628** Row 1: (l) Jim West/Alamy, (r) Carol and Mike Werner/Alamy; Row 2: (l) Image Source Pink/Jupiter Images, (r) Pegaz/Alamy; Row 3: (l) Nick Dolding/zefa/CORBIS, (r) DLILLC/CORBIS; Row 4: (l) Somos Images/CORBIS, (r) Lori Adamski Peek/Getty Images. **629** Row 1: (l) James Worrell/Stone/Getty Images, (r)

Pixland/Jupiter Images; Row 2: (l) Masterfile, (r) Jose Luis Pelaez, Inc./Getty Images; Row 3: (l) Thinkstock Images/Jupiter Images, (r) Stockbyte/Getty Images; Row 4: (l) Brand X Pictures/Jupiter Images, (r) Patrick Lynch/Alamy. **630** Row 1: (l) fotovisage/Alamy, (r) Ligia Botero/The Image Bank/Getty Images; Row 2: (l) Tomi Junger/Alamy, (r) Stockbyte/Alamy; Row 3: (l) Image Source Pink/Getty Images, (r) Alberto Fresco/Alamy; Row 4: (l) CORBIS RF/Alamy, (r) Visions of America, LLC/Alamy. **631** Row 1: (l) Japack Company/CORBIS, (r) John Lund/Paula Zacharias/Blend Images/Getty Images; Row 2: (l) Chase Jarvis/CORBIS, (r) Blend Images/Alamy; Row 3: (l) ImageState/Alamy, (r) Kim Karpeles/Alamy; Row 4: (l) Jamie Grill/Blend Images/CORBIS, (r) Ken Seet/CORBIS. **632** Row 1: (l) Roy McMahon/CORBIS, (r) Thinkstock Images/Jupiter Images; Row 2: (l) Tony Lilley/Alamy, (r) Masterfile; Row 3: (l) A. Carrasco Ragel/epa/CORBIS, (r) CORBIS/Jupiter Images; Row 4: (l) CORBIS/Jupiter Images, (r) Steve Wisbauer/Digital Vision/Getty Images. **633** Row 1: (l) Marco Garcia/Getty Images, (r) Philippe Chevreull/CORBIS; Row 2: (l) M Stock/Alamy, (r) Spencer Grant/PhotoEdit; Row 3: (l) ColorBlind Images/Iconica/Getty Images, (r) Jon Feingersh/Blend Images/Getty Images; Row 4: (l) Flint/CORBIS, (r) David Young-Wolff/PhotoEdit. **634** Row 1: (l) Jeff Greenberg/PhotoEdit, (r) DK Limited/CORBIS; Row 2: (l) Digital Vision/Alamy, (r) Harry Sieplinga/HMS Images/The Image Bank/Getty Images; Row 3: (l) Michael Melford/Riser/Getty Images, (r) Don Hammond/Design Pics/CORBIS; Row 4: (l) Malcolm Case-Green/Alamy, (r) Patrik Giardino/CORBIS. **635** Row 1: (l) Jeff Cadge/Riser/Getty Images, (r) Georgette Douwma/Photographer's Choice/Getty Images; Row 2: (l) Jeff Greenberg/Alamy, (r) Jim West/Alamy; Row 3: (l) Creatas Images/Jupiter Images, (r) Masterfile; Row 4: (l) Radius Images/Jupiter Images, (r) Bertrand Gardel/Hemis/CORBIS. **636** (tl) CORBIS/Jupiter Images; (tr) Mary Kate Denny/PhotoEdit, (mr) tbkmedia.de/Alamy; (mr) Digital Vision/Alamy; (bl) les polders/Alamy; (br) Thinkstock/CORBIS.

ILLUSTRATIONS:

xix Murray Kimber. **xx** Jean-Manuel Duvivier. **034–041** ("Growing Together") Elizabeth Rosen. **043–044** ("My People") Sara Tyson. **089–097** ("How Ananse Gave Wisdom to the World") Frank Morrison. **110–117** Jean-Manuel Duvivier. **132–139** ("Mathematics") Karen Blessen. **170–175** Dale Glasgow. **213–221** ("Alphabet City Ballet") Chris Vallo. **223–226** ("You Can Get It If You Really Want") CJ Zea. **245** Jashar Awan. **249–259** ("Two Were Left") S.D. Nelson. **286–288** ("Test Your Survival Skills") Chris Vallo. **342–346** ("The Jay and the Peacocks") Keith Baker. **356–364** ("Cochlear Implants: Two Sides of the Story") Jim Bartosik. **389–392** ("I'm Nobody") Sara Beazley. **415–427** ("Luck") Andrew Holder. **442–451** ("The Scholarship Jacket") Kent Floris. **467–481** ("The Gift of the Magi") James Bentley. **483–486** ("Shoulders") Murray Kimber.

652